Good Teachers for Tomorrow's Schools

Moral Development and Citizenship Education

Series Editors

Wiel Veugelers (*University of Humanistic Studies, Utrecht, The Netherlands*)
Kirsi Tirri (*University of Helsinki, Finland*)

Founding Editor

Fritz Oser†

Editorial Board

Nimrod Aloni (*Kibbutzim College of Education, Tel Aviv, Israel*)
Marvin Berkowitz (*University of Missouri–St.Louis, USA*)
Horst Biedermann (*St. Gallen University of Teacher Education, Switzerland*)
Maria Rosa Buxarrais (*University of Barcelona, Spain*)
Helen Haste (*University of Bath, UK/Harvard University, USA*)
Dana Moree (*Charles University, Prague, Czech Republic*)
Clark Power (*University of Notre Dame, USA*)
Jasmine Sim (*National Institute of Education, Singapore*)
Joel Westheimer (*University of Ottawa, Canada*)

VOLUME 16

The titles published in this series are listed at *brill.com/mora*

Good Teachers for Tomorrow's Schools

Purpose, Values, and Talents in Education

Edited by

Elina Kuusisto, Martin Ubani,
Petri Nokelainen and Auli Toom

BRILL
SENSE

LEIDEN | BOSTON

All chapters in this book have undergone peer review.

The Library of Congress Cataloging-in-Publication Data is available online at http://catalog.loc.gov

Typeface for the Latin, Greek, and Cyrillic scripts: "Brill". See and download: brill.com/brill-typeface.

ISSN 2352-5770
ISBN 978-90-04-46498-8 (paperback)
ISBN 978-90-04-46499-5 (hardback)
ISBN 978-90-04-46500-8 (e-book)

Copyright 2021 by Koninklijke Brill NV, Leiden, The Netherlands.
Koninklijke Brill NV incorporates the imprints Brill, Brill Hes & De Graaf, Brill Nijhoff, Brill Rodopi, Brill Sense, Hotei Publishing, mentis Verlag, Verlag Ferdinand Schöningh and Wilhelm Fink Verlag.
All rights reserved. No part of this publication may be reproduced, translated, stored in a retrieval system, or transmitted in any form or by any means, electronic, mechanical, photocopying, recording or otherwise, without prior written permission from the publisher. Requests for re-use and/or translations must be addressed to Koninklijke Brill NV via brill.com or copyright.com.

This book is printed on acid-free paper and produced in a sustainable manner.

Contents

List of Figures and Tables   ix
Notes on Contributors   xi

Introduction   1
   Elina Kuusisto, Auli Toom, Martin Ubani and Petri Nokelainen

PART 1
Ethical and Purposeful Teachers and Teaching

1   Equity and Quality as Aims of Education: Teachers' Role in Educational Ecosystems   19
      Hannele Niemi

2   The New Professionalism? How Good Teachers Continue to Teach to Their Best and Well in Challenging Reform Contexts   37
      Christopher Day

3   Teachers' Moral Authenticity: Searching for Balance between Role and Person   57
      Jukka Husu and Auli Toom

4   Design and Implementation of the National Aims for Finnish Teacher Education during 2016–2019   75
      Jari Lavonen

5   Promoting Purpose Development in Schools and Beyond: A Complex, Dynamic, Bioecological Developmental Systems Perspective   91
      Matthew Joseph

6   What Is above Everything? Conceptions of the Sacred among Finnish Youth   111
      Mette Ranta, Henrietta Grönlund and Anne Birgitta Pessi

7 Children's and Youths' Perspectives on Value Diversity in Education: Implications for Teacher Education and Educator Professionalism 129
     Arniika Kuusisto and Arto Kallioniemi

8 The Learning Ambience of Values Pedagogy 148
     Terence Lovat

9 Religious Literacy as a 21st Century Skill for All Teachers 166
     Martin Ubani

PART 2
Supporting Talent Development with a Growth Mindset

10 Education of the Gifted and Talented in Finland 195
     Elina Kuusisto, Sonja Laine and Inkeri Rissanen

11 Recognition, Expectation, and Differentiation for Mathematical Talent Development of Young Gifted English Learners 217
     Jenny Yang, Sonmi Jo, James Campbell and Seokhee Cho

12 Reaching for Medals and Vocational Excellence? WorldSkills Competition Success in Relation to Goal Orientations and Metacognitive and Resource Management Strategies 240
     Petri Nokelainen and Heta Rintala

13 Measuring Apprentices' Intrapreneurship Competence in Vocational Education and Training (VET): An Interdisciplinary Model-Based Assessment 257
     Susanne Weber, Clemens Draxler, Frank Achtenhagen, Sandra Bley, Michaela Wiethe-Körprich, Christine Kreuzer and Can Gürer

14 Creative Talent as Emergent Event: A Neurodiversity Perspective 280
     Ananí M. Vasquez, Mirka Koro and Ronald A. Beghetto

15 A Socio-Cultural Approach to Growth-Mindset Pedagogy: Maker-Pedagogy as a Tool for Developing the Next-Generation Growth Mindset 296
     Jenni Laurell, Aino Seitamaa, Kati Sormunen, Pirita Seitamaa-Hakkarainen, Tiina Korhonen and Kai Hakkarainen

16 Experimental Evidence on Connections between Speech and Music: Possible Applications on Learning   313
    Minna Huotilainen and Teija Kujala

Epilogue: Growth Mindset and Purpose in Critical-Democratic Citizenship Education   331
    Wiel Veugelers

Index   341

Figures and Tables

Figures

1.1	Fundamental and transversal characteristics of good teachers.	6
3.1	The role and personal characteristics of teachers' moral authenticity.	62
7.1	Emerging professionalism through value learning trajectories (Lamminmäki-Vartia et al., 2020, on the basis of Kuusisto & Gearon, 2017a).	132
13.1	Theoretical competence model for intrapreneurship (cognition).	264
13.2	Example task from dimension I: Creating a GANTT-Chart (observation).	266
13.3	Example task from dimension II: Perspective Taking and Reasoning (observation).	270
13.4	Empirical IP competence model (Wright-map) (interpretation).	271

Tables

1.1	Characteristics of good teachers and good teaching.	2
6.1	Total distribution in categories of conceptions of the sacred (adapted from Ranta et al., 2016).	117
7.1	Selection of empirical studies used in the present examination.	134
10.1	Educational trends and gifted education in Finland.	197
10.2	A summary of the critical factors of talent development identified in Finnish empirical studies.	204
11.1	Gifted kindergarten EL students observed in each class of two schools (N = 8).	225
11.2	Student motivation levels in regular and after-school Project BRIDGE'S math classes.	226
11.3	Comparison of motivation levels in students with different levels of English proficiency and math ability, pre- and post-implementation of the BRIDGE math program.	226
11.4	Observation scale of teachers' instructional strategies for teaching math.	229
11.5	Mean and standard deviation of frequency of strategies and math open-response scores.	231
11.6	Two-level hierarchical linear modeling of Open-response assessment scores with Talk Moves and pre-test scores.	232
11.7	Effects of teachers' use of instructional strategies on students' Open-response assessment scores.	233

12.1 Goal orientation items.   246
12.2 Metacognitive and resource management strategy items.   247
12.3 Bivariate correlations between goal orientations and metacognitive and resource management strategies ($N = 137$).   248
12.4 Association of achievement goal orientations with WorldSkills competition success.   250
12.5 Association of metacognition and self-regulation with WorldSkills competition success.   250
14.1 Concepts as used in this chapter and their descriptions.   284
16.1 Key similarities and differences between the acoustic signals and expressive features of speech and music.   316

Notes on Contributors

Frank Achtenhagen
(Dr. rer. pol., 1969, Free University Berlin) is Professor Emeritus of Georg-August-University of Göttingen, Chair of Business Education and Human Resource Development. He has published nationally and internationally. He is editor of the Brill Sense series *Professional and VET Learning*.

Ronald A. Beghetto
(PhD) is the Pinnacle West Presidential Chair & Professor for the Mary Lou Fulton Teachers College at Arizona State University. He is Editor for the *Journal of Creative Behavior*, Book Series Editor for *Creative Theory & Action in Education* (Springer), and Creativity Advisor for the LEGO Foundation.

Sandra Bley
(Dr. oec. publ., 2010; Ludwig-Maximilians-University Munich | LMU, Munich School of Management) is Professor for Vocational Education and Training at Rosenheim Technical University of Applied Sciences, Faculty of Wood Technology and Construction. She has published nationally and internationally.

James Campbell
(PhD, 1968, New York University) is a professor at St. John's University. He is the principal investigator of the American Olympiad studies and has published extensively on factors that contribute to the development of exceptional talent.

Seokhee Cho
(PhD, 1986, University of Alberta) is a professor at St. John's University. She has written and published extensively on gifted and talent development of students in the U.S. and internationally, including mathematical talents of gifted English Language Learners.

Christopher Day
(CertEd; MA; DPhil; PhD; DLitt; LRAM; FRSA, FAcSS) is Professor of Education at School of Education at University of Nottingham, UK.

Clemens Draxler
(PhD, Dr. rer. nat., 2007, University of Kiel; Dr. habil., 2017, University of Bamberg) is Priv.-Doz. at UMIT, The Tyrolean Private University for Health Sciences,

Medical Informatics and Technology, Psychology and Medical Sciences. He has published nationally and internationally especially in the fields of statistics.

Henrietta Grönlund
(DTh, 2012, University of Helsinki) is Professor of Urban Theology at that university. She has published on questions of prosocial behaviour and well-being, especially in relation to religion and values (e.g., in the *Palgrave Handbook of Global Philanthropy*, 2015).

Can Gürer
is Junior Scientist, Univ.-Ass. Dipl.-Psych. at UMIT, The Tyrolean Private University for Health Sciences, Medical Informatics and Technology, Psychology and Medical Sciences. He has published nationally and internationally.

Kai Hakkarainen
is a Professor of Education at the Department of Education, University of Helsinki. He has developed recognized theoretical frameworks technology-mediated collaborative learning and knowledge creation, carried associated design experiments (knowledge building, progressive inquiry, learning by making) at K-12 education.

Minna Huotilainen
(PhD, 1997, Aalto University [previously Helsinki University of Technology]) is a Professor of Educational Sciences at the University of Helsinki. Her background is in the neuroscience of auditory perception, memory, attention and musical and language functions. Currently, she aims at applying brain research as a research method in the field of education.

Jukka Husu
(PhD) is Full Professor of Teacher Education and Dean at the Faculty of Education at University of Turku, Finland.

Sonmi Jo
(PhD, 2009, University of Arizona) is a research director of Project BRIDGE funded by U.S. Department of Education at St. John's University. Her expertise is in STEM education for the gifted, non-traditional identification assessments, and creativity education.

Matthew Joseph
(PhD, 2009, Stanford University) is an Associate Professor of Education at Duquesne University. He has published widely on the topic of purpose devel-

opment across the life span, and is currently writing a book on purpose and complexity.

Arto Kallioniemi
(DTh, 1997, University of Helsinki) is Professor of Religious Education at that university. He also holds UNESCO chair on Values, Dialogue and Human Rights. He works currently as Vice Dean (International Affairs, Societal Interaction and Equality) at the Faculty of Educational Sciences.

Tiina Korhonen
(PhD, 2017, University of Helsinki) is a university lecturer for Learning Innovations in Digital Society at that university. She is the head of the nationwide Innokas Network coordinated by the University of Helsinki, organizing Innovation Education activities in 700 Finnish schools.

Mirka Koro
(PhD, 2001, University of Helsinki) is a Professor of qualitative research and Director of doctoral programs at the Mary Lou Fulton Teachers College, ASU. Her scholarship intersects methodology, philosophy, and socio-cultural critique.

Christine Kreuzer
(Dr. oec. publ., 2018, Ludwig-Maximilians-University Munich | LMU, Munich School of Management) is Product Manager Digital Learning at Airport Munich. She has published nationally and internationally.

Teija Kujala
(PhD, 1997, University of Helsinki) is Professor of Psychology at that university. She has published over 150 peer-reviewed international articles focusing on audition, language and its impairments, learning, and plasticity.

Arniika Kuusisto
(PhD, 2011, University of Helsinki) is Professor in Child and Youth Studies at Stockholm University, Sweden, Research Director and Docent at the University of Helsinki, Finland, and Honorary Research Fellow at the University of Oxford, UK.

Elina Kuusisto
(DTh, 2011, University of Helsinki) works as a University Lecturer (diversity and inclusive education) at the Tampere University, Finland. She has published on teacher ethics, school pedagogy and talent development, particularly on purpose, ethical sensitivity and growth mindset.

Sonja Laine

(PhD, 2016, University of Helsinki) is a Lecturer at the Viikki Teacher Training School and a postdoctoral researcher at the Department of Education at the University of Helsinki. Her main research interests are gifted education, and teachers' and students' mindsets in learning.

Jenni Laurell

(MEd, 2017) works as a doctoral researcher at the University of Helsinki in the SEDUCE doctoral program. Her doctoral research investigates social aspects of students' mindset of intelligence and giftedness as well as students' creative mindset. Kirsi Tirri is her supervisor jointly with Kai Hakkarainen and her research is part of the Growing Mind research project.

Jari Lavonen

(PhD, 1996, University of Helsinki) is a Professor of Science Education. He has been researching both science education for the last 31 years and published 150 refereed scientific papers in journals and books.

Terence Lovat

(University of Newcastle, Australia, Emeritus Professor, Education & Theology) is the author of many research publications, investigator of many research projects. He has honorary appointments at the universities of Oxford, UK, Glasgow UK, and Royal Roads, Canada.

Hannele Niemi

(PhD, 1978) is Professor, Research Director in educational sciences at the University of Helsinki, also nominated as UNESCO Chair in education. She has published many books and articles on education in Finland and globally e.g., *Miracle of education: The principles and practices of teaching and learning in Finnish schools* (Sense, 2016) and *The teacher's role in the changing globalizing world* (Brill, 2018).

Petri Nokelainen

(PhD, 2008, University of Tampere) is a Full Professor of Engineering Pedagogy at the Tampere University, Finland. His research interests cover teaching and learning related to engineering higher education and workplace learning.

Anne Birgitta Pessi

(DTh, 2004, University of Helsinki) is a Professor of Church and Social Studies at that university. Her projects have focused mostly on compassion and altruism, particularly in relation to spirituality and religion.

Mette Ranta
(PhD, 2015, University of Jyväskylä) is Post-Doctoral Researcher at the Faculty of Educational Sciences, University of Helsinki. She specializes in youth life course development and educational transitions, and has publications on youth well-being, agency, and financial independence.

Heta Rintala
(PhD, 2020, Tampere University) is a post doc researcher in Häme University of Applied Sciences, Finland. Her research interests focus on vocational education and training (VET), particularly VET systems and learning environments.

Inkeri Rissanen
(PhD, 2014, University of Helsinki) is a post-doctoral researcher at Tampere University, Faculty of Education and Culture. Her research in the areas of intercultural education, worldview education and growth mindsets in education has been published in key international journals.

Aino Seitamaa
(MEd, 2021) is a research assistant in the Growing Mind research project. She has studied Finnish students' mindsets on intelligence, giftedness and creativity and participated in writing research papers on the mindsets, in-service teacher training and learning analytics.

Pirita Seitamaa-Hakkarainen
is a Professor of Craft Science at the University of Helsinki, Faculty of Educational Sciences. Her research interests focus on maker-centered pedagogy as well as the facilitation of collaborative design through technology-enhanced learning.

Kati Sormunen
(PhD, 2020, University of Helsinki) works as a researcher and a teacher educator at that university. She is specialized in the areas of of technology-enhanced inclusive education as well as programming, robotics and other technology education.

Auli Toom
(PhD) is a Full Professor of Higher Education and Director of the Centre for University Teaching and Learning at the University of Helsinki, Finland.

Martin Ubani
(PhD, 2007, University of Helsinki) is a Professor of Religious Education at the University of Eastern Finland. Recently he co-edited the volume *Contextualis-*

ing dialogue, secularisation and pluralism. Religion in Finnish public education (Waxmann, 2019).

Ananí M. Vasquez
is a doctoral student at Mary Lou Fulton Teachers College, Arizona State University. She is section editor for *Current Issues in Education*, a member of equity and diversity committees for TAG and NAGC and the AERA Autism Spectrum Research committee.

Wiel Veugelers
is Professor of Education (Emeritus) at the University of Humanistic Studies Utrecht. He is editor of the Brill Sense book series *Moral Development and Citizenship Education* and associate editor of the *Journal of Moral Education*.

Susanne Weber
(Dr. rer. pol., 1994, Georg-August-University of Göttingen) is Full Professor and Director of the Institute for Human Resource Education and Management at Ludwig-Maximilians-University Munich | LMU, Munich School of Management. She is editor of Brill series *Professional and VET Learning*.

Michaela Wiethe-Körprich
(Dr. oec. publ., 2017, Ludwig-Maximilians-University Munich | LMU, Munich School of Management) is Manager Health Management at Linde AG. She has published nationally and internationally.

Jenny Yang
(EdD, 2013, St. John's University) is an adjunct assistant professor at that university. She has published and presented studies on gifted English learners, including Effects of M3 Curriculum on Mathematics and English Proficiency Achievement of Mathematically Promising English Language Learners.

Introduction

Elina Kuusisto, Auli Toom, Martin Ubani and Petri Nokelainen

This volume discusses the characteristics of good teachers and the teaching that is needed in today's and tomorrow's schools. The focus is on research-based perspectives, with contributions from several internationally renowned scholars on what constitutes good and quality in teaching-studying-learning processes. As an outcome, the book provides insights into how, in attending not only to the cognitive but also to the affective, behavioral, moral and spiritual domains, teachers are able to support holistic growth and learning among their students in schools of the 21st century.

There is a pressing demand for research-based information on what produces foundational teacher capabilities for developing and implementing sound practices in evolving and complex educational contexts. Teachers in schools nowadays are challenged to create inclusive learning environments and safe spaces for encountering diversity in values, cultures and religions, as well as in (dis)ability and talent. Classrooms are micro-cosmoses in which local and global problems, predicaments, and challenges of the medical (pandemics), ecological (global warming), political (liberal democracies into populist regimes), social (growing social-economic gaps and millions of refugees), and cultural (commercialization and digitization of everyday life) crises are confronted and addressed. Current and prospective future demands highlight the need to educate teachers who are capable of reflecting on and implementing good teaching in the classroom.

One could argue that everyone knows intuitively what good teaching is, and what makes a good teacher. However, given the complex nature of the instructional process and of teaching as a phenomenon, it has proved difficult or even impossible on the scientific level to define teaching or teachers as "good" (e.g., Bakx, 2015; Korthagen, 2004). In this Introduction, therefore, we consider the characteristics of a good teacher and good teaching in terms of the traditions of teacher education identified by Zeichner and Liston (1990). These traditions reflect what was considered the ideal teacher and ideal teaching in different historical phases and research strands during the 20th century. Zeichner and Liston's study was set in the United States, but the same teacher-education traditions have been identified in other countries and cultures, including Finland (Tirri, 1993) and Australia (Gore, 2001). As Table I.1 shows, in identifying and analyzing the main characteristics of a good teacher we also utilize Gore's (2001) and Korthagen's (2004, 2017) approaches to teacher education, Bakx et

TABLE 1.1 Characteristics of good teachers and good teaching

Teacher education traditions (Zeichner & Liston, 1990)	Classroom practice as a framework for teacher education (Gore, 2001)	The holistic approach in teacher education (Korthagen, 2004, 2017)	Research traditions in studying quality teaching (Bakx et al., 2015, 2019)	Aspects of the ideal teacher (Clark & Peterson, 1986; Toom, 2006)	The main characteristics of good teachers
Academic tradition	Intellectual quality	Competences	Professional knowledge studies	Competent and reflective professional	KNOWLEDGE Professional competence
Social-efficiency tradition	Supportive classroom environment	Behavior	Effectiveness studies	Capable decision maker	SKILLS Systematic, stimulating
Developmentalist tradition	Relevance	Beliefs, identity, mission	Studies on perceptions and professional identity	Constructivist teacher	CHARACTER Empathetic, motivated
Social reconstructionist tradition	Recognition of difference	Beliefs, conceptions and skills integrated	Studies on educational equity and teacher integrity	Agentic, ethical teacher	SOCIAL ACTIVITY Agentic, ethical, autonomous

al.'s (2015, 2019) categories of research traditions in studies on quality teaching, as well as Clark and Peterson's (1986) and Toom's (2006) perspectives on the teacher-thinking paradigm.

Zeichner and Liston (1990) identified four traditions of teacher education: academic, social efficiency, developmentalist and social reconstructionist (Table I.1). Teachers following the *academic tradition* are subject-matter specialists with the requisite intellectual qualities and disciplinary knowledge (Zeichner & Liston, 1990; Gore, 2001). They are also experts in educational sciences, which became a new scientific domain of teacher education in the 1980s. As Shulman (1987) states in his seminal work, teachers need both *subject matter knowledge* and *pedagogical content knowledge:* they know *how* subject matter can and should be taught to different students. This approach has been widely theorized. German and European traditions refer to specific knowledge about teaching different subjects as subject didactics (*Fachdidaktik*) (Kansanen et al., 2000), or more recently as subject-specific pedagogy. In line with the academic tradition, Gore (2001) highlights the development of deep understanding and higher-order thinking among teachers and, through them, in pupils. Korthagen (2004, see also Toom, 2017), in turn, writes about *teacher competences* in terms of knowledge, skills and attitudes as indicative of potential teaching capability. Bakx et al. (2015, 2019) refer to professional knowledge as one strand in studies on teaching quality, the implication being that good teachers have a strong knowledge base related to the subjects they teach, as well as a pedagogical understanding of what and how subjects should be taught to different students. In other words, within this framework a good teacher is a competent and reflective professional (Clark & Peterson, 1986; Toom, 2006).

Scholars started to investigate and break down the components of effective teaching when the *social efficiency tradition* was established in the 1920s. They were interested in how students' learning outcomes and achievements were best and most effectively enhanced. Observable teacher traits and teaching activities were examined empirically within the behaviorist paradigm (Zeichner, 1983; Clark, 1986). Following the cognitive approach in psychology and the educational sciences, the social-efficacy tradition broadened the scope to incorporate teacher thinking and reflection, thereby creating a basis for research-based teacher education (Zeichner & Liston, 1990; Kansanen et al., 2000). At this point, the key research areas included the complexity of teacher thinking, ethical issues related to teaching, and the development of methodology and research strategies (Day et al., 1993). Regardless of the changes in paradigm, effective teaching continues to interest teacher educators, researchers and policy makers (e.g., Bardach & Klassen, 2020; Burrough et al., 2019; Goe et al., 2008; Hattie, 2008; Podolsky et al., 2019; Wayne & Youngs, 2003). Teachers intent on building a supportive classroom environment and optimizing student learning need both teaching and classroom-management skills (Bakx et al., 2015; Gore, 2001; Korthagen, 2004, Tirri, 1993), as well as decision-making capability (Clark & Peterson, 1986). It is essential for teachers at the beginning of their professional careers to master basic teaching skills and to build a constructive learning environment in the classroom: such attributes could strengthen self-esteem (Tirri, 1993) and feelings of adequacy among newly qualified teachers, and even prevent them from leaving the profession early in their careers (Heikonen et al., 2017).

The roots of the *developmentalist tradition* lie in the Child Study movement of the 19th century: a good teacher is perceived as a naturalist, an artist and a researcher (Zeichner & Liston, 1990). *Naturalist* in this context means that teachers observe children's behavior in natural settings and build curricula based on their interests and development, resulting in child-centered pedagogy or student-centered teacher education. Being an *artist*, in turn, refers to living one's life to the fullest, and putting the emphasis on personal and artistic development (see also Eisner, 2002): in this sense, teachers in themselves are seen as instruments. Finally, being a *researcher* implies an experimental attitude and the use of inquiry as a means for building curricula and developing teaching practices. This whole tradition could also be termed humanistic teacher education in that it is influenced by humanistic psychology (Zeichner & Liston, 1990). Humanist-based teacher education highlights personal growth, self-actualization, and the person of the teacher (Korthagen, 2004). Even though this was not widely supported, the focus has once again turned to the teacher's self and personal characteristics through the notions of positive and transpersonal psychology with their emphasis on positive traits, virtues and character strengths to promote subjective wellbeing and learning (Korthagen, 2004). We should also point out the importance for teaching, studying, and learning of teacher characteristics such as friendliness, enthusiasm, flexibility, humor, a caring nature, and trustworthiness, as reported in studies on effectiveness (e.g., Tirri, 1993) and in research on perception in which students describe their views on good teachers (Bakx et al., 2015, 2019).

According to Korthagen's (2004) onion model, the core qualities of a good teacher are beliefs, identity and mission. *Beliefs* refer to the meaning systems teachers develop during their lives and their school histories concerning their own intelligence and learning abilities, and the nature of knowledge, for example. These beliefs have cognitive, as well as emotional, volitional, and behavioral aspects (Korthagen, 2004; see also Pajares, 1992). Beliefs are close to *Gestalts*, which "refer to cohesive wholes of earlier experiences, role models, needs, values, feelings images and routines, which are – often unconsciously

– evoked by concrete situations" (Korthagen, 2004, p. 81). Belief systems should be acknowledged during teacher education so that student teachers will learn to change their own meaning systems on the one hand, and on the other hand they will notice their future pupils' beliefs and intervene should they threaten their studying and learning processes. *Identity* reflects how one defines oneself and responds to questions such as "Who am I? What kind of teacher do I want to be?" (Korthagen, 2004; see also Beijaard et al., 2004). Korthagen (2004) distinguishes between personal identity, teacher identity and the teacher's professional identity. *Mission* in this context implies a deep and personal understanding of what inspires one in teaching, or what one sees as one's personal calling in the world (Korthagen, 2004). It relates to the spiritual or transpersonal level of teaching in that it means becoming aware of the meaning of one's own existence and finding personal relevance (Gore, 2001). Mission is a close reflection of purpose and of becoming a purposeful teacher (Kuusisto & Tirri, 2021; Tirri, 2018).

According to the *social reconstructionist* tradition, a good teacher is a socially active person who believes in a more just society and could therefore be described as a transformative intellectual (Zeichner & Liston, 1990). It is a tradition that was promoted by Kirkpatrick and Dewey, for example, but had only a marginal status in US teacher education in the 20th century (Zeichner & Liston, 1990). However, at the beginning of the 21st century it was "rare to find educational policies or programs that do not make reference to attending to diversity, teaching for equality" (Gore, 2001, pp. 124–125). Current views about the agentic teacher (e.g., Toom, Pyhältö et al., 2015) are close to the social reconstructionist tradition according to which a teacher is an autonomous and active professional who is able to advance equal education for all students in the classroom and to advocate a moral purpose through professional practice (Tirri & Husu, 2002; see also Kansanen et al., 2000 on autonomous teachers).

Having considered the four traditions of teacher education and teacher research, we conclude that having professional knowledge, teaching skills, a good character and social awareness are fundamental attributes of a good teacher (Table I.1): someone who is a competent professional, systematic and stimulating in their teaching, has empathy and motivation, and aims to make the world a better place. Moreover, regardless of the tradition, it seems that *research or inquiry*, *reflection* and *morality* are permeable or transversal characteristics that are embedded in (almost all) traditions (Figure I.1). The moral core of teaching (Tirri et al., 2012) is identifiable especially in discussions about professionalism (e.g., Kansanen et al., 2000), character (e.g., Gore, 2001; Korthagen, 2004), and agency (Toom, Pyhältö et al., 2015) in teachers. Aspects of morality have not been equally acknowledged or pondered upon in studies about teacher effectiveness, except in findings that highlight the importance of a caring attitude, friendliness and fairness (e.g., Bakx et al., 2014; Tirri, 1993). All in all, a good teacher demonstrates features of moral expertise in pedagogical encounters, namely ethical sensitivity, judgement, motivation and action (Bebeau et al., 1999). It is argued that, of these, ethical sensitivity is the most crucial in terms of identifying and resolving moral dilemmas in schools (Tirri, 1999, 2019).

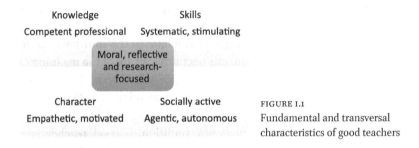

FIGURE I.1 Fundamental and transversal characteristics of good teachers

The chapters to follow focus on good teaching and good teachers from perspectives concerning the fundamental and transversal features of what constitutes a good teacher. More specifically, it is argued that good teachers in tomorrow's schools will need capabilities that reflect the purpose of education, values in education, and talents in education: these are discussed in detail in the two parts of the present volume.

Part 1 reflects on *ethical and purposeful teachers and teaching* by discussing foundations of teaching from different viewpoints. In a fragmented and differentiated world, teachers need a clear vision for their work: why, what and how they are teaching. Teaching with a purpose as well as teaching for a purpose (Tirri et al., 2018) are important elements in making the teaching-studying-learning process personally relevant and meaningful for students and teachers.

In Chapter 1, Hannele Niemi elaborates on equity and quality as aims of education, especially regarding the teacher's role in educational ecosystems. She emphasizes the status of teachers as key persons in providing high-quality education for students. Added to this, macro-level structures and conditions as well as active dialogue and collaboration between teachers and all educational stakeholders must be guaranteed. Niemi also describes teacher commitment to professional ethical standards as an anchor for educational equity and quality.

Christopher Day explores the various perspectives on the new meanings of teacher professionalism in Chapter 2, entitled "The New Professionalism? How Good Teachers Continue to Teach to Their Best and Well in Challenging Reform

Contexts." He analyzes how pressures related to functionally oriented teaching and learning, teacher effectiveness, and the development of new learning technologies influence the teacher as an expert pedagogue and knowledge holder. In the midst of all the changes, he argues, teacher professionalism is still expressed through individual agency, service commitment with a moral purpose, resilience, and collective autonomy.

In Chapter 3, "Teachers' Moral Authenticity: Searching for Balance between Role and Person," Jukka Husu and Auli Toom discuss morally authentic action among teachers, which they define as an essential professional competence. Authenticity is understood as a disposition to act on reason and to make deliberate decisions in demanding classroom situations by balancing role- and person-related perspectives. The empirical study they report explored the ways in which student teachers defined and applied their moral authenticities during their teaching. They identified three types of moral authenticity: *authenticity in moral appearance, authenticity in moral effect*, and *authenticity in moral commitment*. The results highlight the need to support future teachers to act successfully and authentically in challenging moral situations.

Chapter 4, "Design and Implementation of the National Aims for Finnish Teacher Education during 2016–2019" authored by Jari Lavonen, reflects on the design of national goals that were developed by the Finnish Teacher Education Forum through a collaborative brainstorming process. The goals in question include building a broad and solid knowledge base and developing competences related to generating novel ideas and educational innovations, as well as for developing expertise among teachers and their schools. The chapter analyzes how these set goals were put into practice and realized in Finnish teacher education through the development projects. The importance of the continuous, collaborative and research-based development of teacher education is highlighted.

After these chapters, the question of ethical and purposeful teachers and teaching is deliberated in the contexts of moral and religious education. The contributing authors discuss the foundational role and pervasiveness of moral aspects in good teaching, and demonstrate the importance of discussing such aspects within the teacher-education curriculum (Toom, Husu et al., 2015). Teachers in multicultural schools negotiate among students, parents and the school community, and find shared value systems to form a common ground for education. Values and moral education are embedded in all interactions in schools (Jackson et al., 1993). Religious education could be an explicit context in which to support students in terms of value construction as well as moral and spiritual development.

Chapter 5 entitled "Promoting Purpose Development in Schools and Beyond: A Complex, Dynamic, Bioecological Developmental Systems Perspective," written by Matthew Joseph, extends Damon et al.'s (2003) seminal work on purpose that is meaningful to oneself, active engagement and self-transcendence. According to this definition, purpose is a particular life goal that differs from a general sense of purpose and meaning. Having reviewed studies on purpose development, Joseph shows how little is known about it and how it has typically been viewed as a linear process. However, as with moral and identity development, purpose development seems to be an idiographic, stochastic and non-linear process. The author argues that new approaches, and systemic theories in particular, are needed to enhance understanding of how purpose develops during the life span, especially during adolescence. He also claims that without a systemic approach, interventions and programs might only affect individual components of purpose that are not absorbed into a coherent whole. Joseph concludes that the focus in supporting youth purpose should be on best practices in teaching, given that, in the end, good teaching for purpose is for the most part simply good teaching.

The following two chapters (Chapters 6 and 7) continue with a focus on children and youth. Mette Ranta, Henrietta Grönlund and Anne Birgitta Pessi's contribution is entitled "What Is Above Everything? Conceptions of the Sacred among Finnish Youth," and it concerns the spiritual dimension of educational values. According to the authors, what is considered sacred sheds light on what is perhaps the deepest level of meaning and value among students. The younger generation seem to link both individuality and communality in their understanding of the sacred. Given that teachers tend to represent older generations, there is a need for new insights into the roles of sacredness and values in purposeful education. Therefore, even if their empirical data is based on young adults, the authors draw valuable conclusions with implications for teachers and public education. They conclude that if teachers are to understand and support youth, their identity construction, sense of purpose and wellbeing through education, they must address questions related to values and conceptions of the sacred, and reflect on their own stance with regard to these issues.

Chapter 7 entitled "Children's and Youths' Perspectives on Value Diversity in Education: Implications for Teacher Education and Educator Professionalism" authored by Arniika Kuusisto and Arto Kallioniemi, is based on empirical results showing how Finnish children and youth approach value diversity. Drawing on the work of Schwartz (1992, 1997, 2012), the authors refer to values in terms of what are considered important, be they individual or group-level aims, goals and life-guiding principles, which are nevertheless consistent across situations and contexts. After discussing their findings concerning the life worlds of children and youth with reference to worldviews and values, they challenge organizers of public and teacher education, as well as teachers, to take on the task of self-development to meet the requirements of the superdiversity that is present in the lived realities of societies and their citizens.

Chapter 8, by Terence Lovat, is a theoretical overview entitled "The Learning Ambience of Values Pedagogy." It is based on findings from several projects within the Australian Values Education Program (2003–2010), but Lovat also draws on other literature to further his cause. In his thoughtful contribution he describes what he considers are the key features of a positive learning environment in values education, namely calmness, positive relationships, and safety and security. With reference to these features he reminds educators of what remain the fundamentals of all good teaching and teacher education. Accordingly, as he argues, they could be used as tools for combatting instrumentalism.

In Chapter 9, Martin Ubani, in turn, focuses on professional skills related to teaching religion in his theory-based contribution entitled "Religious Literacy as a 21st Century Skill for All Teachers." He argues that religious literacy is an essential skill in facilitating good and ethical professional pedagogical practice in 21st-century public education. Indeed, it has recently been described in academic, policy-related, and public discussions as one constituent of good citizenship. Drawing from several sources, Ubani describes religious literacy as a necessary competence to facilitate the "critical reading" of religion in different contexts, which would also be applicable to different topics and practices in public education. According to him, religious literacy should incorporate a broad understanding of religion: its personal, communal, societal, institutional, cultural, local and global aspects. At the beginning of the chapter, he outlines the theoretical and scientific bases of religious literacy in public education, connecting it to Hirsch's (1987) cultural literacy, the new literacy movement and multiliteracy, and finally to the framework of 21st-century learning skills. Next, Ubani explores religious literacy as a professional skill of teachers in public education. He contextualizes the topic in Finnish public education and subsequently in Finnish teacher education, although it is also applicable to other contexts. He suggests that teacher education would benefit from the broader conceptual application of religious literacy to professional practice, to be understood as a quality criterion that would facilitate the supply of skillful and ethical teachers for 21st-century schools.

Part 2 of this volume concentrates on *supporting talent development with a growth mindset*. The contributions of this section offer empirical perspectives on developing multiple intelligences (Gardner, 1999; Tirri & Nokelainen, 2011) and theoretical considerations on developing creative talents in particular. In both instances, giftedness and talents are understood as developmental processes. The majority of the chapters discuss the multiple ways in which implicit beliefs (i.e., mindsets, e.g., Dweck, 2000, 2006) are present in talent development and are communicated in teaching-studying-learning processes. The various authors discuss the prerequisites of good teaching for talent development, emphasizing the importance of identifying these belief systems and enhancing growth mindset pedagogy (Rissanen et al., 2019). Differentiation among the key tools is used to create personalized learning trajectories that take individual differences into account. Good teaching embraces all students regardless of whether they are challenged or gifted in their learning: it guides them to find their own place in the world, and to strengthen their leaning-to-learn skills and attitudes towards lifelong-learning.

Elina Kuusisto, Sonja Laine and Inkeri Rissanen begin Chapter 10 with an overview of the history and current state of gifted education in Finland, noting that the needs of gifted students were not addressed in national-level curricula until the 2010s. They continue with a summary of Finnish empirical studies investigating the gifted and talented who have been educated within the Finnish system. They show in their analysis that research in this area has focused mainly on individual, contextual, and coincidental factors of talent development, and they acknowledge that educational policies based on equality and inclusiveness may be inherently challenging in terms of recognizing and developing giftedness. In the final part of the chapter they discuss growth mindset pedagogy, suggesting that it may provide the tools to overcome such challenges in the education of the gifted and talented in Finland.

The focus in Chapter 11, entitled "Recognition, Expectation, and Differentiation for Mathematical Talent Development of Young Gifted English Learners" and authored by Jenny Yang, Jo Sonmi, James Campbell, and Seokhee Cho, is on the Project BRIDGE Math program. The program offers differentiated teaching to scaffold learning processes, especially among gifted kindergarten students for whom English is the second language, in other words English learners (EL). The Project is built on three theoretical approaches: the recognition (R) of giftedness, setting high expectations (E), and matching unique learning needs and curricula through differentiation (D). In the empirical analysis the writers introduce two studies on talent development from the perspectives of gifted ELs and their teachers. They found that gifted ELs were more motivated to learn during the program lessons than in regular classes, and that the instructional strategy of the teachers, particularly so-called Talk Moves, was a significant predictor of mathematical reasoning and communication skills. Talk Moves refer to specific language-based methods that are intended to facilitate mathematical discussion. Examples include: revoicing (the teacher repeats the students' messages), repeating (the student is asked to repeat), reasoning (students are asked to reason why they agree or disagree with other students), adding on (students are asked to incorporate another student's answer), and waiting (the teacher gives time for students to answer). According to the findings, good practice in the context of Mathematics and gifted English learners includes curated teaching that recognizes giftedness, offers challenges and differentiates teaching, especially through scaffolding with Talk Moves.

Chapter 12, written by Petri Nokelainen and Heta Rintala, is entitled "Reaching for Medals and Vocational Excellence? WorldSkills Competition Success in Relation to Goal Orientations and Metacognitive and Resource Management Strategies." The authors investigate how such orientations and strategies among Finnish students in vocational education relate to their success in international WorldSkills competitions. Data for this survey study ($N = 137$) was collected from four different teams representing Finland in the WorldSkills competitions that took place in 2009, 2011, 2013, and 2017. According to the results, most successful competitors have higher levels of mastery and performance-approach goal orientations than other competitors. When learning new skills, they also utilize metacognitive strategies more effectively than less successful competitors. These findings imply a need in vocational education and training to nurture adaptive learning patterns by providing meaningful learning environments as well as relevant and authentic job-related tasks integrating theory and practice.

Chapter 13, entitled "Measuring Apprentices' Intrapreneurship Competence in Vocational Education and Training (VET): An Interdisciplinary Model-based Assessment" is a collaborative contribution involving Susanne Weber, Clemens Draxler, Frank Achtenhagen, Sandra Bley, Michaela Wiethe-Körprich, Christine Kreuzer, and Can Gürer. Weber and her colleagues investigate technology-based performance assessments of intrapreneurship (IP) competence among apprentices in vocational education and training (VET). They focus on two competence dimensions, namely idea generation (I) and planning and implementing (II). Rasch modeling results based on an extensive German nationwide sample (932 students from 28 VET schools) reveal four proficiency levels of IP competence, and that 16% of the apprentices reached the highest level. The authors suggest that VET teachers could use these technology-based performance assessments to give their students more precise guidance in the learning and development of IP competence.

The next chapters focus more closely on the development of creativity among students who are recognizable as gifted and those who have learning challenges and disabilities.

Chapter 14, "Creative Talent as an Emergent Event: A Neurodiversity Perspective" written by Anani M. Vasquez, Mirka Koro, and Ronald A. Beghetto introduces the novel concept of *creative talent as an emergent event* (CTEE).

CTEE is defined as *dynamic manifestations of diverse strengths, interests, and happenings recognized by oneself and others in the on-going interactions, processes and artifacts of social situations and contexts.* Emphasizing the dynamic and developmental nature of giftedness and talent, the authors explore systemic and contextual aspects of talent development. Creative talents are considered from the perspective of neurodiversity, which refers to both dynamic capabilities and "limitless modes of interrelating in lived experience." They point out the importance of documenting creative talent events, a process they label a living biography. In other words, good teaching as perceived in this chapter involves teachers, parents and students in gathering evidence and artifacts that illustrate emerging creative talent events, and in acknowledging neurodiversity in all educational contexts.

Chapter 15, "A Socio-Cultural Approach to Growth-Mindset Pedagogy: Maker-Pedagogy as a Tool for Developing the Next-Generation Growth Mindset" written by Jenni Laurell, Aino Seitamaa, Kati Sormunen, Pirita Seitamaa-Hakkarainen, Tiina Korhonen and Kai Hakkarainen discusses Carol Dweck's notion of implicit theories (i.e., mindsets) and its educational manifestation in growth mindset pedagogy (Rissanen et al., 2019). They base their analysis on socio-cultural theory, pointing out that mindsets are not only individual dispositions, as traditionally perceived in psychology, but also social representations. They further emphasize their relevance not only in the context of intelligence and giftedness, but also in the domain of creativity. Justifying their arguments with empirical results, they show how maker pedagogy can foster a creativity-related growth mindset, for example when mainstream students and students with special educational needs collaborate in co-invention projects.

In the final Chapter 16, entitled "Experimental Evidence on Connections between Speech and Music: Possible Applications on Learning," Minna Huotilainen and Teija Kujala discuss the benefits of music in education. They summarize empirical neuro-studies showing that music and speech share similar neural processes. This and the ability of the brain to change and adapt (brain plasticity) means that musical training could be beneficial for auditory systems, the neural processing of speech signals and the development of reading skills. For these reasons, music has been and should be utilized in special education to enhance learning among students with learning difficulties, specifically related to language-learning, and learners with dyslexia or impaired hearing. According to the authors, good teachers take brain plasticity seriously in internalizing and exercising a growth mindset, and by understanding and exploiting the potential of music in enhancing learning.

This volume, which is based on theoretical and empirical research, discusses good teaching for schools in the future from the perspectives of school pedagogy, educational psychology, and neuropsychology. In combining the German and Nordic traditions of school pedagogy with American traditions of pedagogy and psychology, it builds significant bridges between historically separate fields of study and makes a meaningful contribution to existing literature. With its holistic perspective on the characteristics of good teaching it thus makes a unique contribution to the field.

All good teaching has to be backed up with good research. One prerequisite of such research is critical evaluation conducted by the wider academic community. All the chapters in the three sections have been double-blind peer-reviewed by esteemed scholars and the whole book was evaluated by two leading experts.

This volume also celebrates Professor Kirsi Tirri's (1961–) long and successful career in academia, hence the focus on the research topics that are relevant to her life work and research collaboration. Fittingly, it ends with an epilogue "Growth Mindset and Purpose in Critical-Democratic Citizenship Education" written by Professor emeritus Wiel Veugelers. He argues that concepts such as growth mindset and purpose should be posed more in a societal and political context. It is a strong plea for enhancing a social reconstructionist tradition in research on teaching and teacher education. Veugelers serves as editor of the *Moral Development and Citizenship Education* series. This series has published two of Kirsi Tirri's books (Tirri, 2008; Tirri & Nokelainen, 2011), as well as the current volume. Kirsi Tirri and Wiel Veugelers have a long history of collaboration in which this series has had and continues to have an important role.

We would like to express our gratitude to Wiel Veugelers as editor for accepting this volume in the series *Moral Development and Citizenship Education*, and to John Bennett, Henriët Graafland and Jolanda Karada from Brill Sense for running the process efficiently and competently. We are also grateful to the reviewers who were willing to contribute to the project.

References

Bakx, A., Koopman, M., Den Brok, P., & De Kruijf, J. (2015). Pupils' views on good primary school teachers. *Teachers and Teaching: Theory and Practice, 21*(5), 543–564. doi:10.1080/13540602.2014.995477

Bakx, A., Van Houtert, T., van de Brand, M., & Hornstra, L. (2019). A comparison of high-ability pupils' views vs. regular ability pupils' views of characteristics of good primary school teachers. *Educational Studies, 45*(1), 35–56. doi:10.1080/03055698.2017.1390443

Bardach, L., & Klassen, R. M. (2020). Smart teachers, successful students? A systematic review of the literature on teachers' cognitive abilities and teacher effectiveness. *Educational Research Review, 30*. https://doi.org/10.1016/j.edurev.2020.100312

Bebeau, M., Rest, J., & Narvaez, D. (1999). Beyond the promise: A perspective on research in moral education. *Educational Researcher, 28*(4), 18–26.

Beijaard, D., Meijer, P. C., & Verloop, N. (2004). Reconsidering research on teachers' professional identity. *Teaching and Teacher Education, 20*, 107–128.

Burroughs, N., Gardner, J., Lee, Y., Guo, S., Touitou, I., Jansen, K., & Schmidt, W. (2019). A review on the literature on teacher effectiveness and student outcomes. In N. Burroughs, J. Gardner, Y. Lee, S. Guo, I. Touitou, K. Jansen, & W. Schmidt (Eds.), *Teaching for excellence and equity. Analyzing teacher characteristics, behaviors and student outcomes with TIMSS* (pp. 6–16). Springer.

Clark, C. M. (1986). Ten years of conceptual development in research on teacher thinking. In M. Ben-Peretz, R. Bromme, & R. Halkes (Eds.), *Advances of research on teacher thinking* (pp. 7–20). Swets.

Clark, C. M., & Peterson, P. L. (1986). Teachers' thought processes. In M. C. Wittrock (Ed.), *Handbook of research on teaching* (3rd ed., pp. 255–296). Macmillan.

Day, C., Calderhead, J., & Denicolo, P. (Eds.). (1993). *Research on teacher thinking: Understanding professional development*. The Falmer Press.

Damon, W., Menon, J., & Bronk, K. C. (2003). The development of purpose during adolescence. *Applied Developmental Science, 7*, 119–128.

Dweck, C. S. (2000). *Self-theories: Their role in motivation, personality and development*. Psychology Press.

Dweck, C. S. (2006). *Mindset: The new psychology of success*. Random House.

Eisner, E. W. (2002). What can education learn from the arts about the practice of education? *Journal of Curriculum and Supervision, 18*(1), 4–16.

Gardner, H. (1999). *Intelligence reframed: Multiple intelligence for the 21st century*. Basic Books.

Goe, L., Bell, C., & Little, O. (2008). *Approaches to evaluating teacher effectiveness: A research synthesis*. National Comprehensive Center for Teacher Quality. http://files.eric.ed.gov/fulltext/ED521228.pdf

Gore, J. (2001). Beyond our differences: A reassembling of what matters in teacher education. *Journal of Teacher Education, 52*(2), 124–135.

Hattie, J. (2008). *Visible learning: A synthesis of over 800 meta-analyses relating to achievement*. Routledge.

Heikonen, L., Pietarinen, J., Pyhältö, K., Toom, A., & Soini, T. (2017). Early-career teachers' sense of professional agency in the classroom: Associations with turnover intentions and perceived inadequacy in teacher-student interaction. *Asia-Pacific Journal of Teacher Education, 45*(3), 250–266.

Hirsch, E. (1987). *Cultural literacy: What every American needs to know*. Houghton Mifflin.

Jackson, P. W., Boostrom, R. E., & Hansen, D. T. (1993). *The moral life in schools*. Jossey-Bass.

Kansanen, P., Tirri, K., Meri, M., Krokfors, L., Husu, J., & Jyrhämä, R. (2000). *Teachers' pedagogical thinking: Theoretical landscapes, practical challenges*. Peter Lang.

Korthagen, F. A. J. (2004). In search of the essence of a good teacher: Towards a more holistic approach in teacher education. *Teaching and Teacher Education, 20*, 77–97.

Korthagen, F. A. J. (2017). Inconvenient truths about teacher learning: Towards professional development 3.0. *Teachers and Teaching, 23*(4), 387–405. doi:10.1080/13540602.2016.1211523

Kuusisto, E., & Tirri, K. (2021). The challenge of educating purposeful teachers in Finland. *Education Sciences, 11*(1), 29. https://doi.org/10.3390/educsci11010029

Pajares, M. F. (1992). Teachers' beliefs and educational research: Cleaning up a messy construct. *Review of Educational Research, 62*(3), 307–332.

Podolsky, A., Kini, T., & Darling-Hammond, L. (2019). Does teaching experience increase teacher effectiveness? A review of US research. *Journal of Professional Capital and Community*. doi:10.1108/jpcc-12-2018-0032

Rissanen, I., Kuusisto, E., Tuominen, M., & Tirri, K. (2019). In search of a growth mindset pedagogy: A case study of one teacher's classroom practices in a Finnish elementary school. *Teaching and Teacher Education, 77*, 204–213. doi:10.1016/j.tate.2018.10.002

Schwartz, S. H. (1992). Universals in the content and structure of values: Theoretical advances and empirical tests in 20 countries. In M. P. Zanna (Ed.), *Advances in experimental social psychology* (Vol. 25, pp. 1–65). Academic Press. https://doi.org/10.1016/S0065-2601(08)60281-6

Schwartz, S. H. (1997). Values and culture. In D. Munro, S. Carr, & J. Schumaker (Eds.), *Motivation and culture* (pp. 69–84). Routledge.

Schwartz, S. H. (2012). An overview of the Schwartz theory of basic values. *Online Readings in Psychology and Culture, 2*(1). https://doi.org/10.9707/2307-0919.1116

Shulman, L. (1987). Knowledge and teaching: Foundations of the new reform. *Harvard Educational Review, 57*, 1–22.

Tirri, K. (1993). *Evaluating teacher effectiveness by self-assessment: A cross-cultural study* [Doctoral dissertation, University of Helsinki]. Research report 122. Department of Teacher Education.

Tirri, K. (1999). Teachers' perceptions of moral dilemmas at school. *Journal of Moral Education, 28*(1), 31–47.

Tirri, K. (Ed.). (2008). *Moral sensibilities in urban education*. Sense Publishers.

Tirri, K. (2018). Purposeful teacher. In R. Monyai (Ed.), *Teacher education in the 21st century*. InTechOpen. doi:10.5772/intechopen.83437

Tirri, K. (2019). Ethical sensitivity in teaching and teacher education. In M. A. Peters (Ed.), *Encyclopedia of teacher education*. Springer. https://doi.org/10.1007/978-981-13-1179-6_183-1

Tirri, K., Campbell, E., Gearon, L., & Lovat, T. (Eds.). (2012). The moral core of teaching. *Education Research International* [Special issue].

Tirri, K., & Husu, J. (2002). Care and responsibility "in the best interest of the child": Relational voices of ethical dilemmas in teaching. *Teachers and Teaching: Theory and Practice, 8*(1), 65–80.

Tirri, K., Moran, S., & Mariano, J. M. (2018). Introduction. In K. Tirri, S. Moran, & J. M. Mariano (Eds.), *Education for purposeful teaching around the world* (pp. 1–6). Routledge.

Tirri, K., & Nokelainen, P. (2011). *Measuring multiple intelligences and moral sensitivities in education*. Sense Publishers.

Toom, A. (2006). *Tacit pedagogical knowing: At the core of teacher's professionality* [Doctoral dissertation, University of Helsinki]. Research reports 276. Department of Applied Sciences of Education.

Toom, A. (2017). Teachers' professional and pedagogical competencies: A complex divide between teacher work, teacher knowledge and teacher education. In J. Clandinin & J. Husu (Eds.), *The Sage handbook of research on teacher education* (pp. 803–819). Sage Publishers.

Toom, A., Husu, J., & Tirri, K. (2015). Cultivating student teachers' moral competencies in teaching during teacher education. In C. J. Craig & L. Orland-Barak (Eds.), *International teacher education: Promising pedagogies* (Part C: Advances in research on teaching) (Vol. 22C, pp. 13–31). Emerald Publishing. doi:10.1108/S1479-368720150000026001

Toom, A., Pyhältö, K., & O'Connell Rust, F. (2015). Teacher's professional agency in contradictory times [Editorial]. *Teachers and Teaching: Theory and Practice, 21*(6), 615–623. http://dx.doi.org/10.1080/13540602.2015.1044334

Wayne, A. J., & Youngs, P. (2003). Teacher characteristics and student achievement gains: A review. *Review of Educational Research, 73*(1), 89–122.

Zeichner, K. M. (1983). Alternative paradigms of teacher education. *Journal of Teacher Education, 34*, 3–9.

Zeichner, K. M., & Liston, D. P. (1990). Traditions of reform in U.S. teacher education. *Journal of Teacher Education, 40*(2), 3–20.

PART 1

Ethical and Purposeful Teachers and Teaching

CHAPTER 1

Equity and Quality as Aims of Education

Teachers' Role in Educational Ecosystems

Hannele Niemi

Abstract

With increasing access to education worldwide, the quality of education, including the development of skills and competences for learning in schools or adulthood, has become an urgent challenge. In this chapter, questions of equity and quality in education are explored from the viewpoint of educational ecosystems. The major aim is to analyze teachers' role in the system. Teachers are the cornerstones of education, but they cannot improve schools alone. Developing schools' provision of high-quality learning to all children demands macro-level structures and school conditions where teachers can work as real professionals. Interaction and interconnectedness between and within different levels of the system is also necessary. In the teaching profession, teachers' commitment to ethical standards provides a basis from which to integrate equity and quality, but it requires both active dialogue between partners at the national and local levels and continuous professional development.

Keywords

equity – quality – education – teachers' role – educational ecosystems

1   Increasing Inequalities

Globally, access to education has increased over the last 20 years. More than 90% of children have the opportunity to go to school at the primary level (UIS, 2020). In the last 20 years, there has been a huge push towards providing education to most children. However, recent statistics suggest that inequalities in education remain the reality, even though access has been improved. More than 250 million children are out of school when the secondary level is considered (UNESCO, 2018; World Bank, 2018). Access to the secondary level is still difficult because of low learning performance or failure to complete primary school entirely (UNESCO Institute for Statistics [UIS], 2019; UNESCO, 2018;

World Bank, 2018). Future scenarios in education are highly alarming. Forecasts indicate that by 2030, more than half of the world's young people—over 800 million – will not have basic skills in reading and math (e.g., Education Commission, 2016). In the 2019–20 school year, we faced a new challenge from the COVID-19 pandemic. It has closed schools in 132 countries for 1,048,817,181 students and has affected 59.9% of total enrolled learners worldwide (UIS, 2019), deepening the existing gap in learning opportunities. Global statistics from recent years also demonstrate that there are huge differences in students' learning outcomes from country to country, especially in reading and math skills (World Bank, 2018). In some countries, after four years in schools, students cannot read sentences or perform the easiest mathematical tasks. From an equity point of view, access to education, though it is a basic and necessary condition of equity, is not enough to achieve it (see UIS, 2019; World Bank, 2018; European Commission, 2017). One must also question what the quality of education is and how equity and quality of education are connected.

Both concepts – equity and quality – have been discussed for decades in education (e.g., Gorard & Smith, 2004; Organisation for Economic Co-operation and Development [OECD], 2012, 2018; Trifonas, 2003), and their definitions and indicators vary. Often the concepts have been investigated separately or approaches to them have been narrow (e.g., focusing on equal opportunities that emphasize equal chances). Equity requires taking a wider perspective and setting demands for breaking barriers, asserting that different learners must be supported in such a way as to allow them to use equal opportunities. Discussions on the quality of education have often assessed only students' performances without focusing on the real reasons for success or failure in schools, neglecting inputs like macro-level investments in teacher education or unequal structures in society in a wider sense. Altogether, many traditional factors of educational marginalization, such as gender and residence, combined with income, language, minority status, and disability, particularly in low-income or conflict-affected countries (UIS, 2019), prevent students' learning performances. This is the case in many developing, low income countries, but it is not unknown in mid- and even high-income countries. The reasons are often political, system-wide deficiencies in educational structures, teachers' low competences, family poverty, or attitudinal factors, such as parents who do not recognize the value of schooling or the common attitude and belief that females do not need an education (OECD, 2012; UIS, 2019; World Bank, 2018).

Recent analyses and discussions have revealed that equity and quality should be connected (Garira, 2020; Kyriakides et al., 2019; OECD, 2012, 2018). Equity is not only about providing access to education: it also requires support to help students enter educational paths. Equity also includes the idea that quality learning requires high-standard educational services that promote learning for those who have difficulties. Quality should be connected with inputs, processes, and outputs, as well as their interrelationships. In addition, these concepts should be set in their wider ecological contexts, ensuring that different learners are supported at all levels of education.

In this chapter, equity is seen as a policy-making term in the context of an educational ecosystem meaning that learning opportunities for all types of different learners are supported not only by national or local educational authorities and stakeholders but also through teachers' work. It involves more than providing equal opportunities. Quality of learning is understood as the growth of learners' capacity to manage their learning and have a readiness to continue it based on previous knowledge construction. It goes beyond the repetition of knowledge and setting requirements for schools and teachers to provide knowledge that is meaningful and relevant to learners and their futures. Quality of learning is an indicator of the quality of the educational system, but quality of education is more than students' performances. It also involves the quality of inputs into educational services at different levels of the system. It requires that the system is working in a way that is interconnected with its different parts, and that teachers' work is tied to all levels of the system to aim towards equity and quality.

In this chapter, questions of equity and quality in education are reflected upon from the viewpoint of the educational ecosystem and teachers' roles in it. The aim is to analyze teachers' opportunities and challenges in promoting equity and quality in education. Even though teachers play an important role, we have to ask how they can really contribute to education. The first concept of the ecosystem will be introduced and analyzed to explore how teachers can promote equity and quality in education.

2 The Educational Ecosystem Widens Concepts of Quality and Equity

The concept of ecosystems is rooted in biology (e.g., Dowd, 2019; Mars et al., 2012). The most important features of ecosystems are the interconnectedness of their constituents and the information flows that exist throughout the system. Diversity is also an essential feature in the natural ecosystem, ensuring the functioning of the system. We have learned from ecological studies that systems function well when their different parts work together.

The concept of ecosystems has emerged in medicine and health care (Kahn et al., 2012; Walpole et al., 2016), the social sciences (Oksanen & Hautamäki, 2015; Schwinda et al., 2016), and educational discussions (Niemi, 2016a, 2021;

Niemi et al., 2014). Ecosystems have also been used in technological environments to describe the importance of different partners working together (Moore, 2006). Mars et al. (2012) analyze the value of this concept, noting that the metaphor has provided a fresh lens through which to view a world that is inherently interconnected.

The concepts of education systems and educational ecosystems share many features, but the ecosystem approach places an emphasis on the interconnectedness between different parts and actors. Niemi (2016a, 2021) notes that an educational ecosystem has complex connections and processes that interact with different levels of society and social structures. We can refer to a macro-level, which consists of all the structures of the entire educational system, from childhood to adult education. These structures include the national curriculum, educational evaluation systems, and life-long learning strategies for ensuring competences throughout the course of life. Essential viewpoints for this level involve exploring how these structures promote or hinder equity and quality and how teachers can contribute to these goals. In education, there are also meso- or mid-level units, such as schools and other educational institutions, with their own structures and social practices, such as leadership figures and their roles and responsibilities at the institutional and community levels. This level consists of a variety of processes, including how inclusion and other aspects of equity are implemented in schools. We can also observe micro-level ecosystems, where individuals, such as students in the classroom and teachers as representatives of their profession, are influenced by their individual characteristics and backgrounds. Ecosystem thinking also regards connections with other systems in society as crucial, such as connections with health care, social services, and even housing and living circumstances. Ecosystems include the idea that changes are systemic: that is, reforms for equity demand changes in many parts in the system. This connection also helps us to see how equity and quality are interdependent. Garira (2020) and Pischetola and de Miranda (2020) claim that we need a systemic approach, particularly when equity and quality are important aims of the system. When looking at teachers' roles in education, there is always a danger that we will see their roles too simply, only considering how they work as knowledge transmitters. In the next section, teachers' work is reflected upon through the ecosystem lens.

3 Teachers as Part of Educational Ecosystems

Teachers are regarded as cornerstones in the educational system (e.g., Cochran-Smith, 2020; Darling-Hammond, 2005, 2017; Darling-Hammond & Lieberman,

2012; Council of the European Union, 2014; Lefty & Fraser, 2020). The European Commission (2017, p. 8) expresses "High quality, motivated and valued teachers are at the heart of excellent education." Teachers can make a difference in students' life, and this evidence has been available for decades; (e.g., European Commission, 2013; Good et al., 1975; Hattie, 2003; Maloney et al., 2019; Niemi & Lavonen, 2020). Already in the 1990s Hargreaves and Fullan (1992) regarded teachers as change agents in education. However, we also have evidence (e.g., Andrews, 2020; Vallory, 2020) that teachers have very few opportunities to work as change agents because of political conditions, historical roots or deficiencies in teacher education systems. The essential question is what kinds of teachers' professional roles and working conditions are needed so that teachers can work for equity and quality.

When analyzing teachers' role in the ecosystem, we can see educational systems are complex, they have long historical roots, and they are connected with political purposes. This can be found in many countries in different parts of the world (e.g., Lefty & Fraser, 2020). When looking more closely inside the system, we can see that teachers are seen as the most important parts in the system. However, the differences between countries and what is expected from teachers can be huge (Lefty & Fraser, 2020).

Often a strong connection with the economy of the country, aiming at boosting the market economy, providing a more competent work force or expectations and demands of innovations can be ice-breakers e.g., for new industry. In China (Liao & Zhou, 2020), teacher education can be described with metaphors that suggest how it has served national political aims in the 20th century, being first the cornerstones for national reconstruction then the engine for boosting economic growth, thereafter an equalizer harmonizing society, and finally a window for envisioning a global agenda. In Finland the role of teachers' in national identity formation and welfare have been important (Niemi, 2016b; Niemi & Lavonen, 2020). Teachers' work is always connected with wider societal aims, not only with what happens in classrooms.

3.1   *Teacher Work Depends on the Macro Level*

Education is part of society and in educational systems we can identify different levels. A macro level of the system, national regulations, defines how an education structure is organized and what are educational levels e.g., early childhood care and education, primary and secondary level, adult education and higher education. The macro level also consists of regulations for the national curriculum, evaluations and inclusion policy and how teachers are trained. Many practices are rooted in societal processes and also in a nation's history (Lefty & Fraser, 2020; Niemi, 2016b; Niemi & Lavonen, 2020). Nationally, political aims are often reflected in curricula and learning materials that impact on teachers' work. In some countries, especially in the USA, the evaluation system is based on standardized testing, competitiveness and rankings, often also setting teachers in ranking order based on their students' performances (LeTendre, 2018). In some countries, such as Finland, equity and quality are connected with a national policy (Kumpulainen & Lankinen, 2016) and set goals are connected with the entire educational system, teacher education being part of it. Globally, there has been much debate how international measurements, such as PISA, determine schools and teachers' work (Zhao, 2020). Many researchers' demand more focus on contextual factors and quality culture and the quality of educational services. The fact is that some countries lack essential knowledge about educational performances (World Bank, 2018) and this also sets limits for enhancing equity and quality. How much teachers can influence the quality of teaching and learning depends on their competences but also to the extent that they really can contribute to the system if it is regulated by structures which they cannot influence.

The kind of professional role society has given to teachers is decisive. The concept of a profession is often used to describe medical doctors' or lawyers' work. Professions are societal institutions that have specific features, such as a long, high-quality education in institutions that have been audited or accredited, quality criteria for entering a profession, a codified body of knowledge as a basis for the profession, wide autonomy and responsibility to develop one's own work and an ethical code of conduct for working in the profession (e.g., Cruess et al., 2004). The extent to which teachers can be seen as professionals has been debated for a long time (Hargreaves & Fullan, 1992; Howsam, 1976; Lefty & Fraser, 2020; Niemi, Toom et al., 2018; Tom, 1984). Teachers can of course be seen as representatives of a profession but this role requires structures and conditions to work as agents who can act and make improvements in their work.

Teachers can make a difference, but the failure of students does not depend on their poor abilities nor on their teachers. An irrelevant curriculum and lack of support (Field et al., 2007; OECD, 2012) are the real reasons behind the failure. If teachers are very tied to the details of the national curriculum and testing strengthens that, teachers' opportunities to modify teaching to local and individual needs is very limited. And vice versa, in contexts where teachers have high competence, professional autonomy and other macro level systems support their work, they can implement their professional role and introduce education that matters in students' learning. We have also learned that teachers can make a difference in both centralized and decentralized education systems; Singapore, for example, is a centralized system and Finland is a representative decentralized system. Both are countries that have a good educational reputation. They are culturally, politically and geographical different, but the common aspect is a strong teacher education, effective support and respect for teachers from local or national authorities (Low, 2018; Niemi, Lavonen et al., 2018; Tan & Liu, 2015). The status of teachers, provided by the macro-level decisions, is essential for making the teaching profession attractive for talented and motivated applicants. In some countries, for example England (Andrews, 2020) and the USA (Lefty & Fraser, 2020; LeTendre, 2018) a macro-level trend is de-professionalization of teachers' work (Milner, 2013). It leads to a situation where official qualifications are neither required nor is short-term practical training. This has an influence on teachers' work, most often lowering the attractiveness of the teaching occupation and discouraging staying in the profession (Goodwin, 2014).

From the ecosystem perspective, it is also decisive how macro-level structures, for example the teachers' professional role and status, curriculum and evaluation systems and teacher education are working together to ensure equity and quality. If each macro level part is working very separately and there is not the required information flow in the ecosystems, the coherence of the system is missing, it is fragmented, and the system loses its effectiveness. Also, if some parts, for example high stake testing, dominates, the system can be very biased and narrow and can set barriers for student progress, particularly if the inclusion policy is weak or missing. In these cases, teachers have a very limited chance to influence work in their profession.

3.2 *Teachers at an Institution Level*

Schools and other educational institutes are mid-level structures in educational systems. Teachers' work depends on macro-level regulation and on their professional role but their work happens mainly in school communities. The extent to which students can have high quality education and be treated equally, and for equity to be ensured, depends on the teacher's capacity. Tan and Liu (2015, p. ix) have pointed out that teacher effectiveness in our global world is in a continuous process of change: "In this challenging time, we need teachers who inculcate in their students a deep love for learning, and empower then so that they can become self-directed and collaborative learners." Teachers can have a significant impact on their students' lives (Kyriakides et al., 2019) by promoting equality and preventing discrimination.

A teacher matters, but school is more than individual teachers (Vangrieken et al., 2017). School is a social construction that has values, norms and practices that have grown and been maintained by a social community. This is important when thinking about student diversity and inclusion. The macro-level regulations, for example about all students' right for high quality learning, is not necessarily realized if the teachers' or even the whole school community's attitudes do not fully accept the inclusion (e.g., Saloviita, 2020). Even in cases where laws are in place, teachers may not be able to implement them because of attitudinal restrictions that are often connected with a lack of resources or competence. In these cases, such laws become powerless. On the other hand, teachers can make a difference, even in the most difficult conditions. Teachers' moral commitment to their profession is a strong resource for integrating equity and quality (Goodlad et al., 1990; Niemi, 2014; Oser, 1991, 1994; Tirri, 1999, 2008, 2019; Tirri & Husu, 2002; Tirri & Toom, 2020; Tom, 1984). A professional code of ethics often outlines teachers' main responsibilities to their students and defines their role in students' lives. In some countries, such as Ireland, teachers' code of conduct covers interaction with students, colleagues, and the whole school community (Teaching Council, 2016), and in Finland responsibilities also cover contributions to society (Ethical Committee for the Teaching Profession, 2020). Toom and Husu (2016) have pointed out that teachers' work is wide and their responsibilities cover relationships with students, parents, colleagues, and involve developing learning environments. The work is often hard and teachers need to collaborate with others and share the challenges they meet in their work.

Fritz Oser (1921, 1994) and Kirsi Tirri (1999) have analyzed teachers' work from the perspective of moral dilemmas, pointing out how important ethical reflections are in teachers' work. Oser has created a model that consists of justice, caring and truthfulness, pointing out that teachers should keep them all integrated. A dilemma may well develop if all of them are not implemented. A core of the profession is the moral commitment of teachers and how they work in real situations in schools.

From the ecosystem viewpoint, teachers' individual efforts are needed but the school works as a community. It is essential that interconnectedness, information flow and diversity create a living unity that aims at equity and quality. In schools, there can also be departments based on subject matters, and teachers are working alone, without collegial support and cooperation. The culture of a school depends on leadership and how responsibilities and power have been divided in a school community (e.g., Hilty, 2011; Lieberman & Friedrich, 2010). Teacher leadership is a concept that describes how teachers can be influential in a school community.

3.3   *Teachers at the Micro Level*

A teacher is also a person and has his/her individual features. Teachers' professional development and growth have been investigated for decades using different conceptualizations (Avalos, 2011; Blömeke & Kaiser, 2017; Caena, 2014; Hargreaves & Fullan, 1992). Teachers are described in terms of expertise development, teachers' agency, identity formation, life histories, and constructivist conceptual change (e.g., Dreyfus & Dreyfus, 1986; Feiman-Nemser, 2008; Hargreaves & Fullan, 1992; Huberman, 1992; Livingston, 2018; Maskit, 2011; Schön, 1987). In all these theories, teachers are seen as learners who need to adapt to the demands of the profession. Recently, theories of dynamic and adaptive expertise (Beltramo, 2017; van Tartwijk et al., 2017; Männikkö & Husu, 2019) have brought to the fore the changing situations in which teachers work (see also Lee & Tan, 2018). The work requires teachers to renew their own capacities. Teachers' development is seen as adaptive, reflective, and reformative. As Anthony et al. (2015, p. 109) describe, expertise is understood as "not being directly related to teaching experience – the traditional novice versus expert division – but rather, as a component of professionalism."

Teachers need continuous learning and the learning that happens in the contexts and situations in schools are important learning opportunities (Schultz & Ravitch, 2013). Development happens where professional demands and teachers' own personal microsystem are integrated. This can involve cultural positions, family, traditions, values, worldviews, different disciplines and their values, norms. The teacher's own personality is an important tool in the teaching profession. However, the teacher's role that is connected to the curriculum and to ethical standards goes beyond the teacher's own personal features or e.g., his or her own personal values and attitudes.

Teachers are not free in the sense that they can implement their own personal missions without taking into account societal requirements, and the aims of curricula and evaluation systems. All teacher has their own ecosystem with their own histories, memories and experiences. Teachers need to integrate these experiences into their own professional commitments. Even though teaching is not a vocation in the traditional sense, it requires one to serve even in the worst conditions, nevertheless commitments to ethical codes and a deep interest in human development makes it meaningful. To be active agents, teachers also need support.

4 Conclusions

Teachers cannot change education alone. This chapter raises the question what is needed so that teachers can really promote equity and quality in education. Teachers work in a local context and in specific situations. However, teaching happens in an educational ecosystem that has macro-level structures and regulations, school communities as mid-level institutions of the ecosystem, and finally teachers have their own personal professional development processes at their micro levels. They all impact on teachers' capacities to promote equity and quality in education.

The concept of the educational ecosystem is based on the assumption that different levels are interconnected vertically between levels and there is active cooperation horizontally within each level. Teachers can make a difference in their students' lives but certain conditions are required where parts of the system are in interaction and there are continuous discussions on the values and aims of education in society and also on democracy as an essential aim of society (Zeichner, 2020). Teachers' opportunities to promote equity and quality and to integrate them into their daily work depends on the philosophical premises on which education is seen as an ecosystem.

Educational ecosystems need common visions and cooperation and they must be open to interaction, diversity and information flow. Teachers and teacher education should be in active dialogue with different levels of the educational system (Dehghan, 2020; Niemi, 2016a). Their professional role should be accepted and also supported by macro-level structures and practices, e.g., in teacher education and curriculum and evaluation systems. Without professional competence, autonomy and trust it is very difficult to be in charge of professional responsibilities.

While the ecosystem metaphor is a useful tool for understanding and predicting the conditions that shape and influence systems, it is important to understand the differences between biological and human ecosystems. Biological systems are not supported by the conscious plans of different constituents, whereas to be effective, human organizations and systems must be based on conscious human actions, strategic aims, and commitments. This sets frames and conditions how teachers really can contribute in the system. In educational ecosystems it is a necessary condition that partners and actors are connected, that they are committed to common aims, that they share information, and that they regard diversity as a resource. We have evidence how hierarchy, bureaucracy, fragmentation, lack of communication cause ineffectiveness in education, resulting in subsystems that are separated into segmented territories, each of which has its own aims, social practices, and power structures.

It is worth noting that systems can work very effectively if there is a common aim and all actors are committed to that aim. However, there is also a danger. The ecosystem cannot be based on a top-down management serving power structures and political tools without real dialogue about allowing inclusion and diversity (Burns et al., 2016). Pursiainen (2002, p. 43) writes that professional institutions are phenomena of a free society and warns "A totalitarian society does not recognize genuine professionalism. A totalitarian society is based on the idea that there is only one and only one right perspective from which all things must be assessed and from which all decisions must be made." In free societies, professional freedom is based on trust and the idea that professionals will serve the common interests of all. If this trust were to be broken, professional freedom and authority would soon be questioned (Pursiainen, 2002).

Teachers' opportunities to work for equity and quality in education is a philosophical value issue that has connections to all levels of the educational ecosystem. Equity and equality are required at all practical levels throughout the system. Andreas Schleicher (2012) presents the following outlines for combining equity and quality:

- *Combining ambitious standards with strong support.* This requires a shift away from mere control over the resources and content of education and towards a focus on outcomes – directing services towards individual students based on their needs, including services for students requiring special educational or social assistance. It also needs educational networks between individual schools and between schools and other institutions to enable teachers and schools to improve their performance.
- *Government and schools sharing decision-making responsibility.* Schools need to choose their own responses to the local conditions. This involves knowing how to use the results from evaluations and assessments in order to reveal the best practices and identify shared problems. Both teachers and schools can improve their performance and develop more supportive and productive learning environments.
- *Engaging with an increasingly diverse student body to improve equity in education.* Raising performance levels depends critically on the capacity of education systems to address the needs of poorly performing students and schools.
- *Fair and inclusive education design.* The structure of education systems and the pathways through that system can help or hinder equity. Traditionally, education systems have sorted students into different tracks, institutions and streams according to attainment. This sorting sometimes increases inequalities and inequities.

Developing schools towards high-quality learning for all children demands macro-level structures and school conditions where teachers can work as real professionals. In the teaching profession, teachers' commitment to ethical standards gives a basis to integrate equity and quality but it needs active dialogue between partners at both national and local levels and continuous professional development. Connecting equity and quality, demands that in education human actors, unlike natural ecosystems, anticipate the future and create conditions that have an impact beyond the present setting and that teachers are part of these processes. To this end, educational actors must work together to design, adapt, and create systems that lead to lifelong learning and high-quality education for all. This is a key mission of education.

References

Andrews, R. (2020). Crisis and opportunity in teacher preparation in England. In L. Lefty & J. Fraser (Eds.), *Teaching the world's teachers* (pp. 132–152). Johns Hopkins University Press.

Anthony, G., Hunter, J., & Hunter, R. (2015). Prospective teachers' development of adaptive expertise. *Teaching and Teacher Education, 49*, 108–117. https://doi.org/10.1016/j.tate.2015.03.010

Avalos, B. (2011). Teacher professional development in teaching and teacher education over ten years. *Teaching and Teacher Education, 27*(1), 10–20. https://doi.org/10.1016/j.tate.2010.08.007

Beltramo, J. L. (2017). Developing adaptive teaching practices through participation in cogenerative dialogues. *Teaching and Teacher Education, 63*, 326–337. https://doi.org/10.1016/j.tate.2017.01.007

Blömeke, S., & Kaiser, G. (2017). Understanding the development of teachers' professional competencies as personally, situationally and socially determined. In D. J. Clandinin & J. Husu (Eds.), *The Sage handbook of research on teacher education* (2 volume set, pp. 783–802). Sage Publications.

Burns, T., Köster, F., & Fuster, M. (2016). *Education governance in action: Lessons from case studies*. OECD Publishing. http://dx.doi.org/10.1787/9789264262829-en

Caena, F. (2014). Teacher competence frameworks in Europe: Policy-as-discourse and policy-as-practice. *European Journal of Education, 49*(3), 311–331. https://doi.org/10.1111/ejed.12088

Cochran-Smith, M. (2020). Teacher education for justice and equity: 40 years of advocacy. *Action in Teacher Education, 42*(1), 49–59. doi:10.1080/01626620.2019.1702120

Council of the European Union. (2014). Council conclusions of 20 May 2014 on effective teacher education. *Official Journal of the European Union, C183*, 22–24.

Cruess, S. R., Johnston, S., & Cruess, R. L. (2004). "Profession": A working definition for medical educators. *Teaching and Learning in Medicine, 16*(1), 74–76. https://doi.org/10.1207/s15328015tlm1601_15

Darling-Hammond, L. (2005). Teaching as a profession: Lessons in teacher preparation and professional development. *Phi Delta Kappan, 87*(3), 237–240. https://doi.org/10.1177/003172170508700318

Darling-Hammond, L. (2017). Teacher education around the world: What can we learn from international practice? *European Journal of Teacher Education, 40*(3), 291–309. https://doi.org/10.1080/02619768.2017.1315399

Darling-Hammond, L., & Lieberman, A. (Eds.). (2012). *Teacher education around the world: Changing policies and practices*. Routledge.

Dehghan, F. (2020). Teachers' perceptions of professionalism: A top-down or a bottom-up decision-making process? *Professional Development in Education*, 1–10. https://doi.org/10.1080/19415257.2020.1725597

Dowd, M. (2019). *Ecosystem: Definition, types, structure & examples*. Sciencing. https://sciencing.com/ecosystem-definition-types-structure-examples-13719218.html

Dreyfus, H. L., & Dreyfus, S. E. (1986). *Mind over machine: The power of human intuition and expertise in the era of the computer*. Basil Blackwell.

Education Commission. (2016). *The learning generation. Investing in education for a changing world*. The International Commission on Financing Global Education Opportunity. http://report.educationcommission.org/report/

Ethical Committee for the Teaching Profession. (2020). *Professional ethics. Teachers-values and ethical principles*. The Trade Union of Education in Finland [OAJ]. https://www.oaj.fi/en/education/ethical-principles-of-teaching/teachers-values-and-ethical-principles/

European Commission. (2013). *Supporting teacher competence development for better learning outcomes*. https://ec.europa.eu/assets/eac/education/experts-groups/2011-2013/teacher/teachercomp_en.pdf

European Commission. (2017). *School development and excellent teaching for a great start in life. Communication from the Commission to the European Parliament. The Council, the European Economic and Social Committee and the Committee of the Regions*. Brussels. https://op.europa.eu/en/publication-detail/-/publication/aa9ffc00-4524-11e7-aea8-01aa75ed71a1

Feiman-Nemser, S. (2008). Teacher learning. How do teachers learn to teach? In M. Cochran Smith, S. D. Feiman-Nemser, & D. McIntyre (Eds.), *Handbook of research on teacher education. Enduring questions in changing contexts* (pp. 697–705). Routledge/Taylor & Francis.

Field, S., Kuczera, M., & Pont, B. (2007). *No more failures: Ten steps to equity in education*. OECD.

Garira, E. (2020). A Proposed unified conceptual framework for quality of education in schools. *Sage Open, 10*(1). https://doi.org/10.1177/2158244019899445

Good, T. L., Biddle, B. J., & Brophy, J. E. (1975). *Teachers make a difference*. Holt, Rinehart & Winston.

Goodlad, J. I., Soder, R., & Sirotnik, K. A. (Eds.). (1990). *The moral dimensions of teaching*. Jossey-Bass.

Goodwin A. L. (2014). Perspectives on high performing education systems in Finland, Hong Kong, China, South Korea and Singapore: What lessons for the U.S.? In S. Lee, W. Lee, & E. Low (Eds.), *Educational policy innovations* (pp. 185–199). Springer. https://doi.org/10.1007/978-981-4560-08-5_11

Gorard, S., & Smith, E. (2004). An international comparison of equity in education systems. *Comparative Education, 40*(1), 15–28. doi:10.1080/0305006042000184863

Hargreaves, A., & Fullan, M. G. (1992). Introduction. In A. Hargreaves & M. Fullan (Eds.), *Understanding teacher development* (pp. 1–19). Teacher College Press.

Hattie, J. A. C. (2003, October). *Teachers make a difference: What is the research evidence?* [Paper presentation]. Australian Council for Educational Research Conference, Melbourne, Australia. http://research.acer.edu.au/research_conference_2003/4/

Hilty. E. B. (Ed.). (2011). *Teacher leadership. The "new" foundations of teacher education.* Peter Lang.

Howsam, R. (1976). *Educating a profession.* American Association of Colleges for Teacher Education.

Huberman, M. (1992). Teacher development and instructional mastery. In A. Hargreaves & M. Fullan (Eds.), *Understanding teacher development* (pp. 216–241). Longman Publishers.

Kahn, L. H., Monath, T. P., Bokma, B. H., Glbbd, E. P., & Aguirre, A. A. (2012). One health, one medicine. In A. A. Aguirre, R. S. Ostfeld, & P. Daszak (Eds.), *New directions in conservation medicine: Applied cases of ecological health* (pp. 33–44). Oxford University Press.

Kumpulainen, K., & Lankinen, T. (2016). Striving for educational equity and excellence: Evaluation and assessment in Finnish basic education. In H. Niemi, A. Toom, & A. Kallioniemi (Eds.), *Miracle of education: The principles and practices of teaching and learning in Finnish schools* (2nd ed., pp. 71–82). Sense Publishers.

Kyriakides, L., Creemers, B. P. M., & Charalambous, E. (2019). Searching for differential teacher and school effectiveness in terms of student socioeconomic status and gender: Implications for promoting equity. *School Effectiveness and School Improvement, 30*(3), 286–308.

Lee, W. O., & Tan, J. P.-L. (2018). The new roles for twenty-first-century teachers: Facilitator, knowledge broker, and pedagogical weaver. In H. Niemi, A. Toom, A. Kallioniemi, & J. Lavonen (Eds.), *The teacher's role in the changing globalizing world: Resources and challenges related to the professional work of teaching* (pp. 11–31). Brill | Sense.

Lefty, L., & Fraser, J. W. (2020). Changing paths and enduring debates in US American teacher education. In L. Lefty & J. Fraser (Eds.), *Teaching the world's teachers* (pp. 281–300). Johns Hopkins University Press.

LeTendre, G. K. (2018). Teaching in the USA: Decentralization, inequality, and professional autonomy. In H. Niemi, A. Toom, A. Kallioniemi, & J. Lavonen (Eds.), *The *teacher's role in the changing globalizing world: Resources and challenges related to the professional work of teaching practices* (pp. 91–108). Brill | Sense.

Lieberman, A., & Friedrich, L. D. (2010). *How teachers become leaders*. Teacher College Press.

Liao, W., & Zhou, Y. (2020). Teacher education reform and national development in China (1978–2107). In L. Lefty & J. Fraser (Eds.), *Teaching the world's teachers* (pp. 111–131). Johns Hopkins University Press.

Livingston, K. (2018). Multiple influences on teachers in changing environments. *European Journal of Teacher Education, 41*(2), 135–137. https://doi.org/10.1080/02619768.2018.1432318

Low, E.-L. (2018). The changing roles of teachers and teacher learning in the twenty-first century: The Singapore story. In H. Niemi, A. Toom, A. Kallioniemi, & J. Lavonen (Eds.), *The teacher's role in the changing globalizing world: Resources and challenges related to the professional work of teaching practices* (pp. 125–140). Brill | Sense. https://doi.org/10.1163/9789004372573_009

Maloney, T., Hayes, N., Crawford-Garrett, K., & Sassi, K. (2019). Preparing and supporting teachers for equity and racial justice: Creating culturally relevant, collective, intergenerational, co-created spaces. *Review of Education, Pedagogy, and Cultural Studies, 41*, 252–281.

Männikkö, I., & Husu, J. (2019). Examining teachers' adaptive expertise through personal practical theories. *Teaching and Teacher Education, 77*, 126–137. https://doi.org/10.1016/j.tate.2018.09.016

Mars, M., Bronstein, J., & Lusch, R. (2012). The value of a metaphor: Organizations and ecosystems. *Organizational Dynamics, 41*(4), 271–280.

Maskit, D. (2011). Teachers' attitudes toward pedagogical changes during various stages of professional development. *Teaching and Teacher Education, 27*(5), 851–860. https://doi.org/10.1016/j.tate.2011.01.009

Milner, H. R. (2013). *Policy reforms and de-professionalization of teaching*. National Education Policy Center. http://nepc.colorado.edu/publication/policy-reforms-deprofessionalization

Moore, J. F. (2006). Business ecosystems and the view from the firm. *The Antitrust Bulletin, 51*(1), 31–75.

Niemi, H. (2014). Purposeful policy and practice for equity and quality – A Finnish case. In S. K. Lee, W. Lee, & E. L. Low (Eds.), *Education policy innovations*. Springer.

Niemi, H. (2016a). Building partnerships in an educational ecosystem: Editorial. *CEPS Journal, 6*(3), 5–15.

Niemi, H. (2016b). The societal factors contributing to education and schooling in Finland. In H. Niemi, A. Kallioniemi, & A. Toom (Eds.), *The miracle of education: The principles and practices of teaching and learning in Finnish schools* (2nd ed., pp. 24–40). Sense Publishers.

Niemi, H. (2021). Teacher education at the crossroads – Educational ecosystems for equity and quality of learning. In X. Zhu & H. Song (Eds.), *Envisioning the teaching and learning of teachers for excellence and equity in education* (pp. 5–23). Springer.

Niemi, H., & Lavonen, J. (2020). Teacher education in Finland: Persistent efforts for high-quality teachers. In L. Lefty & J. Fraser (Eds.), *Teaching the world's teachers* (pp. 153–178). Johns Hopkins University Press.

Niemi, H., Lavonen, J., Kallioniemi, A., & Toom, A. (2018). The role of teachers in the Finnish educational system. In H. Niemi, A. Toom, A. Kallioniemi, & J. Lavonen (Eds.), *The teacher's role in the changing globalizing world* (pp. 47–61). Brill | Sense. https://doi.org/10.1163/9789004372573_004

Niemi, H., Multisilta, J., Lipponen, L., & Vivitsou, V. (Eds.). (2014). *Finnish innovations and technologies in schools. Towards new ecosystems of learning.* Sense Publishers.

Niemi, H., Toom, A., Kallioniemi, A., & Lavonen, J. (Eds.). (2018). *The teacher's role in the changing globalizing world.* Brill | Sense. https://doi.org/10.1163/9789004372573_001

OECD. (2018). *Equity in education: Breaking down barriers to social mobility.* PISA, OECD Publishing. https://doi.org/10.1787/9789264073234-en

Oksanen, K., & Hautamäki, A. (2015). Sustainable innovation: A competitive advantage for innovation ecosystems. *Technology Innovation Management Review, 5*(10), 24–30.

Organisation for Economic Co-operation and Development (OECD). (2012). *Equity and quality in education: Supporting disadvantaged students and schools.* OECD Publishing. https://www.oecd-ilibrary.org/docserver/9789264130852-en.pdf?expires=1603811705&id=id&accname=ocid194948&checksum=ED0BFE160E3A84E9CFAF1606C2E9B13F

Oser, F. K. (1991). Professional morality: A discourse approach (the case of the teaching profession). In W. Kurtines & J. Gewirtz (Eds.), *Handbook of moral behaviour and development* (pp. 191–228). Lawrence Erlbaum.

Oser, F. K. (1994). Moral perspectives on teaching. *Review of Research in Education, 20,* 57–128.

Pischetola, M., & de Miranda, L. V. T. (2020). Systemic thinking in education and a situated perspective on teaching. *Ciência & Educação, 26,* https://doi.org/10.1590/1516-731320200015

Pursiainen, T. (2002). Ammattien etiikka [The nucleus of professional ethics]. In Ethical Committee for the Teaching Profession (Ed.), *Etiikka koulun Arjessa* [*Ethics in the everyday life in schools*] (pp. 35–44; English summary, pp. 146–147). The Trade Union of Education in Finland, Otava.

Saloviita, T. (2020). Attitudes of teachers towards inclusive education in Finland. *Scandinavian Journal of Educational Research, 64*(2), 270–282. https://doi.org/10.1080/00313831.2018.1541819

Schleicher, A. (Ed.). (2012). *Preparing teachers and developing school leaders for the 21st century: Lessons from around the world.* OECD Publishing. http://dx.doi.org/10.1787/9789264xxxxxx-en

Schön, D. A. (1987). *Educating the reflective practitioner: Toward a new design for teaching and learning in the professions.* Jossey-Bass.

Schultz, K., & Ravitch, S. M. (2013). Narratives of learning to teach: Taking on professional identities. *Journal of Teacher Education, 64*(1), 35–46. https://doi.org/10.1177/0022487112458801

Schwinda, J., Gilardia, K., Beasleyb, V., Mazeta, J., & Smitha, W. (2016). Advancing the 'one health' workforce by integrating ecosystem health practice into veterinary medical education: The Environment Summer Institute. *Health Education Journal, 75*(2), 170–183.

Tan, O.-S., & Liu, W.-C. (Eds.). (2015). *Teacher effectiveness. Capacity building in a complex learning era.* Cengage Learning Asia.

Teaching Council. (2016). *Code of professional conduct for teachers* (2nd updated ed.). https://www.teachingcouncil.ie/en/publications/fitness-to-teach/code-of-professional-conduct-for-teachers1.pdf

Tirri, K. (1999). Teachers' perceptions of moral dilemmas at school. *Journal of Moral Education, 28*(1), 31–47.

Tirri, K. (Ed.). (2008). *Educating moral sensibilities in urban schools.* Sense Publishers.

Tirri, K. (2019). Ethical sensitivity in teaching and teacher education. In M. A. Peters (Ed.), *Encyclopedia of teacher education* (Springer Nature) (pp. 1–5). Springer Science+Business Media. https://doi.org/10.1007/978-981-13-1179-6_183-1

Tirri, K., & Husu, J. (2002). Care and responsibility in "the best interest of the child": Relational voices of ethical dilemmas in teaching. *Teachers and Teaching, 8*(1), 65–80.

Tirri, K., & Toom, A. (2020). The moral role of pedagogy as the science and art of teaching. In K. Tirri & A. Toom (Eds.), *Pedagogy in basic and higher education: Current developments and challenges* (pp. 3–13). IntechOpen.

Tom, A. (1984). *Teaching as a moral craft.* Longman.

Toom, A., & Husu, J. (2016). Finnish teachers as 'makers of the many': Balancing between broad pedagogical freedom and responsibility. In H. Niemi, A. Toom, & A. Kallioniemi (Eds.), *Miracle of education: The principles and practices of teaching and learning in Finnish schools* (pp. 41–55). Sense Publishers.

Trifonas, P. P. (Ed.). (2003). *Pedagogies of difference rethinking education for social justice.* Routledge.

UNESCO. (2018). *One in every five children, adolescents and youth is out of school worldwide.* UNESCO Institute for Statistics. http://uis.unesco.org/sites/default/files/documents/fs48-one-five-children-adolescents-youth-out-school-2018-en.pdf

UNESCO Institute for Statistics (UIS). (2019, October). *Combining data on out-of-school children, completion and learning to offer a more comprehensive view on SDG 4*. Information Paper No. 61. UNESCO-UIS. http://uis.unesco.org/sites/default/files/documents/ip61-combining-data-out-of-school-children-completion-learning-offer-more-comprehensive-view-sdg4.pdf

Vallory, E. (2020). Preparing teachers for the schools we have or for the school we want? Challenges and changes in Catalonia (Spain). In L. Lefty & J. Fraser (Eds.), *Teaching the world's teachers* (pp. 89–110). Johns Hopkins University Press.

van Tartwijk, J., Zwart, R., & Wubbels, T. (2017). Developing teachers' competences with the focus on adaptive expertise in teaching. In D. J. Clandinin & J. Husu (Eds.), *The Sage handbook of research on teacher education* (2 volume set; pp. 820–835). Sage Publications.

Vangrieken, K., Meredith, C., Packer, T., & Kyndt, E. (2017). Teacher communities as a context for professional development: A systematic review. *Teaching and Teacher Education, 61*, 47–59. https://doi.org/10.1016/j.tate.2016.10.001

Walpole, S. C., Pearson, D., Coad, J., & Barna, S. (2016). What do tomorrow's doctors need to learn about ecosystems? *Medical Teacher, 38*(4), 338–356.

World Bank. (2018). *World development report 2018: Learning to realize education's promise*. https://doi.org/10.1596/978-1-4648-1096-1

Zeichner, K. (2020). Preparing teachers as democratic professionals. *Action in Teacher Education, 42*(1), 38–48. https://doi.org/10.1080/01626620.2019.1700847

Zhao, Y. (2020). Two decades of havoc: A synthesis of criticism against PISA. *Journal of Educational Change, 21*, 245–266.

CHAPTER 2

The New Professionalism?
How Good Teachers Continue to Teach to Their Best and Well in Challenging Reform Contexts

Christopher Day

Abstract

Teacher professionalism has long been defined as being composed of a strong technical culture, service ethic, professional commitment, and autonomy. They have been regarded as the pillars which have defined teachers' professionalism. In recent years, however, interpretations of service and autonomy have been contested, as the purposes and practices of school-based education, and teachers' roles and accountabilities, have become subject to change as a result of the increased international policy press for functionally oriented teaching and learning, 'value-added' teacher effectiveness, and developments of new learning technologies which challenge the teacher as expert pedagogue and knowledge holder. This chapter will explore different, conflicting perspectives on the new meanings of professionalism. It will acknowledge that external pressures have created new conditions of service, but that, whilst such pressures influence, they do not necessarily shape how teachers' professionalism and, in particular, their autonomy, may be enacted. Indeed, there is much evidence to suggest that these core elements of professionalism are alive and active in teachers who teach to their best and well; and that these teachers' professionalism continues to be expressed through their individual agency, service commitment (moral purpose), resilience and collegial autonomy.

Keywords

teacher professionalism – autonomy – service commitment

1 Introduction

Teacher professionalism has long been understood in the academic literature (Furlong et al., 2000; Talbert & McLaughlin, 1994) as being composed of a strong technical culture (knowledge base); service ethic (inner core of strong, shared beliefs in serving clients' needs); professional commitment (strong individual and collective identity); and professional autonomy (control over classroom practice). The OECD (2016) report on professionalism, drawing upon teachers' own perspectives (OECD, 2014), extended these to include peer networks – opportunities for information exchange and support necessary to maintain high standards of teaching – indicating a trend towards more collaborative work as an essential part of teachers' professionalism. Whilst there seem to be few disagreements about these key features of professionalism, there are clear divisions about how they are enacted in schools. There are also relatively few texts which seek to identify differences in the extent to which different kinds of professionalism contribute to teacher effectiveness, what 'effectiveness' means, whether this is a stable or changing concept, and whether such effectiveness might be defined in different ways when related to individual or collective educational beliefs, practices and contexts. Although the overall view of professionalism continues to be associated with a period of training resulting in a strong knowledge base, service ethic, and professional commitment, teachers' rights to define educational purposes through the formal curriculum, interpret clients' needs and exercise discretionary judgements in the classroom (autonomy) are enacted in different ways. Moreover, the pace of movement away from the teacher's individual authority and autonomy towards the managerially compliant has taken different forms in different jurisdictions.

The first part of this chapter will, therefore, examine competing perspectives on the meaning of teacher professionalism. It will un-pack policy makers' perspectives, and place these in contrast to those of findings from much academic research. The second part will discuss changes in meanings-in-practice of teacher autonomy and service ethic in different contexts. The third part will examine relationships between these and teachers' identities, and consider how the changing governance structures, accountability and leadership contexts of schools contribute to emerging interpretations of teachers' enactment of individual classroom autonomy as expressed through new forms of collegially driven decision making The final part will discuss what it means to be a 'good' professional, and what kinds of teacher identities are associated with teachers who 'go the extra mile' in their work in schools and classrooms as principled professionals whose educational beliefs are located in their service ethic through both their mindsets and 'moral competence in pedagogical encounters' (Tirri, 2014, p. 600).

2   Redefining Teacher Professionalism: Competing Perspectives

2.1   *The Policy Voice*

Debates about the meaning of professionalism are not new. In his seminal work, Friedson uses the word 'professionalism' to refer to, 'the institutional circumstances in which members of occupations rather than managers control work,' asserting that, 'The organized occupation creates the circumstances under which its members are free of control by those who employ them' (Friedson, 2001, p. 12). There is, however, a difficulty in claiming this as an inalienable right for all teachers, since the evidence from empirical research is that not all teachers provide the same quality of opportunities for learning in the same ways or to the same degree for all their students at all times and in all circumstances. It follows that being 'free of control' does not guarantee that all members of the teaching profession can be expected to teach to their best and well. Moreover, because teaching is a public service:

> rarely do teachers own their professional standards to the extent other professionals do, and rarely do they work with the level of autonomy and in the collaborative work culture that people in other knowledge-based professions take for granted. (Schleicher, 2018, p. 96)

Perhaps this is why teaching has long been identified as a 'semi-profession' (Etzioni, 1969). As far back as 1994, David Hargreaves, architect of what was to become England's national 'self-improving' school system (Hargreaves, 1994), identified a shift towards a 'new professionalism':

> At its core, the new professionalism involves a movement away from the teacher's traditional authority and autonomy towards new forms of relationships with colleagues, with students and with parents. These relationships are becoming closer as well as more intense and collaborative, involving more explicit negotiation of roles and responsibilities .... (Hargreaves, 1994, p. 424)

Essentially, Hargreaves' words heralded a developing erosion of the traditional individual authority enjoyed by many teachers to make their own informed decisions about the way in which they progressed teaching and learning in their classrooms, as governments have sought improvements in students' academic outcomes, and promoted educational opportunities for a wider range of students than previously, through a series of measures which have sought to improve schooling through the introduction and imposition of choice and accountability policies.

Schools in many countries across the world have been subject to a similar raft of government-initiated reforms over the past three decades. These are seen as a means of building the human, economic, and social capital of citizens who live and work in increasingly competitive and turbulent global environments. Many governments have done so by increasing their direct interventions in school governance structures, school leadership and management and the curriculum in order to raise standards and increase opportunities for all students.

Perhaps as a tacit admission of the inability of central governments to achieve success through these reforms, in recent years, emerging new governance structures of schools in many countries, East and West, seem to be placing more importance on school-based control of standards of teaching and learning through the establishment of school co-operatives (e.g., formally constituted clusters, trusts, partnerships, federations, co-operatives). Whilst these new configurations appear to give more autonomy to schools in the way they conduct their work, centralised control of curriculum, teaching standards, high stakes accountability and corporate management practices remain in place. These have effectively narrowed teachers' and schools' room to exercise discretionary judgements about what is taught, processes of teaching, learning and student assessment, and what are defined as valuable student outcomes. 'Effective' schools and the professionalism of teachers are identified by governments by their abilities to contribute to the progress and achievement of their students in national tests and examinations. Within the curriculum, there is a hierarchy of subjects which are regarded as the most valuable, and those which are regarded as desirable but less important. There is evidence that subjects regarded as less valuable, often related to the Arts (Hall & Thompson, 2017), now are receiving less time and attention in many jurisdictions.

The 'added value' that teachers' work brings to students in all areas is also now more transparent, an established norm for schools in many countries, whether through regimes of increasingly sophisticated internal systems of monitoring of 'evidence-informed' teaching, through internal 'regimes of truth' (Hall & Noyes, 2009), nationally developed teaching and school leadership standards, and external school inspections. It has also become widely accepted by policy makers and schools that:

> Without evidence of all students making at least one year's growth for a year's input there is a reduced right to local control or autonomy ... [and that] .... It seems more reasonable to consider that the collective of the adults in schools should be responsible for all students' learning. (Hattie, 2016, p. v)

In many countries the reforms have been characterised as 'neoliberal' policies that emphasise devolved governance, diversification of teacher qualification routes, setting and monitoring regional and national standards of teaching (e.g., Apple, 2006; Ozga, 1995). Two common elements of these reforms are a focus upon equity, and an emphasis on raising students' academic attainment.

This movement towards more narrowly defined measures of school 'effectiveness' has been popularised by the name GERM (Sahlberg, 2012), a neoliberal 'global educational reform movement.' However, whilst GERM identified a similar general direction of travel by governments, there are substantial differences between them in strategy and pace of implementation. Differences in national cultures and educational and policy histories and current practices have resulted in differences in reforms. It is also important to examine how schools and teachers respond to these, and not to assume that they passively comply.

2.2   Researcher Voices

It is argued that contrary to the intention of policy reforms, which increase standardisation and narrow the curriculum, increased high stakes accountability and the dominance of corporate management practices, 'not only fail to reduce inequalities but exacerbate and reproduce existing class and race inequalities in schooling' (Fuller & Stevenson, 2019, p. 1). These claims continue to be disputed by policy makers, despite evidence to the contrary in terms of results in tests and public examinations which show that a significant achievement gap between students from disadvantaged and advantaged communities continues (e.g., Strand, 2014).

Among the consequences of external policy reforms for schools and teachers have been increased workloads, intensification of the teaching task, and more transparent contractual accountabilities through public, results-driven assessment (e.g., Apple, 2006; Ball, 2012a; Castells, 1997; Ozga, 2008; Power, 2004). It is claimed that one effect of reforms is that the professional space for teachers to exercise individual discretionary judgment in their classrooms has changed such that it has limited rather than enhanced their scope for this, and that reforms have led to 'the erosion of responsible, accountable and democratic professionalism' (Biesta, 2015, p. 82) as neoliberal policies have burdened individuals 'with tasks that used to be the responsibilities of governments and the state' (Biesta, 2015, p. 76).

Many researchers suggest also that, in the round, the reforms have led to the 'de-professionalisation' of teachers, whose job now, they suggest, is to carry out the demands of government, with school principals in the role of government proxies. Academic communities have responded to the increased interventionist roles of governments in different ways. Among the multitude of research strands, there are at least six which are dominant in the research literature:

i.   *Sociologically-oriented studies* which are highly critical of 'neoliberal' policy and its effects upon teacher professionalism (Ball, 2012b; Hyslop-

Margison, 2010; Ozga, 2008; Sachs, 2016; Sachs & Mockler, 2012) and 'performativity' cultures in schools (Ball, 2003); and a multitude of accounts of increasing erosion of teacher morale, accompanied by recruitment, attrition and retention problems (Borman & Dowling, 2008). There have always been tensions between 'organisational' and 'occupational' dominance of expertise (Abbott, 1991, p. 32). Many of these draw upon the work of social theorists, especially Foucault (Ball, 2012b) and Bourdieu (1986) to provide critiques of 'market-driven' policies as resulting in the unequal distribution of power. In this research, managerial, bureaucratic agendas are claimed to determine what teachers do, how they do it, and to what end. Researchers claim that they damage teachers' abilities to, 'make a living while controlling their own work' (Friedson, 2001, p. 17), so that, 'When individuals cease to control a large proportion of their own work, the skills essential to doing these tasks self reflectively and well, atrophy and are forgotten' (Apple, 1992, p. 22);

ii. *School effectiveness, empirical studies*, which, though robust, have been claimed to serve the 'functionalist' needs of policy makers. These are conducted largely by quantitatively oriented researchers, have sought to identify the characteristics of 'effective' schools in relation to students' measurable results, many including a strong 'social justice' strand in their work. Such studies continue to be criticised as serving the policy agenda, focussing upon the, 'extent (…) schools, teachers, or programmes contribute to student performance' (Marks, 2017, p. 148);

iii. *School-improvement studies*, which promote school-based inquiries into needs identified by schools themselves as organisations. Here, research merges with development. Researchers encourage and support school-led 'cadres' of teachers, usually led by senior leaders in the school and tightly focussed upon organisationally determined agendas (Hopkins, 2003);

iv. *Action research/practitioner research studies* in which academics engage closely with teachers in empowering individual and collaborative research;

v. *Teacher research*, through which scholars from different academic disciplines combine theoretical and empirical research which is aimed at understanding teachers, their work and lives, and the contexts and conditions which influence their professionalism; and

vi. *Curriculum research*, which seeks to understand what and how students learn and what would be valuable for them to experience as they attend school.

It will be seen from this very brief tour of these academic research strands that whilst some focus upon critique, others focus on understanding, and others focus upon assisting schools and teachers in their development. It is reasonable to surmise that, whilst all acknowledge the power and prevalence of policy reforms, those occupying some of the strands are decidedly pessimistic about their consequences for teachers' professionalism, whilst others are less so.

Critics claim, then, that, 'a growing number of global actors have gained greater control over the rules for classifying and framing the good teacher' (Robertson, 2012, p. 589). However, as noted many years ago, there is a difference between 'classification' and 'framing.' The former centres on the use of power, whereas the latter centres on the use of control, for example, by school principals and teachers, over the selection, organisation and pacing of knowledge in practice (Bernstein, 1971). While Bernstein developed these theories in relation to curriculum, I am using them here in order to draw attention to the possibilities for controlled, agential responses by schools and their teachers to the external power of reforms which are antithetical to their educational beliefs, identities and practices, and which challenge their identity as professionals. Rather than characterise these as 'resistance,' it may be more accurate to formulate them in terms of assertions of their own interpretations of professionalism as characterised by productive professional identity, represented through a strong sense of service (moral purpose), commitment, resilience, and professional autonomy.

3   Changing Contexts, Changing Practices: From Individual to Collegial Autonomy?

There are different perceptions now of the degrees of autonomy afforded to teachers. For example, Volume 1 of TALIS (OECD, 2019) 'examines the level of professionalism in teaching and to what extent teachers see their profession as offering relevant and attractive careers.' Among its five 'pillars' which outline the attraction of teaching is, 'the degree of autonomy that teachers and school leaders enjoy in their daily work, to make decisions and apply expert judgement and to inform policy development at all levels of the system, so that professionalism can flourish' (p. 26). Mausethagen and Mølstad (2015) defined autonomy as having three characteristics: (i) pedagogical freedom and control; ii) the will and capacity to justify practices; (iii) a local responsibility (p. 30). Their empirical research examined autonomy in Norwegian schools in the context of shifts in curriculum control relationships at national, municipality and school levels. In Norway, as in many other countries:

> ... the emphasis of educational policy has shifted from a somewhat traditional interpretation of autonomy – where teachers enjoyed a high degree of classroom autonomy, coupled with a limited evaluation of student outcomes – to placing more responsibility on local actors (municipalities, schools and teachers) and their documentation on succeeding in improving student outcomes and the overall quality and efficiency of teaching. (Mausethagen & Mølstad, 2015, pp. 30–31)

A related examination of professional autonomy in practice in the emerging localised accountability architectures has been developed by another Norwegian researcher. He questioned the validity of the work of those who hold a general view of the meaning of professional autonomy by locating variations in its practice that are likely to occur in devolved systems of school governance.

> Could it be that the literature on the de-professionalism of the teaching profession jumps to a questionable conclusion? Is it too quick to assume that the general loss of professional autonomy implies that professionals actually lose their autonomy at the level of practice? (Frostenson, 2015, p. 20)

He developed a three-level typology in order to debate the question he posed:
- *'General professional autonomy'* which refers to changes in the frames within which teachers work (governance, school systems, reforms through which government influence through determining curriculum 'legitimate,' pedagogies, and assessment measures).
- *'Collegial professional autonomy'* – decentralisation has increased collective autonomy, as against individual autonomy in schools, as in the case of England's move to embrace 'systems' management through the establishment of multi-academy trusts, chains, teaching school allowances and other forms of collegial arrangements in which individual managers (Chief Executive Officers or Executive Headteachers) have the authority to influence teachers' work (Evetts, 2011). However, in practice most of these systems operate through the exercise of increased autonomy in collegial form. Thus, individual autonomy in the form of decision-making power need not automatically imply decreased autonomy at the level of practice since collective forms of work preferred by school management may require it.

- *'Individual professional autonomy'* – here a 'substantial sphere of action and decision-making ... (is) ... tied to the professional practice of the individual teacher' (Frostenson, 2015, p. 24). He identifies a key tension in the practice of individual autonomy as 'in the use of metrics, or other forms of evaluation as decisive criteria for quality in which the teacher becomes accountable rather than responsible, implying that the teacher loses the traditionally enjoyed mandate of trust' (Frostenson, 2015, p. 25).

Frostenson argued that the effect of the widespread and continuing distributed configurations of school governance is that the degree of autonomy that individual teachers have has become more constrained in recent years as their work accountabilities have become more closely aligned with the internal demands of school as a collective. So, there are now tensions between individual teachers' freedom to choose (individual autonomy) and responsibility for choice (collegial autonomy). From a pessimistic perspective, this seems to confirm an increase in 'managerial' as against 'occupational' professionalism, by placing the responsibility for degrees of individual versus collegial autonomy directly upon school leaders. Seen from a less pessimistic perspective, this hands control of this aspect of professionalism to the professionals themselves. What is certain, is that what it means to be autonomous in one school and one system might be something quite different in another. Mausethagen and Mølstad (2015) concluded, as do I, that:

> Autonomy may be viewed as a continuum where the performative and individual aspects of teachers' work are related to the organisational and collective aspects of their profession. (p. 32)

This implies that it is possible for schools in local, regional and national governance systems which appear to be designed to control their work, to exercise agency, rather than passively comply. Yet, at the same time, there must be a limit on the degree of agency exercised by schools where such agency does not result in student learning gains.

4 Professional Identity: Sustaining Commitment, Resilience and Agency

There is now a corpus of empirical research which has found that there are many schools which continue to create time and space for teaching and learning which go beyond, but do not ignore, central policy interventions, and in which teachers' purposes and practices demonstrate both individual and collegiate forms of a professionalism that transcend mere functionality. Examples of this can be found in research literature on successful school leadership in many countries (Ärlestig et al., 2016). These show similarities in their identification of educational purposes, values, service ethic, and associations between these and productive professional identities, commitment, resilience and perceived and 'value-added' effectiveness.

Teacher beliefs have been characterised as:

> The interconnected affective, conceptual, and evaluative perspectives that teachers develop about themselves, their students, student learning, methods of instruction, curriculum, and schools as social institutions. (Zembylas & Chubbuck, 2015, p. 174)

They underpin teacher identities, strength of agency, and are the drivers of commitment and the capacities for the everyday resilience that all teachers need to be able to sustain their willingness and ability to teach to their best and well (Day, 2017). These contribute to the strength or weakness of teachers' professional identity which stands at the core of teachers' professionalism. Identity

> provides a framework for teachers to construct their own ideas of 'how to be,' 'how to act,' how to understand their work and their place in society. Importantly, teacher identity is not something that is fixed nor is it imposed; rather it is negotiated through experience and the sense that is made of that experience. (Sachs, 2005, p. 15)

In times of challenge, it is teachers' strength of identity which is likely to determine the choices that they make between, for example, being unquestioningly compliant with changes which they do not believe will benefit their students, or finding ways to 'translate' or 'reinterpret' these so that they will be of use in the contexts in which they work. If the latter, then it can be said that they are continuing to assert their individual professionalism. So it does not necessarily follow that strong pressures from others, even those in powerful positions, will have entirely negative effects upon teachers' service ethic, commitment, resilience and autonomy, as expressed through their professional identities.

The choices teachers make will be suggestive of strong or weak levels of what psychologists term 'efficacy' and sociologists term 'agency.' Bandura has claimed that personal efficacy beliefs are capabilities or capacities, not a fixed state, but subject to social influence, so that, 'When faced with obstacles, setbacks, and failures, those who doubt their capabilities slacken their efforts, give up, or settle for mediocre solutions. Those who have a strong belief in their capabilities redouble their effort to master the challenges'(Bandura, 2000, p. 120). Teachers' individual and collective efficacy – merging diverse individual goals in support of common organisational goals – are closely associated with their individual and collective sense of agency (Eteläpelto et al., 2013; Hitlin & Elder, 2007). Many empirical studies (e.g., Day, 2011; Day et al., 2007) have found that teacher efficacy and agency continue to be possessed by teachers with moral purposes who teach to their best and well, despite existing political and social circumstances and ideologies; and that teachers who express their agency through positive relationships with their students are more likely to be effective and resilient than those who do not (Spilt et al., 2011; Soini et al., 2016). Such findings suggest that changes in external environments and policies which appear to promote a narrow, 'functionalist,' 'managerialist dominated' and 'technicist' cultures of teaching and learning influence, but do not always determine, how individuals feel or act.

It is not that oppressive structures and discourses do not exist, and that these do not affect teacher professionalism and identity. Rather, it is not necessarily the case that their existence, by definition, must always result in negative effects on the professionalism of all teachers. There is a wide range of international research on improving, effective, and successful schools which demonstrates how their teachers mediate, resist, and find productive room to manoeuvre, asserting their individual and collective sense of agency within a sense of positive identity.

Research which focuses upon understanding teachers' work and lives confirms this, finding that there are different levels of teachers' service ethic, commitment and resilience, and that these may vary within and between teachers in accordance with the relative strengths of their beliefs, motivations, commitment, resilience, efficacy, agency, and wellbeing, and the influences of school culture, often associated with the quality of school leadership (Leithwood & Riehl, 2007; Mansfield et al., 2012; Palmer, 2007).

There are variations, also, between the professionalism of teachers with different work orientations: whether, for example, they regard teaching as just a job, as a career, or a 'calling,' contributing to the greater individual and collective good (Seligman, 2002); and between teachers in different career phases (Huberman, 1989). In the USA, Fessler and Christenson (1992) noted a dynamic ebb and flow among teachers as they responded to changed personal and organisational contexts. A four-year national multi-perspective, multi-method study of the work, lives and effectiveness of teachers in primary and secondary schools in England (Day et al., 2007) found that: (i) there were perceived qualitative, and significant statistical associations between teachers' levels of commitment, capacities for resilience, and effectiveness; (ii) commitment and capacities for resilience varied over time within and between their professional experience phases; (iii) this was influenced positively or negatively by policy, organisational, and personal/professional contexts; (iv) school contexts (supportive/unsupportive leaders, and or colleagues, student classroom behaviour), and personal life events were perceived to have the biggest influence on teacher commitment, capacity for resilience, and effectiveness; and (v) teachers in later phases were more likely, but not necessarily, to be less committed and less resilient than others.

Commitment and resilience have been found to be predictors of teachers' performance, burnout, and attrition, as well as having an important influence on students' cognitive, social, behavioural, and affective outcomes (Day & Hong, 2016; Firestone, 1996); and may be enhanced or diminished by factors such as student behaviour, collegial and administrative support, parental demands, and national educational policies. The current worldwide pandemic has added to the demands on and challenges to students, schools and teachers as they seek to develop new ways of teaching and recalibrate their roles and relationships with students, though at the time of writing it is too early to judge the effects on teachers' professionalism. What we do know, however, is that for commitment to endure, regardless of circumstance, requires a capacity for resilience. Resilience has been traditionally associated with 'bouncing back' from the trauma of adverse physical and psychologically threatening experiences, actions or events. Downes (2017) later conceptualised resilience, not in terms of 'bouncing back,' with the implication that the original 'shape' may be regained, but in terms of dynamic transition points in space between individuals and their environments in which they are able to exercise spatial-relational agency as they co-exist in mutual tension.

5 Moral Competencies in and beyond Pedagogical Encounters

Research on resilient teachers and resilient schools (Day & Gu, 2014) found that teachers' capacity for resilience was not stable, but fluctuated according to their willingness, commitment and ability to manage potentially conflicting forces of different magnitudes successfully; and that they were helped or hindered in this by the strength of their inner commitment to teaching, often referred to as 'moral purpose' (Goodlad, 1992), and by the nature of the interactions with colleagues within the workplace. This leads to questions about the purposes of professionals in schools. Should teachers, for example, focus primarily upon achieving academic excellence solely through their strong content and pedagogical technical knowledge base? Is that the only necessary quality necessary to communicate their professionalism and, through this, be effective? Or should they enact a broader definition of the purposes of their work, through demonstrating their service ethic, professional commitment and autonomy through their individual and collective identities?

What is agreed by researchers, policy makers and parents is that teachers' qualities and practicesare at the heart of school performance and educational outcomes. Their willingness, capacities and abilities to teach to their best and well – to apply their values, content and pedagogical knowledge and skills – are fundamental to students' opportunities to progress and achieve.

Regardless of external social contexts and conditions in which teachers work, all students, whether at school or university, are entitled to be taught by teachers who are willing and able to teach well and to their best. What teaching to one's best and well means will be subject to the norms of different countries and cultures, and these change over time. An important issue for all in this century is whether it is enough for teachers to fulfil the 'performativity' demands of policies which focus primarily on raising levels of academic achievement for all. Consideration of values education and the place of moral purpose in teachers' work seems to have taken a 'back seat,' or been put on the 'back burner' by policy makers as they have focused unrelentingly on 'delivering' measurable student performances in order to increase their value in building their capacities and qualifications to enter the workforce. Yet 'good' schools and 'good' teachers expect to provide through who they are and what they do (their professionalism) the broader education envisioned, for example, by John Dewey:

> Perhaps the greatest of all pedagogical fallacies is the notion that a person learns only the subject he is studying at the time. Collateral learning in the way of formation of enduring attitudes, of likes and dislikes, may be and often is much more important than the spelling lesson or lesson in geography or history that is learned. For these attitudes are fundamentally what count in the future. The most important attitude that can be formed is that of the desire to go on learning. (Dewey, 1938/1997, p. 48)

Those who recruit and prepare and support them share in the responsibility for encouraging, if not defining, a clear understanding of the broader purposes of education, a view of the 'good' society, equity and continuing love of learning. They should be able to reflect critically and be clear about the preferred 'shape' of their professional identities, how they define 'commitment,' their values, dispositions, virtues, a range of pedagogies, differentiating between the learning needs of every student, their expectations of themselves and others, their capacities for resilience and how to manage the emotional dimensions of teaching and learning. Similarly, schools themselves, and especially their leaders, need to support this core, 'what it takes to be a good teacher' curriculum. Whatever new teachers bring with them may be fragile and will need nurturing; and, since needs and contexts change over teachers' career lives, more experienced teachers' sense of identity, commitment and resilience are likely to need revisiting and renewing in the middle and later phases of their working lives (OECD, 2011).

There is little doubt that responses to the question 'What is teaching about?' will depend on the political and cultural heritage of the country or jurisdiction and/or individual values. These might range from those primarily concerned with universal suffrage for all (equity, social justice) through to various interpretations of democracy, preparation for work, social reproduction, citizenship, 'eudaimonia,' indoctrination, or revolution by the 'oppressed.' Yet regardless of the rights and wrongs of the different positions taken, all protagonists would subscribe to the view that it is the beliefs, values, identities, efficacy, agency, commitment, resilience and relational qualities of teachers that are key to the achievement of both broad and narrow educational purposes. As this chapter reminds us, governments have attempted to re(de)fine the nature of professionalism by developing national teacher qualification frameworks and in-service teaching standards, often expressed as competences, and putting into place various means of monitoring and judging to what extent these standards are being reached and even surpassed. In effect, they are intended to reflect, if not represent, what education is about. Yet critics continue to claim that how policy makers are defining this is in much less equitable, more narrowly academic and reductionist and functionalist ways than are desirable, and that, contrary to their intentions, they have resulted in a lower, rather than higher, commitment of teachers to their work. Biesta views the 'tendencies' that are currently influencing how 'good education' and 'professionalism' area as undermining opportunities for teacher professionalism:

> I argue that three tendencies that are often presented as developments in the ongoing professionalisation of teaching and that can be found in different forms and guises in schools, colleges and universities – treating students as customers; being accountable; and replacing subjective judgement with scientific evidence – are undermining rather than enhancing opportunities for teacher professionalism. (Biesta, 2015, p. 75)

Whilst these three tendencies have the potential to erode previous notions associated with professionalism and replace them with others, I have argued that this does not have to be so, and that there are many examples of schools and teachers with productive, positive professional identities, commitment and resilience under-pinned by strong moral purposes. Although the unfettered right to individual autonomy has been replaced in many, though not all, countries by collegial autonomy, and notions of teachers' as expert knowledge holders are being replaced by those of teachers as 'curators' of knowledge as the technological revolution continues unabated, the evidence of how schools and their teachers are responding gives cause for optimism that teacher professionalism may still be in a healthy state. In schools and among teachers where professionalism of the kinds identified in this chapter flourishes, there is a palpable and strong service ethic, efficacy and agency, and professional commitment, capacity for resilience, and sense of autonomy. In these schools, teacher professionalism is alive and well, despite the alienating influences of excessive bureaucracy, the rise of flawed direct cause and effect assumptions about relationships between the quality of teaching and the quality of learning (Fenstermacher & Richardson, 2005), and of policies which emphasise 'managerialist' and 'performativity' cultures.

6   Conclusions

This chapter has examined evidence for claims by some researchers that policy-driven reforms threaten teachers' professionalism, and thus their ability to offer a 'good' education, and engage in 'meaningful' professional conduct; and that they have produced:

> a situation where measurement has become an end in itself rather than a means to achieve a good education in the fullest and broadest sense of the term. (Biesta, 2015, p. 83)

They may well have produced 'a situation,' but they have not, in my experiences and those of many other researchers, teacher educators, school principals, students and parents, resulted in a loss of the professionalism of the many teachers who continue, through their service ethic (moral purpose), sense of productive professionalism, and within this a commitment to both individual and collegial autonomy, with an abiding commitment to educate and inspire a developing ambition to learn and achieve among their students.

Good teaching requires teachers who are clear about their professional purposes, those of the organisation, parents, and their governments (some or all of which may be conflicting), and who are willing and able to manage these in classrooms in which students are likely to exhibit the results of a variety of motivations, abilities and behaviours, regardless of personal and professional circumstance. Good teaching may include, but continues to be more than, meeting sets of standards, and greater than the sum of competences, however these may be defined. Narrowly-framed competences are one part, but only one part, of the necessary toolkit which teachers need in order to teach to their best and well. They are not useful when used as sticks to ensure compliance. Fundamentally, in order to exercise 'discretionary capital' (Hargreaves & Fullan, 2012), teachers need to be able to 'read' and understand the classroom, school, pupil and policy contexts in which they work, to exercise 'considered' judgements, and to manage the emotional cauldrons of classroom lives.

> Teaching is unavoidably a moral endeavour … Education (and schooling as a means to it) serves more expansive demands than scores of academic achievement, and thus the contributions that teachers make to the moral life of classrooms, to the moral lives that our … students lead, and to the character of our society, are critical. (Sanger & Osguthorpe, 2011, p. 570)

References

Abbott, A. (1991). The order of professionalisation. *Work and Occupations, 18*, 355–384.

Apple, M. W. (1992). Educational reform and educational crisis. *Journal of Research in Science Teaching.* https://doi.org/10.1002/tea.3660290804

Apple, M. W. (2006). *Educating the 'right' way: Markets, standards, God, and inequality* (2nd ed.). Routledge.

Ärlestig, H., Day, C., & Johansson, O. (Eds.). (2016). *A decade of research on school principals.* Springer.

Ball, S. J. (2003). The teacher's soul and the terrors of performativity. *Journal of Education Policy, 18*(2), 215–228.

Ball, S. J. (2012a). *Global education Inc: New policy networks and the neo-liberal imaginary.* Routledge.

Ball, S. J. (2012b). *Foucault, power, and education.* Routledge.

Bandura, A. (2000). Cultivate self-efficacy for personal and organizational effectiveness. In E. A. Locke (Ed.), *The Blackwell handbook of principles of organizational behavior* (pp. 120–136). Blackwell.

Bernstein, B. (1971). On the classification and framing of educational knowledge. In M. Young (Ed.), *Knowledge and control* (pp. 47–76). Collier MacMillan.

Borman, G. D., & Dowling, N. M. (2008). Teacher attrition and retention: A meta-analytic and narrative review of the research. *Review of Educational Research, 78*(3), 367–409.

Bourdieu, P. (1986). The forms of capital. In J. Richardson (Ed.), *Handbook of theory and research for the sociology of education* (pp. 241–258). Greenwood.

Biesta, G. (2015). What is education for? On good education, teacher judgement, and educational professionalism. *European Journal of Education, 50*(1), 75–87.

Castells, M. (1997). *The power of identity: The information age: Economy, society and culture Volume II*. Blackwell.

Day, C. (2011). The new lives of teachers. *Teacher Educational Quarterly, 19,* 35–377.

Day, C. (2017). *Teachers' worlds and work: Understanding complexity, building quality*. Taylor & Francis.

Day, C. (2018). Professional identity matters: Agency, emotions and resilience. In P. Schutz, J. Hong, & F. D. Cross (Eds.), *Research on teacher identity. Mapping challenges and innovations* (pp. 61–71). Springer.

Day, C., & Gu, Q. (2014). *Resilient teachers, resilient schools: Building and sustaining quality in testing times*. Routledge.

Day, C., Gu, Q., & Sammons, P. (2016). The impact of leadership on student outcomes: How successful school leaders use transformational and instructional strategies to make a difference. *Educational Administration Quarterly, 52*(2), 221–258. doi:10.1177/0031161X15616863

Day, C., & Hong, J. (2016). Influences on the capacities for emotional resilience of teachers in schools serving disadvantaged urban communities: Challenges of living on the edge. *Teaching and Teacher education, 59,* 115–125.

Day, C., Sammons, P., & Stobart, G. (2007). *Teachers matter: Connecting work, lives and effectiveness*. McGraw-Hill Education.

Dewey, J. (1997). *Experience and education*. Touchstone. (Original work published 1938)

Downes, P. (2017). Extended paper: Reconceptualising foundational assumptions of resilience: A cross-cultural, spatial systems domain of relevance for agency and phenomenology in resilience. *International Journal of Emotional Education, 9*(1), 99–120.

Eteläpelto, A., Vahasantanen, K., Hokka, P., & Paloniemi, S. (2013). What is agency? Conceptualizing professional agency at work. *Educational Research Review, 10,* 45–65.

Etzioni, A. (1969). *The semi-professions and their organization: Teachers, nurses, social works*. Free Press.

Evetts, J. (2011). A new professionalism? Challenges and opportunities. *Current Sociology, 59,* 406–422. doi:10.1177/0011392111402585

Fenstermacher, G. D., & Richardson, V. (2005). On making determinations of quality in teaching. *Teachers College Record, 107*(1), 186–213.

Fessler, R., & Christensen, J. (Eds.). (1992). *Teacher career cycle: Understanding and guiding the professional development of teachers.* Allyn & Bacon.

Firestone, W. A. (1996). Leadership: Roles or functions? In K. A. Leithwood, J. D. Chapman, P. Hallinger, & A. Hart (Eds.), *International handbook of educational leadership and administration* (pp. 395–418). Kluwer Academic Publishers.

Friedson, E. (2001). *Professionalism, the third logic: On the practice of knowledge.* University of Chicago Press.

Frostenson, M. (2015). Three forms of professional autonomy: De-professionalisation of teachers in a new light. *Nordic Journal of Studies in Educational Policy, 1*(2). doi:10.3402/nstep.v1.28464

Fuller, K., & Stevenson, H. (2019). Global education reform: Understanding the movement. *Educational Review, 71*(1), pp. 1–4. https://doi.org/10.1080/00131911.2019.1532718

Furlong, J., Barton, L., Miles, S., & Whitty, G. (2000). *Teacher education in transition: Reforming professionalism?* Open University Press.

Goodlad, J. (1992). The moral dimensions of schooling and teacher education. *Journal of Moral Education, 21*, 87–97.

Hall, C., & Noyes, A. (2009). New regimes of truth: The impact of performative school self evaluation systems on teachers' professional identities. *Teaching and teacher education, 25*(6), 850–856.

Hall, C., & Thompson, P. (2017). *Inspiring school change: Transforming education through the creative arts.* Routledge.

Hargreaves, A., & Fullan, M. (2012). *Professional capital: Transforming teaching in every school.* Teachers College Press.

Hargreaves, D. H. (1994). The new professionalism: The synthesis of professional and institutional development. *Teaching and Teacher Education, 10*(4), 423–438.

Hattie, J. (2016, July 11). *Third annual visible learning conference: Mindframes and maximizers.* Washington, DC.

Hitlin, S., & Elder, G. H. Jr. (2007). Understanding 'agency': Clarifying a curiously abstract concept. *Sociological Theory, 25*(2), 170–191.

Hopkins, D. (2003). *School improvement for real.* Routledge.

Huberman, M. (1989). The professional life cycle of teachers. *Teachers College Record, 91*(1), 31–57.

Hyslop-Margison, E. J., & Dale, J. (2010). *Paulo Freire: Teaching for freedom and transformation.* Springer.

Leithwood, K., & Riehl, C. (2005). What we know about successful school leadership. In W. Firestone & C. Riehl (Eds.), *A new agenda: Directions for research on educational leadership* (pp. 22–47). Teachers College Press.

Mansfield, C. F., Beltman, S., Price, A., & McConney, A. (2012). 'Don't sweat the small stuff': Understanding teacher resilience at the chalkface. *Teaching and Teacher Education, 28*(3), 357–367.

Marks, G. N. (2017). Is adjusting for prior achievement sufficient for school effectiveness studies? *Educational Research and Evaluation, 23*(5–6), 148–162.

Mausethagen, S., & Mølstad, C. E. (2015). Shifts in curriculum control: Contesting ideas of teacher autonomy. *Nordic Journal of Studies in Educational Policy, 2*. https://doi.org/10.3402/nstep.v1.28520

OECD. (2011). *OECD work on education*. OECD Publishing.

OECD. (2014). *TALIS 2013 results: An international perspective on teaching and learning*. TALIS OECD Publishing.

OECD. (2016). *Teacher professionalism*. OECD Publishing.

OECD. (2019). *TALIS 2018 Results (Volume 1). Teachers and school leaders as lifelong learners*. TALIS OECD Publishing.

Ozga, J. (1995). Deskilling a profession: Professionalism, deprofessionalisation and the new managerialism. In H. Busher & R. Saran (Eds.), *Managing teachers as professionals in schools* (pp. 21–37). Kogan Page Limited.

Ozga, J. (2008). Governing knowledge: Research steering and research quality. *European Educational Research Journal, 7*(3), pp. 261–272.

Palmer, D. (2007). What is the best way to motivate students in science? *Teaching Science-The Journal of the Australian Science Teachers Association, 53*(1), 38–42.

Power, M. (2004). *The audit explosion*. Demos.

Robertson, S. L. (2012). Placing teachers in global governance agendas. *Comparative Education Review, 56*(4), 584–607.

Sachs, J. (2005). Teacher education and the development of professional identity: Learning to be a teacher. In P. Denicolo & M. Kompf (Eds.), *Connecting policy and practice: Challenges for teaching and learning in schools and universities* (pp. 5–21). Routledge.

Sachs, J. (2016). Teacher professionalism: Why are we still talk about it? *Teachers and Teaching, 22*(4), 413–425.

Sachs, J., & Mockler, N. (2012). Performance cultures of teaching: Threat or opportunity? In C. Day (Ed.), *The Routledge handbook of teacher and school development* (pp. 33–43). Routledge.

Sahlberg, P. (2012, June 30). *How GERM is infecting schools around the world?* https://pasisahlberg.com/text-test/

Sanger, M. N., & Osguthorpe, R. D. (2011). Teacher education, preservice teacher beliefs, and the moral work of teaching. *Teaching and Teacher Education, 27*(3), 569–578.

Schleicher, A. (2018). *How to build a 21st-century school system?* OECD.

Seligman, M. (2002). *Authentic happiness: Using the new positive psychology to realize your potential for lasting fulfillment*. Free Press.

Soini, T., Pietarinen, J., & Pyhalto, K. (2016). What if teacher learns in the classroom? *Teacher Development, 20*(3), 380–397.

Spilt, J. L., Koomen, H. M. Y., & Thijs, J. T. (2011). Teacher wellbeing: The importance of teacher student relationships. *Educational Psychology Review, 23*, 457–477. doi:10.1007/s10648-011-9170-y

Strand, S. (2014). School effects and ethnic, gender and socio-economic gaps in educational achievement at age 11. *Oxford Review of Education, 40*(2), 223–245.

Talbert, J. E., & Mclaughlin, M. W. (1994). Teacher professionalism in local school contexts. *American Journal of Education, 102*(2), 123–153.

Tirri, K. (2014). The last 40 years in Finnish teacher education. *Journal of Education for Teaching, 40*(5), 600–609.

Zembylas, M., & Chubbuck, S. M. (2014). The intersection of identity, beliefs, and politics in conceptualizing teacher identity. In H. Fives & M. G. Gill (Eds.), *International handbook of research on teachers' beliefs* (pp. 173–189). Taylor & Francis.

CHAPTER 3

Teachers' Moral Authenticity

Searching for Balance between Role and Person

Jukka Husu and Auli Toom

Abstract

Teachers' morally authentic action is an essential professional competence, but challenging to perform in real classroom situations. Although teachers are often aware of their external task demands and have also internalized their professional role requirements, it is often difficult for them to deal authentically in challenging moral situations in classrooms. Authenticity can be seen as a disposition to act on reasons and exercising in making decisions and constant deliberation. When practicing authenticity, teachers balance their thoughts and actions both with situational appropriate professional demands and personal preferences. This study explores ways teachers define and apply their *moral authenticities* during teaching. The study is based on qualitative data from student teachers' practicum portfolios where they reported pedagogical dilemmas from their teaching practice. The analysis of qualitative case data (N = 110) revealed three different moral authenticities that were constructed from student teachers' action reports: *authenticity in moral appearance*, *authenticity in moral effect*, and *authenticity in moral commitment*. The results emphasize the need to provide teachers with such competencies that help them to manage successfully and authentically in challenging moral situations. Implications for pre-service and in-service teacher education are also discussed.

Keywords

teacher authenticity – moral qualities – teacher education

1   Introduction

During the last decades, authenticity has been increasingly discussed in many fields in society (Potter, 2010). In general, authenticity relates to the quality of something to be experienced as real and true. For example, Heidegger (2001) made a distinction between a conventional, false, and inauthentic surface level and a true and authentic depth level of being. While this kind of deep level of authenticity is demanding to use in research, the concept of ethics of authenticity (Taylor, 1991) provides more possibilities to observe human beings and their actions. According to Taylor (1991), authenticity is the freedom to decide for oneself rather than being shaped by external influences. However, authenticity also means acting in accordance with ethical values and esteemed cultural norms in dialogue with others, and it is not equal with freedom to pursue solely personal preferences (p. 66).

In education, teachers have been encouraged to be authentic that is believed to be integral to their professional success and satisfaction. Teacher authenticity is assumed to promote good and effective teaching. As Bialystok (2017) notes, "if teachers are not sincere or not accurate, we have good reason to worry about the quality of the education being imparted to students. But as authenticity is a self-relation, it is thought that teachers must be "true to themselves" in order to uphold a truthful relation with those they teach" (p. 13). Thus, authenticity has been emphasized for positive teacher–student relationships and as an essential support for good learning (De Bruyckere & Kirschner, 2016; Kreber et al., 2007). The concept and practice of *authenticity* constitutes a crucial link between teaching and the achievement of students' learning and development outcomes at school level (Iverson et al., 2008). As Kreber (2010a) notes, the question of interest is not only whether teachers can create a unique identity as teacher from within themselves, but whether "there might be a way of being a teacher that is uniquely their own (i.e., their person) while at the same time linked, and committed, to something significant that lies beyond themselves (i.e., their professional roles).

Teacher education programs have been explored through authenticity (Darling-Hammond & Snyder, 2000; Iverson et al., 2008; Tellez, 1996), and its use as a tool to support teacher learning both in pre- and in-service teacher education (Kreber, 2010a, 2010b; Walton & Rusznyak, 2016). Many teacher educators tend to agree that increased authenticity of teaching activities will improve teacher candidates' learning experiences. Often, teacher candidates are advised to "just be yourself." However, as De Bruyckere and Kirschner (2016) remind us, "just being yourself" can be a too demanding task for inexperienced student teachers. Thus, before increasing the number of authentic experiences in teacher education, we have to determine more exactly what actually characterizes authentic learning tasks (Cranton, 2006; Cranton & Carusetta, 2004; Kreber et al., 2007; Serrano et al., 2018).

Teaching as an authentic endeavor comes close to teaching as a moral enterprise (Cook-Sather & Barker-Doyle, 2017). Sanger (2017) views teaching as a "morally significant endeavor" but notes that teachers usually do not develop a sophisticated professional knowledge or concepts related to the moral work of teaching during teacher education. Both pre-service and in-service teachers report (i) believing that morality varies and is subjective to some degree; (ii) being conflicted about how to address differences between school values and those students bring from their home; and (iii) having a high sense of self-efficacy for serving as good role models for their students (Sanger, 2017, p. 348).

The pervasive moral qualities of teaching become understandable for student teachers when they are considered through the tasks of education and schooling in their institutional and curricular contexts (Dewey, 1927; Dzur, 2008), and through the quality of everyday interactions between teachers and students (Husu & Tirri, 2007). Teachers are in a central position of responsibility in these pedagogical relationships (van Manen, 2000) to promote student learning, cultivate their capabilities, and build a favorable and hopeful atmosphere for learning. While students cannot be forced to participate in these asymmetric pedagogical interactions (Kansanen et al., 2000), they should be guided with care and thoughtful use of pedagogical expertise (Noddings, 1998). All these institutional and individual factors contribute to a good ethos of education (Husu & Tirri, 2007), and the moral work of teaching becomes realized through these complexities of everyday schooling and education.

This study explores the moral authenticities in teaching in their various orientations student teachers employ. Our aim is to clarify the role *authenticity* plays in student teachers' professional learning, and the pedagogies they adopt during teacher education. The specific research task of this study can be addressed as follows: How do student teachers present their moral authenticities in their pedagogical case descriptions?

2   Characteristics and Contexts of Moral Authenticity

2.1   *Teacher Authenticity*

Laursen (2005) notes that the personal quality of a teacher is often experienced as a unified whole by students, and the concept of authenticity denotes this quality. It reveals linkages between teachers' role and personal prescriptions, moral characteristics, pedagogies and their various authenticities (Buchmann, 1986; Floden & Buchmann, 1993; Jackson, 1986; Kreber, 2010a; Marinell, 2008; Taylor 1991). The authenticity stance implies that teaching activities are experienced and justified by larger, organized contexts that enable activities to go beyond mere personal particulars (Wiggins, 1993).

When teachers practice the virtue of authenticity (Sockett, 2009), they balance their thinking and actions both with situationally appropriate role demands and their personal preferences (Buchmann, 1986). Thus, authenticity can be seen as a disposition to act on different reasons, and it is exercised in making decisions and built up in constant deliberation: much in a same way as skills – both intellectual and practical – in teaching situations. This is because authenticity consists of pedagogical actions that (i) are routinely performed by teachers; (ii) involve working with students; (iii) promote knowledge of practice of teaching; (iv) prompt teachers' self-reflection, and (v) serve formative purposes in teaching (Iverson et al., 2008).

2.2 Role Perspectives in Teacher Authenticity: Determining Guiding Norms

Role theory (Biddle & Thomas, 1966) concerns important features of social and professional life, characteristic behavior patterns, and offers a valuable perspective for considering teacher authenticity as well. It explains roles by presuming that persons are members of social and professional positions and hold expectations for their own behaviors and those of others. Its vocabulary and concerns are popular among social scientists and practitioners, and role concepts have generated a lot of research (see e.g., Beck, 2008; Brophy, 1982; Buchmann 1986; Bullough et al., 1984; Floden & Buchmann, 1993; Hansen, 1993; Holt-Reynolds 2000; Su et al., 2017; Turner, 1978; Wilson, 1962).

According to the authenticity stance, it is crucial to understand teaching as a role word. Roles embody high aspirations, and in school context provide certain mechanisms for guiding action in their light. The roles are parts that teachers play in our schools, they do not describe individuals and they apply regardless of teachers' personal opinions. In order to fulfil their mandate correctly, teachers cannot operate in an informal, ad hoc manner, even from the viewpoint of authenticity (Buchmann, 1986; Lortie, 1975). As Hansen (2001) notes, "the question of what it means to be a person in the role of teacher is best answered ... from a context of tradition and practice" (p. 19). An individual person becomes a teacher through embracing the responsibilities of the work and through engaging in the social world of the school and classroom.

Professionally, this involves critically questioning the world outside of teachers themselves. Teachers should be aware of the characteristics and preferences of learners and others including how they are the same and different from their own (Cranton & Carusetta, 2004). Moral action for the good of others and larger community requires the capacity for mutuality and interdependence in pedagogical relationships (Edwards, 2017). It requires understanding of and commitment to one's own interests in interaction with understanding and commitment to the interests of others. Here, to act ethically, requires the ability to use multiple understandings, and to be able to engage in relationships with others grounded in appreciation of their differences (Cranton, 2006; Baxter Magolda, 2009).

2.3 Personal Characteristics in Authenticity: Individual Qualities Defining Teacher's Work

As noted, teachers are expected to act within the limits of their role. In addition to their role-oriented skills, teachers have to find ways for their subjectivity and personal adaptations in teaching. In practice, they have to discover their own strengths and their own ways to teach (Männikkö & Husu, 2019). Here, the challenges are real because everyone likes to be told that "being oneself" or "the firm following of the rules or code ethics" is all right, even laudable. But what are these own strengths and own ways to teach? Teacher autonomy and self-realization are indisputably teacher's personal goods. However, as Buchmann (1986) emphasizes, schools are for children, and children's autonomy and self-realization depend in part what they learn in schools. Thus, "self-realization in teaching is not a good in itself, but only insofar as pursuing self-realization leads to appropriate student learning" (p. 538). Teachers are persons, but being one's self in teaching is not enough. Person must be paired with teachers' role obligations.

Similar to moral qualities, authenticity in teaching is founded on continuing development of a teachers' sense of self. Becoming authentic is, in many ways, individuation. However, it is not only being genuine, but also understanding what genuine means in specific contexts (Toom & Husu, 2018). Therefore, instead of "honesty," authenticity can usefully be thought of as coherence (Hunt, 2006). This coherence needs to be both internal (Does what teachers are doing match what they believe?) and external (To what extent is what teachers are doing consistent with the standards, structures, and constraints of their work?). As Kornelsen (2006) notes, this calls for teachers "to bring qualities of mind, character, and practice transcending skillful application of technique[s of teaching]" (p. 80).

Becoming an authentic teacher is a developmental process that builds on experience, responsibility, and reflection in particular contexts (Cranton & Carusetta, 2004). Authenticity does not mean conditions where individuals make judgments for themselves alone and without external obligations: authenticity always occurs in its social and institutional contexts (Taylor, 1991). Thus, it is important note that besides teachers' role expectations and personal characteristics, contextual factors and local structures contribute much to teacher's possibilities to work and regulate their professional actions. Figure 3.1 describes the institutional and individual fundamentals and their respective role and personal elements (external expectations and internal dispositions/needs) characterizing teachers' moral authenticities.

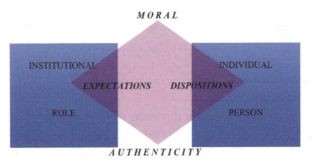

FIGURE 3.1
The role and personal characteristics of teachers' moral authenticity

As Figure 3.1 shows, we define moral authenticity as a subjective experience between a teacher's individual characters and institutional expectations. By internal experiences, we refer to a teacher's dispositions consisting of thoughts, feelings, values, and behavioural preferences; by external expectations we mean demands that come from a school context where a teacher is working along with his/her general and particular professional role requirements. This view of authenticity adopts a phenomenological stance that privileges a teacher's experience of authenticity. We assume that teachers are capable of reflecting on and assessing the correspondence between their internal personal experiences and external role demands. Also, we view moral authenticity as a continuum rather than an individual trait or institutional weight. We do not differentiate between authentic and inauthentic teachers but instead aim to examine the spectrum of their experiences at a particular moment of their career, and to consider the generative potential of increasing authenticity in teaching profession.

3 The Study

This study is a part of our wider research project, where the aim is to analyze the moral dimensions of teacher's knowing in reflecting on caring pedagogical principles and actions (see e.g., Husu & Toom, 2008; Tirri et al., 2013; Toom & Husu, 2018; Toom et al., 2015).

3.1 Data Sources

The data were collected from 110 primary school student teachers as part of their advanced educational major studies during teacher education at the University of Helsinki, Finland. The general aim of the course was to focus on the dimensions of teacher's pedagogical knowing, construction of personal practical theory of teaching as well as enhance competencies for teaching. Student teachers got deeper insights into teacher's work, how to understand the instructional process in its wholeness, and supported their learning of one's own thinking and action through integrating theory and practice.

The data were collected as part of student teachers' course tasks by using the case report procedure (Thomas, 2011; Yin, 2003). The student teachers wrote a reflective case description of a real-life pedagogical dilemma they had experienced during their teaching practice period and provided professional, personal and situational interpretations to their cases (Blomberg et al., 2014; Lampert & Ball, 1998; Shulman, 1992; Strike, 1993).

3.2 Data Analysis and Interpretation

We used holistic units of analysis (Miles et al., 2014) to allow the researchers to create an overall picture of the data. To identify the student teachers' moral authenticities, we handled each case description (f = 110) as a single unit of analysis. The coding was conducted using abductive content analysis (Timmermans & Tavory, 2012). This means that theory-driven coding categories were adopted, but the categories were modified to fit the data.

In the coding of the student teachers' case descriptions, we modified and applied Kreber's (2007, 2010a, 2010b) theorizations on teacher's authenticity: pedagogical practices, quality and goal of interaction, and Fuller and Bown's (1975) three-stage model of teacher development from self-centered approaches towards task- and impact-oriented ways to interpret professional actions (cf. Conway & Clark, 2003; Hagger et al., 2008). With the help of these theory-driven interpretations, we analyzed what kind of moral authenticities were emphasized in each case description. With the help of these theories, we came to employ the following three categories:

1. *Authenticity in moral appearance* refers to teacher's active efforts to map out the information related to teaching experience and its associations. The category consisted of e.g., the following features: care for students; care for the subject and interest in engaging students with the subject ideas that matter; making educational decisions and acting in ways that are in the interest of students; practicing a constructive developmental pedagogy; consistency between values and actions.
2. *Authenticity in moral effect* is related to teacher's considerations about the influence that their work as teachers has on students' learning and on educational matters as whole. The category consisted of e.g., the following features: promoting the authenticity of others; reflecting on purposes in education and teaching; critically reflecting on how certain norms and practices have come about.
3. *Authenticity in moral commitment* includes comments on teacher's personal characteristics, self-confidence and integrity in teaching, caring

relationships with pupils, continuous dialogue with larger professional context as well as passion to teaching profession.

Our holistic units of analysis (Miles et al., 2014) allowed us to create an overall picture of the data. After careful reading, the first phase in the data analysis was the division of the whole case data into analysis units, which ranged in length from some short sentences to longer pieces of text. Secondly, the content of the unit was then read analytically, in order to find out how it represented student teachers' authenticities in *moral appearance, moral effect*, and *moral commitment* in candidates' professional actions. Thirdly, the statements were identified with one of the three forms of authenticity. The transition between the forms of authenticity were not clear-cut in nature, rather the categories employed were elusive and included connections to various contents of authenticities. The identification was made according to the most emphasized content of authenticity in each data unit.

To assure the validity and reliability of the results the whole analysis was done by two researchers. Throughout the data analysis, the coded classifications were systematically re-read, and the categories were cross-checked. The two researchers also continuously identified, discussed, and checked all the coding units and categories (Braun & Clarke, 2006). In addition, the theoretical coherence of the category system was considered (Morse, 2018).

4   Findings

4.1   *Authenticity in Moral Appearance*

Within the goals of this category, the student teachers highlighted the importance of professional task of teaching in its full meaning. They cared about the subject of teaching and presented reasons why it mattered from the viewpoint of pupils' learning, which was a priority for them. The data excerpts below present the quality of this authenticity:

> I started the lesson and gave instructions for pupils. One girl raised her hand and suggested an alternative way of action. The girl did not care about the instructions, but rather wanted the lesson to proceed in an alternative way. Many pupils started to complain the girl. I was a little bit confused, but still, was able to make a decision and say that I appreciate your suggestion, but I just told you the instructions and I have chosen the way of action to the topic we have today. The girl did not accept this, but tried to persuade me. I didn't know her beforehand, but I felt that it

is wise to be strict now. The lesson proceeded as I had instructed. (PEDA-
GOGICAL PRACTICES, S8, female)

After few days or even hours, the same situation happened again. The girl suggested changes to the lessons that were not so bad all the time. The only difference was that other pupils did not accompany her. I also realized that the girl tried to control other's actions even during the breaks. I had acted in a reasonable way. During these lessons, I reflected on various teaching methods, their usefulness for pupils. From time to time, I started to ask pupils' suggestions to certain subject areas. I tried to take into account that the suggestions came from different pupils. (QUALITY OF INTERACTION, S8, female)

It is good that teacher is able to follow her justified plans. Still, the teacher has to keep in mind that when changing, the plans are even more versatile. Student participation has a strong motivational power and it has influence on their work satisfaction. (GOAL, S8, female)

As the excerpts from this category show, student teachers were truly interested in the questions pupils asked and aimed at engaging in dialogue with them. Also, their reflections evidenced concern for pupil learning. The student teachers seemed to possess knowledge of how the classroom context and their ways of teaching influenced on pupils' learning activities. In their case reports, student teachers described their professional actions through various teaching methods by which they aimed to promote emotionally safe learning environment, pupils' independent thinking, and understanding of different perspectives of topics in question. Student teachers' investments to teaching and pupil learning were obvious, and they were willing to improve their pedagogy continuously. Essential in this moral authenticity, as student teachers mentioned, was to bring always one's own true self and interest of subject into teaching.

The data consisted of manifold task-oriented authenticities: different teaching contents from various disciplines or subject areas, the physical classroom including the size of the class and the room arrangement, the psychological environment within the learning group, the school norms and the general school culture, and the roles the particular school expected teachers to maintain. The student teachers reported all these task-related characteristics, but their emphasis was more often on content and context issues than critically reflecting the pedagogical norms and expectations related to their larger psychosocial contexts.

In line with the data, this group of student teachers seemed to have a sort of process response/reflection to the requirements of teaching and learning situations. They reflected how conscientiously they had been identifying their particular goals, and how effective they had been in supporting pupil learning? The sources of knowledge used in reflection were often experience-based but they also justified their actions with research-based views and arguments. Approximately, one third of the student teachers case descriptions (n = 43/110) represented this orientation.

4.2   *Authenticity in Moral Effect*

This second category revealed that authenticity is not an on-off phenomenon, that a teacher possesses it or not, but rather that it is an ongoing developmental process of becoming more authentic. With authenticity in moral effect, a small number of student teachers (n = 11/110) succeeded to develop this sort of capacity for their pupils, in close pedagogical encounters with them. It is through this authentic capacity that they could recognize the same kind of legitimacy also in pupils with whom they worked. In order to be authentic in this sense, teachers were able to give space for their pupils to act and flourish.

Within this category, student teachers considered their goals both through the impact of their being as a teacher and their practical actions to pupils' learning and growth as well as authenticity in them. The quality of this sort of authenticity is described in the following excerpts:

> I act in a way that pupils have a possibility to participate to the collective project and feel their contribution meaningful and important. Everyone has to participate and strive towards the aims of the project collaboratively with others. Still, there was always tricky action from some pupils' side. I had to be able to construct an alternative lesson plan very quickly. I had to trust others, school assistant and pupils quite a lot. Many things had to function, so that we all were able to manage the situation and even learn collaboration skills, feel joy and creativity, which all are mentioned in the curriculum. (PEDAGOGICAL PRACTICES, S19, male)

> I realized that I will not manage with my original lesson plan, so I have to make a new plan and change my teaching method. I have to trust to pupils' way of acting as independent groups, who all choose their leader and divide the tasks between the members of the group. Actually, through this kind of working, the groups felt that they were doing their own work and were willing to complete the task. (QUALITY OF INTERACTION, S19, male)

My original boring plan that everyone does the same thing became impossible when there were more pupils than I had expected and I was forced to trust in groups' work. I think that trust was the key to activate pupils and intensive contribution from all group members. Even pupils themselves valued their collaboration and active participation. Everyone was willing to contribute, although they did totally different tasks. Participation happened differently than I had planned. Courage to change the plan and understand the resources outside yourself were encouraging, and this was a hopeful experience. (GOAL, S19, male)

A precondition for this kind of authenticity was that student teachers felt to be defined by themselves, not by other people's expectations. However, this did not mean complete self-disclosure, but rather a developing self-efficacy as a teacher. Student teachers explained their moral authenticities by describing their interactions and relationships with pupils: their ways of inspiring and stimulating enthusiasm towards learning, and especially encouraging authenticity in their pupils. Based on their preferences, this group of student teachers seemed to possess a sort of premise response/reflection to the requirements of their teaching and learning situations. They reflected how and why their pedagogical actions were helpful or failed to help their pupils to engage in meaningful and productive learning experiences and results. What possible alternatives there were? How and why it mattered that they provided choices, support, and collaboration to their pupils?

Within this category of authenticity in moral effects, student teachers reflected on their personal reasons and premises of professional pedagogical work as teachers, but also more general purposes of teaching and education. Furthermore, they also presented critical notions on the prevailing pedagogies and ideologies of education.

4.3   *Authenticity in Moral Commitment*

Within authenticity in moral commitment, student teachers described their goals through themselves as candid and dedicated teachers. They emphasized their sincerity and openness in interactive teaching situations – being true to their personality and character. They saw it important not to hide anything or not faking to ensure the real interaction with pupils. Student teachers liked to gain such self-confidence that they would be able to define their own ways of being a teacher rather than to conform to expectations of others. The following data excerpts present the quality of this authenticity in moral commitment:

> There were two disrupting pupils at the arts lesson. Their disruption (talking loud, own show, etc.) started immediately after the pupils entered the classroom. I relied on the way of action that had been successful before; I acted in a "strict manner." I asked for silence with a very resounding and tight voice, so that we would be able to start working. My actions caused only much more racket on girls' side. (PEDAGOGICAL PRACTICES, S5, female)

> Tension still existed in the classroom, but both pupils and I seemed to avoid provoking each other. I tried to speak more friendly than usual, and the girls talked in a less aggressive manner and with silent voice. Still, the girls did not work, but only were hanging around in the classroom and observed the situation. (QUALITY OF INTERACTION, S5, female)

> I became sad, because the girls didn't know me and didn't know that I work as a teacher because I truly care about kids and young people. Just because of that I have the courage to be who I am and set requirements at the classroom. The other thing was that I had not been in such situations never before. Previous disruptive pupils and classes had accepted my demanding and decorous way of action. These pupils have also noticed that when things are going well, also they can influence and also I am more relaxed. (GOAL, S5, female)

In their professional actions, they emphasized themselves as truly being in the teacher role, and strived to build caring and trustworthy relationships with their pupils. In addition to personal characteristics, student teachers pondered their personal enthusiasm towards subjects they were teaching. They had understood the importance of a committed teacher professionalism towards which they were willing to proceed.

Within this interpretative category, student teachers showed explicit self-awareness and they eagerly articulated their values to clarify their views and actions in classrooms. They felt strong congruence between their own (and in most cases also professional) values and actions. In their case reports, they articulated their 'own teaching stories' where they brought themselves in the middle of their classrooms to guide their actions, but also their students' learning activities. They often reported genuine passion for teaching and related caringly to their pupils' learning and development. They wanted to find best ways to teach their pupils and sought to fit to the requirements of each case. Based on their preferences, they seemed to have a sort of habitual response/reflection to the requirements of teaching and learning situations.

Authenticity in moral commitment was most often presented in student teachers' case descriptions (n = 56/110).

5 Discussion

As we have shown, teaching can be structured from the viewpoints of authenticities in *moral appearance*, *moral effect*, and *moral commitment* and pedagogies related to them. While the adaptation of role standards is an integral part of teaching profession, also teachers' personal characteristics and virtuous authenticities are important traits of a competent professional. An interesting question is what would happen if one of these three elements would be missing from teachers' actions? What kind of pedagogical practice would result? In line with these questions, De Bruyckere and Kirschner (2016) give one answer as they prompt that "authentic teacher needs to break out of the harness of the curriculum to give students and learners a unique and relevant experience … [by] taking the lead to put the student in the centre" (p. 12).

Student teachers' moral authenticities play a key role in determining whether and how they are able to mobilize their intellectual resources and professional commitments in impacting their students' learning in the future. From the viewpoint of teacher education, pedagogical authenticities set high demands. Teacher candidates come to teacher education with their experiences and personal orientations. As they learn to teach, they need help in mediating their personal orientations in relation to professional contexts and practices It is also important to remember that authenticities can be mediated for student teachers to some extent. The virtuous pedagogical authenticities are professional states or ways of being towards which student teachers should, and can be guided. But ultimately – it is up to their deliberation as to the kind of orientation to their work they will follow.

In this chapter, we have explored the conditions of teachers' moral authenticities in order to make teachers' work more visible and give them more control over what they are doing (Husu & Clandinin, 2017). However, our purpose has not been to present the "foreground," that is the results of "what works," but instead to highlight the "background" of professional action. We have tried out a constructive synthesis of various positions that often appear separate and disconnected or even in conflict. However, we do not intend to propose a final static or inflexible state of affairs. What we have tried to do is to present a temporary condition in which dialogue between different positions can encourage further discussion and hopefully lead to better understandings of teachers' professional actions.

References

Baxter Magolda, M. B. (2009). Educating students for self-authorship: Learning partnerships to achieve complex outcomes. In C. Kreber (Ed.), *The universities and its disciplines: Teaching and learning within and beyond disciplinary boundaries* (pp. 143–156). Routledge.

Beck, S. (2008). The teacher's role and approaches in a knowledge society. *Cambridge Journal of Education, 38*(4), 465–481.

Bialystok, L. (2017). Authenticity in education. In *Oxford research encyclopedia of education*. Retrieved January 28, 2021, from https://oxfordre.com/education/view/10.1093/acrefore/9780190264093.001.0001/acrefore-9780190264093-e-168

Biddle, B. J., & Thomas, E. J. (Eds.). (1966). *Role theory: Concepts and research*. John Wiley & Sons.

Blomberg, G., Sherin, M. G., Renkl, A., Glogger, I., & Seidel, T. (2014). Understanding video as a tool for teacher education: Investigating instructional strategies to promote reflection. *Instructional Science, 42*, 443–463. https://doi.org/10.1007/s11251-013-9281-6

Braun, V., & Clarke, V. (2006). Using thematic analysis in psychology. *Qualitative Research in Psychology, 3*, 77–101.

Brophy, J. E. (1982). How teachers influence what is taught and learned in classrooms. *Elementary School Journal, 83*(1), 1–14.

Buchmann, M. (1986). Role over person: Morality and authenticity in teaching. *Teachers College Record, 87*(4), 529–543.

Bullough, R. V., Gitlin, A. D., & Goldstein, S. L. (1984). Ideology, teacher role, and resistance. *Teachers College Record, 86*(2), 339–358.

Conway, P. F., & Clark, C. M. (2003). The journey inward and outward. A re-examination of Fuller's concern-based model of teacher development. *Teaching and Teacher Education, 19*, 465–482.

Cook-Sather, A., & Baker-Doyle, K. (2017). Developing teachers' capacity for moral reasoning and imagination in teacher education. In D. J. Clandinin & J. Husu (Eds.), *The Sage handbook of research on teacher education* (pp. 354–368). Sage Publications.

Cranton, P. (2006). Integrating perspectives of authenticity. *New Directions for Adult and Continuing Education, 111*, 83–87.

Cranton, P., & Carusetta, E. (2004). Perspectives on authenticity. *Adult Education Quarterly, 55*(1), 5–23.

Darling-Hammond, L., & Snyder, J. (2000). Authentic assessment of teaching in context. *Teaching and Teacher Education, 16*(5–6), 523–545.

De Bruyckere, P., & Kirschner, P. A. (2016). Authentic teachers: Student criteria perceiving authenticity of teachers. *Cogent Education, 3*(1). doi:10.1080/2331186X.2016.1247609

Dewey, J. (1927). *The public and its problems.* Reprinted in J. A. Boydston (Ed.), *John Dewey, The later works: 1925–1953* (Vol. 2, pp. 253–372). Southern Illinois University Press.

Dzur, A. W. (2008). *Democratic professionalism: Citizen participation and the reconstruction of professional ethics, identity, and practice.* The Pennsylvania State University Press.

Edwards, A. (2017). The dialectic of person and practice: How cultural-historical accounts of agency can inform teacher education. In D. J. Clandinin & J. Husu (Eds.), *The Sage handbook of research on teacher education* (pp. 269–285). Sage Publications.

Floden, R. E., & Buchmann, M. (1993). Between routines and anarchy: Preparing teachers for uncertainty. In R. E. Floden & M. Buchmann (Eds.), *Detachment and concern. Conversations in the philosophy of teaching and teacher education* (pp. 211–221). Cassell.

Fuller, F. F., & Bown, O. H. (1975). Becoming a teacher. In K. Ryan (Ed.), *Teacher education* (74th Yearbook of the National Society of Education, pp. 25–52). University of Chicago Press.

Hagger, H., Burn, K., Mutton, T., & Brindley, S. (2008). Practice makes perfect? Learning to learn as a teacher. *Oxford Review of Education, 34*(2), 159–178.

Hansen, D. T. (1993). From role to person: The moral layeredness of classroom teaching. *American Educational Research Journal, 30*(4), 651–674.

Hansen, D. T. (2001). *Exploring the moral heart of teaching: Toward a teacher's creed.* Teachers College Press.

Heidegger, M. (2001). *Being and time.* Blackwell. (Original work published 1962)

Holt-Reynolds, D. (2000). What does the teacher do? Constructivist pedagogies and prospective teachers' beliefs about the role of a teacher. *Teaching and Teacher Education, 16*, 21–32.

Hunt, R. (2006). Institutional constraints on authenticity in teaching. *New Directions for Adult and Continuing Education, 111*, 51–62.

Husu, J., & Clandinin, J. D. (2017). Pushing boundaries for research on teacher education: Making teacher education matter. In D. J. Clandinin & J. Husu (Eds.), *The Sage handbook of research on teacher education* (pp. 1169–1180). Sage Publications.

Husu, J., & Tirri, K. (2007). Developing whole school pedagogical values – A case of going through the ethos of "good schooling." *Teaching and Teacher Education, 23*(4), 390–401. doi:10.1016/j.tate.2006.12.015

Husu, J., & Toom, A. (2008). Ethics, moral, politics – The (un)broken circle of good and caring pedagogical practice. In A. Kallioniemi, A. Toom, M. Ubani, H. Linnansaari, & K. Kumpulainen (Eds.), *Cultivating humanity: Education – values – new discoveries* (pp. 215–230). Finnish Educational Research Association.

Iverson, H. L., Lewis, M. A., & Talbot III, R. M. (2008). Building a framework for determining the authenticity of instructional tasks within teacher education programs. *Teaching and Teacher Education, 24*(2), 290–302. doi:10.1016/j.tate.2007.09.003

Jackson, P. (1986). *The practice of teaching.* Teachers College Press.

Kansanen, P., Tirri, K., Meri, M., Krokfors, L., Husu, J., & Jyrhämä, R. (2000). *Teachers' pedagogical thinking. Theoretical landscapes, practical challenges.* Peter Lang Publishing.

Kornelsen, L. (2006). Teaching with presence. *New Directions for Adult and Continuing Education, 111,* 73–82.

Kreber, C. (2010a). Academics' teacher identities, authenticity and pedagogy. *Studies in Higher Education, 35*(2), 171–194.

Kreber, C. (2010b). Courage and compassion in the striving for authenticity: States of complacency, compliance, and contestation. *Adult Education Quarterly, 60*(2), 177–198.

Kreber, C., Klampfleitner, M., McCune, V., & Bayne, S. (2007). What do you mean by "authentic"? A comparative review of the literature on conceptions of authenticity in teaching. *Adult Education Quarterly, 58*(1), 22–43.

Lampert, M., & Ball, D. L. (1998). *Teaching, multimedia, and mathematics. Investigations of real practice.* Teachers College Press.

Laursen, P. E. (2005). The authentic teacher. In D. Beijaard, P. C. Meijer, G. Morine-Dershimer, & H. Tillema (Eds.), *Teacher professional development in changing conditions* (pp. 199–212). Springer.

Lortie, D. (1975). *Schoolteacher: A sociological study.* The University of Chicago Press.

Männikkö, I., & Husu, J. (2019). Examining teachers' adaptive expertise through personal practical theories. *Teaching and Teacher Education, 77,* 126–137. doi:10.1016/j.tate.2018.09.016

Marinell, W. H. (2008). Capturing authenticity, transforming perception. *Harvard Educational Review, 78*(3), 529–548.

Miles, M. B., Huberman, A. M., & Saldaña, J. (2014). *Qualitative data analysis: A methods sourcebook.* Sage.

Morse, J. (2018). Reframing rigor in qualitative inquiry. In N. K. Denzin & Y. S. Lincoln (Eds.), *The Sage handbook of qualitative research* (5th ed., pp. 796–817). Sage Publications.

Noddings, N. (1998). An ethic of caring and its implications for instructional arrangements. *American Journal of Education, 96*(2), 215–230.

Potter, A. (2010). *The authenticity hoax: How we got lost finding ourselves.* Harper/HarperCollins.

Sanger, M. (2017). Teacher beliefs and the moral work of teaching in teacher education. In D. J. Clandinin & J. Husu (Eds.), *The Sage handbook of research on teacher education* (pp. 339–353). Sage Publications.

Serrano, M. M., O'Brien, M., Roberts, K., & Whyte, D. (2018). Critical pedagogy and assessment in higher education: The ideal of 'authenticity' in learning. *Active Learning in Higher Education, 19*(1), 9–21.

Shulman, J. H. (1992). Toward a pedagogy of cases. In J. H. Shulman (Ed.), *Case methods in teacher education* (pp. 1–30). Teachers College Press.

Sockett, H. (2009). Dispositions as virtues: The complexity of the construct. *Journal of Teacher Education, 60*(3), 291–303.

Strike, K. A. (1993). Teaching ethical reasoning using cases. In K. A. Strike & P. Lance Ternasky (Eds.), *Ethics for professionals in education: Perspectives for preparation and practice* (pp. 102–116). Teachers College Press.

Su, Y., Feng, L., & Hsu, C.-H. (2017). Accountability or authenticity? The alignment of professional development and teacher evaluation. *Teachers and Teaching: Theory and practice, 23*(6), 717–728. doi:10.1080/13540602.2016.1255189

Taylor, C. (1991). *The ethics of authenticity*. Harvard University Press.

Tellez, K. (1996). Authentic assessment. In J. Sikula, T. J. Buttery, & E. Guyton (Eds.), *Handbook of research on teacher education* (2nd ed., pp. 704–721). Macmillan.

Thomas, G. (2011). The case: Generalisation, theory and phronesis in case study. *Oxford Review of Education, 37*(1), 21–35.

Timmermans, S., & Tavory, I. (2012). Theory construction in qualitative research: From grounded theory to abductive analysis. *Sociological Theory, 30*(3), 167–186.

Tirri, K., Toom, A., & Husu, J. (2013). The moral matters of teaching: A Finnish perspective. In C. J. Graig, P. C. Meijer, & J. Broeckmans (Eds.), *From teacher thinking to teachers and teaching: The evolution of a research community* (pp. 223–239). Emerald Group Publishing.

Toom, A., & Husu, J. (2018). Teacher's work in changing educational contexts: Balancing the role and the person. In H. Niemi, A. Toom, A. Kallioniemi, & J. Lavonen (Eds.), *The teacher's role in the changing globalizing world: Resources and challenges related to the professional work of teaching* (pp. 1–9). Brill | Sense.

Toom, A., Husu, J., & Tirri, K. (2015). Cultivating student teachers' moral competencies in teaching during teacher education. In C. J. Craig & L. Orland-Barak (Eds.), *International teacher education: Promising pedagogies* (Part C, pp. 13–31). Emerald Group Publishing.

Turner, R. H. (1978). The role and the person. *The American Journal of Sociology, 84*(1), 1–23.

van Manen, M. (2000). Moral language and pedagogical experience. *Journal of Curriculum Studies, 32*(2), 315–327. doi:10.1080/002202700182781

Walton, E., & Rusznyak, L. (2016). Approaches to assessing preservice teachers' learning in authentic and rigorous ways: The case of an inclusive education module. *Perspectives in Education, 34*(1), 84–101.

Wiggins, G. (1993). Assessment: Authenticity, context, and validity. *Phi Delta Kappan*, *75*(3), 200–208, 210–214.

Wilson, B. R. (1962). The teacher's role: A sociological analysis. *The British Journal of Sociology*, *13*(1), 15–32.

Yin, R. K. (2003). *Case study research: Design and methods.* Sage Publications.

CHAPTER 4

Design and Implementation of the National Aims for Finnish Teacher Education during 2016–2019

Jari Lavonen

Abstract

The chapter summarises the analysis and reflections on the national aims for Finnish teacher education undertaken by the Finnish Teacher Education Forum over a span of three years. The forum consisted of 70 experts, representing universities, applied universities, principals, teachers, students and other relevant stakeholders. Members of the forum discussed research outcomes related to teacher education and generated ideas for revising it at national and local meetings of the forum and through a web-based brainstorming session. In 2016, three strategic aims were identified for teachers' pre- and in-service education and for their continuous lifelong professional learning: a broad and solid knowledge base; competences for generating novel ideas and educational innovations; and competences for developing teachers' own expertise as well as that of their schools. Furthermore, the forum laid down six concrete guidelines to direct the development of teacher education and financed 45 pilot projects. Typically, the projects, which involved several universities and providers of education, were collaborative and contextual in nature. In addition to the national and local meetings, these projects helped realise the strategic aims of teacher education practices and supported the professional learning of teacher educators

Keywords

education policy – teacher education strategy – teacher educator

1   Introduction

National-level goals or aims for teacher education are typically laid down in national or state-level documents, often called teacher education standards or strategies or shortly teacher standards. These documents describe the competences and values a teacher should possess or what a teacher should know and be able to do (Cochran-Smith, 2006; Ingvarson, 2002; Torrance & Forde, 2017). This chapter introduces how the Teacher Education Development Programme or national level teacher education strategy was designed and implemented in Finland during years 2016 to 2019. A collaborative design approach was used as it is known to positively influence the design and implementation process and support teacher educators' learning (Burns & Köster, 2016; Kitchen & Figg, 2011; Maier & Schmidt, 2015).

Globally, competences needed by teachers have been identified by the Organisation for Economic Co-operation and Development (OECD) on the basis of their Teaching and Learning International Survey (TALIS) 2018 (OECD, 2019, 2020). TALIS, administered in 48 countries, covers teacher education and initial policy and practices; teachers' instructional and professional practices, self-efficacy and job satisfaction; school leadership, environments and climate; and teacher feedback and development. The survey findings guide policies on teacher education, school leadership and teaching, with a special emphasis on aspects that affect student learning.

According to OECD policy recommendations, teachers should possess deep and broad professional knowledge in order to influence student learning. This professional knowledge includes, firstly, knowledge about a discipline, knowledge about the curriculum in that discipline and knowledge about students and how they learn in that discipline. Second, they require knowledge about professional practices in order to select appropriate teaching or instructional techniques, such as collaborative learning, or in order to create an environment that is conducive to learning. Importantly, teachers should be able to support students from different backgrounds with varied needs, engage them in learning and promote tolerance and social cohesion (cf. Tirri & Laine, 2017). They should themselves engage actively in formative assessment and give feedback to students to ensure that they feel valued and included. Third, teachers need enquiry and research skills that allow them to be lifelong learners and progress in their profession. Finally, in addition to these aims related to teacher education strategies, Finland's teacher education programme also emphasises teachers' ethical and moral competences (Kuusisto & Tirri, 2019).

Most countries focus on the first two areas of knowledge or competences as well as the competences for professional learning. For example, the Australian Professional Standards for Teachers (APST, 2014) groups teacher competences into three domains: professional knowledge, which covers knowledge about students, how they learn and knowledge about content and how to teach it; professional practices, which include planning and implementation of effective teaching and learning strategies, creating and maintaining a supportive and safe learning environment, assessing, providing feedback and reporting on student learning; and professional engagement, which includes teachers' own engagement in professional learning and with colleagues, parents and the community. Another example of teacher standards is the UK Teachers' Standards (Department for Education, 2011/2013), which emphasise professional knowledge and practices and expect teachers to demonstrate consistently high levels of personal and professional conduct.

However, the three areas of competences outlined above are no longer adequate for teachers. Today, providers of education, like school districts or municipalities, expect teachers to participate in leadership activities and in collaboration efforts, such as working in teams as well as with other schools and parents. In fact, teachers surveyed in TALIS (OECD, 2019, 2020) reported a high frequency of such activities in their schools. Teacher collaboration enables the setting of common teaching and learning goals not only for the classroom but for the whole school. It also facilitates the monitoring of goal achievement. With the teacher profession turning more challenging in the current times, teachers are constantly required to multi-task, which includes, for example, organising an inclusive class and using education technology. Teachers today also need an innovation orientation for effectively overcoming new challenges.

Given the growing needs, teacher education standards or strategies are challenging to design and implement. It is also difficult to involve relevant partners in a collaboration or make a sustainable change to teacher education programmes and practices (Darling-Hammond, 2017). It is common for standards, reforms or development programmes to be made by a small, nominated group of experts. For instance, Beach et al. (2014, p. 167) observed, on the basis of their long-term policy analysis of Sweden, that Swedish reforms are too strongly controlled by the government alone. However, in her study focusing on the design and implementation of teacher education policy aims, Darling-Hammond (2017) noted that successful national-level strategies or reforms call for the participation of teacher educators and teachers in professional standard-setting. In a similar vein, Russell et al. (2001) argued, on the basis of their review of teacher education reforms, that collaboration is not only important to policy design but also an aim of teacher education. Collaboration in defining the aims of teacher education ensures that the aims are acceptable to all the stakeholders, and their implementation is considered in the teacher education programmes. According to Slater (2010), the key characteristics of collaboration in the context of education improvement are as follows: joint work or interdependence, parity or equality among participants and voluntary participation. Given the varied factors that influence the design and implementation of national-level teacher education standards, an analysis of such strategies across countries can offer important insights.

2   Role of Teachers and Teacher Education in Finnish Society

In Finland, admission to teacher profession is selective, and competent teachers are available throughout the country. In Finland's decentralised education system, traditional universities are responsible for planning teacher education programmes and implementing these five-year masters' level programmes autonomously. However, collaboratively agreed-on national aims for teacher education communicate shared ideas and characteristics that are valued in the teacher profession (Tirri, 2014; Tirri & Ubani, 2013).

An important characteristic of Finnish education is collaborative development of local curricula and classroom-level assessment practices. Finland has never based its quality assurance on standardised testing, unlike countries following an outcome-based education model. Nor has Finland used school inspectors since the early 1990s. The quality of education has been advanced through a decentralised approach, which emphasises national-level guideline-type strategic documents, such as framework curricula. Local curriculum processes have inspired and empowered teachers and principals to develop the local curriculum, to improve their own work processes and to enhance the quality of education (Holappa, 2007).

A salient characteristic of teacher education in Finland has been its emphasis on research (Eklund, 2018; Tirri, 2014). Accordingly, student teachers learn both how to consume and to produce educational knowledge. This research knowledge is needed for a broad conception of local planning, the development of teaching and school practices and for the assessment of teaching and learning. Consequently, teachers play an important role in the decentralised Finnish educational system.

3   Documents as Sources of Information

Collaborative design and implementation of the national Teacher Education Development Programme as described in this chapter were based on documents, such as notes, memos, commitments and statements from different stakeholders, created during the years 2016–2019. Memos were written during 12 full-day meetings of the entire forum and seven regional meetings and executive committee meetings. The executive committee consisted of ten experts, with three representing universities, four from the Ministry of Education and Culture (MEC) and three from stakeholder organisations. The executive committee met every month for a four-hour meeting – 30 sessions in all from 2016 to 2019 – and discussed, for example, the outcomes of the literature review, policy documents of other countries and brainstormed processes and their outcomes. Moreover, the committee planned the forum meetings and drafted the minutes of those meetings. In total, this chapter is based on 95 standard pages of memos – with each memo document named in the format *Memo of the executive committee meeting, DD/MM/YY* – and one 78-page document titled *Summary of pilot project evaluations*, which contained data collected from the directors of the pilot projects (Lavonen et al., 2020).

Document analysis is a systematic procedure for reviewing or evaluating documents in order to elicit meaning, gain understanding and develop empirical knowledge (Corbin & Strauss, 2008). In the context of this study, document analysis was used to understand the design and implementation process of the education development programme and the collaboration between the stakeholders during the process. Information and insights derived from the documents have been used to write the text, as described by Bowen (2009).

To extract information and insights, the documents were skimmed through (superficial examination), read (thorough examination) and interpreted (Corbin & Strauss, 2008). They were read several times in order to identify all the aspects related to the design of the development programme. Limitations of document analysis (Bowen, 2009) relevant to this case were as follows: (1) insufficient detail because the documents were produced for the forum's internal use and not for research use and (2) biased selectivity in writing because they were written according to the ministry's procedures and mainly in order to note issues important to internal processes. To overcome these limitations, the researchers used their own notes and presentations to aid recall (Patton, 1990).

4 Collaborative Planning of National Aims for Teacher Education

To identify challenges and advance teacher education, in February 2016, the MEC appointed a Finnish Teacher Education Forum (MEC, 2016) or 70 experts from universities, national-level administrative offices and partner organisations for teacher education, such as the Association of Finnish Local and Regional Authorities and the Trade Union of Education (OAJ). The forum was asked to collaboratively work on a Development Programme for Teachers' Pre-, Introductory and In-Service Education (later programme). To design the development programme, the forum studied the research outcomes related to teacher education and the brainstorming outcomes related to the revision of teacher education at the national level.

The challenges to Finnish education were identified from the OECD, PISA and TALIS (OECD, 2013, 2014) surveys and national-level monitoring reports, which were produced by the Finnish Education Evaluation Centre, Karvi. The recognised challenges were discussed and summarised in the forum meetings (*'The presentation of the forum director summarised the challenges at student, classroom, school and city level,' Memo of the forum meeting, 25/5/16*):

Challenges stemming from the school environment that influence teacher education:
- student-level challenges, such as a decrease in learning outcomes, an increase in the variation of the learning outcomes and the varied needs of individual learners;
- classroom-level challenges, such as guiding students in active and collaborative learning, processes in heterogeneous and multi-cultural classrooms and supporting students in learning twenty-first century competencies according to new curricula;
- school- and city-level challenges, such as a lack of collaboration among teachers, lack of quality work at the local level and lack of pedagogical leadership that supports teachers' professional learning;
- challenges in teachers' pedagogical competences, collaboration and innovative orientation and a lack of willingness or competence for personal professional learning; and
- society-level challenges, such as the number of young people who drop out of education or the labour market and an increase in inequality as well as the influence of digitalisation, such as artificial intelligence and automation, on the education sector.

A review of literature on teachers and teacher education (Husu & Toom, 2016) highlighted several issues, which were discussed at the forum meetings and considered during the design of the development programme. These included research outcomes related to the role of education in society; teaching learners with different needs; the design and use of educational innovations, such as education technology, in teaching and learning; and finally, the impact of research related to teachers and teacher education on the design of the development programme. The review shed light on several models for categorising teacher knowledge and competencies. For instance, it revealed that in addition to various domains of teacher knowledge, student teachers should be willing and able to learn new competences. For example, inclusive education and co-teaching may be competences that teachers may not have learned in their initial days, but they should be able to learn them on the job (Beijaard et al., 2007; Korthagen, 2016, 2017). However, learnings from the literature review are not easy to implement in practice because one's understanding of teacher knowledge (competence) depends on the national education policy and how teacher professionalism or effectiveness is understood; how teachers' professional learning and collaboration are organised; and how the school as a learning community (school development) is organised (Leana, 2011) ('*Discussed the content of the literature review and a guideline was prepared,*' Memo of the executive committee meeting, *13/4/16*). This is why the Finnish Teacher Education Forum adopted a process-like and dialogical working approach and emphasised the reaching of a consensus among actors.

In order to broadly gather views from teacher educators and stakeholders, the forum decided to organise a national web-based brainstorming session on the revision of teacher education. The aim of the brainstorming session was to capture teacher educators' and teachers' views on what they considered important to teacher education. A call to participate in the brainstorming process was sent to teacher educators in all Finnish universities as well as to all teachers and administrative employees working in the field of education, both at the national and local level, in order to decentralise the idea-generation process and enable all the stakeholders to participate in the reform process (Cochran-Smith et al., 2018). The participants were first guided on generating ideas important to teacher education. Next, they were asked to evaluate or rank ideas contributed by others. Results showed that the most important student priorities for teacher education are learning-to-learn skills, along with interaction and collaboration skills. Overall, the competences involved in generating ideas and engaging in change- and research-based action and collaboration enable teachers to participate collaboratively in the development of classroom practices and culture, particularly in school contexts. Further, most of the top-ranked skills and competences identified are needed outside the classroom. This implies that in teacher education, participants believe that more attention should be paid to the skills and competences needed for effective teacher collaboration. Interaction and collaboration skills as well as digitalisation skills are needed in a classroom environment ('*In the evaluation discussion, it was agreed that network-based brainstorming together with the hearing of stakeholders in the executive committee meetings offered a broad view on what kind of aims different parties and stakeholders emphasise in teacher education,*' Memo of the executive committee meeting, *19/2/18*).

Between autumn 2016 and spring 2019, the Finnish Teacher Education Forum organised 12 nationwide meetings, seven local meetings and several thematic group meetings. During 2016, these meetings supported the collaborative efforts to meet the challenges and aims of teacher education and facilitated the drafting of the Development Programme for Teachers' Pre-, Introductory and In-Service Education (MEC, 2016).

The final outcome of the design process– the Development Programme for Teachers Pre-, Introductory and In-Service Education – specified three strategic competence aims for teachers' pre- and in-service education and their

continuous lifelong professional learning. Although these aims do not cover everything, they do guide the development of teacher education. According to this document, a professional teacher should
- have a broad and solid knowledge base about the relevant subject matter and pedagogy; about how to engage learners with different needs; about collaboration, interaction, digital and research skills; about schools' societal and business connections; and about ethical codes.
- be able to generate novel ideas and educational innovations while developing the local curriculum; while planning inclusive education; and in designing and adopting of the pedagogical innovations.
have the willingness and competences required for professional learning; for developing the schools' operations and environments, especially the school culture and versatile learning environments; and for using the digital tools necessary for maintaining and creating different networks and partnerships with students, parents and other stakeholders (*'In the meeting, the strategic aims outlined covered the following areas: broad basic competences; research competences; leadership; partnerships and networks; sustainable development and global citizenship,'* Memo of the upper secondary school section of the forum meeting, 18/3/16; *'It was agreed that the strategy will consists of three elements: a vision, strategic aims and actions,'* Memo of the executive committee meeting, 26/2/16).

In addition to the strategic competence aims, the development programme included six concrete strategic guidelines that directed the development of teacher education as well as the pilot projects, which have been and continue to be implemented in two phases: between the years 2017–2019 and 2019–2021. The strategic guidelines for the pilot projects were as follows:
- A teacher education programme's structure, objectives and organisation will better support the cumulative development of competences needed by a teacher both inside and outside the classroom.
- Teacher education will be strengthened through close collaboration, networking and by building a culture of doing things together.
- Teacher education institutions will promote teacher education with well-functioning structures and successful student admissions.
- The programmes, learning environments and teaching/learning methods used in teacher education will be improved to strengthen teachers' expertise in generating ideas and pedagogical innovations.
- Strategic leadership among education providers, schools and other education institutes will be strengthened.

– Training programmes and teaching/learning practices will be based on research, and student teachers will be expected to learn research skills.

5 Implementation of National Aims through Development Projects

The national Development Programme for Teachers' Pre-, Introductory and In-Service Education (MEC, 2016) was implemented through research-oriented pilot projects, national seminars and workshops and local and regional meetings. In all, 31 collaborative and networking pilot projects were financed during 2017 and 2019, and 14 pilot projects are to be rolled out during 2019–2021 by the MEC through the allocation of 27 million euros. The call for proposals for pilot projects emphasised the aims and actions introduced in the development programme. It also highlighted the collaboration between pre- and in-service teacher education, collaboration with universities and schools and the research-based orientation of the projects ('*The funded projects were introduced and discussed,*' *Memo of the executive committee meeting, 17/8/18*).

All universities, engaged in teacher education, coordinated at least one pilot project. Two universities of applied sciences coordinated two common projects. Each project had at least one partner university, and one project enlisted all universities as partners. The pilot projects involved networking with the municipalities, and 129 out of 456 municipalities participated as partners in the projects. Their participation was important because they are responsible for teachers' professional learning ('*The municipality collaboration was discussed …,*' *Memo of the executive committee meeting, 1/9/18*).

To monitor the progress of the pilot projects, a self-evaluation questionnaire was distributed among the directors of the pilot projects in September 2018. They were asked to identify the focus areas for their pilot projects from a list (multiple options could be selected), which was based on the aims introduced in the call for proposals earlier. In total, 26 pilot project directors indicated that 'a new model for teacher competence' was the main focus for their pilot projects, while 24 indicated that 'teaching and supervision in teacher education' was their main focus. Other focus areas included digital learning and new learning environments (19), development of supervised teaching practice (15), multi-professional collaboration (14), development of leadership and school networks (12), multi-lingual learning and multi-cultural classrooms (10), equality and gender-sensitive education (8) and development of special needs education (6). Additionally, the directors of pilot projects highlighted the importance of collaboration among teacher educators and active implementation of new ideas in teacher education programmes and activities ('*Summary of pilot project evaluations,*' 10/10/18). For a better understanding of the evaluations, three pilot projects examples are presented below.

A good example of a multi-disciplinary and collaborative project was 'Supporting each other!' [Tuetaan yhdessä!],[1] which aimed to develop pedagogy and support the learning of various learners. The project was implemented jointly by all Finnish universities and with the involvement of several municipalities. Project outcomes included a model for pedagogical counselling of special education teachers, development of teachers' professional skills and developing strength-based pedagogy. The project offered interactive online material for teacher educators.

OpenDigi[2] was a consortium of several universities. The project aim was to form regional development communities (consisting of researchers, teacher educators, teacher students, primary teachers) and create approaches for producing and sharing research-based digital learning material for teachers' pre- and in-service education. The project partners designed, implemented and analysed regional development community models and supported digital teaching and learning in Finnish teacher education.

Creative expertise – building bridges between teachers' pre- and in-service education[3] – was a teacher education project, grounded in systemic thinking and research-based knowledge. The project developed models within the contexts of phenomenon-based teaching and lifelong learning of teachers. Teacher educators and teacher students were supported through a collaboration between universities and schools, while they relied on hybrid learning environments (combining digital and physical environments) and expertise from various disciplines. The focus was on diverse themes in learning and teaching, such as multi-literacy and language awareness, the equal school, a research-minded approach to working, student motivation and cross-curricular cooperation.

The Finnish Education Evaluation Centre evaluated the implementation of the Development Programme for Teachers Pre-, Introductory and In-Service Education by analysing the pilot project documents, surveying the projects, and interviewing stakeholders and project experts. The centre found that the teacher education reform model developed by the Teacher Education Forum had several strengths, including networking and bringing together different experts and stakeholders. Networking, in particular, was vital to the implementation of all strategic competence aims, including the emphasis on the 21st century competences. Most pilot projects were recognised to have a strong emphasis on community building and collaboration. The evaluation report also noted challenges and future targets for implementation, such as creating a clear plan for supporting the achievement of the strategic competence aims.

It also called for monitoring the effectiveness of the pilot projects during and after its completion in 2023–2024 (Niemi et al., 2018).

6 Discussion

The aim of this chapter has been to describe the collaborative design and implementation of the national Development Programme for Teachers Pre-, Introductory and In-Service Education. A large forum comprising many actors, several national and local meetings and a brainstorming session at the national level were undertaken to serve the interests of teacher education community and other relevant stakeholders, including education policymakers. Diverse groups were involved to ensure strategy planning was not controlled by a small number of people (Beach et al., 2014, p. 167).

Two important characteristics of the Finnish educational context are decentralisation and autonomy at the teacher, school, municipality and university level. Decentralisation allows teachers and teacher educators to address local contexts and education research outcomes in their work. These factors are strongly linked to the Finnish way of interpreting teacher and teacher educators' professionalism and the status of teachers and teacher education in Finnish society. However, they also complicate the development of national strategies or national-level guidelines. Hence, it becomes important to engage autonomous teacher education institutes and teacher educators themselves in the planning of national strategies. Doing so ensures ownership of the strategies and facilitates their adoption (Madalińska-Michalak et al., 2018). Researchers also argue that teacher educators should be seen as reformers rather than as objects or targets of reforms or as local implementers of larger policies. By enlisting the support of multiple actors through various efforts –collaboration, national- and local-level meetings and a national brainstorming session with teacher educators – the development programme has engaged teacher educators not only in the design of the strategy but also in its adoption (Koenraad & van der Hoeff, 2013).

However, developing a national-level framework for teacher education through collaboration has not been an easy process. In this context, voluntary participation served as a key characteristic of collaboration (Slater, 2010). Voluntary participation implied that different individuals attended different meetings, which made it difficult to achieve consensus even though joint work and interdependence are important to collaboration.

A unique feature in the designing of the development programme was a national-level web-based brainstorming process, in which various teacher educators, teachers and stakeholders participated. This brainstorming process offered different inputs to the strategy process than forum meetings and literature review. The outcomes emphasised the importance of learning-to-learn skills, along with interaction and collaboration skills, especially in the initial teacher education and professional learning. Another outcome of the brainstorming process was the emphasis on learning competences related to generating ideas, being ready for change and collaborating through partnerships and networks. The outcomes suggested that teacher education should prioritise skills and competences needed for collaborative and creative processes.

The forum recognised three strategic competence aims to be emphasised in teachers' pre- and in-service education. These aims were explained as applicable to the whole career, similar to the approach used, for example, in Scotland (Torrance & Forde, 2017). The aims stated that student teachers and teachers should, first, have a broad and solid knowledge base, which covers depth of knowledge in the relevant subject matter and pedagogy. Second, they should become better in generating novel ideas and educational innovations while designing local curricula or planning inclusive education. Third, they should have the competences required for professional learning and for the development of the professional community (MEC, 2016). These aims are not easy to achieve through traditional teacher education courses and instead require diverse learning contexts and activities. These contexts include university course work, field work and research-oriented work. The achievement of these aims are dependent on a wide array of factors, such as opportunities for developing professional knowledge, including classroom observation and teacher modelling (Flores, 2019).

Research competence has been an integral component a Finnish teacher knowledge base, since the launch of masters level teacher education in the 1970s (Tirri, 2014). Research orientation in teacher education has allowed Finnish teachers to develop the competences needed for professional learning, planning the local curriculum and teaching and assessment activities. This type of orientation is typically not included in the teacher knowledge base.

The three strategic competence aims to partly solve the challenges in Finnish education. The competences outlined for teachers' knowledge base include those needed for tackling the diverse needs of individual learners as well as those needed to guide students in active and collaborative learning processes within heterogeneous and multi-cultural classrooms. The aims related to the development of the professional community imply that teachers need better collaboration and pedagogical leadership competences. Finally, the aim of generating novel ideas and educational innovations focuses on the need to solve problems or overcome challenges at the local level. Creativity is needed, for example, to design versatile digital and physical learning environments as well as inclusive ones.

Comparison of the Finnish teacher education development programme with the teacher standards of other countries, such as Australia and the UK, reveals that the former emphasises quality teaching and learning, similar to the others (APST, 2014; Department for Education, 2011). Further, in keeping with the other standards, the Finnish programme prioritises teachers' professional learning and their professional engagement with teacher education colleagues and parents. However, the standards of the other countries do not consider academic orientation or research competence as important for teachers. Further, they do not focus on the teachers' active role in generating novel solutions for classroom teaching. Overall, the aims of the Finnish teacher education development programme are in line with the daily activities captured in TALIS. In particular, the Finnish aims address the competences teachers need in activities outside the classroom for various collaborations.

Implementing a new strategy, a development project or a reform programme in teacher education or engaging teacher educators in the implementation of such project is a challenging endeavour (Beach et al., 2014, p. 167). Therefore, the Finnish Teacher Education Forum has adopted a participatory approach for implementation. In practice, several pilot projects have been executed to support the implementation of the programme. The implementation of the Teacher Education Development Programme through pilot projects offers a supportive environment for teacher educators and teachers in their autonomous roles (Müller et al., 2010). Collaboration and networking provide forums for discussing the strategic aims and their implementation, in addition to supporting the national planning and implementation of the development programme (Kitchen & Figg, 2011; Paavola & Hakkarainen, 2014). Collaboration and networking in practice involved teacher educators within one university and between universities as well as stakeholders and other parties in education, such as the MEC, providers of education or municipalities and teachers. These 'supportive' features for the implementation of the development programme also helped teachers' and teacher educators' professional learning (Maier & Schmidt, 2015). This was important because the implementation was assumed to occur through teacher educators' professional learning within the pilot projects. The memo documents, the main document, the *summary of pilot project evaluations* and descriptions of three pilot projects show that the teacher educators collaborated and actively implemented the new ideas in the teacher education activities. However, it is not easy to determine the influence of *collaborative* strategy planning on the implementation of the strategy. This aspect can be explored in future research.

Notes

1 https://tuetaan.wordpress.com/
2 OpenDigi (2019). OpenDigi Teacher education development project. https://opendigi.fi/
3 https://www.jyu.fi/edupsy/fi/tutkimus/tutkimushankkeet/kotisivut/ula

References

APST. (2014). *Australian professional standards for teachers*. Australian Institute for Teaching and School Leadership. http://www.aitsl.edu.au/australian-professional-standards-for-teachers/standards/list

Beach, D., Bagley, C., Eriksson, A., & Player-Koro, C. (2014). Changing teacher education in Sweden: Using meta-ethnographic analysis to understand and describe policy making and educational changes. *Teaching and Teacher Education, 44*, 160–167.

Beijaard, D., Korthagen, F., & Verloop, N. (2007). Understanding how teachers learn as a prerequisite for promoting teacher learning. *Teachers and Teaching: Theory and Practice, 13*(2), 105–108.

Bowen, G. A. (2009). Document analysis as a qualitative research method. *Qualitative Research Journal, 9*(2), 27–40.

Burns, T., & Köster, F. (Eds.). (2016). *Governing education in a complex world. Educational research and innovation*. OECD Publishing.

Cochran-Smith, M. (2006). *Policy, practice, and politics in teacher education*. Corwin Press.

Cochran-Smith, M., Keefe, E. S., & Carney, M. C. (2018). Teacher educators as reformers: Competing agendas. *European Journal of Teacher Education, 41*(5), 572–90.

Corbin, J., & Strauss, A. (2008). *Basics of qualitative research: Techniques and procedures for developing grounded theory* (3rd ed.). Sage.

Darling-Hammond, L. (2017). Teacher education around the world: What can we learn from international practice? *European Journal of Teacher Education, 40*(3), 291–309.

Department for Education. (2013). *Teachers' standards: Guidance for school leaders, school staff and governing bodies*. DfE. (Original work published 2011) https://assets.publishing.service.gov.uk/government/uploads/system/uploads/attachment_data/file/665520/Teachers__Standards.pdf

Eklund, G. (2018). Master's thesis as part of research-based teacher education: A Finnish case. *Journal of Teacher Education and Educators, 8*(1), 5–20.

Flores, M. A. (2019). Learning to be a teacher: Mentoring, collaboration and professional practice. *European Journal of Teacher Education, 42*(5), 535–38.

Holappa, A.-S. (2007). *Perusopetuksen opetussuunnitelma 2000-luvulla – uudistus paikallisina prosesseina kahdessa kaupungissa* [*The renewal of the basic education curriculum: Case study in two cities*] [Doctoral dissertation, Univerisity of Oulu]. Jultika. http://urn.fi/urn:isbn:9789514286032

Husu, J., & Toom, A. (2016). *Opettajat ja opettajankoulutus – suuntia tulevaan: Selvitys ajankohtaisesta opettaja- ja opettajankoulutustutkimuksesta opettajankoulutuksen kehittämisohjelman laatimisen tueksi* [*Teachers and teacher education – New directions for future: A report on current teacher education research for the Teacher Education Development Programme*]. Opetus- ja kulttuuriministeriö [Ministry of Education and Culture].

Ingvarson, L. (2002). *Development of a national standards framework for the teaching profession*. https://research.acer.edu.au/teaching_standards/7

Kitchen, J., & Figg, C. (2011). Establishing and sustaining teacher educator professional development in a self-study community of practice: Pre-tenure teacher educators developing professionally. *Teaching and Teacher Education, 27*(5), 880–90.

Koenraad, T., & van der Hoeff, A. (2013). National competence standards for initial teacher education: A result of collaboration by faculties of education in the Netherlands. *Journal of Teacher Education and Educators, 2*(2), 167–194.

Korthagen, F. A. J. (2016). The pedagogy of teacher education. In J. Loughran & M. L. Hamilton (Eds.), *International handbook of teacher education* (Vol. 1, pp. 311–346). Springer.

Korthagen, F. A. J. (2017). A foundation for effective teacher education: Teacher education pedagogy based on situated learning. In D. J. Clandinin & J. Husu (Eds.), *Handbook of research on teacher education* (Vol. 1, pp. 528–544). Sage.

Kuusisto, E., & Tirri, K. (2019). Teachers' moral competence in pedagogical encounters. In W. Veugelers (Ed.), *Education for democratic intercultural citizenship* (pp. 81–106). Brill Sense.

Lavonen, J., Mahlamäki-Kultanen, S., Vahtıvuori-Hänninen, S., & Mikkola, A. (2020). A collaborative design for a Finnish teacher education development programme. *Journal of Teacher Education and Educators, 9*(2), 241–262.

Leana, C. R. (2011). The missing link in school reform. *Stanford Social Innovation Review, 9*(4), 30–35.

Madalińska-Michalak, J., O'Doherty, T., & Flores, M. A. (2018). Teachers and teacher education in uncertain times. *European Journal of Teacher Education, 41*(5), 567–571.

Maier, R., & Schmidt, A. (2015). Explaining organizational knowledge creation with a knowledge maturing model. *Knowledge Management Research & Practice, 13*(4), 361–81.

Ministry of Education and Culture (MEC). (2016). *Opettajankoulutuksen kehittämisohjelma* [*Development programme for teachers' pre- and in-service education*].

https://minedu.fi/artikkeli/-/asset_publisher/opettajankoulutuksen-kehittamisohjelma-julkistettiin-opetnitelmallisesti-lapi-tyour

Niemi, H., Erma, T., Lipponen, L., Pietilä, M., Rintala, R., Ruokamo, H., Saarivirta, T., Moitus, S., Frisk, T., & Stylman V. (2018). *Maailman parhaiksi opettajiksi – Vuosina 2016–2018 toimineen Opettajankoulutusfoorumin arviointi* [*The world's most competent teachers – Evaluation of the Teacher Education Forum in 2016–2018*]. Kansallinen koulutuksen arviointikeskus [Finnish Education Evaluation Center].

OECD. (2013). *PISA 2012. Results in focus. What 15-year-olds know and what they can do with what they know.* OECD Publishing. http://www.oecd.org/pisa/keyfindings/pisa-2012-results-overview.pdf

OECD. (2014). *Talis 2013 results: An international perspective on teaching and learning.* OECD Publishing. http://www.oecd-ilibrary.org/education/talis-2013-results_9789264196261-en

OECD. (2019). *TALIS 2018 results (Volume I): Teachers and school leaders as lifelong learners.* TALIS, OECD Publishing. https://doi.org/10.1787/1d0bc92a-en

OECD. (2020). *TALIS 2018 results (Volume II): Teachers and school leaders as valued professionals.* TALIS, OECD Publishing. https://doi.org/10.1787/19cf08df-en

Paavola, S., & Hakkarainen, K. (2014). Trialogical approach for knowledge creation. In S. C. Tan, H. J. So, & J. Yeo (Eds.), *Knowledge creation in education* (pp. 53–73). Springer Singapore.

Patton, M. Q. (1990). *Qualitative evaluation and research methods* (2nd ed.). Sage.

Russell, T., McPherson, S., & Martin, A. K. (2001). Coherence and collaboration in teacher education reform. *Canadian Journal of Education, 26*(1), 37–55.

Slater, L. (2010) *Collaboration: A framework for school improvement.*

Tirri, K. (2014). The last 40 years in Finnish teacher education. *Journal of Education for Teaching, 40*(5), 600–609.

Tirri, K., & Laine, S. (2017). Teacher education in inclusive education. In D. J. Clandinin & J. Husu (Eds.), *The Sage handbook of research on teacher education* (Vol. 2, pp. 761–776). Sage.

Tirri, K., & Ubani, M. (2013). Education of Finnish student teachers for purposeful teaching. *Journal of Education for Teaching, 39*(19), 21–29.

Torrance, D., & Forde, C. (2017). Redefining what it means to be a teacher through professional standards: Implications for continuing teacher education. *European Journal of Teacher Education, 40*(1), 110–126.

CHAPTER 5

Promoting Purpose Development in Schools and Beyond

A Complex, Dynamic, Bioecological Developmental Systems Perspective

Matthew Joseph

Abstract

Purpose development is a complex, dynamic, highly individualized process that is interdependently influenced by coactions among individuals in the context of their multiple ecological levels over time. Traditional approaches to investigating purpose development have provided preliminary insights into how it may be fostered (inside and outside of the classroom), though the methods employed in these studies have largely failed to account for the complexity and unpredictability that is inherent in the purpose development process. The present work reviews the purpose development literature and highlights findings that may provide insights into teaching for purpose, while acknowledging their limitations. Three contemporary developmental frameworks – Bronfenbrenner's Bioecological Systems Model, the Relational Developmental Systems perspective, and the Complex Dynamic Systems approach – are offered as lenses intended to advance theorizing about and empirical studies of how purpose develops, and how to promote it in schools and beyond.

Keywords

youth purpose – developmental systems – complex dynamic systems

1   Introduction

Imagine you are a high school science teacher in a large, predominantly white, relatively affluent, high-performing public school district in a mid-sized city. You look at your roster before the first day of school, and the profile of a student named Ranielle catches your eye. The district's student information system indicates that Ranielle is a Black female, and was a strong performer in her previous science classes. You are eager to learn more about Ranielle's interest in science, and potential to excel as a student from an underrepresented group in a STEM discipline. As a teacher educated about and invested in your potential role as a support for developing young people's purposes in life, you wonder: How might you play a part in Ranielle's purpose development journey?

Not all teachers view themselves as key supports in the development of purpose in their students, but a wealth of literature in the domains of educational psychology and youth development suggest they certainly can be, and often are (Malin, 2018; Tirri, 2018; Tirri & Ubani, 2013). There is a good deal of empirical support for the approaches teachers can take to promote certain aspects of youth purpose development in their students (Bundick & Tirri, 2014; Koshy & Mariano, 2011; Moran et al., 2013). Teachers who understand and are enacting their own purposes are particularly well-equipped to model and support their students' purpose development (Quinn, 2016; Tirri & Kuusisto, 2016). In this hypothetical example wherein you are Ranielle's new science teacher – and, as luck would have it, well-read in the purpose literature and a purposeful teacher yourself – you may feel like you have numerous arrows in your purpose development quiver, and are eager to play your part.

In reality, of course, you occupy but one microsystem (the high school science classroom) in the multitude of layered ecologies that comprise Ranielle's day-to-day existence (Bronfenbrenner, 2005). Moreover, learning science is but one of myriad proximal academic goals to which Ranielle aspires, among the myriad other proximal as well as distal goals to which she will quite normatively attend as an adolescent (e.g., maintaining friendships, managing familial responsibilities, achieving in extracurricular domains, having fun). As such, what you do as Ranielle's teacher toward *any* developmental end – whether advancing her scientific knowledge, or boosting her academic self-efficacy in the sciences, or promoting her exploration of STEM careers – can only be fully understood in the context of the influences of and interactions among these other ecologies (Elder, 1998). That is, Ranielle's purpose development in your classroom is perforce influenced by how her other microsystems (e.g., family, peer networks, faith community) interact with yours, how the actors across those microsystems might directly and indirectly interact with you or affect Ranielle's experience in your class, and how the broader society and subcultures within which Ranielle is embedded influences her values, priorities, decisions, and actions (Burrow & Hill, 2020).

The present chapter builds on the work of Tirri and her colleagues (Bundick & Tirri, 2014, 2018; Tirri & Kuusisto, 2016; Tirri & Ubani, 2013) and complements the emerging literature on teaching for purpose in the school context (Malin, 2018), by zooming out from the microsystem of the classroom to better understand other factors that might affect students' purpose development and teachers' roles in supporting them. Though youth purpose research has advanced significantly in terms of identifying different forms and correlates of purpose, it is surprising that relatively little is known about how purpose actually *develops* (Bronk, 2014; Malin et al., 2019). In particular, there have been few empirical studies investigating between-person differences in within-person purpose changes throughout adolescence, what factors influence these changes, and how different purpose trajectories lead to different outcomes (Burrow & Hill, 2020). As such, the present work seeks not only to review the (somewhat limited) current evidence on what might promote certain aspects of purpose development, but also to push the field forward toward applying three powerful developmental models – Bronfenbrenner's Bioecological Systems Model (2005), the Relational Developmental Systems perspective (e.g., Elder, 1998; Lerner, 2018), and the Complex Dynamic Systems approach (Hilpert & Marchand, 2018) – in the service of advancing a more holistic and comprehensive understanding. The primary question addressed in this chapter is, how might education and youth development researchers and practitioners acknowledge and move beyond the limitations of traditional approaches to investigating and promoting the development of youth purpose in classrooms and beyond?

2   What Is Youth[1] Purpose?

Across the psychological literature, the term "purpose" has been defined in numerous ways (see Bronk, 2014, for a review). For most of the 20th century, "purpose" was used (mostly in studies of adults) more or less synonymously with the term "meaning" to refer to a general sense that one matters, that one's life is coherent, that one is goal-directed, that one's activities are worthwhile; the phrase "sense of meaning and purpose" is commonly used in this literature to refer to some variation or amalgam of these. In particular, Ryff's (1989) conception of "purpose in life" as well as Steger et al.'s (2006) notion of "meaning in life" have been widely adopted in the social/personality psychology and well-being literatures to reflect this general "sense of meaning and purpose" approach.

Damon et al.'s (2003) definition of "youth purpose" – which defines purpose as a personally meaningful, actively engaged, self-transcendent life goal – has become the most prevalent in the youth development and educational psychology literatures. These authors disentangled "meaning" and "purpose," with the former referring to the broader "sense of meaning and purpose" idea and the latter being restricted to a particular type of life goal that encapsulates each of the aforementioned dimensions. McKnight and Kashdan (2009) similarly viewed purpose as a life aim, emphasizing its self-organizing property that guides goal setting, decision making, and provides a compass for behavior (though they diverge from Damon et al. (2003) in their omission of a beyond-the-self focus). It is not the objective of the present work to advance one conceptualization over another; each has been independently fruitful toward generating a wealth of research toward a broader understanding of how purpose functions. Indeed, there are developmental benefits to promoting young people's general sense of purpose as well as their purposeful life goals (Burrow et al., 2018). That said, the present work will focus primarily on the Damon et al. (2003) conceptualization, given its heralded position in the youth development and educational psychology literatures.

3. What Do We Know about Youth Purpose Development?

The first day of school has arrived, and you ask each student to share two things when they introduce themselves: (a) something you couldn't gather from their student profile that they believe is important for you to really know them, and (b) something they hope to learn in your class this year. When it is Ranielle's turn, she reveals matter-of-factly that she recently came out as genderqueer, prefers the pronoun "they" and the nickname "Rani," and is part of a blended family living most of the time with their biological mother (who is Black) and stepfather (who is white). They also express that, as a devout Christian, they hope to learn more about how science and religion intersect. How might this new knowledge help shape how you teach Rani for purpose?

The youth purpose literature has burgeoned since Damon et al.'s (2003) seminal work. Space constraints preclude a comprehensive review of the topic here (for that, see Bronk, 2014). The brief review presented in this section was conducted using search terms such as "youth purpose," "purpose development," "purpose interventions," and "teaching/educating for purpose" in common psychology-related academic search engines including PsycINFO and PsycLIT, and general academic search engines including EBSCO's Academic Search Elite and Google Scholar, with a focus on peer-reviewed articles and book/handbook chapters published since 2003. Sources were selected based on their attention to youth purpose *development* (not merely forms or correlates of purpose, or descriptive studies of purposeful youth) and relevance to the educational domain.

Youth purpose primarily focuses on the developmental stage of adolescence. Pre-adolescents typically have not yet developed the cognitive capacities necessary to meaningfully explore and commit to a life purpose (Van Dyke & Elias, 2007); however, the development of initiative, goal exploration, future orientation, and other individual capacities in these earlier years lay important groundwork for purpose development in adolescence and beyond (Bronk, 2014). Moreover, purpose development certainly continues into adulthood, though it is likely to be qualitatively different given the formative nature of the adolescent years toward longer-term life pursuits (Damon, 2008).

According to Hill and Burrow (2020), in the adolescent years "determining where one wants to go is an integral component of knowing who one is" (p. 15). Adolescents have likely developed the cognitive skills to start to make sense of how the goals they explored in preceding stages will help define them. In that regard, identity development and purpose development are, while distinct (Damon & Bundick, 2018), also inextricably intertwined (Hill & Burrow, 2012). Indeed, one well-established conception of the purpose development process adapts Marcia's (1966) identity status model in advancing the notions of "purpose exploration" and "purpose commitment" (Burrow & Hill, 2011; Burrow et al., 2010).

In general, purpose exploration has been found to be largely adaptive toward purpose development in the adolescent years, whereas the evidence regarding purpose commitment in adolescence is mixed (Bronk, 2014). For example, youth who commit to life goals before they have engaged in sufficient identity development or understand the resources (e.g., educational, psychological) necessary to pursue those goals may be apt to "lose" their purpose (Malin et al., 2014, 2019). So far, the youth purpose literature has yet to offer clear insights into what the optimal developmental timing might be for purpose commitment to take hold and remain stable into one's adult years (Burrow et al., 2018), though it is clear that for some youth, adolescence is formative in their purpose development (Bronk, 2014).

McKnight and Kashdan (2009) suggested there are three different developmental pathways to identifying a life purpose: (1) proactive engagement, (2) reactions to significant life events, and (3) social learning. The "proactive pathway" involves a relatively linear process from purpose exploration to purpose commitment, followed by purpose pursuit. The "reactive pathway" involves one's experience of a significant, typically unexpected life event (such as the loss of a loved one); as such, purpose commitment (to an aim related to the significant event) was likely not preceded by much purpose exploration. The "social learning pathway" involves a young person observing someone engaged in a desired life pursuit, which the young person then adopts. As with the proactive pathway, purpose exploration precedes purpose commitment, but the exploration process is less deliberate and more vicarious. Hill et al. (2014) found in their empirical investigation of these pathways that scores on a proactive pathway measure were, on average, higher than scores on both the reactive and social learning pathway measures, suggesting it is the most common pathway. However, the pathways were not mutually exclusive; proactive pathway scores were significantly correlated with both the reactive and social learning pathway scores, suggesting some interplay among the pathways.

Malin et al. (2019) investigated purpose transitions over two years across four age cohorts from early adolescence through emerging adulthood. They found that for early adolescents, the primary mechanism for developing purpose was through empathy; for middle adolescents, purpose was facilitated by tethering life goals to career goals; in later adolescence, the transition from high school to either higher education or the working world largely resulted in purpose discontinuity; and, in emerging adulthood, purpose development was strongly influenced by one's career path (for example, those in the helping professions were more likely to sustain their purpose, whereas those in artistic fields – as well as those who had trouble finding employment – were more likely to lose theirs).

In addition to these potential pathways to purpose development, the literature has provided some insights into possible precursors of purpose and promising intervention strategies.[2] Youth who develop purpose are often those who have previously engaged in personally meaningful, self-transcendent activities, such as volunteer experiences, faith-based activities, and different forms of creative expression (Bronk, 2012). Participation in service-learning courses has been shown to be related to college students' purpose development, especially when they are provided reflective feedback on their experiences (Shin et al., 2018). Opportunities to reflect upon and discuss one's life goals has also been found to promote different aspects of youth purpose (Bundick, 2011; Pizzolato et al., 2011). Supportive adults, including teachers as well as parents and other family members, in addition to close friends, have further been found to provide general social support to youth that connects to purpose development (Malin et al., 2014; Moran et al., 2013). Moreover, some intervention programs have shown promise toward promoting purpose, including a career-focused purpose intervention (Dik et al., 2011) and an online purpose exploration and gratitude intervention (Bronk et al., 2019).

Additionally, there are numerous examples of purpose development programs focused on changing schoolwide cultures. For example, Cohen's (1993) purpose-centered system of education used a project-based model through which students investigated personally meaningful social problems and applied subject matter from their courses to possible solutions (see Koshy & Mariano, 2011). Similarly, Malin (2018) highlights the successes of multiple educational non-profit organizations that work with schools toward student purpose development using more of a consultation/coaching model, such as the Quaglia Institute for Student Aspirations, The Future Project, and Project Wayfinder. These whole-school-focused purpose development approaches have showed promise, though rigorous academic study of their efficacy remains ongoing.

4 How Three Powerful Developmental Models Can Help Us Better Understand Purpose Development

Bronfenbrenner's (2005) Bioecological Systems Model and the Relational Developmental Systems approach (e.g., Elder, 1998; Lerner, 2018) are not new in the field of youth development; however, their application to purpose development has been underappreciated. The Complex Dynamic Systems perspective (Hilpert & Marchand, 2018) is the newer developmental model on the block, though it is a close cousin to the Relational Developmental Systems approach and has been fruitfully applied to constructs similar to purpose development (e.g., identity development, student engagement). It should be noted that it is *not* the primary objective in explicating these frameworks to be prescriptive toward teaching for purpose; indeed, given the lack of empirical research applying these models directly to purpose development, prescription is premature. The primary objective is instead to illuminate the numerous factors external to the classroom that are likely to inform educators' proximal efforts to promote students' purpose development. How this information might apply to the practice of teaching for purpose will be addressed later in the chapter.

4.1 *Purpose Development through Bronfenbrenner's Bioecological Systems Lens*

Invoking Bronfenbrenner's work is seemingly *de rigueur* in much of the purpose development literature, and to that end many scholars have importantly and appropriately heeded his call to apprehend the role of context, especially cultural and international differences (Damon & Malin, 2019; Tirri et al., 2016). However, it is rare that such studies explicitly consider the development of youth purpose from a truly holistic and integrative ecological perspective; only very recently has the field begun to address the myriad interconnected influences on an individual youth's purpose development as situated within each of Bronfenbrenner's (2005) bioecological systems (see Burrow & Hill, 2020).

Bronfenbrenner's original Ecological Systems Model (1979) described four ecological systems that comprise a person's life. The microsystem is one's immediate environment and comprises direct relationships (such as family and friends) and interactions with organizations (such as school). Rani's interactions with you as their teacher and their fellow classmates are prevalent in the classroom microsystem. The mesosystem refers to interrelationships between different microsystems – typically among the people that inhabit them. For example, Rani's mesosystem, in relation to your classroom, might involve their parents' communications with you. Exosystems have indirect effects on the individuals' developmental outcomes; they do not actively participate in this ecological level. If Rani's parents are struggling with work-life balance, for example, this may affect the parents' ability to help Rani with their homework, which in turn may affect their learning in your classroom. The macrosystem refers to broader societal and/or cultural values, an individual's economic conditions and access to material resources, and structures that permit or inhibit opportunities. For Rani, their awareness of cultural scripts regarding the roles of women (or gender non-binary people), and people of color in the sciences may influence how they approach your class; indeed, their potential experiences of racial, gender, and gender identity socialization and marginalization are likely to influence not only their classroom learning but their purpose development in general (Sumner et al., 2018).

Bronfenbrenner (2005) later updated his model and renamed it the Bioecological Systems Model to recenter the person in their ecological context. He posited a Process-Person-Context-Time (PPCT) model to explain how "human development takes place through the processes of progressively more complex reciprocal interaction between an active, evolving biopsychological human organism and the persons, objects, and symbols in its immediate external environment" (Bronfenbrenner, 2005, p. 5). The first element, Process, refers primarily to these interactions that occur regularly over extended periods of time, or "proximal processes." Your interactions with Rani in and outside of the classroom over the course of the school year would be an example of a proximal process. Bronfenbrenner suggested these proximal processes are "the primary engines of development" (Bronfenbrenner, 2005, p. 6) that allow for the actualization of developmental potentials. Through these proximal processes, the second element – the Person (Rani) – and the individual characteristics and dispositions they bring with them to your classroom interactions (their identities, previous knowledge, values, developmental capacities, etc.) will intersect with what is happening within and across the levels of the four aforementioned ecological systems (i.e., the Context).

The Time element is reflected in a newly introduced ecological level of Bronfenbrenner's (2005) updated model, the chronosystem. The chronosystem accounts for the changes that occur across these systems over time. For the typical adolescent, the list of normative changes that occur throughout a school year (e.g., identity development, shifting values, relationships with friends or significant others) is long. Moreover, cohorts of students will be affected by historical events in their communities, nations, and the world around them (e.g., racial unrest, economic downturns, global pandemics) that influence their experiences as a group differently than other cohorts (Elder, 1998). As such, not only will Rani's values and aspirations likely change across the school year, but their cohort may (on average) hold different values and aspirations compared to previous cohorts.

How (and whether) Rani – or any other student – takes up the support and opportunities you provide for purpose development will in some form and to some degree be influenced by these multiple layers of their context, all of which interact dynamically over time.

4.2 Purpose Development through the Relational Developmental Systems Lens

Relational Developmental Systems (RDS) might be thought of as a metatheoretical framework comprising a suite of interconnected developmental theories (e.g., Elder, 1998; Lerner, 1982; Overton, 2015), undergirded by Bronfenbrenner's Bioecological Systems Theory (2005). The present work provides a brief conceptual overview of RDS, and how its core tenets may be brought to bear on purpose development.

In contrast to traditional Newtonian-based research approaches that view normative development as a linear unfolding of epigenetic potentialities and attempt to reduce systems to their constituent parts, RDS adopts a more integrative, holistic, "process-relational" approach (Overton, 2015) focusing on how individuals agentically coact with others and their contexts over time (Lerner, 2018). Brandtstädter (1998) referred to these individual-context relations as "developmental regulations," and when they are mutually beneficial, he called them "adaptive." Adaptive developmental regulations, according to Lerner and his colleagues (2019; Gestsdóttir & Lerner, 2008), are promoted by intentional self-regulation, which involves deliberately regulating one's behaviors, thoughts, attention, and emotions to achieve one's goals. The process involves wisely selecting goals, optimizing one's resources in pursuit of those goals, and compensating through goal disinvestment or redirection as required by the changing nature of the environment and development of the individual (see Baltes & Baltes, 1990). As such, RDS views development as *necessarily* nonlinear, dynamic, and complex.

Purpose development maps nicely onto the notion of intentional self-regulation; purposeful life goals are (typically) intentionally selected, pursued through optimization, and sometimes involve compensatory mechanisms when different means are necessary to achieve the aim or the aim shifts. Linver et al. (2018) found in a sample of adolescents that, controlling for demographic factors, intentional self-regulation was significantly and strongly correlated with having found a life purpose. Additionally, self-transcendent goals are more likely to be held by young people who intentionally self-regulate (Mueller et al., 2011).

Elder's (1998) life course framework further supports the RDS perspective that "the developing person is viewed as a dynamic whole, not as separate strands, facets, or domains such as emotion, cognition, and motivation" and "the course of development is embedded in a dynamic system of social interchanges and interdependencies across and within levels" (Elder et al., 2015, p. 19). Thus, a young person's purpose development influences and is influenced by the coaction of their intra-individual capacities (including emotional, cognitive and motivational, as well as moral, physical, social, spiritual, etc.) along with their inter-individual interactions and relationships, as embedded within their ecological layers. Rani's purpose development may be interdependent not only with their internal cognitive and moral development, but also with their racial identity, gender identity, and/or spiritual development. And these individual developmental processes will be influenced by how Rani agentically navigates their relationships with people (e.g., their parents) and organizations (e.g., their church's youth group) within and across their ecological levels.

RDS further advances that, since "no two people develop across life with the same series of time and place relations … human development is fundamentally idiographic" (Lerner, 2018, pp. 267–268). This developmental uniqueness presents challenges both to the study of purpose development and its practical application. Most research on youth purpose – and positive youth development in general – takes a nomothetic, linear approach (Lerner et al., 2019) that assumes (a) a reducible set of factors in a system that combine in predicable ways to produce an outcome; (b) that can be measured (quantitatively and/or qualitatively) and analyzed using descriptive and/or linear methods (ostensibly to uncover causal relations); (c) the results of which are generalizable to most youth; and (d) in turn, (ostensibly) well-suited to inform broad policy and practice (see Burrow et al., 2018). Among the few youth purpose studies that have employed idiographic (person-centered), longitudinal, mixed-method approaches, results have showed non-linear developmental trajectories (e.g.,

Linver et al., 2018; Malin et al., 2014). The role of such non-linear development has also been uncovered in adjacent fields such as moral development (Kim & Sankey, 2009) and identity development (Kaplan & Garner, 2017). Moreover, inferences made from quantitative investigations (in this field and across the social sciences) are typically based on aggregated data, which assumes ergodicity (where average interindividual-level behavior reflects intraindividual-level behavior); however, it is not always true – and may even be rare – that what happens "on average" is a good predictor of the experience of an individual person or subgroup (Fisher et al, 2018; Rose, 2016). The ideographic, non-ergotic, non-linear nature of purpose development thus requires new approaches to its investigation as well.

4.3 Purpose Development through a Complex Dynamic Systems Lens

A few weeks into the term, you notice Rani is having trouble concentrating, dozing off in class and not alert when called on to answer a question. You ask to speak with them after class, at which point they share they have been kicked out of their house and are jumping between the basement couches at friends' houses and a local homeless shelter. They hint that conflict as arisen with their parents over their gender identification, which does not align with their religious beliefs. How might this new contextual knowledge inform how you teach Rani for purpose (and in general)?

The RDS lens on purpose development clearly explicates its complex, dynamic, and idiographic properties. Another important element of purpose development that RDS implies (but is not central to most of RDS theories[3]) is that of stochasticity, or the role of randomness in development. It could not be foreseen that Rani would be kicked out of their house when they came out publicly as genderqueer, but that unpredictable event may have profound consequences for their development, including purpose development.

In contrast to the more static, "standard approach" to studying developmental phenomena – in which outcomes are determined to be predictable (or not) based entirely upon on the values of variables reflecting parts of a system at a particular time (van Geert & Steenbeek, 2005) – stochastic, dynamic models for understanding developmental phenomenon are more probabilistic, suggesting outcomes are not highly predictable but instead more or less likely depending on the initial conditions, changing features, and inherent randomness of the situations and environments (and actors inhabiting them). Research employing this so-called "standard approach" involves the static measurement of a (supposedly) reducible set of factors in a system that combine in (supposedly) predicable ways, (supposedly) revealed through linear analysis, to produce a "predictable" outcome. Given the reliance to date on this approach in the majority of purpose research, much of what we "know" about purpose development is bounded by the limitations of these methods.

Supporting this perspective, Moran (2020) asserted that "a coherent, ecological-dynamic model of life purpose aim and practice has been lacking in the life purpose literature" (p. 637). To address this important gap, she propounds a new "dynamic life momentum model" to better understand how purpose develops in practice. This model reflects the "reciprocal, symbiotic relationship between individuals and life situations that co-produce cultural ecosystems" (p. 629) and aims to capture "the direction, speed and commitment to a specific prosocial aim that is maintained by a person repeatedly using the processes in the model to make – and learn from making – contributions to others" (p. 638). The model incorporates aspects of RDS, including intra- and inter-individual feedback loops informing one's purpose aims, actions, and assessments of positive impact, as well as the influence of sociocultural factors. Though the model has yet to be tested empirically, it represents an ambitious and important advance in the quest to account for the inherently complex, dynamic, and ecological nature of purpose development.

Another approach to understanding the complex and dynamic nature of purpose development entails drawing on existing theories that have been applied to related constructs. Perhaps the most compelling of these is Complex Dynamic Systems (CDS) theory (Hilpert & Marchand, 2018), which has recently been used as a framework for understanding two purpose-related processes: identity development (Kaplan & Garner, 2017) and students' engagement in school (Symonds et al., 2019).[4] A full treatment of the CDS approach and its analytical tools is beyond the scope of this chapter; the primary objective here is to introduce the tenets of the theory and some preliminary propositions for how they might map onto purpose development, in hopes of inspiring future theoretical and empirical work.

CDS holds that certain phenomena arise dynamically and unpredictably from a constellation of factors interacting within and upon a given system (Hilpert & Marchand, 2018). Dynamic human systems comprise people interacting with each other and the structures within which they are embedded, as well as the conscious and unconscious psychological substrates within a person (e.g., emotions, goals, character strengths) interacting to define one's experience and inform behavior. According to CDS, these interpersonal and intrapersonal coactions strive toward order, or "self-organization." This notion echoes the "self-organizing life aim" element of McKnight and Kashdan's (2009) purpose definition. When self-organized coactions harmonize into repeated, stable patterns, they reflect what is called an "attractor" state. Attractors often manifest intrapersonally in persistent attitudes and beliefs; thus, they may offer a new scheme for understanding "stable and generalized intentions" per Damon et al.'s (2003) purpose definition.

Dynamic systems are in a constant state of "becoming," which involves the interconnectedness among all of the system's elements, and multidirectional and simultaneous effects of the behavior of each of the elements on all of the other elements. In CDS theory, this is called "emergence." Emergence among the interrelations of elements within a system can affect higher-order structures (e.g., experiences inform the selection of life goals), just as the higher-order structures can affect the emergence process (e.g., life goals frame the selection of experiences) (see Kaplan & Garner, 2017). The continuous emergence process of the dynamic system leads to iterative changes, wherein any new iteration of the system follows from the previous iteration and provides the basis for the next iteration. Whereas this iterative process and interdependence among the systems' elements typically manifests in stability (such as when purpose exploration coheres into a purpose commitment through the "proactive pathway"), these are also the same conditions that can lead to rapid and unexpected changes when any element of the system is sufficiently perturbed (such as when one experiences a discrete incidence of injustice, loss, or trauma that precipitates the "reactive pathway" to purpose). These "irregularities" can have disproportionate effects on the rest of the system (such as a shift in purpose commitment that reorganizes one's proximal and distal goal structures). The immediate effects of the irregularities are often too small to detect and only discernible over time (van Geert & Steenbeek, 2005), such as when a teacher proposes a question in class that sparks a student's interest that results in a virtuous cycle leading to a purpose commitment (as in the real case of a 12-year-old purpose exemplar named Ryan Hreljac, documented in Damon, 2008).

To be sure, as Rani's high school science teacher, it is not your job to understand how attractor states and emergence and self-organizing coactions operate to promote purpose development in your classroom. Again, the intentions of this explication are to further highlight the incredible complexity of the purpose development process, and nudge scholars toward incorporating these advances in developmental science into their theoretical and empirical work such that this inherent complexity is better understood. With this improved understanding, educators like you will be better equipped with more arrows in your purpose development quiver, and the knowledge to discern when and which ones to pull.

5   Implications for Teaching Practice to Promote Purpose Development

At the end of your first term, you assign a short paper in which you ask the students to reflect on their life purpose and imagine how science might be related to it. Rani candidly shares in their paper that they like science, but their purpose in life is to serve a higher power and they think sometimes science conflicts with their belief system. How might this new knowledge (re)frame how you teach Rani for purpose?

The overarching messages of this chapter – that we don't really know much about purpose development; and what we do "know" may be tenuous, limited by a reliance on traditional empirical methods that, while not invalid, are perhaps not as well suited to investigate complex, dynamic, stochastic phenomena (like purpose development) as contemporary developmental models – may leave you wondering, *What can I, one teacher in one classroom, actually meaningfully do to promote Rani's purpose development?*

Absent a complex, dynamic, bioecological systems perspective, one might be tempted to conclude that since purpose is a life goal composed of discernible dimensions (e.g., personal meaningfulness, self-transcendence, engagement), it can be deconstructed into its constituent parts and each of them fostered individually. Whereas there is likely to be no harm in this approach – after all, students being oriented toward meaning, or engaging in prosocial behavior, or persisting toward goals, are desirable ends in themselves – the contemporary developmental theories reviewed herein would cast doubt on the sum of these constituent parts necessarily adding up to become purpose. That is to say, purpose development may in fact be promoted by engaging students in gratitude interventions or asking them to reflect on and discuss their life goals, or integrating service-learning components into the classroom. Alternatively, this elemental approach may only affect individual components of purpose (e.g., self-transcendent orientation, goal commitment) that never meld with the other components into a coherent, engaged, meaningful, stable, self-transcendent life goal.

A different, though perhaps more radical takeaway might be that, instead of feeling compelled to ascertain all of the necessary information about each student's bioecological profile, along with interactions among and changes in their levels over time, to ensure you are as equipped as possible to pull the right arrows out of your purpose development quiver, you might instead simply consider focusing more broadly on implementing best practices in teaching for purpose *in general* (such as providing opportunities to choose personally meaningful topics for projects, pointing out the consequences of one's actions, and encouraging reflection on how one's long-term goals might connect to the course material; Malin, 2018). Incidentally, these reflect best pedagogical practices and the tenets of authentic instruction, independent of whether the end is purpose development or learning in general (Bundick & Tirri, 2014; Mariano, 2014). To invoke Lapsley (2016), just as "good character education is just good education" (p. 296), good teaching for purpose is, in large part, simply good teaching.

Beyond following these practical guidelines that reflect what good teachers already do, for those willing and able to invest beyond the classroom in their students' purpose development, another consideration might be to encourage and be available to connect individually with any student who seeks you out as a potential purpose mentor. Moreover, a purpose mentorship program could be formalized at the school level, wherein teachers with particular areas of expertise are matched with students who self-identify as having an interest in purpose exploration in those areas. The youth mentorship literature has shown that mentors can serve as role models and supports for facilitating identity development (Rhodes, 2005), and that mentor and mentorship quality are positively related to having a sense of meaning/purpose (Schwartz et al., 2013). Innovative approaches to youth mentoring are being developed that might permit teacher-student purpose mentoring to take place in and across classroom settings that involve shared mentoring responsibilities and might extend over multiple academic years (Schwartz & Rhodes, 2016).

6 Concluding Statement

Purpose development is a complex, dynamic, highly individualized process that is influenced by one's multiple ecological levels over time. The lack of empirical research drawing on contemporary models of development that properly account for this complexity calls into question the limited research that currently exists on promoting purpose development. Rani's example shows us that a small number of static pieces of information may tell us little about what purposes young people have and what factors may influence their development, and how initial conditions can change in unpredictable and highly consequential ways. The present chapter thus serves to highlight the practical challenges inherent in promoting purpose development, to temper our presumptions about how purpose development operates, and as a call to action among scholars of purpose to take these deficiencies seriously and work toward advancing our understanding through the application of these models to our research.

At the same time, there is at least a preliminary corpus of empirical findings that, even with their unknown veracity, represent a starting point for informing practice. Though we cannot (yet?) predict precisely how, why, when, or under what conditions purpose develops for any given young person, and cannot (yet?) offer clear prescriptions for promoting purpose development (in the classroom and beyond), we can say with at least measured confidence that when it comes to promoting youth purpose, we teachers, parents, any and all supportive adults invested in developing young people – we matter.

Notes

1 There is some debate in the youth purpose literature about what ages comprise "youth" (Burrow et al., 2018). Given the focus of this volume on teaching for purpose, the present work will primarily concentrate on purpose development among adolescents.
2 Given that much of this evidence is based on correlational studies and descriptive qualitative data, causal developmental inferences may be premature.
3 One exception is Elder's (1998) life course theory, which explicitly acknowledges the potential role of developmental "turning points." However, this theory does not attempt to account for the random nature of these events.
4 Space constraints preclude thorough treatments of these models; however, given they provide accessible and exhaustive explications of how CDS can be applied to purpose-related constructs, they may offer fruitful templates for further theory and research on purpose development.

References

Baltes, P. B., & Baltes, M. M. (1990). Psychological perspectives on successful aging: The model of selective optimization with compensation. In P. B. Baltes & M. M. Baltes (Eds.), *Successful aging: Perspectives from the behavioral sciences* (pp. 1–34). Cambridge University Press.

Brandtstädter, J. (1998). Action perspectives on human development. In W. Damon (Series Ed.) & R. M. Lerner (Vol. Ed.), *Handbook of child psychology: Theoretical models of human development* (5th ed., Vol. 1, pp. 807–863). Wiley.

Bronfenbrenner, U. (1979). *The ecology of human development*. Harvard University Press.

Bronfenbrenner, U. (2005). *Making human beings human: Bioecological perspectives on human development*. Sage.

Bronk, K. C. (2012). A grounded theory of youth purpose. *Journal of Adolescent Research, 27*, 78–109.

Bronk, K. C. (2014). *Purpose in life: A critical component of optimal youth development*. Springer Science & Business Media.

Bronk, K. C., Baumsteiger, R., Mangan, S., Riches, B., Dubon, V., Benavides, C., & Bono, G. (2019). Fostering purpose among young adults: Effective online interventions. *Journal of Character Education, 15*(2), 21–38.

Bundick, M. J. (2011). The benefits of reflecting on and discussing purpose in life in emerging adulthood. *New Directions for Youth Development, 132,* 89–103.

Bundick, M. J., & Tirri, K. (2014). Student perceptions of teacher support and competencies for fostering youth purpose and positive youth development: Perspectives from two countries. *Applied Developmental Science, 18*(3), 148–162.

Burrow, A., & Hill, P. L. (2011). Purpose as a form of identity capital for positive youth adjustment. *Developmental Psychology, 47*(4), 1196–1206.

Burrow, A., & Hill, P. L. (Eds.). (2020). *The ecology of purposeful living across the lifespan: Developmental, educational, and social perspectives.* Springer.

Burrow, A. L., Hill, P. L., Ratner, K., & Sumner, R. (2018). A better tomorrow: Toward a stronger science of youth purpose. *Research in Human Development, 15*(2), 167–180.

Burrow, A. L., O'Dell, A., & Hill, P. (2010). Profiles of a developmental asset: Youth purpose as a context for hope and well-being. *Journal of Youth and Adolescence, 39,* 1265–1273.

Cohen, A. (1993). A new educational paradigm. *Phi Delta Kappan, 74*(10), 791–795.

Damon, W. (2008). *The path to purpose: Helping children find their calling in life.* Free Press.

Damon, W., & Bundick, M. (2018). Purpose. In M. Bornstein (Ed.), *The Sage encyclopedia of lifespan human development* (pp. 1791–1792). Sage Publications, Inc.

Damon, W., & Malin, H. (2019). The development of purpose: An international perspective. In L. Jensen (Ed.), *The Oxford handbook of moral development* (pp. 110–127). Oxford University Press.

Damon, W., Menon, J. L., & Bronk, K. C. (2003). The development of purpose during adolescence. *Journal of Applied Developmental Science, 7*(3), 119–128.

Dik, B. J., Steger, M. F., Gibson, A., & Peisner, W. (2011). Make your work matter: Development and pilot evaluations of a purpose-centered career education intervention. *New Directions for Youth Development, 132,* 59–73.

Elder, G. H. Jr. (1998). The life course as developmental theory. *Child Development, 69*(1), 1–12.

Elder, G. H. Jr., Shanahan, M. J., & Jennings, J. A. (2015). Human development in time and place. In R. Lerner, M. H. Bornstein, & T. Leventhal (Eds.), *Handbook of child psychology and developmental science* (pp. 6–54). Wiley.

Fisher, A. J., Medaglia, J. D., & Jeronimus, B. F. (2018). Lack of group-to-individual generalizability is a threat to human subjects research. *Proceedings of the National Academy of Sciences, 115*(27), E6106–E6115.

Gestsdóttir, G., & Lerner, R. M. (2008). Positive development in adolescence: The development and role of intentional self regulation. *Human Development, 51,* 202–224.

Hill, P. L., & Burrow, A. L. (2012). Viewing purpose through an Eriksonian lens. *Identity: An International Journal of Theory and Research, 12*(1), 74–91.

Hill, P. L., & Burrow, A. L. (2020). Introduction: The purpose of studying purpose and the need for an ecological perspective. In A. Burrow & P. L. Hill (Eds.), *The ecology of purposeful living across the lifespan: Developmental, educational, and social perspectives* (pp. 1–9). Springer.

Hill, P. L., Sumner, R., & Burrow, A. L. (2014). Understanding the pathways to purpose: Examining personality and well-being correlates across adulthood. *The Journal of Positive Psychology, 9*(3), 227–234.

Hilpert, J. C., & Marchand, G. C. (2018). Complex systems research in educational psychology: Aligning theory and method. *Educational Psychologist, 53*(3), 185–202.

Kaplan, A., & Garner, J. K. (2017). A complex dynamic systems perspective on identity and its development: The dynamic systems model of role identity. *Developmental Psychology, 53*(11), 2036–2051.

Kim, M., & Sankey, D. (2009). Towards a dynamic systems approach to moral development and moral education: A response to the JME Special Issue, September 2008. *Journal of Moral Education, 38*(3), 283–298.

Koshy, S. I., & Mariano, J. M. (2011). Promoting youth purpose: A review of the literature. *New Directions for Youth Development, 132*, 13–29.

Lapsley, D. (2016). Teaching moral development. In M. Cecil Smith & N. Defrates-Densch (Eds.), *Challenges and innovations in educational psychology teaching and learning* (pp. 287–302). Information Age Publishing.

Lerner, R. M. (1982). Children and adolescents as producers of their own development. *Developmental Review, 2*(4), 342–370.

Lerner, R. M. (2018). Character development among youth: Linking lives in time and place. *International Journal of Behavioral Development, 42*(2), 267–277.

Lerner, R. M., Tirrell, J. M., Dowling, E. M., Geldhof, G. J., Gestsdóttir, S., Lerner, J. V., King, P. E., Williams, K., Iraheta, G., & Sim, A. T. (2019). The end of the beginning: Evidence and absences studying positive youth development in a global context. *Adolescent Research Review, 4*(1), 1–14.

Linver, M. R., Urban, J. B., MacDonnell, M., Roberts, E. D., Quinn, J., Samtani, S., Doubledee, R., Gama, L., & Morgan, D. (2018). Mixed methods in youth purpose: An examination of adolescent self-regulation and purpose. *Research in Human Development, 15*(2), 118–138.

Malin, H. (2018). *Teaching for purpose: Preparing students for lives of meaning*. Harvard Education Press.

Malin, H., Liauw, I., & Remington, K. (2019). Early adolescent purpose development and perceived supports for purpose at school. *Journal of Character Education, 15*(2), 1–20.

Malin, H., Reilly, T. S., Quinn, B., & Moran, S. (2014). Adolescent purpose development: Exploring empathy, discovering roles, shifting priorities, and creating pathways. *Journal of Research on Adolescence, 24*(1), 186–199.

Marcia, J. E. (1966). Development and validation of ego-identity status. *Journal of Personality and Social Psychology, 3*, 551–558.

Mariano, J. M. (2014). Introduction to special section: Understanding paths to youth purpose – Why content and contexts matter. *Applied Developmental Science, 18*(3), 139–147.

McKnight, P. E., & Kashdan, T. (2009). Purpose in life as a system the creates and sustains health and well-being: An integrative, testable theory. *Review of General Psychology, 13*(3), 242–251.

Moran, S. (2020). How practicing our purpose aim contributes to a cultural common good, and vice versa. In A. Burrow & P. L. Hill (Eds.), *The ecology of purposeful living across the lifespan: Developmental, educational, and social perspectives* (pp. 199–232). Springer.

Moran, S., Bundick, M., Malin, H., & Reilly, T. S. (2013). How supportive of their specific purposes do youth believe their family and friends are? *Journal of Adolescent Research, 28*(3), 348–377.

Mueller, M. K., Phelps, E., Bowers, E. P., Agans, J. P., Urban, J. B., & Lerner, R. M. (2011). Youth development program participation and intentional self-regulation skills: Contextual and individual bases of pathways to positive youth development. *Journal of Adolescence, 34*(6), 1115–1125.

Overton, W. F. (2015). Process and relational developmental systems. In W. F. Overton & P. C. M. Molenaar (Eds.), *Handbook of child psychology and developmental science: Theory and method* (7th ed., Vol. 1, pp. 9–62). Wiley.

Pizzolato, J. E., Brown, E. L., & Kanny, M. A. (2011). Purpose plus: Supporting youth purpose, control, and academic achievement. *New Directions for Youth Development, 132*, 75–88.

Quinn, B. P. (2016). Learning from the wisdom of practice: Teachers' educational purposes as pathways to supporting adolescent purpose in secondary classrooms. *Journal of Education for Teaching, 42*(5), 602–623.

Rhodes, J. E. (2005). A model of youth mentoring. In D. L. Dubois & M. K. Karcher (Eds.), *Handbook of youth mentoring* (pp. 30–43). Sage.

Rose, T. (2016). *The end of average: How to succeed in a world that values sameness*. Penguin UK.

Ryff, C. D. (1989). Happiness is everything, or is it? Explorations on the meaning of psychological well-being. *Journal of Personality and Social Psychology, 57*, 1069–1081.

Schwartz, S. E. O., Chan, C., Rhodes, J. E., & Scales, P. (2013). Community developmental assets and positive youth development: The role of natural mentors. *Research in Human Development, 10*, 141–162.

Schwartz, S. E. O., & Rhodes, J. E. (2016). From treatment to empowerment: New approaches to youth mentoring. *American Journal of Community Psychology, 58*(1–2), 150–157.

Shin, J., Kim, M. S., Hwang, H., & Lee, B. Y. (2018). Effects of intrinsic motivation and informative feedback in service-learning on the development of college students' life purpose. *Journal of Moral Education, 47*(2), 159–174.

Steger, M. F., Frazier, P., Oishi, S., & Kaler, M. (2006). The meaning in life questionnaire: Assessing the presence of and search for meaning in life. *Journal of Counseling Psychology, 53,* 80–93.

Sumner, R., Burrow, A. L., & Hill, P. L. (2018). The development of purpose in life among adolescents who experience marginalization: Potential opportunities and obstacles. *American Psychologist, 73*(6), 740–752.

Symonds, J. E., Kaplan, A., Upadyaya, K., Salmela-Aro, K., Skinner, E., & Eccles, J. S. (2019). *Momentary student engagement as a dynamic developmental system.* PsyArXiv. doi:10.31234/osf.io/fuy7p

Tirri, K. (2018). The purposeful teacher. In R. B. Monyai (Ed.), *Teacher education in the 21st century.* IntechOpen. doi:10.5772/intechopen.83437

Tirri, K., & Kuusisto, E. (2016). Finnish student teachers' perceptions on the role of purpose in teaching. *Journal of Education for Teaching, 42*(5), 532–540.

Tirri, K., Moran, S., & Mariano, J. M. (2016). Education for purposeful teaching around the world. *Journal of Education for Teaching, 42*(5), 526–531.

Tirri, K., & Ubani, M. (2013). Education of Finnish student teachers for purposeful teaching. *Journal of Education for Teaching, 39*(1), 21–29.

Van Dyke, C. J., & Elias, M. J. (2007). How forgiveness, purpose, and religiosity are related to the mental health and well-being of youth: A review of the literature. *Mental Health, Religion, & Culture, 10*(4), 395–415.

van Geert, P., & Steenbeek, H. (2005). Explaining after by before: Basic aspects of a dynamic systems approach to the study of development. *Developmental Review, 25,* 408–442.

CHAPTER 6

What Is above Everything?

Conceptions of the Sacred among Finnish Youth

Mette Ranta, Henrietta Grönlund and Anne Birgitta Pessi

Abstract

Individuals' conceptions and understandings of the sacred illustrate the deepest levels of their identity and spirituality. Our chapter presents the findings of our research based on representative data from Finnish youth (Ranta et al., 2016). We examine how understandings of the sacred are related to religiosity and non-religiosity, and how the definitions vary across gender. Interestingly, more than in older age groups, youth link elements of both individuality and togetherness to their understanding of the sacred. Our study reflects cultural interpretations of what the sacred means for Finnish youth. All in all, in order for teachers to understand young peoples' world view, sense of purpose, and values, exploration of these understandings is crucial. This will help the teachers of tomorrow's schools to support the wellbeing and identity construction of youth.

Keywords

identity – individuality – religiosity – spirituality – the sacred – values – youth – young people

1   Introduction

What is most important to you? What do you value the most? In what do you want to invest most of your money? What about your time? The answers to such questions deeply illustrate our values.

Values provide an empirical window into the core of every individual's personal identity (Grönlund, 2011; Hitlin, 2007). Values, by definition, are trans-situational, relatively stable principles or desirable goals that guide individuals' actions (Schwartz, 2007). Among young people, values play a significant role in how individuals see themselves in the community (Lindh & Korhonen, 2010). As values are a pivotal element of everyone's identity, understanding their students' values is crucial for teachers to support these young people as they develop and construct their identities. That is, good teachers of tomorrow will understand the importance – and to some extent the content – of their students' values. Identity formation requires active identity work. While healthy psychological development occurs throughout the lifespan, according to the classic work of Erikson (1968), gaining a sense of identity is a core developmental task throughout adolescence. This is the case especially in individualized societies like the Western ones (Erikson, 1968), where individuals are expected to make significant decisions and find their life path on their own (Miles, 2000).

In this chapter, we argue that the concept of the sacred provides a similar window on the deepest – or even deeper – level of meaningful issues as values. As we illustrate in our theoretical framework, the sacred is something set aside and set above everything else. It is the most secured and important of all valued matters. There is plenty of research on the values of children, youth and young adults (Daniel et al., 2012; Döring, 2010; Lindh & Korhonen, 2010; Reeskens & Vandecasteele, 2017; Sortheix et al., 2019; Uzefovsky et al., 2016; Vecchione et al., 2016, 2020; Weber, 2017), as well as some research on the role of these values in identity formation (Andrews, 1973; Erentaitė et al., 2019; Grönlund, 2011; Knafo & Schwartz, 2010). Much less empirical research has been done on young people's views and experiences on the sacred. Values and the sacred are not the same, and we discuss their relationship in this chapter. Religion and spirituality have been studied relatively extensively, also regarding younger age groups, but most quantitative studies have focused on institutionalized religion (Collins-Mayo & Dandelion, 2016; Sjöborg, 2013; Storm & Voas, 2012). Although a growing number of studies have emerged on the role of religion in youth development (Lerner et al., 2008), there has been a call for empirical studies concerning its relation to young adults' religiosity or spirituality (De Haan et al., 2011). Research is crucial; As noted by Oser and Scarlett (1991) and Tamminen (1991), few phenomena may be as integral across human development as religious and spiritual concerns. As Tirri and Quinn (2010) have concluded, youth who engage in their quest for self within a spiritual context potentially have the advantages of inspirational ideology, community support and transcendent understanding in striving to achieve the authentic balance between care of self and care for others, both of which are crucial for sustained purpose.

As a concept, of course, the sacred intertwines with religion and with spirituality. Currently, the spirituality and religiosity of young people are in flux. In Finland, the religious landscape has changed from strong institutionalized Evangelical Lutheranism to an emphasis on globalism, secularism, and new religious movements; this is reflected in how students themselves see the role of religion in the school setting (Kuusisto et al., 2016). At the individual level, one significant change has been the shift from religious upbringing in the family to religiosity construction through one's own search (Niemelä, 2006). However, Finnish research shows that religious family upbringing is highly influential for determining the scope of religiousness among young people (Niemelä, 2006; Räsänen, 2010). This landscape underscores the need to explore the views and experiences of younger age groups related to religion. The sacred is one aspect of this.

As Paden (2003, 2009) has stated, the sacred continues to be observable whenever identities are challenged and at stake. The core motivation of this chapter is to understand young people's views on the sacred. We ask: what is sacred for young people, and how can understanding their concept and views of the sacred help in understanding their values and life stage? Such knowledge will allow the teachers of tomorrow to better understand and support young people and their identity formation.

2 The Sacred as a Window on Young People's Values

The sacred is a concept and phenomenon which can be understood and defined in many different ways. Our view of the sacred draws from a line of research that decouples it from religion. Although religion continues to be one central sphere of life, which defines, controls, and applies the sacred, the sacred can also be used as an analytic category separate from religion (Knott, 2013; Stausberg, 2017). In the Finnish language, "sacred" (*pyhä*) has been regarded as an old, pre-Christian liminal term that signifies something that has a special status. It distinguishes the untouchable or supernatural from the mundane and ordinary. The term has also carried meanings such as good, secure, pure and taken (Anttonen, 2010; Saarikivi, 2017). The sacred is a line that sets aside issues that one is not willing or able to negotiate about. As such, sacred is not only a matter of religion. It resembles a wider logic of drawing boundaries that is typical for the human mind (Durkheim, 1912/1995; Anttonen, 2000, pp. 277–281, 2010, pp. 122–125). This viewpoint builds on the Durkheimian approach to the sacred as separated and protected from the profane, the realm of everyday activities, things, places, or activities of supreme value or ultimate significance (Knott, 2013).

As such, the sacred can be applied to secular contents, allowing it to be recognized and experienced by religious and non-religious people alike. In this, it resembles spirituality. As Hill et al. (2000) note, not all conceptions of spirituality are linked to religion, though the use of the term spirituality apart from religion has a surprisingly short history (Sheldrake, 1992; Wulff, 1997).

How then do the concepts of the sacred and spirituality relate to each other? They are deeply intertwined. For Hill and colleagues (2000), for instance, spirituality refers to the feelings, thoughts, experiences, and behaviours that arise from a search for the sacred. The term "search" here refers to attempts to identify, articulate, maintain, or transform, and the term "sacred" refers to a divine being, divine object, Ultimate Reality, or Ultimate Truth as perceived by the individual. They note that the term "spiritual" is often used in modern discourse as a substitute for words like "fulfilling" or "important"; but ideologies, activities, and lifestyles are not spiritual unless they involve considerations of the sacred (Hill et al., 2000, pp. 64, 66). Not all definitions of spirituality explicate the sacred. Yet the concepts circle around the same phenomena; the sacred and spiritualty are always beautifully entangled. For Reich (1998), spirituality involves transcendence or a commitment to ideas and/or institutions that go beyond the self in time or place (cf. Lerner et al., 2008; Tirri & Quinn, 2010). Exploring the sacred thus furthers understanding of spirituality – and vice versa, research on spirituality enriches studies of the sacred.

Decoupling the sacred – and spirituality – from religion does not, however, indicate that the role of religion should be overlooked. Religions have been the predominant contexts that have coordinated and defined the sacred in most societies, also Finland. This continues to influence the ways in which the sacred is understood and the concept used. For example, Pargament and Mahoney (2005) and Pargament et al. (2017) take a psychological approach to the sacred and the ways in which individuals can experience and perceive it. They view the sacred as having a core and a wider ring. At the core of the sacred are concepts that refer to a transcendent reality, and on a wider ring are aspects of life that are not transcendental but take on deeper meaning and value. The non-transcendental objects, issues, or places can be sanctified as illuminations of the transcendent in this world, but they can also be sanctified without presupposing a transcendental reality. In the latter case, qualities from the realm of the transcendent are nevertheless transferred to the object or issue. In this sense, even though secular objects and issues can be viewed as sacred without an idea of the transcendent, the qualities that originally refer to a transcendent reality, continue to influence the experience.

Although the above psychological viewpoint highlights the role of the individual, the sacred continues to be a question of community and context. Their roles cannot be overlooked when analyzing the conceptions of individuals, and this includes the religious context. Durkheim (1912/1995) approached the sacred (and religion) essentially as something that binds a community together. Even if in individualistic (and in terms of religion, relatively secularized) contexts, (religious) communities have less direct power to define the sacred, and processes of group identification and commitment are increasingly fragmented and dynamic, individuals still negotiate with and position themselves in relation to different communities, or communal and societal discourses. Discourses displayed by the media, families, and religious traditions are utilized in individual negotiations and identifications with, as well as separations from, the sacred of religious and other communities or groups (Knott, 2013). Individual and communal conceptions of the sacred always interact, and influence one another. Thus, even if the sacred can be viewed as an utterly personal experience, emotion, or category of meaning, these experiences and conceptions always reflect their – religious and broader – context (Knott, 2013; Pargament 2017; Taves, 2013).

The sacred is a window on issues and objects of the utmost importance, and thus comes close to the concept of values. Like the sacred, personal values are constructed in dynamic relationship with the relevant groups of people and within the cultural context. Values are normative and justified but they are often also emotional and to some extent unrecognized (Schwartz, 2007); just like our experiences of the sacred. Young people's values – by definition – demonstrate their beliefs, their desirable goals that guide their actions and decision-making, and what is important to them at an early stage (Schwartz, 2007, 2012).

Thus, to put it somewhat simply: Following the definition of the sacred as something set aside and above everything, values illustrate what is important to young people, and the sacred illustrates what is *most* important to them. The present chapter focuses on the latter by reviewing our previous research (Ranta et al., 2016) on young adults' conceptions of the sacred in Finland. In the following section, we re-examine our findings from this study, focusing on the importance of the sacred in the educational context, and then return to the distinction between values and the sacred in our discussion, particularly concerning future studies.

3 Bridging the Individualized Sacred with Traditional and Communal Religion

3.1 *Method*

In our earlier research (Ranta et al., 2016), we examined how the sacred is interpreted and experienced by Finnish youth. Our data came from a self-report questionnaire collected in 2011 from young adults aged 19–35 ($N = 334$), taken from an extensive and nationally representative population sample in Finland

(N = 1,285). The questionnaire concerned various issues ranging from wellbeing to values and to pro-sociality. We focused on the responses to the open-ended question: "Please tell us what the sacred, sacredness, means to you? Where and how can you experience it?" Relating to the multifaceted nature of the framework of the sacred, our inquiry thus covered elements ranging from understandings to emotions, and from experiences to views on spaces and places.

This was the first time these personal understandings and experiences of the sacred had been studied with such extensive survey data in Finland. Internationally, empirical research on the views and experiences of the sacred are rare, and even more so, among youth. What is actually typical for the experiences, reflections, and understandings of the sacred by the Finnish youth, and how do their conceptions differ in comparison to the adult population? We also examined how the understandings of the sacred relate to the role of subjective religiosity, spirituality, and gender. How do sacred components in life differ between individuals, and groups, such as young men and women?

In the data-determined content analysis, the qualitative data were classified into 15 categories (Table 6.1). Then, the answers were categorized using a thematic analytical approach. The qualitative analyses portrayed how young adults show great heterogeneity in their conceptions of the sacred, as well as enthusiasm towards the topic in general with their – often lengthy – in-depth responses. The responses often included various intertwined elements and in these cases were placed in several categories.

3.2 *Findings*

What did we find? As seen in Table 6.1, Finnish young people primarily highlight subjectivity and personal issues concerning the individual in their understanding of the sacred, including oneself, individuality, personal opinions, and thinking (28% of participants), as well as rest, peace and the home (28% of participants). For example (a direct quotation from the data):

> The sacred is something big, respected, and a secret. To me, God is sacred. But also everyday personal things can be sacred and one does not want to share them with anyone other than close ones whom one trusts. The sacred can be experienced in everyday life, everywhere: at home and in different places such as the church, in nature, in one's own mind, and so on.

The meaning of the sacred is multifaceted, and this is clear in the thoughts of the young people who responded to the question. Even if the big picture illustrates individuality, more communal elements are evident. The church as a location or as an institution came to a close third place (24% of participants):

TABLE 6.1 Total distribution in categories of conceptions of the sacred (adapted from Ranta et al., 2016)

Category	Entire sample (n = 1,835)		19–35 years (n = 473)	
	%	% of cases	%	% of cases
Individual, myself, my opinions, thinking	9	21	14	28
Rest, peace, the home as a location	14	31	13	28
Location, church, institution	13	28	12	24
Nature	13	29	10	21
Love, close ones, home with family	9	21	11	22
Nothing, doubt, difficult to say, difficult	8	17	11	22
The 'sacred' as a concept	7	15	8	17
Belief, religion	9	20	8	16
Others, helping, contact	6	14	4	9
Ritual	3	7	3	6
Human dignity, new life, children	3	6	4	7
Finland, independence	0.7	2	0.2	0.4
Death, grave	3	6	2	3
Art, music, science	2	3	0.6	1
Health	0.1	0.2	0	0

Note: The n refers to the number of meaning categories of responses in the entire sample and the youth subsample, not the size of the sample (entire sample, N = 1,285; youth aged 19–35, N = 334), in reference to the Multiple Response Sets data used.

> Sacred means quieting down at God's word, the Bible, and explaining it. The sacred and sacredness are religious concepts that are also present in everyday life, although one usually stops at them only on holidays. Sacred things (God, Jesus, the Holy Spirit, etc.) bring peace, joy and freedom. It's almost too difficult to explain.

Another young person noted:

> The sacred means becoming aware of the presence of God, in Christianity. I can experience it at church/congregational events, in the middle of nature, or together with others while praying. A leisurely ambiance is important for experiencing the sacred.

Interestingly, we did not find significant gender differences in the young people's conceptions of the sacred. The core is the same: individual responses were most prominent for both young men – "The sacred is a [...] very personal matter. One can experience it wherever and whenever one wishes" – and young women – "The sacred means peace and it is personal, my most own."

While the differences between age groups were minor, older respondents highlighted the themes of rest, peace, and the home as well as nature as sacred, and more so than young respondents. Another major age-related difference was the fact that Finnish young people showed more feelings of doubt related to the sacred in their responses, or felt that the question was difficult for them, even to the point that they felt that they had no actual experiences of the sacred:

> Sacred is a swear word when it is used for something [...] beyond the real world that turns out to produce mainly negative energy in those who dare to examine it reasonably. A good thing may thus turn into a burden when it is not dared to be questioned or developed.

Interestingly, young people's conceptions of the sacred, which often related to subjectivity and individuality, were also often intertwined with togetherness, close social relationships, and solidarity;

> To me, the sacred means understanding the fact that we are all connected to each other (the entire universe), and living with this truth every second. One can sense the sacred within oneself and in others, wherever and whenever.

The notion of combined subjectivity and close social relationships support previous research on healthy identity development in late adolescence, in particular. Campbell et al. (1984) showed this, emphasizing young people's individuality, connectedness, and emotional affection for the family. The individuating and reflective stage of faith emblematic of adolescence and young adulthood provides both an opportunity and a responsibility for questioning one's religious beliefs and moral issues in relation to those of others and institutionalized religion (Fowler, 2001). Thinking about teachers in both schools and higher education, it is crucial to acknowledge how multifaceted young people's contemplation of the sacred is.

It seems that young people see the self and individual rights as especially protected and untouchable. This is well in line with Finnish society's current emphases on authenticity and individual rights, which are especially adopted by young adults who have grown up in an individualist age. In our view, these results reflect the life phase these young people are currently experiencing, and the developmental tasks of finding one's own identity, values, and life path. The fact that young people also view social ties and solidarity as sacred highlights that holding individuality and subjectivity sacred does not mean selfishness or egoism.

Issues around values, spirituality, and the sacred are not easy ones, nor everyday concrete matters. The younger the participants, the more they reflected doubt and difficulty in their responses to the open-ended question. Moreover, 30% of young participants in the study did not respond to this question at all. Both non-response and the notions of bewilderment or doubt suggest an extended "identity crisis" characteristic for the prolonged youth phase of individualized contemporary society (Côté, 2000).

After categorizing the participants into four levels of religiosity based on their subjective religiosity, spirituality, and praying as a form of traditional religious practice, we found that the most religious participants expressed religious conceptions of the sacred and themes related to the church as an institution. While the most unreligious youth expressed more doubt and difficulty in their understanding of the sacred, the other prominent conceptions such as rest, peace and home, love and close ones, or individuality were important for all the young people irrespective of their level of religiosity.

4   Conclusions – And Food for Thought

Psychosocial development has traditionally (e.g., Brandtstädter, 1998; Bronfenbrenner, 1977) been seen as following a specific path that is regulated by physical maturation, agency, and aspirations, as well as by societal and cultural values. In a societal context of identity exploration and instability, the search for not only individualistic sacredness but also togetherness and connection through social relationships is strong, which comes close to classical perceptions of religion and communal functions of the sacred. Societal change and increased heterogeneity among young people have resulted in a trend towards individualization, subjectivity, and a lifestyle of increased independence, self-determination and self-realization (Miles, 2000). This trend is not entirely positive since uncertainty and lack of social support are also on the rise. Such a landscape calls for studies on values and the sacred.

In our 2016 study (Ranta et al., 2016), young respondents emphasized different personal and individual conceptions of the sacred. The qualitative nature of our data made investigating this theme especially intriguing, as the participants responded with enthusiasm to portray their concepts of the sacred. Finnish young people clearly relate to the concept of the sacred, finding it interesting and meaningful. Our study shows that individual viewpoints and subjective experiences of the sacred were central to young people's concept of the sacred. Traditional viewpoints of the sacred as related to religion, beliefs, and the church as an institution were also strongly represented. These were often intertwined with personal pondering about the meaning of the sacred. The prominent conceptions of the sacred in our findings, related to subjectivity and individuality, were also very much intertwined with togetherness, close social relationships, and solidarity. Considering teachers, this overall finding underscores the conclusion by Tirri and Quinn (2010): Educators hit the mark when they are able to provide an optimal balance between commitment to the wellbeing of the self and others.

While our young respondents clearly expressed such subjectivity and individuality in their conceptions of the sacred, many expressed a sense of doubt or difficulty in responding to such a question. In this sense, the study portrays the significance of the sacred for young people's age-normative development and ongoing identity construction, key issues for this life phase. While our study focused on young adults aged 19–35, further research is needed on the ongoing developmental processes in this life stage, namely in terms of identity and faith development. Older participants reflected more on themes of rest, peace, the home, and nature in their conceptions of the sacred. Major gender differences among youth were not found.

With rapid societal change, individualization increases in parallel with a need for community and belonging. In our 2016 study (Ranta et al., 2016), the psychological value of social relationships for Finnish youth was clearly evident. Young people long for a sense of community or belonging, which refers to the sum of social relationships that arise from social interaction and common experiences and lead to attachment between individuals (Colclough & Sitaraman, 2005). This experience of belonging is relevant for wellbeing and social identity (Davidson & Cotter, 1991; Prezza et al., 2001; Prezza & Constantini, 1998). Individuals need to have a sense of being part of a larger entity, whether it is a small personal social circle or a larger social network (Henderson et al., 2007; Kehily, 2007). Maintaining a sense of, or membership in, a community such as a circle of friends or a school class, creates an important source of trust and wellbeing through peer group conformity. For young people in today's society, this includes many means of communicating and connecting on social media that is not dependent on physically bounded interaction (Ellison et al., 2007).

Religious identity, a self-definition of one's religious values and beliefs, is defined in late adolescence (Erikson, 1968). This identity based on personal characteristics sets the possibility of achieving a spiritual identity over the course of childhood and adolescence (Templeton & Eccles, 2006). For the young people in our study (Ranta et al., 2016), personal pondering, reflecting a sense of personal sacredness, individual viewpoints and subjective experiences were central, illustrating a subjective turn of values and religiosity. However, our study also found that traditional conceptions of the sacred as analyzed by classical theorists of religion and sociology (e.g., Durkheim, 1912/1995) were also important. Aspects of transcendence and the church as an institution were strongly present in the young people's responses, reflecting their values and religiosity. Their emphasis on individuality gives way to underlining formal versions of religiosity in adulthood – young people did not focus on these so much.

5 Vistas for Teachers and Researchers

If teachers – and others – are to understand and support young people in their identity construction; it is essential that they explore and contemplate young people's values and conception of the sacred. While our study (Ranta et al., 2016) used data from Finnish young adults aged 19–35, it offers insight into conceptions of the sacred among younger school-aged Finns prior the critical transition to adulthood. The issues which young people underline as sacred play a vital role in their positive development, wellbeing, and sense of meaning. All this should be supported by teachers in discussions on the students' own beliefs, values, and identity beyond traditional religious education (in school). The symbolic status of the sacred can be a tool for promoting positive development – even more so during societal and religious change, as identified in Finnish society today. Religion as lived and experienced as a cultural resource enables personal orientation (Henriksen, 2016); understanding the sacred is a means for supporting young people's positive development and identity formation.

While Finnish young people strive for individualization, they use the concept of the sacred in relation to others, communities, and close social relationships. Concrete ideas about how to use our findings in the everyday context of schools will be much better designed by teachers than by us. Foremost, our findings encourage explanations and discussions on the sacred, and definitely not only in religious education classes. Our findings firmly illustrate that young people are not strangers to the concept of the sacred, but certainly have multifaceted thoughts and emotions about it.

The closer young people come to the verge of independence, the more instability they experience, especially in their transition towards adulthood, further education and work (Arnett, 2006). As post-industrial societies become more complex, psychological functioning becomes increasingly important (Heckhausen, 1999). The extensive review of Meeus et al. (1999) shows how slow development of identity results in low psychological wellbeing. Self-worth and a notion of "who am I?" is set against a cultural standard. This question relates to identity formation, ponderation upon the meaning and purpose of life (Tirri & Quinn, 2010). Individuals construct their own life course by selecting, through individual agency, their own experiences, social relationships, and settings but within the opportunities and constraints provided by historic, economic and political circumstances (Elder & Johnson, 2003; Settersten, 2003).

To what extent do our findings on their views of the sacred reflect young people's values? Does the sacred seem to be valued above all other valued matters? Our findings cohere with those of other researchers on the subject. Young Finns find values related to personal wellbeing and the rights of individuals, such as health, freedom, and human rights, important. They also find communities and social ties central as family, relationships, and love are among the most important things to them (Haikkola & Myllyniemi, 2020; Pekkarinen & Myllyniemi, 2019).

This being true, young people's values about the sacred differ from their experience of it; their relation fascinating and complex. Despite the similarities between these concepts, our recent representative research on more than 6,000 Finns (Pessi et al., 2018) showed that even though some connections are found, individuals' conceptions of the sacred are not explained by their values. In that study, respondents who held values directed to themselves (e.g., power, wealth, success) as important, considered issues related to themselves such as health and their own opinions as sacred more often than those who did not find such values important. Similarly, respondents who held universalistic, self-transcending values (e.g., egalitarianism, social justice, nature conservation) as important, considered human dignity, nature, and helping and communality more often than those who did not find such values important. However, this study found that the correlations between value directions and conceptions of the sacred were relatively low. In fact, values – even combined with gender, age, education, political orientation, living area, and language – only explained less than 20% of the conceptions of the sacred.

Even though the sacred and values resonate, and the sacred illustrates some of the most important issues for an individual, the sacred is not the same as values. The sacred sets apart the most particular and ultimate. We maintain that it reaches an even deeper layer of meaningful issues, objects, and values: the things that need to be protected not only because they are important or viewed as right and good, but because they have supreme value.

To conclude, the sacred is not the same as values, religion, or spirituality, but it can illustrate their roles and importance in the identities of individuals, and in this case, Finnish young people. At the same time, the sacred is always a question of community and context, and individuals negotiate with and position themselves in relation to different communities, or communal and societal discourses. In relation to religiosity, young adults want to adopt an independent and active role instead of seeing themselves as religious in a fixed or standardized way (Sjöborg, 2013). This is true for the sacred in particular, and in general when young adults shape and reflect upon their identities, but the reflection happens in relation to existing discourses and contexts.

The sacred as a concept, which young people recognize and can use, opens a door to investigating, discussing, and understanding their most important values, spirituality, and life stage. For young people, spirituality is a means for understanding oneself and the world, in addition to speaking of experiences of transcendence (King et al., 2014). Authenticity, morality, values, and the sacred are deeply intertwined, as illustrated by a quote from our data: "To me, my own moral conceptualizations are sacred, uppermost judgment."

If teachers understand and ponder these issues – also with their students – they will be better equipped to support and promote not only young people's identity development but also meaningfulness and sense of purpose, which in turn are crucial to wellbeing (Ivtzan et al., 2011; Pessi, 2017). As Tirri and Quinn (2010) have concluded, by taking into account the range of spiritual sensitivities, those who wish to encourage a sense of purpose in young people are planting on fertile ground. The same is very much true for sensitivity to the sacred.

References

Andrews, J. (1973). The relationship of values to identity achievement status. *Journal of Youth and Adolescence, 2*(2), 133–138.

Anttonen, V. (2000). Sacred. In W. Braun & R. T. McCutcheon (Eds.), *Guide to the study of religion* (pp. 271–282). Cassell.

Anttonen, V. (2010). *Uskontotieteen maastot ja kartat* [*The terrains and maps of religious studies*]. Suomalaisen Kirjallisuuden Seura [The Finnish Literature Society].

Arnett, J. J. (2006). Emerging adulthood in Europe: A response to Bynner. *Journal of Youth Studies, 9*(1), 111–123.

Brandtstädter, J. (1998). Action theory in developmental psychology. In R. M. Lerner (Ed.), *Handbook of child psychology: Theoretical models of human development* (5th ed., Vol. 1, pp. 807–863). Wiley.

Bronfenbrenner, U. (1977). Toward an experimental ecology of human development. *American Psychologist, 32*(7), 513–531.

Campbell, E., Adams, G. R., & Dobson, W. R. (1984). Familial correlates of identity formation in late adolescence: A study of the predictive utility of connectedness and individuality in family relations. *Journal of Youth and Adolescence, 13*(6), 509–525.

Colclough, G., & Sitaraman, B. (2005). Community and social capital: What is the difference? *Sociological Inquiry, 75*(4), 474–496.

Collins-Mayo, S., & Dandelion, P. (Eds.). (2016). *Religion and youth: Theology and religion in interdisciplinary series in association with the BSA Sociology of Religion Study Group.* Ashgate.

Côté, J. E. (2000). *Arrested adulthood: The changing nature of maturity and identity.* NYU Press.

Daniel, E., Schiefer, D., Möllering, A., Benish-Weisman, M., Boehnke, K., & Knafo, A. (2012). Value differentiation in adolescence: The role of age and cultural complexity. *Child Development, 83*(1), 322–336.

Davidson, W. B., & Cotter, P. R. (1991). The relationship between sense of community and subjective wellbeing: A first look. *Journal of Community Psychology, 19*(3), 246–253.

De Haan, L. G., Yonker, J. E., & Affholter, C. (2011). More than enjoying the sunset: Conceptualization and measurement of religiosity for adolescents and emerging adults and its implications for developmental inquiry. *Journal of Psychology & Christianity, 30*(3), 184–195.

Durkheim, E. (1995). *The elementary forms of religious life* (J. Ward, Trans.). Free Press. (Original work published 1912)

Döring, A. K. (2010). Assessing children's values: An exploratory study. *Journal of Psychoeducational Assessment, 28*(6), 564–577.

Elder, G. H. Jr., & Johnson, M. K. (2003). The life course and aging: Challenges, lessons, and new directions. In R. A. Settersten Jr. (Ed.), *Invitation to the life course. Toward new understandings of later life* (pp. 49–81). Baywood.

Ellison, N. B., Steinfield, C., & Lampe, C. (2007). The benefits of Facebook 'friends": Social capital and college students' use of online social network sites. *Journal of Computer-Mediated Communication, 12*(4), 1143–1168.

Erentaitė, R., Vosylis, R., & Crocetti, E. (2019). Longitudinal associations of identity processing styles with prodiversity and proequality values in adolescence. *Child Development, 90*(5), 1490–1502.

Erikson, E. H. (1968). *Identity, youth and crisis.* W. W. Norton Company.

Fowler, J. W. (2001). Faith development theory and the postmodern challenges. *International Journal for the Psychology of Religion, 11*(3), 159–172.

Grönlund, H. (2011). Identity and volunteering intertwined: Reflections from the values of young adults. *Voluntas, 22*(4), 852–874.

Haikkola, L., & Myllyniemi, S. (Eds.). (2020). *Hyvää työtä! Nuorisobarometri 2019* [*Good work! Youth barometer 2019*]. Valtion nuorisoneuvosto, Nuorisotutkimusseura, Nuorisotutkimusverkosto, Opetus- ja kulttuuriministeriö [Ministry of Education and Culture, The State Youth Council & The Finnish Youth Research Network].

Heckhausen, J. (1999). *Developmental regulation in adulthood. Age-normative and sociostructural constraints as adaptive challenges.* Cambridge University Press.

Henderson, S., Holland, J., McGrellis, S., Sharpe, S., & Thomson, R. (2007). *Inventing adulthoods. A biographical approach to youth transitions.* Sage.

Henriksen, J.-O. (2016). Everyday religion as orientation and transformation: A challenge to theology. *Nordic Journal of Religion and Society, 29*(1), 36–51.

Hill, P. C., Pargament, K. II., Hood, R. W., McCullough, M. E., Jr., Swyers, J. P., Larson, D. B., & Zinnbauer, B. J. (2000). Conceptualizing religion and spirituality: Points of commonality, points of departure. *Journal for the Theory of Social Behaviour, 30*(1), 51–77.

Hitlin, S. (2007). Doing good, feeling good: Values and the self's moral center. *The Journal of Positive Psychology, 2*(4), 249–259.

Ivtzan, I., Chan, C., Gardner, H., & Prashar, K. (2011). Linking religion and spirituality with psychological well-being: Examining self-actualisation, meaning in life, and personal growth initiative. *Journal of Religion and Health, 52*(3), 915–929.

Kehily, M. J. (Ed.). (2007). *Understanding youth: Perspectives, identities and practices.* Sage.

King, P. E., Clardy, C. E., & Ramos, J. S. (2014). Adolescent spiritual exemplars: Exploring spirituality in the lives of diverse youth. *Journal of Adolescent Research, 29*(2), 186–212.

Knafo, A., & Schwartz, S. H. (2010). Identity formation and parent-child value congruence in adolescence. *British Journal of Developmental Psychology, 22*(3), 439–458.

Knott, K. (2013). The secular sacred: In between or both/and? In A. Day, G. Vincett, & C. R. Cotter (Eds.), *Social identities between the sacred and the secular* (pp. 145–169). Ashgate.

Kuusisto, A., Poulter, S., & Kallioniemi, A. (2016). Finnish pupils' views on the place of religion in school. *Religious Education, 112*(2), 110–122.

Lerner, R. M., Roeser, R. W., & Phelps, E. (2008). *Positive youth development and spirituality: From theory to research.* Templeton Foundation Press.

Lindh, K., & Korhonen, V. (2010). *Youth values and value changes from cultural and transnational perspective. Cross-cultural lifelong learning.* Tampere University Press.

Meeus, W., Iedema, J., Helsen, M., & Vollebergh, W. (1999). Patterns of adolescent identity development: Review of literature and longitudinal analysis. *Developmental Review, 19*(4), 419–461.

Miles, S. (2000). *Youth lifestyles in a changing world.* Open University Press.

Niemelä, K. (2006). Does religious upbringing matter? The effect of religious upbringing on the religious and spiritual identity of urban young adults in Finland. In K. Tirri (Ed.), *Religion, spirituality & identity* (pp. 153–169). Peter Lang.

Oser, F. K., & Scarlett, W. G. (Eds.). (1991). *Religious development in childhood and adolescence*. Jossey-Bass.

Paden, W. E. (2003). *Interpreting the sacred: Ways of viewing religion*. Beacon Press.

Paden, W. E. (2009). Reappraising Durkheim for the study and teaching of religion. In P. Clark (Ed.), *The Oxford handbook of the sociology of religion* (pp. 941–961). Oxford University Press.

Pargament, K. I., & Mahoney, A. (2005). Sacred matters: Sanctification as a vital topic for the psychology of religion. *The International Journal for the Psychology of Religion, 15*(3), 179–199.

Pargament, K. I., Oman, D., Pomerleau, J., & Mahoney, A. (2017). Some contributions of a psychological approach to the study of the sacred. *Religion, 47*(4), 718–744.

Pekkarinen, E., & Myllyniemi, S. (2019). Arvot. In E. Pekkarinen & S. Myllyniemi (Eds.), *Vaikutusvaltaa Euroopan laidalla. Nuorisobarometri 2018* [*Influence on the edge of Europe. Youth barometer 2018*]. Valtion nuorisoneuvosto, Nuorisotutkimusseura, Nuorisotutkimusverkosto, Opetus- ja kulttuuriministeriö [Ministry of Education and Culture, The State Youth Council & The Finnish Youth Research Network].

Pessi, A. B. (2017). Dazed and amazed by moonlight: Exploring sense of meaning as the mediator of the effects of religion, belonging, and benevolence on well-being. *Nordic Journal of Religion and Society, 30*(1), 24–42.

Pessi, A. B., Pitkänen, V., Westinen, J., & Grönlund, H. (2018). *Pyhyyden ytimessä. Tutkimus suomalaisten arvoista ja pyhyyden kokemisesta* [*In the core of the sacred. A study on the values and experiences of the sacred among Finns*]. e2 Tutkimus & Suomen Kulttuurirahasto [e2 Research & The Finnish Cultural Foundation].

Prezza, M., Amici, M., Roberti, T., & Tedeschi, G. (2001). Sense of community referred to the whole town: Its relations with neighbouring, loneliness, life satisfaction and area of residence. *Journal of Community Psychology, 29*(1), 29–52.

Prezza, M., & Constantini, S. (1998). Sense of community and life satisfaction: Investigation in three different territorial contexts. *Journal of Community and Applied Social Psychology, 8*(3), 181–194.

Ranta, M., Pessi, A. B., & Grönlund, H. (2016). Young adults' conceptions of the sacred in Finland today. *Young, 25*(1), 45–65.

Räsänen, A. (2010). Teenage religion – Religiousness among Finnish 8th and 9th graders. *Education Inquiry, 1*(3), 143–156.

Reeskens, T., & Vandecasteele, L. (2017). Hard times and European youth. The effect of economic insecurity on human values, social attitudes and well-being. *International Journal of Psychology, 52*(1), 19–27.

Reich, K. (1998). Psychology of religion: What one needs to know. *Zygon: Journal of Religion and Science, 33*(1) 113–120.

Saarikivi, J. (2017). Pyhän käsitteestä ja alkuperästä [On the concept and origin of the sacred]. *Elore, 24*(1), 1–11.

Schwartz, S. H. (2007). Universalism values and the inclusiveness of our moral universe. *Journal of Cross-Cultural Psychology, 38*(6), 711–728.

Schwartz, S. H. (2012). An overview of the Schwartz theory of basic values. *Online Readings in Psychology and Culture, 2*(1).

Settersten, R. A. Jr. (2003). Propositions and controversies in life-course scholarship. In R. A. Settersten Jr. (Ed.), *Invitation to the life course: Toward new understandings of later life* (pp. 15–45). Baywood.

Sheldrake, P. (1992). *Spirituality and history: Questions of interpretation and method.* Crossroads.

Sjöborg, A. (2013). Mapping "religion" – or "something, I don't know what"? Methodological challenges exploring young peoples' relations with "religion." In A. Day & G. Vincett (Eds.), *Social identities between the sacred and the secular* (pp. 191–200). Ashgate.

Sortheix, F. M., Parker, P. D., Lechner, C. M., & Schwartz, S. H. (2019). Changes in young Europeans' values during the global financial crisis. *Social Psychological and Personality Science, 10*(1), 15–25.

Stausberg, M. (2017). The sacred and the holy – From around 1917 to today. *Religion, 47*(4), 549–556.

Storm, I., & Voas, D. (2012). The intergenerational transmission of religious service attendance. *Nordic Journal of Religion & Society, 25*(2), 131–150.

Tamminen, K. (1991). *Religious development in childhood and adolescence: An empirical study.* Finnish Academy of Science and Letters.

Taves, A. (2013). Building blocks of sacralities. In R. F. Paloutzian & C. L. Park (Eds.), *Handbook of the psychology of religion and spirituality* (pp. 138–161). Guilford Press.

Templeton, J. L., & Eccles, J. S. (2006). *The relation between spiritual development and identity processes.* In E. C. Roehlkepartain, P. E. King, L. Wagener, & P. L. Benson (Eds.), *The handbook of spiritual development in childhood and adolescence* (pp. 252–265). Sage Publications, Inc.

Tirri, K., & Quinn, B. (2010). Exploring the role of religion and spirituality in the development of purpose: Case studies of purposeful youth. *British Journal of Religious Education, 32*(3), 201–214.

Uzefovsky, F., Döring, A. K., & Knafo-Noam, A. (2016). Values in middle childhood: Social and genetic contributions. *Social Development, 25*(3), 482–502.

Vecchione, M., Schwartz, S., Alessandri, G., Döring, A. K., Castellani, V., & Caprara, M. G. (2016). Stability and change of basic personal values in early adulthood: An 8-year longitudinal study. *Journal of Research in Personality, 63,* 111–122.

Vecchione, M., Schwartz, S. H., Davidov, E., Cieciuch, J., Alessandri, G., & Marsicano, G. (2020). Stability and change of basic personal values in early adolescence: A 2-year longitudinal study. *Journal of Personality, 88*(3), 447–463.

Weber, J. (2017). Discovering the millennials' personal values orientation: A comparison to two managerial populations. *Journal of Business Ethics, 143*(3), 517–529.

Wulff, D. M. (1997). *Psychology of religion: Classic and contemporary* (2nd ed.). Wiley & Sons.

CHAPTER 7

Children's and Youths' Perspectives on Value Diversity in Education
Implications for Teacher Education and Educator Professionalism

Arniika Kuusisto and Arto Kallioniemi

Abstract

This chapter examines Finnish children's and youths' perspectives on encountering value diversity in education. Our examination builds on an ecological approach (e.g., Bronfenbrenner, 1979, 2005; Sameroff, 2010) to learning and development along individual life trajectories (e.g., Kuusisto, 2011; Kuusisto & Gearon, 2017a; Lamminmäki-Vartia et al., 2020). The empirical findings presented here are based on various mixed methods data sets gathered from children, youths, parents, and professionals, in which our main focus is on the age groups 9 to 10, 12 to 13, and 15 to 16 (N = 2781) in Estonia, Finland and Sweden, and in particular the Finnish sub-sample of 1,301 children. This chapter presents a synthesis across a set of empirical studies, highlighting children's and youths' own perspectives encountering diversity in education. We conclude by discussing children's and youths' value learning trajectories in the changing Finnish society, and how the results can be used to inform teacher education programs and teachers' professional development on (super)diversity in school, thereby contributing to our understanding of educating good teachers for tomorrow's schools and the role of values in education.

Keywords

children – youths – education – diversity – value learning trajectories – teacher professionalism

1   Introduction

This chapter examines Finnish children's and youths' perspectives when encountering value diversity in education. Our examination builds on an ecological approach (e.g., Bronfenbrenner, 1979, 2005; Sameroff, 2010) to learning and development along individual life trajectories (e.g., Kuusisto, 2011; Kuusisto & Gearon, 2017a; Lamminmäki-Vartia et al., 2020). By values we refer to the individual or group level aims, goals and life guiding principles that are consistent across situations and contexts (Kuusisto & Gearon, 2017b; Schwartz, 1992, 1997, 2012) – to put simply, what is regarded as important and valuable. Worldview is here understood, again both at individual and group levels, as the ontological, epistemological and ethical orientation to the environment (Riitaoja et al., 2010); the ontological foundation for values, beliefs and knowledge used in meaning-making and for making choices (Poulter, 2013). Furthermore, worldviews function as a philosophy of life, which plays a critical role in understanding reality and in providing satisfying meanings to life questions. As group values and epistemologies, these function to define understandings of what can be known and how to construct ideas of oneself and "the other" (Poulter et al., 2016, p. 68).

Worldviews are here used for both religious and non-religious traditions and approaches to meaning-making or value systems at the group level. At the individual level, especially as regards the younger generations of children and youths, worldviews are increasingly hybrid in nature, merging elements from a variety of religious, secular, etc. sources or traditions (Helve, 2016). Although the present examination focuses on "value diversity" as in how children and youths perceive and, indeed, "encounter" different group level worldviews, we acknowledge the diversities within these traditions, as well as the necessarily oversimplified operationalizations of these complex phenomena into survey measures in order to be completable by children as young as nine in our youngest samples.

The landscape of values and worldviews in Finnish society has in recent years changed remarkably, both due to increased migration but also due to the polarization of values and worldviews more broadly. For example, Finnish society is becoming increasingly secularized, with a decreased interest in membership of institutional religions. At the same time, there is increased interest in new religious movements and spirituality. Religious socialization in the homes, as in intentional home education aiming to transmit a particular religious tradition and value system, has decreased notably (see e.g., Tervo-Niemelä, 2020). This marks a significant change for the younger generations of children and youths who thereby construct their worldviews increasingly from a number of different sources rather than growing into a particular tradition (e.g., Kuusisto, 2011), and are thus also likely to draw more influences from sources outside the family. One of our data sets informed us that alongside family, school and the Internet were the top three influencers for children and youths when searching for information about religions (Kuusisto & Kallioniemi, 2015). This diversification of worldviews and values is also a part of the everyday in societal educational arenas, where especially the big cities now host a much more varied landscape of religious and non-religious worldviews than just a couple of decades ago. These changes have implications concerning the role of values education and education on religions and worldviews in ECEC and schools.

Finland was one of the 24 participating countries in the International Civic and Citizenship Education study (ICCS) 2016. The Finnish sample included 179 comprehensive schools, some 3,200 eighth-grade students and 2,200 teachers. As regards the measured attitudes on equality and diversity, Finnish teenagers' attitudes to gender equity was on average more positive than in the participating countries. When it comes to equity between ethnic groups, the Finnish responses were on a level with the international average. Girls' attitudes were more positive than the boys'. Attitudes to equity of both genders and ethnic groups were also associated with the level of the youths' civic knowledge and cognitive test results: the higher the results, the more positive the attitudes were. Both in Finland and in the participating countries on average, the attitudes towards equity had become more positive between 2009 and 2016 (International Civic and Citizenship Study ICCS, 2017; University of Jyväskylä, 2018).

2   Emerging Diversity-Related Teacher Professionalism through Value Learning

Through several empirical life history approaches and/or learning trajectory mixed methods data sets (see Table 7.1), we have analyzed the processes of value learning (also as a means to emerging professionalism), and developed a working model that has thereafter been used as an analytical tool (Kuusisto & Gearon, 2017a). Our focus has spanned from early childhood education, school, and teacher education to parents and home education and religious communities.

Building on previous research on teacher professionalism (e.g., Karila, 2008; Rissanen et al., 2018), an ecological systems theory approach (e.g., Bronfenbrenner, 1979, 2005; Sameroff, 2010) and our empirical analyses, Kuusisto and Gearon have developed an analytical model for examining individual value learning trajectories (e.g., Kuusisto & Gearon, 2017a, 2017b, 2019; Gearon & Kuusisto, 2017a, 2017b). The model encompasses six value learning trajectory staging posts, namely: Givens, Positionings, Engagements, Tensions, Negotiations, Resolutions, and, as a result of this value negotiation process, the now altered "Givens" with more informed knowledge for further encounters of similar professional value tensions or the like (Gearon & Kuusisto, 2017). It can be used for examining value learning processes both in childhood and youths and

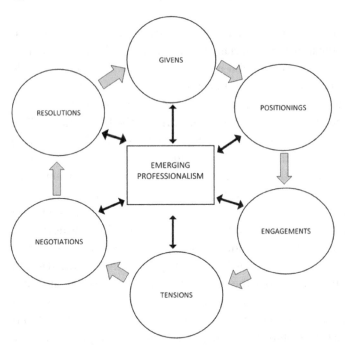

FIGURE 7.1 Emerging professionalism through value learning trajectories
(Lamminmäki-Vartia et al., 2020, on the basis of Kuusisto & Gearon, 2017a)

among students or along professional trajectories. Besides the encountering of value tensions in the specific learning context, it is important to acknowledge the particular broader socio-historical and political context in which the learning context is embedded, as well as the temporality of both the learning-in-time as well as the continuously altering, also diversifying social and societal, and broader global situation. Value learning is situated in relation to societal diversity of values and worldviews, which is reflected, for instance, in the emerging teacher student professionalism in teacher education as a process of professional development through value learning (Lamminmäki-Vartia et al., 2020; Kuusisto & Gearon, 2019) and teachers' professional trajectories (e.g., Luodeslampi et al., 2019).

Later empirical analyses have further contributed to the proof of the concept for, and application of, the model of worldview diversity related to teacher professionalism (see Figure 7.1) (Lamminmäki-Vartia et al., 2020). The figure illustrates how, drawing from student teachers' learning trajectory data (pre-survey, a 6-month process of collaborative learning in a group and as paired with a more experienced in-service teacher, and finally a retrospective interview), the emerging worldview diversity related professionalism develops gradually through the learning process (Lamminmäki-Vartia et al., 2020).

3 Empirical Findings on Encountering Diversity in the Everyday of Children and Youths

Table 7.1 presents a selection of the empirical analyses we have carried out in relation to encountering diversity and individual value learning trajectories. Initially, the EDEN project builds on the research strand originating with Kuusisto's study on value learning trajectories in relation to religious minority socialization (Kuusisto, 2011), and a 2008–2010 research project Multicultural Children and Adults in ECEC (MUCCA), a joint venture between the City of Helsinki Social Services Department (Director Eija Bergman) and the ECEC research unit (Director Mikko Ojala) at the University of Helsinki, which she was responsible for carrying out (Kuusisto, 2010). The project was initiated by the ECEC practitioners, who pointed out the need to locate and further develop good practices related to the then speedily diversified Finnish ECEC. The findings of this MUCCA project led to the realization of a lack of up-to-date knowledge on children's and youths' perspectives on encountering the changing societal situation and increasing diversity also in the older age groups of comprehensive school pupils. A further project design was developed, now working together with Kallioniemi, to gather mixed methods data (N = 1301) from the ages 9, 12, and 15. Later on, the EDEN research project was first expanded internationally to the collaboration with colleagues at Södertörn University (CARDIPS project, with Straarup, Berglund 2011–2012, Vikdahl 2012–2020, Jahnke 2012–2019) and the University of Tartu (Shihaleyev), spanning across Finnish, Swedish and Estonian schools with a similar mixed methods design of an international survey instrument (N = 2781) and interviews with children and youths in Sweden and Estonia as well as teacher interviews. The lower secondary school data was combined for some analyses together with Elina Kuusisto, Kristiina Holm, and Kirsi Tirri, for looking at the gender variance of pupils' interreligious sensitivity (N = 1000), as well as for comparing Finnish teachers' (N = 1008) and students' (N = 1000) responses to a 23-item Intercultural Sensitivity Scale Questionnaire (ICSSQ). The Finnish EDEN project was also supplemented with further data gathering with upper secondary school pupils, age group 16–19. The EDEN project has also been succeeded by the presently ongoing Academy of Finland funded "Growing up radical? The

TABLE 7.1 Selection of empirical studies used in the present examination

Children and youth	Pupils and teachers	Student teachers and professional educators
Diversity in ECEC MUCCA research project (e.g., Kuusisto et al., 2014b)	*Teachers' and students' intercultural sensitivity* (Kuusisto, E. et al., 2015)	*Religious authority and education* (N = 50) (Gearon & Kuusisto, 2017a)
Encountering Diversity in Education EDEN (Survey N = 1900; Interviews N = 38 + 14; ages 6, 9, 12, 15, 18) (e.g., Kuusisto & Kallioniemi, 2015)		*Developing emerging professional competences related to worldview education* (e.g., Lamminmäki-Vartia et al., 2020)
Gender Variance in Interreligious Sensitivity among Finnish Pupils (N = 1000) (Kuusisto et al., 2014a)		*Intercultural, interreligious sensitivities and competences of teacher students* (Rissanen et al., 2016; Kuusisto, E. et al., 2015)
CARDIPS Finnish, Swedish & Estonian data sets (N = 2781) (e.g., Shihaleyev et al., 2019; Kallioniemi et al., 2018)		*Teachers' professional trajectories and value negotiations* (e.g., Luodeslampi et al., 2019; Lamminmäki-Vartia et al., 2020)
REDCO2 (Kavonius et al., 2015a, 2015b)		
Growing up radical? Educational institutions in guiding young people's worldview construction (N = 3617) (e.g., Niemi et al., 2018)		
Socialization and religious social identity (e.g., Kuusisto, 2003, 2011)		

role of educational institutions in guiding young people's worldview construction" (2018–2023; PI A. Kuusisto with L. Gearon, S. Benjamin, and P. Koirikivi; and L. Malkki and A. Kallioniemi as advisory members of the project) looking into the role of schools in supporting pupils' (N = 3617) worldview construction, and in preventing and counteracting extremism and radicalization.

Although the perspectives and research focus vary across data sets, each of these projects contributes towards a further understanding on "diversifying diversities" (Vertovec, 2015, 2019) and how these intersectional complexities have influenced education and value learning in different contexts, plus the knowledge we can draw from these in developing teacher education for diversities.

4 Children's and Youths' Experiences on Diversity in Educational Contexts

Most pupils agreed that religion has at least an acknowledged "place" in the school context. The question of religion's place in schools in Finland has been a much-debated issue, since Finnish society has in recent decades become notably more diversified. The state is neutral, but historically we have had two national churches in Finland: the Evangelical-Lutheran and the Greek Orthodox Church. They have had a big impact on school and education. The majority of the Finnish population (68.7%) belong to the Evangelical-Lutheran Church and 1.1% belong to the Greek Orthodox Church and 1.7% to other religious communities; almost one third of the population (28.5%) do not belong to any religious communities. The number of members of the Evangelical-Lutheran Church has in recent decades been decreasing and at the same time the number of people belonging to other religious communities has been increasing (Salomäki et al., 2020, pp. 49–50). Today the Nordic societal landscape has been described as post-Lutheran (Thurfjell, 2016) or Secular Lutheran (Riitaoja et al., 2010; Poulter et al., 2016).

Pupils see religion as a very important part of life "for religious persons," and many see the role of religion in society as important. Most pupils agreed that religious symbols (wearing a veil for religious reasons, or a crucifix in a necklace) can be visible in school. Many also felt that schools should provide a place for silence, and also considered it important for school meals to include alternatives suitable for those following a diet for religious reasons.

One of the starting points for our research project Encountering Diversity in Education (EDEN) was to generate up-to-date knowledge on children's and youths' experiences on diversity in their everyday contexts, and to thereby also facilitate development of education on religions, worldviews and values in ECEC and schools. The functions and the role of religious education or education on religions and worldviews has been much debated in recent years, both in Finland and internationally. At the same time, the observation has been raised that in changing societies, citizens need a much more multisided and deep knowledge and understanding in this rapidly changing world. Multiple literacies connected to religions and worldviews are also seen as one part of general literacy in the Finnish curriculum. The perspectives connected to religions are intertwined with the processes of negotiating belonging, especially inclusion and exclusion in peer groups. These negotiations and the politics of belonging (Yuval-Davis, 2006), embed intersectional influences of, for example, gender, ethnicity, language, personal worldview (as religious, secular, or hybrid), and culture. This is acutely a question related to minority rights, as well as Universal Human Rights and the Rights of the Child. Increasing migration, increasing transnational movement of families, and the changing population structure have made religions and worldviews in many ways more visible in the everyday of children and youths.

The Finnish approach to religious education can be seen from learning about and learning from approaches which were presented by Grimmit and Ready (1975) and further developed by Grimmit (2000). Learning about religions and worldviews thereby contributes to the multiple literacies and citizenship skills for democratic, multi-value societies. Learning from religions and worldviews relates to how education can give pupils tools with which to construct their own worldviews. In Finland, education on the diversity of religions and worldviews has been seen as a function of the school, and thereby Religious Education, or the alternative Ethics, is a separate and compulsory school subject (Kallioniemi & Ubani, 2016; Åhs, 2020).

Finnish schools are a very central part of society in which different languages, cultures, identities, religions and worldviews are in interaction with each another. Schools contribute to a diverse society in which the local and global are interconnected (NCCBE, 2014, p. 26). The teaching in the subject area proceeds according to nationally set central aims defined in the curriculum. Besides knowledge on religions, the subject area covers a wide range of topics related to values and ethical education. Previous research in values and ethics education, such as research on moral dilemmas identified by pupils (Tirri, 2003) and teachers' moral and ethics (Tirri, 1998, 1999, 2011; Tirri & Kuusisto, E., 2019), is important in informing the future development of the subject area.

In an analysis on the findings from the data of the two older comprehensive school student groups in our EDEN data from Finland (N = 825; age groups 12–13, 15–16), we examined their views on the place of religion both as a formal part of the National Curriculum and as a part of the social interaction and physical environment in their everyday educational context. The pupils' attitudes to the visibility of religions in school was in general rather positive, contrasted by the 15% who either agreed or agreed strongly that religion should not be visible at school. The majority (47%) also agreed that there should be opportunities to discuss religion-related matters at school; 31% had a neutral stance to this statement, whereas a fifth (21%) disagreed or strongly disagreed with it. The openness towards the visibility of religions differed between their peers wearing small, more discreet religious symbols, and the wearing of more visible ones, such as wearing a necklace with a cross (Likert 1–5; M = 3.5), was seen much more positively than the wearing of religion-related clothing, such as a veil (M = 3.2), (t = 7.1, df = 824) (Kuusisto et al., 2017).

Both age and gender variance were present in the findings. Girls, for instance, showed more acceptance for the use of religious symbols in school than boys did: they regarded the wearing of both discreet (M = 3.8, SD = 1.4 vs. boys M = 3.2, SD = 1.4) and visible (M = 3.6, SD = 1.5 vs. boys M = 2.8, SD = 1.4) religious symbols more positively. In both cases the differences were highly significant ($t = 5.5^{***}$, $df = 823$; $t = 7.5^{***}$, $df = 823$). This is in line with previous research (Holm, 2012; Kuusisto et al., 2014a), suggesting that girls are more tolerant toward diversity than boys are. Boys also agreed more often than girls (almost significant difference: $t = 2.8^{*}$, $df = 823$; boys M = 2.6, SD = 1.2 vs. girls M = 2.4, SD = 1.2) that religion should not be visible at school. Previous research also indicates that girls are more religious than boys (e.g., Francis & Robbins, 2005). Age, here measured with the school grade (6th grade age group 12–13 vs. 9th grade age group 15–16), also made a difference in pupils' openness towards the visibility of religions in school. Older pupils (M = 3.7, SD = 1.4) agreed more often than younger ones (M = 3.4, SD = 1.4) that one should have a right to wear at least discreet religious symbols at school. The same also applied to the wearing of religion-related clothing such as a head scarf (M = 3.3, SD = 1.5 vs. M = 3.1, SD = 1.5) – both differences were statistically significant ($t = 3.1^{**}$, $df = 823$; $t = 2.4^{**}$, $df = 823$) (Kuusisto et al., 2017).

The cultural, secular nature of some of the Lutheran majority was exemplified, for instance, in the following quote from the open answers of a ninth grader: "My official religion is EvLuth. But I am an Atheist, I do not believe in God." And about parental affiliation, they state: "Evangelical Lutheran, but they do not believe in God." (9th grader, Helsinki [288]). (Kuusisto et al., 2017.)

Our international mixed methods data sets include samples from Finnish, Swedish and Estonian children and youths in the age groups of 9 to 10, 12 to 13 and 15 to 16 – a purposive non-probability sample of $N = 2781$ – consisted of 713 respondents from Estonia, 1,257 from Finland, and 811 from Sweden. The sampling was purposive, as the researchers were interested in schools with more notable cultural and religious diversity. The proportion of male and female respondents was almost equal (49% and 51%, respectively), as was the distribution between age groups (33% for third graders, 33% for sixth graders, and 34% for ninth graders). We focused in particular on the ways in which the children perceived and encountered diversity in their school context, as well as how this diversity was connected with peer group inclusion and exclusion. About half of the pupils report experiences of having been either frequently or occasionally bullied: 11% report having been bullied frequently, and 41% occasionally. The perceived preconditions for bullying were mainly connected to visible diversity, such as people's appearance (explaining 5% of frequent and 20% of occasional bullying), clothes (3% frequent and 19% occasional), and for who they had as friends (2% frequent and 20% occasional). Immigrant background (1% frequent and 4% occasional), religion (1% frequent and 6% occasional), and home language (2% frequent and 8% occasional) were also mentioned (Schihaleyjev et al., 2020).

Analysis on the country of residence showed variance in this: in Estonia, more than half of the pupils (51%) have experienced occasional and 11% frequent bullying; in Finland, 41% for occasional and 12% for frequent bullying; and in Sweden, 34% of children and youths had experienced occasional and 7% frequent bullying. In Estonia and Finland, the children and youths reported more frequent bullying or victimization because of their appearance, friends, clothes or "something else" than their peers in Sweden. Some of the reasons were also connected to gender: girls reported more bullying related to their appearance than boys did (Schihaleyjev et al., 2020).

Although the actual frequencies in the big data regarding the bullying connected to home language, religiously more observant family background, and migration background are relatively low, we have to remember that so too are the numbers of these pupils in schools. These are in fact factors making children and youths vulnerable to bullying. Of the 1,334 students who responded to the question about their parents' worldview, 632 stated that their parents are Christians, 29 Muslim, 29 some other religion, and 485 told that they practiced no religion. As an indicator for the actual religious commitment in the Secular Lutheran (Poulter et al., 2016) North, we used the question "Have you learned to pray at home?" Children and youths from more religiously devout families were bullied more than their peers from non-religious families in all the listed categories or preconditions behind bullying – not primarily because of religion (Schihalejev et al., 2020). In our data sets age, gender, and place of residence were important factors behind openness or prejudice, or sensitivities to diversity: the older the pupils, the more open attitudes they reported towards diversity, girls being more open and tolerant than boys, and children and youths in bigger cities being more open and tolerant than those residing in smaller cities or towns. This could be seen to support the classic intergroup contact hypothesis, initially proposed by Allport (1954), and the vast research base founded on that: the more opportunities for dialogue, knowledge and personal interaction, the more understanding towards difference.

In another analysis, we (Kuusisto et al., 2014a) examined gender variance in interreligious sensitivity among a non-probability sample of 1,000 Finnish lower secondary school pupils in the age group 12–16. In an analysis on the pupils' self-reported attitudes towards interreligious sensitivity, measured with the Interreligious Sensitivity Scale, the findings again illustrated significant variation between genders in pupils' interreligious sensitivity. In addition, the geographical variance between the Helsinki capital area and one of the two smaller cities, as well as the pupils' own religious affiliation influenced their interreligious sensitivity (Kuusisto et al., 2014a).

As regards the education on religions and worldviews in school, our findings pointed out that most pupils were satisfied with the RE model they had. In an analysis of the follow-up study of the international, EU-wide REDCo study, where Finland was added to the sampling, we compared the data sets from Finnish (N = 406) and Estonian (N = 582) pupils (total N = 988). Again, age was highlighted as an important variable, with the older pupils' (over 16) views about religion in school being more positive than younger pupils' (under 16 years) views. The younger pupils were also more likely to agree with a statement that learning about religion leads to conflicts in the classroom. Older pupils also rated the place of religion in school higher, as well as the role of school in them learning to have respect for everyone, whatever their religion. Older pupils agreed more on the fact that at school they had opportunities to discuss religious issues from different perspectives, and they found topics related to religions more interesting at school than younger pupils did. Older pupils were also more of the opinion that learning about religions at school helps them to understand themselves better (Kallioniemi et al., 2018).

According to pupils, there should be objective teaching about religions and beliefs and about other outlooks on life. In diversified societies, the need for knowledge concerning different religions and worldviews has risen significantly. Present and future citizens need much larger and deeper skills in issues concerning religions and worldviews than previous generations did. In

Finnish society, there are many challenges in developing the current system of religious and worldview education. At present, RE is organized according to pupils' formal membership or affiliation, if any, so the subject is taught in separate teaching groups. In some schools, there can be six different religious education classes (e.g., Lutheran, Orthodox, Catholic, Muslim, Buddhism, and secular ethics). The present RE model has been seen to support religious minority identities (e.g., Rissanen, 2014) through "interpreting" world religions into local, "lived" religions and contexts, thereby possibly contributing towards inclusion and coherence in society, democratic citizenship, and countering extreme and radical thinking. This is where both the local variance in applying worldview education (e.g., Tainio et al., 2018 for the ECEC level) and teacher's implicit theories and moral professionalism (Rissanen et al., 2018) gain a critical role.

5 Discussion and Open Conclusion

Though merely a brief overview of selected results related to diversity in educational settings in Finland, and in particular how children and youths have experienced it in their everyday lives, there are a few points that we would like to conclude with. First of all, we would like to highlight the important role of societal educational contexts in supporting children and young people's value learning and worldview construction. This is not only due to the diminishing role of explicit religious education in families (e.g., Tervo-Niemelä, 2020), but also, as the findings above show, the children and youths themselves appreciate school as a platform for learning and discussion on religions and worldviews. Secondly, we would like to highlight the diverse school context as a space and place for familiarizing oneself with the alternative ways of seeing the world. It is here that students "encounter" values, worldviews, and religions but also have an opportunity to familiarize themselves with and learn to appreciate them. This is of critical importance not only for secular, culturally Christian majority children, but also for children from minority cultural, language, and worldview backgrounds: those who are at present most vulnerable to being bullied in schools (Schihalejev et al., 2020).

What remains in a critical role is how to ensure teacher competences related to worldview diversity so that all student teachers would be equipped to deal with worldview-related sensitivities and moral professionalism. Where the school contributes to a diverse society in which the local and global are interconnected (Finnish National Board of Education, 2016, p. 26), it also needs to ensure that its understanding of Finnishness is broad enough to welcome all the "diversifying diversities" (Vertovec, 2015, 2019) as a part of its perception of "us," so that the minority cultures, languages or religious will no longer trigger peer-group exclusion and bullying. Democratic citizenship education needs to start with the welcoming of diversity at the societal, school and classroom level. Education on religions, worldviews and values that contributes towards this end should foster an increased understanding of a variety of different "lived" perspectives, besides providing knowledge on different traditions.

As regards the implications of the above-presented findings to teacher education and beyond, these complex questions resonate with a solid body of previous research. Rissanen et al. (2018) have analyzed the implications of teachers' implicit theories for moral education, illustrating the multiplicity of ways in which teachers' implicit beliefs are communicated to students and also how these influence teachers' interpretations and endeavors to educate the ethical capabilities of their pupils. Rissanen et al. define moral professionalism in line with Sockett (1993) as the quality of educators' professional practices, thereby judged by professional standards and actualizing in teachers' moral practices and roles in everyday educational contexts (Hanhimäki, 2011). In their review on previous literature, they conclude that the moral dimension of teaching has been seen to include teacher positionings on moral sensitivity, moral judgment, moral motivation, moral behavior, and teachers' professional ethics and values (Bebeau et al., 1999; Narvaez, 2007; Rest, 1983; Tirri et al., 2013). The conclusion is that morally professional teachers need competencies related both to their character and to their conduct if they are to promote learners' holistic development (Tirri, 2011; Tirri et al., 1999). Based on their empirical analysis, Rissanen et al. argue for the importance of implicit theories in research on moral education (Rissanen et al., 2018).

As part of the emerging professionalism of student teachers, future teachers should be even better supported in, and equipped with, a multisided knowledge of "diversifying diversity" or superdiversity (Vertovec, 2015, 2019) in society. As also our student teacher learning diaries illustrate (Lamminmäki-Vartia et al., 2020), teachers should also have an openness to life-long learning and continuously developing professionalism in relation to the lived worldviews of the children, families and colleagues in societal educational contexts. This also necessitates a deeper 'take' on the perspectives of (super)diversity and lived religions in teacher education (Poulter et al., in press). These perspectives should, moreover, be a vital part of teacher education. Students need to be made aware of the complexity of superdiversity and lived religions as part of teacher education. Furthermore, a high level of reflexivity is needed in teacher education. It is of critical importance for student teachers and in-service teachers to understand about peer group sensitivity to diversity – both intercultural and interreligious – in order for them to teach about religions and worldviews sensitively.

Education is always necessarily connected to and embedded on some underlying value basis. Questions related to ethics are accentuated in our rapidly changing society and schools, where diversifying diversities, and multiple values and worldviews, are always present. This means that teachers convey values in their work, consciously or unconsciously. Therefore, it is very important that teachers reflect on their own values and presuppositions critically. Teachers are role models in their approach to diversity, and this is shown in how we talk about diversity and "other" religions, worldviews, traditions and cultures. The questions this raises are many. Do all cultures and worldviews get the same amount of time and space in classroom dialogue? Are they presented in an equally positive light? Does every pupil have the place to be seen and heard? Teachers are in a key position for constructing a positive atmosphere in education and classroom interaction, which is an important element in supporting learning (Day & Johansson, 2008; Biesta, 2010; Kallioniemi et al., 2015, p. 117).

Teachers develop professionalism during and after teacher education, and professional trajectories are a continuous value learning process. Professionalism is constantly being developed through experiences, thus building tacit knowledge into a personal way of dealing with diversities (see the above presented model). Teachers should build a positively appreciative space in the classroom for respectful discussion. As a part of their professional approach, teachers can encourage a positive presence for diversity, both as regards the explicit teaching of worldviews and traditions, and through their example and role model in the respectful encounter of values, worldviews, and religions different to their own.

Acknowledgements

Kuusisto's work was carried out in connection to the Academy of Finland funded (Grant No. 315860) research project "Growing up radical? The role of educational institutions in guiding young people's worldview construction".

References

Åhs, V. (2020). *Worldviews and integrative education. A case study of partially integrative Religious Education and Secular Ethics Education in a Finnish lower secondary school context* [Doctoral dissertation, University of Helsinki]. Unigrafia.

Allport, G. W. (1954). *The nature of prejudice*. Addison-Wesley.
Bebeau, M., Rest, J., & Narvaez, D. (1999). Beyond the promise: A perspective on research in moral education. *Educational Researcher, 28*, 18–26.
Biesta, G. (2010). *Good education in an age of measurement: Ethics, politics, democracy.* Paradigm Publisher.
Bronfenbrenner, U. (1979). *The ecology of human development: experiments by nature and design.* Harvard University Press.
Bronfenbrenner, U. (2005). *Making human beings human: Bioecological perspectives on human development.* Sage.
Day, C., & Johansson, O. (2008). Leadership with a difference in schools serving disadvantaged communities: Arenas for success. In K. Tirri (Ed.), *Educating moral sensibilities in urban schools* (pp. 19–34). Sense Publishers.
Finnish National Board of Education. (2016). *National core curriculum for basic education 2014.* Finnish National Board of Education.
Gearon, L., & Kuusisto, A. (2017a). On theory: Framing value learning in the life trajectory – Epistemology, ethics, the existential. In A. Kuusisto & L. Gearon (Eds.), *Value learning trajectories: Theory, method, context* (pp. 11–30). Waxmann.
Gearon, L., & Kuusisto, A. (2017b). On context: Value learning and life trajectories research in situ – Historical-political systems, spectrums of value, biographical positionings. In A. Kuusisto & L. Gearon (Eds.), *Value learning trajectories: Theory, method, context* (pp. 161–177). Waxmann.
Grimmitt, M. (2000). *Pedagogies of Religious Education: Case studies in the research and development of good pedagogic practice in RE.* McCrimmons.
Grimmitt, M., & Read, G. (1975). *Teaching Christianity in RE.* Mayhew.
Hanhimäki, E. (2011). *Moral professionalism in interaction: Educators' relational moral voices in urban schools* [Doctoral dissertation, University of Helsinki]. Waxmann.
International Civic and Citizenship Study ICCS. (2017). Retrieved November 15, 2020, from http://iccs.iea.nl/home.html
Helve, H. (2016). A longitudinal perspective on worldviews, values and identities. *Journal of Religious Education, 63*, 95–115. doi:10.1007/s40839-016-0021-5
Kallioniemi, A., Honkasalo, V., & Kuusisto, A. (2015). Opettajan yhteiskunnallinen rooli moninaistuvassa koulussa [Teacher's societal role in diversifying school]. In H. Cantell & A. Kallioniemi (Eds.), *Kansankynttilä keinulaudalla. Miten tulevaisuudessa opitaan ja opetetaan? [Teacher on a seesaw: What's the future like for learning and teaching?]* (pp. 109–125). PS-kustannus.
Kallioniemi, A., Schihalejev, O., Kuusisto, A., & Poulter, S. (2018). Estonian and Finnish pupils' experiences of religious issues and views on the place of religion in school. *Religion & Education, 45*(1), 73–88. doi:10.1080/15507394.2017.1355176
Kallioniemi, A., Schihalejev, O., Poulter, S., & Kuusisto, A. (2017). Virolaisten ja suomalaisten nuorten käsityksiä uskonnonopetuksesta koulussa [Perceptions of Estonian

and Finnish youth on instruction on religions at school]. *Teologinen Aikakauskirja* [*Finnish Journal of Theology*], *122*(1), 34–46.

Kallioniemi, A., & Ubani, M. (2016). Religious Education in Finnish school system. In H. Niemi, A. Toom, & A. Kallioniemi (Eds.), *Miracle of education* (pp. 179–190). Sense Publishers.

Karila, K. (2008). A Finnish viewpoint on professionalism in early childhood education. *European Early Childhood Education Research Journal, 16*(2), 210–223. doi:10.1080/13502930802141634

Kavonius, M., Kuusisto, A., & Kallioniemi, A. (2015a). Religious Education and tolerance in the changing Finnish society. *Religious Education Journal of Australia, 31*(1), 18–24.

Kavonius, M., Kuusisto, A., & Kallioniemi, A. (2015b). Pupils' perceptions of worldview diversity and Religious Education in the Finnish comprehensive school. *Journal of Intercultural Studies: An International Journal, 36*(3), 320–337. https://doi.org/10.1080/07256868.2015.1029884

Kuusisto, A. (2003). Transmitting religious values in Adventist home education. *Journal of Beliefs & Values, 24*(3), 283–293. https://doi.org/10.1080/1361767032000156066

Kuusisto, A. (2010). Social networks and identity negotiations of religious minority youth in diverse social contexts. *Ethnic and Racial Studies, 33*(5), 779–796. https://doi.org/10.1080/01419870903254679

Kuusisto, A. (2011). *Growing up in affiliation with a religious community: A case study of Seventh-day Adventist youth in Finland* [Doctoral dissertation, University of Helsinki]. Waxmann.

Kuusisto, A., & Gearon, L. (2017a). The life trajectory of the Finnish religious educator. *Religion and Education, 44*(1), 39–53. doi:10.1080/15507394.2016.1272154

Kuusisto, A., & Gearon, L. (2017b). On method: Researching value learning and life trajectories – Dialogue, diversity and inter-disciplinarity. In A. Kuusisto & L. Gearon (Eds.), *Value learning trajectories: Theory, method, context* (pp. 99–115). Waxmann.

Kuusisto, A., & Gearon, L. (2019). Why teach about religions? Perspectives from Finnish professionals. *Religions, 10*(6), 347. doi:10.3390/rel10060347

Kuusisto, A., & Kallioniemi, A. (2015). Pupils' views of Religious Education in a pluralistic educational context. *Journal of Beliefs and Values, 35*(2), 155–164.

Kuusisto, A., Kallioniemi, A., & Matilainen, M. (2014b). Monikulttuurinen työyhteisö suomalaisen varhaiskasvatuksen kentällä [Multicultural ECEC working community in Finland]. *Kasvatus* [*The Finnish Journal of Education*], *45*(2), 113–126.

Kuusisto, A., Kuusisto, E., Holm, K., & Tirri, K. (2014a). Gender variance in interreligious sensitivity among Finnish pupils. *International Journal of Children's Spirituality, 19*(1), 25–44. https://doi.org/10.1080/1364436X.2014.887560

Kuusisto, A., Poulter, S., & Kallioniemi, A. (2017). Finnish pupils' views on the place of religion in school. *Religious Education, 112*(2), 110–122. doi:10.1080/00344087.2016.1085237

Kuusisto, E., Kuusisto, A., Rissanen, I., Holm, K., & Tirri, K. (2015). Finnish teachers' and students' intercultural sensitivity. *Journal of Religious Education, 63*(2), 65–77. https://doi.org/10.1007/s40839-016-0018-0

Lamminmäki-Vartia, S., Poulter, S., & Kuusisto, A. (2020). Learning trajectory of emerging professionalism: Finnish student teacher negotiating worldview education and ECEC superdiversity. *Contemporary Issues in Early Childhood.* https://doi.org/10.1177/1463949120961598

Luodeslampi, J., Kuusisto, A., & Kallioniemi, A. (2019). Four Religious Education teachers: Four retrospective career trajectories. *Religions, 10*(8), 474. https://doi.org/10.3390/rel10080474

Narvaez, D. (2007). How cognitive and neurobiological sciences inform values education for creatures like us. In D. N. Aspin & J. D. Chapman (Eds.), *Values education and lifelong learning* (pp. 127–146). Springer.

Niemi, P.-M., Benjamin, S., Kuusisto, A., & Gearon, L. (2018). How and why education counters ideological extremism in Finland. *Religions, 9*(12), 420. https://doi.org/10.3390/rel9120420

Poulter, S. (2013). Uskonto julkisessa koulussa: koulu yhteiskunnallisuuden näyttämönä [Religion in public school: school as the scene of society]. *Kasvatus* [*The Finnish Journal of Education*], *44*(2), 162–176.

Poulter, S., Kuusisto, A., & Lamminmäki-Vartia, S. (in press). Developing praxeological understanding in teacher education: A case of worldview education in Finnish ECEC. In H. Harju-Luukkainen, S. Garvis, & J. Kangas (Eds.), *Finnish early childhood education and care – From research to policy and practice.* Springer.

Poulter, S., Riitaoja, A.-L., & Kuusisto, A. (2016). Thinking multicultural education 'otherwise' – From a secularist construction towards a plurality of epistemologies and worldviews. *Globalisation, Societies and Education, 14*(1), 68–86. doi:10.1080/14767724.2014.989964

Rest, J. (1983). Morality. In P. Mussen (Ed.), *Carmichael's manual of child psychology. Volume on Cognitive development* (J. Flavell & E. Markman, Vol. Eds., 4th ed., pp. 556–629). Wiley.

Riitaoja, A.-L., Poulter, S., & Kuusisto, A. (2010). Worldviews and multicultural education in the Finnish context: A critical philosophical approach to theory and practices. *Finnish Journal of Ethnicity and Migration, 5*(3), 87–95. http://www.etmu.fi/fjem/

Rissanen, I. (2014). *Negotiating identity and tradition in single-faith Religious Education: A case study of Islamic Education in Finnish Schools* [Doctoral dissertation, University of Helsinki]. Münster.

Rissanen, I., Kuusisto, E., Hanhimäki, E., & Tirri, K. (2018). The implications of teachers' implicit theories for moral education: A case study from Finland. *Journal of Moral Education, 47*(1), 63–77. doi:10.1080/03057240.2017.1374244

Rissanen, I., Kuusisto, E., & Kuusisto, A. (2016). Developing teachers' intercultural sensitivity: Case study on a pilot course in Finnish teacher education. *Teaching and Teacher Education, 59*, 446–456. https://doi.org/10.1016/j.tate.2016.07.018

Salomäki, H., Hytönen, M., Ketola, K., Salminen, V.-M., & Sohlberg, J. (2020). *Uskonto arjessa ja juhlassa. Suomen evankelis-luterilainen kirkko vuosina 2016–2019* [*Religion in the everyday and festivities: Finnish Evangelical Lutheran Church in 2016–2019*]. Kirkon tutkimuskeskus [Church Research Institute].

Sameroff, A. J. (2010). A unified theory of development: A dialectic integration of nature and nurture. *Child Development, 81*, 6–22.

Schihalejev, O., Kuusisto, A., Vikdahl, L., & Kallioniemi, A. (2020). Religion and children's perceptions of bullying in multicultural schools in Estonia, Finland and Sweden. *Journal of Beliefs & Values, 41*(3), 371–384. doi:10.1080/13617672.2019.1686732

Schwartz, S. H. (1992). Universals in the content and structure of values: Theoretical advances and empirical tests in 20 countries. In M. P. Zanna (Ed.), *Advances in experimental social psychology* (Vol. 25, pp. 1–65). Academic Press. https://doi.org/10.1016/S0065-2601(08)60281-6

Schwartz, S. H. (1997). Values and culture. In D. Munro, S. Carr, & J. Schumaker (Eds.), *Motivation and culture* (pp. 69–84). Routledge.

Schwartz, S. H. (2012). An overview of the Schwartz theory of basic values. *Online Readings in Psychology and Culture, 2*(1). https://doi.org/10.9707/2307-0919.1116

Sockett, H. (1993). *The moral base for teacher professionalism*. Teachers College Press.

Tainio, L., Kallioniemi, A., Hotulainen, R., Ahlholm, M., Ahtiainen, R., Asikainen, M., Avelin, L., Grym, I., Ikkala, J., Laine, M., Lankinen, N., Lehtola, K., Lindgren, E., Rämä, I., Sarkkinen, T., Tamm, M., Tuovila, E., & Virkkala, N. (2019). *Koulujen monet kielet ja uskonnot: Selvitys vähemmistöäidinkielten ja -uskontojen sekä suomi ja ruotsi toisena kielenä -opetuksen tilanteesta eri koulutusasteilla* [*The many languages and religions in schools: An investigation of the teaching of minority mother tongues and religions as well as Finnish and Swedish as a second language at different educational levels*]. Valtioneuvoston kanslia [Prime Minister's Office].

Tervo-Niemelä, K. (2020). Religious upbringing and other religious influences among young adults and changes in faith in the transition to adulthood: A 10-year longitudinal study of young people in Finland. *British Journal of Religious Education*. doi:10.1080/01416200.2020.1740169

Thurfjell, D. (2016). *Varför finns religion* [*Why does religion exist?*]. Molin & Sorgenfrei.

Tirri, K. (1998). *Koulu moraalisena yhteisönä* [*School as a moral community*]. Department of Teacher Education, University of Helsinki.

Tirri, K. (1999). *Opettajan ammattietiikka* [*Teacher's professional ethics*]. WSOY.

Tirri, K. (2003). The moral concerns and orientations of sixth-and ninth-grade students. *Educational Research and Evaluation, 9*(1), 93–108. doi:10.1076/edre.9.1.93.13545

Tirri, K. (2011). Holistic school pedagogy and values: Finnish teachers' and students' perspectives. *International Journal of Educational Research, 50*, 159–165.

Tirri, K., Husu, J., & Kansanen, P. (1999). The epistemological stance between the knower and the known. *Teaching and Teacher Education, 15*, 911–922.

Tirri, K., & Kuusisto, E. (2017). *Opettajan ammattietiikka oppimassa* [*Learning teachers' professional ethics*]. Gaudeamus.

Tirri, K., Toom, A., & Husu, J. (2013). The moral matters of teaching: A Finnish perspective. In C. J. Craig, P. C. Meijer, & J. Broeckmans (Eds.), *Teacher thinking to teachers and teaching: The evolution of a research community* (pp. 223–239). Emerald Publishing.

University of Jyväskylä. (2018). *Finnish teenagers' civic knowledge still of high standard: Confidence in social institutions highest in the world.* https://ktl.jyu.fi/en/current/news/finnish-teenagers2019-civic-knowledge-still-of-high-standard-7th-november-2017

Vertovec, S. (2015). Introduction: Formulating diversity studies. In S. Vertovec (Ed.), *Routledge international handbook of diversity studies* (pp. 1–20). Routledge.

Vertovec, S. (2019). Talking around super-diversity. *Ethnic and Racial Studies, 42*(1), 125–139. doi:10.1080/01419870.2017.1406128

Yuval-Davis, N. (2006). Belonging and the politics of belonging. *Patterns of Prejudice, 40*(3), 197–214. doi:10.1080/00313220600769331

CHAPTER 8

The Learning Ambience of Values Pedagogy

Terence Lovat

Abstract

The chapter will highlight the key features of the learning ambience created by a values pedagogy and the ramifications of these for good teaching. Data will be extracted from the projects that ran as part of the Australian Values Education Program (2003–2010) as well as from germane international work. The key features will be summarised thematically under the headings of Calmness, Positive Relationships and Safety and Security, key features of the persistent implicit effects of the program. Ramifications of such features for efficacious learning will be elicited from allied research, so justifying the notion that values pedagogy is best understood as a direct and holistic, rather than adjunct, pedagogical means of achieving efficacious learning. Persistent cross-referencing will be provided that underline the consistency to be found around these features in the Australian program and international research.

Keywords

values pedagogy – learning ambience – efficacious learning – calmness – positive relationships – safety and security

1   Introduction

The chapter will summarise findings concerning the essence of a values approach to teaching and learning, an approach referred to as values pedagogy. Research and practice demonstrate how it works in establishing a conducive environment for learning (referred to as the implicit dimension) and curriculum implementation (referred to as the explicit dimension). The chapter will focus especially on the implicit dimension, namely, the building of an ambience for learning that allied research shows is essential for efficacious learning to occur. It will focus on three key features of such an ambience, namely, Calmness, Positive Relationships, and Safety and Security. These three features were notable among the implicit effects of the Values Education Program to be found in the various government reports that summarised findings (DEST, 2006; DEEWR, 2008), including the evaluation of the entire program (Lovat et al., 2009).

2   The Nature of Values Pedagogy: A Two-Sided Coin

In my book *The Art and Heart of Good Teaching* (Lovat, 2019a), I refer to the work of Darcia Narvaez (2010, 2014, 2016), the neuropsychologist, who is one of many neuroscientists to emphasise the importance of imagination in building the confidence and mindset essential to what she refers to as "efficacious learning." She ties imagination, emotion and the rational together in suggesting that it is imagination that unlocks the emotions that are needed for sound reasoning. Why? Because reasoning is both rational and emotional. The mind thinks both logically and emotionally; the mind thinks with feeling.

Narvaez focusses on the ways in which human knowing has worked over the millennia of human existence, a process that in a sense is repeated each time a new life comes into the world. Among her specialities is early childhood education where imagination is the key or, if it is not stimulated, the death of efficacious learning. She makes the point however that imagination rarely results from spontaneous impulses. Educators must work out how to stimulate imagination through ensuring the safe environment, wherein students can feel free to take the risks associated with imaginative play, and the guiding hand of craftily planned pedagogy. It is another way of talking about the two-sided coin of values pedagogy, the implicit side being the safe, values-filled learning environment and the explicit being the values-focussed dissemination of curriculum content (Lovat et al., 2011). This chapter will concentrate on the first of these sides, searching out findings that demonstrate the importance of an implicit values-filled learning environment (Lovat, 2019b, 2019c).

By implicit is meant that the learning environment must be characterised by care, trust, respect and encouragement. There is any amount of research that has demonstrated the importance of such a values-filled "ambience," as Fred Newmann (Newmann et al., 2006) described it. Newmann's work focussed on "authentic pedagogy," the pedagogy most associated with teaching that works best, or "quality teaching" (Lovat & Toomey, 2009). He devised and factor-analysed five "pedagogical dynamics," five features or characteristics that seemed to sum up the elements most obviously associated with teaching that was working, achieving its goals, including academic achievement. The most important, the veritable sine qua non, was the "ambience of care and trust." Similar evidence was elicited in an Australian Council for Educational

Research (ACER) study conducted by Ken Rowe (2004). Of the four factors that most obviously contributed to students "doing well," the top two were care and trust, the environment wherein students were confident they were cared for and one they trusted.

The findings from the Australian Values Education Program (AVET) (2003–2010) offered ample evidence that values pedagogy can contribute powerfully to the creation of the ambiences of learning that reflect on Newmann's and Rowe's findings. In subsequent work, data from the findings were analysed under three headings: calmness, a word that continued to press through the evidence; positive relationships, both student to student and teacher to student; and safety and security, something about feeling comfortable and protected.

3   Calmness

The Values Education Study (DEST, 2003), the first major AVET project, spoke of "cohesion" and greater "peace" developing in those schools that engaged in the values pedagogy intervention at the heart of the study. Thereafter, this notion of "calmness," as defined, became a key referent in the studies that followed. It was said to be a crucial factor in schools where efficacious learning was realised. There was some speculation about whether this calmness preceded or followed naturally from such learning. If the former, then there was no need to refer to underlying epistemological, neurological or other scientific issues being at stake. Creating a calm environment can be seen as a pedagogical tool in and of itself. The calmness then works to stem negative behaviour, meaning teachers can pay more attention to the students themselves and the mechanics of teaching.

The alternative view was that the strengthened learning plays its own role in calming the environment. By this explanation, through engaging students in deeper ways of knowing, ones that stimulate the interpretive, critical and imaginative cognitive interests (Habermas, 1972, 1974; Lovat, 2013), the emotional and imaginative parts of the brain such that sound reasoning is impelled (Narvaez, 2010, 2014, 2016; Immordino-Yang, 2011), then learning becomes a richer experience, resulting in a greater sense of calm in the students. If this is accepted, then a cognitive or neurological theory would seem relevant to understanding such a phenomenon. There was evidence pointing both ways in the data and this will be analysed below.

In the Values Education Good Practice Schools Project (VEGPSP) (DEST, 2006; DEEWR, 2008), a longitudinal values pedagogical project in 312 cross-sector schools, the theme of calmness was linked throughout to improvements in both behaviour and learning. The school was said to be a "better place" because values pedagogy had led to students displaying improved self-control and hence becoming better behaved. The way it was phrased, sometimes it seemed the better environment happened first and the improved learning followed. At other times, it was phrased in a way that suggested the opposite. In these cases, the teacher's own pedagogical approach was seen as the main stimulant. That is, when teachers were faced with the challenge of placing values at the heart of the learning environment, they tended to implement more engaging learning activities. Furthermore, through using the discourse of values in addressing behaviour issues themselves, students began adapting better to their learning and, in the accumulated effects of all this, a greater calmness descended:

> ... by creating an environment where these values were constantly shaping classroom activity, student learning was improving, teachers and students were happier, and school was calmer. (DEST, 2006, p. 120)

As the projects moved into their later stages, the link between calmness and effective learning environments became more pronounced. There was also a greater emphasis to be found on the notion of cohesion accompanying calmness, of the explicit links between calm and the inclusive, caring environment, and of the ripple effect down to both student and teacher self-confidence:

> We observed that those teachers whose classrooms were characterised by an inclusive culture of caring and respect and where character development played an important and quite often explicit role in the daily learning of students were those same teachers who also demonstrated a high level of personal development, self-awareness of, and commitment to their own values and beliefs. (DEEWR, 2008, p. 39)

In the Testing and Measuring Study (Lovat et al., 2009; Lovat & Dally, 2018), an evaluative project that followed on from VEGPSP, the above assertions from teachers and others around calmness were confirmed. There was numerous evidence pointing to the following:

> ... a calmer, more caring and more cooperative environment than before the values program. (p. 7)

> ... a "calmer" environment with less conflict and with a reduction in the number of referrals to the planning room. (p. 8)

> ... calmer and more peaceful classrooms, and helped children to be more settled and attentive. (p. 34)
>
> ... calmer, more caring and more cooperative environment than before the values program. (p. 44)
>
> ... the school assumes a calmer, more peaceful ambience, better student-teacher relationships are forged, student and teacher wellbeing improves and parents are more engaged with the school. (p. 68)
>
> The positive effects on school ambience included teacher perceptions of the school being calmer and more peaceful .... (p. 86)
>
> The group felt that there was a direct correlation between the success of the values ... program and the increased calmness and respectfulness observed in classrooms. (p. 101)

In international studies, the notion of calmness in conjunction with improved learning is also evident. Farrer (2010) refers to calmness among both students and staff as one of the features of the values pedagogy she witnessed transforming the West Kidlington, UK, school under the leadership of Neil Hawkes:

> Because everyone's happy and calm, they're learning more. (p. 396)

Farrer refers to calmness as a deliberate strategy that sets the scene for the kind of values pedagogy that leads to enhanced learning. She speaks of the importance of "a moment's silence" before assembly or class as an element in the pedagogy that settles children into a relaxed and receptive state for learning. In this sense, calmness is more a cause than an effect.

In the work of Adalbjarnardottir (2010), Narvaez (2010) and Nielsen (2010), calmness is also referred to as a feature of values pedagogy but one that results from stimulating, imaginative learning, rather than an artefact that impels such learning,

> Whether as cause or effect, or both, the calm classroom, characterized by a range of features including more positive and self-regulated behaviour among students, better organization of curriculum and teaching, learning activities more likely to stimulate the whole person (cognition, emotion, sociality, etc.), more explicit values discourse and ideally a com-

ponent that involves social engagement, seems to be a persistent facet of the learning site where academic diligence is regularly reported. (Lovat et al., 2011, p. 216)

4 Positive Relationships

The issue of improved and positive relationships resulting from values pedagogy, teacher-student and student-student, was prominent from the beginning of the program. In the 2003 study report, we read:

> … the 50 final projects … are underpinned by a clear focus on building more positive relationships within the school as a central consideration for implementing values education on a broader scale. (DEST, 2003, p. 3)

The positive relationships theme persisted throughout and, as with so much of the evidence, became more sophisticated as teachers and researchers had time to reflect on its impact on the learning environment, including explicitly the ways teachers were teaching:

> It was … observed (within the school) that where teachers were seeing the importance of establishing relationships and of respecting their students – this was reflected in the behaviour of their students … Where teachers are embracing values education as something that is important and to be embedded in practice – their pedagogy is enhanced. (DEEWR, 2008, pp. 81–82)

At the heart of the relationships factor lay the issue of language and discourse. The notion of having a "common language" around values was referred to constantly as providing a new means of dealing with issues of behaviour and other transactional matters, as well as offering a deepened focus for how to deal with curriculum content. By means of a shared language, issues could be brokered between teachers and students, and students and students, so alleviating conflict, improving behaviour and ultimately strengthening relationships between the various stakeholders. Similarly, by means of a shared language, issues arising from curriculum content could be grappled with at a deeper level than was common in classroom discourse. These features then had a "ripple effect" on the total learning environment. Hence, reports on the issue of improved relationships were always enmeshed in a matrix of related issues:

... focussed classroom activity, calmer classrooms with students going about their work purposefully, and more respectful behaviour between students. Teachers and students also reported improved relationships between the two groups. Other reports included improved student attendance, fewer reportable behaviour incidents and the observation that students appeared happier. (DEEWR, 2008, p. 27)

In the Testing and Measuring Study (Lovat et al., 2009; Lovat & Dally, 2018), claims such as these were further tested. Claims around matters like attendance and behaviour reports were easily able to be verified through school records of such things. Less easily measurable claims were put to the test in different ways, through interviews and the like. As a result, we were able to elicit evidence of a range of behaviours relevant to improved relationships. In Lovat et al. (2009), these included: teachers recognising the need to respect, listen to (pp. 8, 9, 102, 107), understand (p. 9) and care for students (p. 53). They became more aware of students as persons and their particular needs as they took the time to be interested and listen to them about their lives outside of school (pp. 9, 32, 47, 61, 82). In a reciprocal manner, student respect for teachers increased (pp. 51, 66, 83). The student-teacher relationship was recognised as an important factor in student academic engagement (p. 100). Stronger collegial ties between students and teachers developed (p. 13), so that there was genuine two-way communication (p. 61) and this resulted in a more positive ambience in the classroom: 'the values focus produced more respectful, focused and harmonious classrooms' (p. 100).

Finally, the findings (Lovat et al., 2009) stood up to being tested and measured more formally and the central importance of the relationships factor was confirmed:

> Teachers' and students' comments also suggested that improved relationships between students contributed to a more cooperative and productive learning environment. (p. 6)

> Of student–teacher relationships, there was evidence of a ... rise in levels of politeness and courtesy, open friendliness, better manners, offers of help, and students being more kind and considerate. (p. 9)

> ... consistent findings that values education changes teacher-student relationships so that rather than enforcing minimum standards of behaviour or school work, teachers are more likely to support and encourage students to strive for higher ideals. (p. 12)

THE LEARNING AMBIENCE OF VALUES PEDAGOGY   155

> Teachers' comments suggested that improved relationships between students contributed to a more cooperative and productive learning environment. (p. 37)
>
> ... data ... provided converging evidence about the positive impact of values education on student academic diligence, school ambience, student and teacher relationships and student and teacher wellbeing. (p. 58)
>
> ... teachers also benefited from more mutually respectful relationships with students and from more collegial relationships with other staff. (p. 66)
>
> ... case studies that present data on student – teacher relationships mostly report improved and very positive patterns. (p. 81)
>
> Improvement in students' interpersonal relationships was noted by students, staff and parents and these observed and measurable changes in student behaviour had important repercussions for the schools' ambience. (p. 86)
>
> ... values education helped to develop "more trusting" relationships between staff and students. (p. 87)
>
> ... the quantitative and qualitative evidence ... has demonstrated that a well-crafted and well-managed values education intervention has potential to impact positively on ... student-teacher relationships ... (p. 88)

Clement (2010) draws on a wealth of international research in demonstrating that the issue of relationships lies at the heart of the flow-on effects from values pedagogy of improved behaviour, calmer environments and enhanced academic focus, as a package of factors:

> The development of intrinsic motivation flourishes in the context of secure relationships. (p. 48)

The findings concerning the centrality of relationships to efficacious learning is found in any number of international studies. Carr (2010) proposes that teaching is an inherently relational endeavour and so effective teaching requires positive and supportive relations between teachers and their students:

> ... teaching as both a professional role and an activity is implicated in, or impossible to conceive apart from, human qualities of an inherently "personal" nature, or from interpersonal relationships. (p. 63)

Carr goes on to say that because teaching is by its very nature a "people profession," the kinds of relationships that characterise it are even more integral to its work and its likely success than that of any other profession. The teacher whose relationships with students are not characterised by fair treatment, trust and support is unlikely to be having any positive effect on their students' outcomes or wellbeing.

Robinson and Campbell (2010) point to two main features of a values approach to learning, namely the quality of the learning itself and the quality of the teacher-student relationship, underlining especially the importance of "inclusiveness" on the part of the teacher such that all students know they belong and are valued. It is this kind of relationship that determines their engagement with learning. Tirri (2010) identifies, through her empirical work on professional ethics, that relationships management is crucial to effective professional work for teachers and that part of this management entails the capacity to deal with emotion:

> The skill in understanding and expressing emotions is ... necessary for teachers to establish caring relationships with their students and their families. (p. 159)

Tirri's idea fits well with the neuroscientific evidence I have explored above. The teacher who can deal with emotion is most likely to impel the imagination that Narvaez suggests is central to the sound reasoning needed for learning.

Hawkes (2010) illustrates the centrality of positive relationships to achieving all the benefits of values pedagogy, including the academic effect of improved attention to student work, a view endorsed in this case by a UK inspectorial Ofsted Report (Ofsted, 2007). Meanwhile, Gellel (2010) suggests:

> ... teachers play a fundamental role since it is through the relationships that they establish and develop with students, colleagues and the wider community that they share and facilitate values and holistic development. (p. 163)

Osterman (2010) makes the link between teacher-student relationships and the quality of teaching one of hand-in-glove, the implicit and explicit two sided coin of values pedagogy. It is not just the teacher who establishes good relationships with students who facilitates greater academic impact but the teacher who does this in conjunction with good quality content and effective pedagogical strategies. She labours the point that high quality teaching has its own effect on relationships. In other words, establishing positive relationships is itself part of efficacious pedagogy but so also is the way in which content is disseminated. Osterman also underlines the crucial nature of modelling for good relationships to ensue. It is the way students see the teacher relating to fellow students that is the great determiner of how they will relate themselves. The teacher who employs favouritism, cronyism or discrimination of any kind is modelling precisely these negative behaviours. In contrast, teachers must be the model they want for the class. Osterman (2010) refers to results of a study that illustrated the centrality of positive teacher-student relationships to be inherent to teachers achieving the best academic results:

> ... these teacher behaviors appeared to contribute to a more positive classroom environment where students were engaged in and valued learning and where relationships with peers were governed by friendship and support. (p. 247)

Arthur and Wilson (2010) report on a study from the UK that confirmed relationships as one of a number of key features of programs that nurture student wellbeing, including in the development of character and students' overall growth in knowledge and confidence as learners:

> Above all, the quality of relationships between teachers and students is an essential aspect of character formation in schools. There is a positive relationship between character dimensions, achievement and learning dispositions. (p. 352)

Meanwhile, Dasoo's (2010) report on a South African study with a particularly disadvantaged clientele illustrates dramatically the indispensable nature of promoting and establishing the right sorts of relationships as an inherent and inextricable part of the pedagogy:

> I will present evidence of how a values education initiative has the potential to refocus and nurture the teacher's understanding of the important role he or she plays not only in imparting subject knowledge to a learner but also in creating relationships with them that are indicative of com-

mitment to and care for the development of their character and the eventual role they will play in society. (p. 360)

Sun and Stewart (2010) propose that relationships are '… positively associated with students' motivation, achievement, feelings of belonging and affect in school' (p. 409). Meanwhile, Benninga and Tracz (2010) note that one of the features of the "values" schools that had the most tangible positive academic results were those schools that '… promoted a caring community and positive social relationships' (p. 523). Adalbjarnardottir's (2010) concludes, on the basis of her empirical work, that a teacher's capacity to establish effective and positive relationships with students and among students is a fundamental piece in the puzzle of teacher competence.

5   Safety and Security

As with the calmness and relationships factors, safety and a sense of security in their learning environment came through as crucial in the earliest phase of the values pedagogy program. There were routine comments about safety in the physical environment through to the kind of safety implied in more positive relationships (DEST, 2003, pp. 18, 20, 58). The concept of safety took physical safety as a given; clearly, no efficacious learning will be happening if students do not feel safe and secure. Moreover, it referred back to the issue of relationships, teacher-student and student-student, and the acceptance of difference, gender, ethnicity, religion, etc. that was either a characteristic of the school or not. One of the overt goals for some in developing a values pedagogy was as follows:

> … to re-engineer a school culture so the school could promote and nurture itself as a safe, compassionate, tolerant and inclusive school. (DEST, 2003, p. 96)

> The core school values contribute towards the desirable outcomes of safety, happiness, connectedness, emotional well-being, high self-esteem, exemplary behaviour, citizenship, service, achievement and student self-confidence. (DEST, 2003, p. 131)

As the project rolled out, the safety factor became even more pronounced and the connections with student wellbeing and their academic attention were more obvious. Moreover, the sense that students had agency over their own

THE LEARNING AMBIENCE OF VALUES PEDAGOGY 159

safety through taking responsibility for their own environment became a feature. In turn, this would influence the learning ambience:

> The atmosphere of care and safety generated in a community of inquiry provides a space in which less confident students can try out ideas with the guarantee that they will be listened to. (DEST, 2006, p. 121)

Moreover, the issue of the common language provided by values pedagogy came to be seen as instrumental and inherently related to safety:

> ... a shared school community language that could contribute to positive, safe and inclusive learning communities. (DEST, 2006, p. 181)

As with all the factors, the safety factor came to be seen in more sophisticated light as the projects moved to their later stages. By phase 2 of VEGPSP, the issue of safety was seen as more enmeshed with other pedagogical factors, while the allied notion of possessing a common language persisted:

> The pedagogies engage students in real-life learning, offer opportunity for real practice, provide safe structures for taking risks, and encourage personal reflection and action. (DEEWR, 2008, p. 9)

> (Values pedagogy) ... requires students to scrutinise questions that are difficult to resolve or answer, and focus on listening, thinking, challenging and changing viewpoints within a guided and safe environment. (DEEWR, 2008, p. 28)

> The structured discussion and agreed values that govern the engagement provide safety and support for students as well as an expectation that correction and revision are part of the debating process. It promotes critical thinking and encourages an obligation to respect one's fellow inquirers. It attempts to produce better thinkers and more caring members of society, who accept differences and, at the same time, submit conflicts to reasonable scrutiny. All participants are expected to respect one another as thoughtful members of the group who communally seek to better understand the issue at hand. (DEEWR, 2008, p. 28)

> The pedagogy gives students responsibility but recognises the inherent risks of this and accordingly provides for student safety and support. (DEEWR, 2008, p. 32)

> Participation in values education projects can provide a safe learning environment for teachers to expand their repertoires of practice through the sharing of strategies and supportive debriefing. (DEEWR, 2008, p. 60)

The many claims around the centrality of safety and security as a feature of the learning environment where wellbeing and learning are intertwined were confirmed when put to the test in the empirical project designed to test all the claims of the earlier projects:

> When values education was explicit, a common language was established among students, staff and families. This not only led to greater understanding of the targeted values but also provided a positive focus for redirecting children's inappropriate behaviour. Teachers perceived that explicitly teaching values and developing empathy in students resulted in more responsible, focused and cooperative classrooms and equipped students to strive for better learning and social outcomes. (Lovat et al., 2009, p. 88)

Toomey (2010) notes the link between the introduction of values language and student patterning of behaviour. Similarly, Dally (2010) observed that values language provides a positive focus and "consistent expectations" when discussing appropriate and inappropriate classroom behaviour with other teachers, students and parents (p. 514). This constitutes in itself a safety factor.

Similarly, the theme was easy to find in international research. Tirri (2010) notes that students report safety as a feature of those environments where values pedagogy is being implemented. Similarly, Osterman (2010) identifies the setting up of "safe space" in which students feel respected and are safe to practise respect for their fellows as an artefact of the kind of teacher practice that is most associated with academic performance. Spooner-Lane et al. (2010) also note safe space as one of the enmeshed features of those sites where teachers both establish the right relationships and provide overall high class pedagogy:

> ... teachers must possess certain capabilities that will allow them to provide high quality instruction in a safe, supportive, and stimulating learning environment and design and manage individual and group learning experiences that are intellectually stimulating. (p. 383)

Narvaez (2010) cites her own earlier work in making the connection between the safety of the physical environment and the potential psychological security that is necessary to the effective learning ambience. She notes the distraction from learning that ensues when students feel unsafe and become preoccupied by their insecurity:

> When climates are unsafe to the individual, they will provoke a "security ethic" in which self-safety becomes a major focus and priority for action. (p. 667)

Brew and Beatty (2010) tie the notion of the safe environment to the overall social cohesion experienced by the student and hence the strengthening of this environment's potential to support enhanced academic success:

> Among interrelated outcomes are increases in student sense of safety and belonging, parent and community partnership involvement in school and student academic performance, along with decreases in bullying, vandalism, absenteeism and discipline problems. (p. 680)

Adalbjarnardottir (2010) emphasises the importance of the safety factor in her analysis of teachers undergoing professional development in an effort to enhance their learning environments:

> ... as teachers create a caring and safe classroom atmosphere, students can feel free to express their ideas, feel they are heard, and feel the need to listen to each other – and feel motivated to argue, debate, and reach agreement. (p. 744)

6   Conclusion

As I identify in the book referred to at the outset of this chapter, *The Art and Heart of Good Teaching* (Lovat, 2019a), the findings herein have ramifications far beyond those pertaining to the species of education known as values education, character education, moral education and the like. As John Dewey (1964), Richard S. Peters (1981) and David Carr (2006, 2010) have argued in their own ways, and as the most basic perusal of the Islamic educational tradition would attest (Lovat, 2019d), all education is moral education. Hence, its values dimension, implicit and explicit, must comprise an indispensable component of efficacious learning. As I have written elsewhere (Lovat, 2019c), the noise created by Western education's obsession with instrumentalism cannot drown out this fundamental, age-old truth. Nonetheless, the obsession can and often does limit if not damage the effectiveness of Western education in its quest to provide the knowledge, skills and dispositions essential for survival, success and wellbeing among young people facing the challenges of a rapidly changing, increasingly uncertain world. The findings of the Australian Values Education Program, in part outlined in this chapter, serve to remind Western educators of some of the fundamentals of good teaching and teacher education that can too easily be buried in a world bent on instrumental ends. Let me finish with words from the summative text colleagues and I compiled at the tail end of the program:

> It seems the jury is well and truly in that ambience is one of the most significant keys to academic improvement. Furthermore, this ambience is characterized across vastly different research domains in a remarkably predictable way. What then is this predictable characterization? In which ambience does this improvement occur? Once again, the evidence suggests that it occurs in the ambience characterized by calmness, by positive teacher-student relationships and by safety and security in both basic and sophisticated senses. No doubt, there are other words that could be used and other emphases drawn out but we are at the point of saying that, in all likelihood, any of these characterizations would be reducible to one or all of these key features. Hence, it is clear what constitutes the main implicit aspect of values pedagogy, namely, the ambience of learning as understood above, and this all makes perfect sense. It is in accord entirely with the pedagogical work of Newmann .... The ambience of support and trust is a *sine qua non* of the pedagogy that produces the best holistic results. (Lovat et al., 2011, p. 224)

References

Adalbjarnardottir, S. (2010). Passion and purpose: Teacher professional development and student social and civic growth. In T. Lovat, R. Toomey, & N. Clement (Eds.), *International research handbook on values education and student wellbeing* (pp. 737–764). Springer.

Arthur, J., & Wilson, K. (2010). New research directions in character and values education in the UK. In T. Lovat, R. Toomey, & N. Clement (Eds.), *International research handbook on values education and student wellbeing* (pp. 339–358). Springer.

Benninga, J., & Tracz, S. (2010). Continuity and discontinuity in character education. In T. Lovat, R. Toomey, & N. Clement (Eds.), *International research handbook on values education and student wellbeing* (pp. 521–548). Springer.

Brew, C., & Beatty, B. (2010). Valuing social and emotional connectedness among learners at all levels. In T. Lovat, R. Toomey, & N. Clement (Eds.), *International research handbook on values education and student wellbeing* (pp. 675–702). Springer.

Carr, D. (2006). Professional and personal values and virtues in education and teaching. *Oxford Review of Education, 32,* 171–183.

Carr, D. (2010). Personal and professional values in teaching. In T. Lovat, R. Toomey, & N. Clement (Eds.), *International research handbook on values education and student wellbeing* (pp. 63–74). Springer.

Clement, N. (2010). Student wellbeing at school: The actualisation of values in education. In T. Lovat, R. Toomey, & N. Clement (Eds.), *International research handbook on values education and student wellbeing* (pp. 37–62). Springer.

Dally, K. (2010). A teacher's duty: An examination of the short-term impact of values education on Australian primary school teachers and students. In T. Lovat, R. Toomey, & N. Clement (Eds.), *International research handbook on values education and student wellbeing* (pp. 503–520). Springer.

Dasoo, N. (2010). Nurturing teacher wellbeing through values education. In T. Lovat, R. Toomey, & N. Clement (Eds.), *International research handbook on values education and student wellbeing* (pp. 359–376). Springer.

DEEWR. (2008). *At the heart of what we do: Values education at the centre of schooling.* Report of the Values Education Good Practice Schools Project – Stage 2. Curriculum Corporation. Retrieved September 12, 2016, from http://www.curriculum.edu.au/values/val_vegps2_final_report,26142.html

DEST. (2003). *Values education study.* (Executive summary final report) Curriculum Corporation. Retrieved September 12, 2016, from http://www.curriculum.edu.au/verve/_resources/VES_Final_Report14Nov.pdf

DEST. (2006). *Implementing the national framework for values education in Australian schools: Report of the Values Education Good Practice Schools Project – Stage 1: Final report, September 2006.* Curriculum Corporation. Retrieved 12 September, 2016, from http://www.curriculum.edu.au/verve/_resources/VEGPS1_FINAL_REPORT_081106.pdf

Dewey, J. (1964). *John Dewey on education: Selected writings.* Modern Library.

Farrer, F. (2010). Re-visiting the 'quiet revolution.' In T. Lovat, R. Toomey, & N. Clement (Eds.), *International research handbook on values education and student wellbeing* (pp. 395–408). Springer.

Gellel, A. (2010). Teachers as key players in values education: Implications for teacher formation. In T. Lovat, R. Toomey, & N. Clement (Eds.), *International research handbook on values education and student wellbeing* (pp. 163–178). Springer.

Habermas, J. (1972). *Knowledge and human interests* (J. Shapiro, Trans.). Heinemann.

Habermas, J. (1974). *Theory and practice* (J. Viertal, Trans.). Heinemann.

Hawkes, N. (2010). Values education and the national curriculum in England. In T. Lovat, R. Toomey, & N. Clement (Eds.), *International research handbook on values education and student wellbeing* (pp. 225–238). Springer.

Immordino-Yang, M. H. (2011). Implications of affective and social neuroscience for educational theory. *Educational Philosophy and Theory, 43*(1), 98–103.

Lovat, T. (2013). Jurgen Habermas: Education's reluctant hero. In M. Murphy (Ed.), *Social theory and educational research: Understanding Foucault, Habermas, Derrida and Bourdieu* (pp. 69–83). Routledge.

Lovat, T. (2019a). *The art and heart of good teaching: Values as the pedagogy.* Springer Nature.

Lovat, T. (2019b). Values education, efficacious learning and the Islamic connection: An Australian case study. In K. Tirri (Ed.), *Encyclopedia of teacher education.* Springer Nature. https://link.springer.com/referenceworkentry/10.1007%2F978-981-13-1179-6_186-1

Lovat, T. (2019c). Values as the pedagogy: Countering instrumentalism. In K. Tirri (Ed.), *Pedagogy and pedagogical challenges.* IntechOpen. https://www.intechopen.com/online-first/values-as-the-pedagogy-countering-instrumentalism

Lovat, T. (2019d). Islamic education today and yesterday: Principal themes and their potential to enlighten Western education. In M. Huda, J. Safar, A. Mohamed, K. Jasmi, & B. Basiron (Eds.), *Global perspectives on teaching and learning paths in Islamic education* (pp. 1–20). IGI Global.

Lovat, T., & Dally, K. (2018). Testing and measuring the impact of character education on the learning environment and its outcomes. *Journal of Character Education, 14*(2), 1–22.

Lovat, T., & Toomey, R. (Eds.). (2009). *Values education and quality teaching: The double helix effect.* Springer.

Lovat, T., Toomey, R., Dally, K., & Clement, N. (2009). *Project to test and measure the impact of values education on student effects and school ambience.* Report for the Australian Government Department of Education, Employment and Workplace Relations (DEEWR) by The University of Newcastle, Australia. DEEWR. http://www.curriculum.edu.au/verve/_resources/Project_to_Test_and_Measure_the_Impact_of_Values_Education.pdf

Lovat, T., Dally, K., Clement, N., & Toomey, R. (2011). *Values pedagogy and student achievement: Contemporary research evidence.* Springer.

Narvaez, D. (2010). Building a sustaining classroom climate for purposeful ethical citizenship. In T. Lovat, R. Toomey, & N. Clement (Eds.), *International research handbook on values education and student wellbeing* (pp. 659–674). Springer.

Narvaez, D. (2014). *Neurobiology and the development of human morality: Evolution, culture, and wisdom.* W. W. Norton & Company.

Narvaez, D. (2016). *Embodied morality: Protectionism, engagement and imagination.* Palgrave Macmillan.

Newmann, F. M., & Associates. (1996). *Authentic achievement: Restructuring schools for intellectual quality.* Jossey-Bass Publishers.

Nielsen, T. (2010). Towards pedagogy of giving for wellbeing and social engagement. In T. Lovat, R. Toomey, & N. Clement (Eds.), *International research handbook on values education and student wellbeing* (pp. 617–630). Springer.

Ofsted. (2007). *Inspection report: West Kidlington Primary School, 21–22 March, 2007.* Office for Standards in Education.

Osterman, K. (2010). Teacher practice and students' sense of belonging. In T. Lovat, R. Toomey, & N. Clement (Eds.), *International research handbook on values education and student wellbeing* (pp. 239–260). Springer.

Peters, R. S. (1981). *Moral development and moral education.* George Allen & Unwin.

Robinson, W., & Campbell, R. (2010). School values and effective pedagogy: Case studies of two leading edge schools in England. In T. Lovat, R. Toomey, & N. Clement (Eds.), *International research handbook on values education and student wellbeing* (pp. 75–90). Springer.

Rowe, K. (2004). In good hands: The importance of teacher quality. *Educare News, 149,* 4–14.

Spooner-Lane, R., Curtis, E., & Mergler, A. (2010). Embracing philosophy and raising the standard of pre-service teacher education programs. In T. Lovat, R. Toomey, & N. Clement (Eds.), *International research handbook on values education and student wellbeing* (pp. 377–394). Springer.

Sun, J., & Stewart, D. (2010). Promoting student resilience and wellbeing: Asia-Pacific resilient children and communities project. In T. Lovat, R. Toomey, & N. Clement (Eds.), *International research handbook on values education and student wellbeing* (pp. 409–426). Springer.

Tirri, K. (2010). Teacher values underlying professional ethics. In T. Lovat, R. Toomey, & N. Clement (Eds.), *International research handbook on values education and student wellbeing* (pp. 153–162). Springer.

Toomey, R. (2010). Values education, instructional scaffolding and student wellbeing. In T. Lovat, R. Toomey, & N. Clement (Eds.), *International research handbook on values education and student wellbeing* (pp. 19–36). Springer.

CHAPTER 9

Religious Literacy as a 21st Century Skill for All Teachers

Martin Ubani

Abstract

The purpose of this chapter is to conceptualize religious literacy as a 21st century skill for all teachers. The chapter begins by describing the background and content of religious literacy in modern scholarly discussions. Then, a proposition for domains of religious literacy within the professional competence of all teachers is presented. I advocate that religious literacy is not only a content or curricular objective, but that critical teachers should have knowledge of religious literacy as a quality criterion for good practice in public education and as a legitimacy tool in meeting the demand for recognizing religion in public education and in society. Finally, recommendations for teacher education in the 21st century are presented. The discussion is contextualized mainly within Finnish public education.

Keywords

21st century skills – religious literacy – teacher education – school

1   Introduction

This chapter conceptualizes religious literacy as a 21st century skill for all teachers based on an analysis of previous literature from different fields. "21st century skills," "new learning skills," "transferable skills" and "generic skills" have been at the forefront of international educational policy since the late 1980's (Darling-Hammond, 2006; Dede, 2009; Geisinger, 2016; Guilland et al., 2017; Newton & Newton, 2014; Niemi et al., 2018; Niemi & Multisilta, 2016; Oliver & St. Jorre, 2018; Tynjälä et al., 2016; Viinikka & Ubani, 2019; Virtanen & Tynjälä, 2019; Wang et al., 2018). Consequently, key policymakers have issued statements grounding public education on these foundations (European Commission, 2013; Organization for Economic Co-operation and Development

[OECD], 2005). The integral notion in this initiative has been maintaining the competitiveness of societies (OECD, 2018) and the question of what skills the citizens of today and tomorrow should have in order to be able to navigate in diverse, evolving and complex knowledge societies. As societies have changed from industrial to information and knowledge societies, the requirement for new kinds of skills for domains such as learning, problem-solving, collaboration, empathy and entrepreneurship is thought to have grown in relevance (Binkley et al., 2012; Griffin el al., 2012). Also, digitalization has called for new skills, such as digital literacy, or updating of already recognized skills, such as information literacy (Lankshear & Knobel, 2011). Consequently, there are several listings and sets of "new skills" in the literature, such as the Assessment and Teaching of 21st Century Skills (ATC21) (Wang et al., 2018) and the Partnership for 21st Century Learning (Battelle for Kids, 2007).

Much of the discussion in the chapter will be contextualized in Finnish public education. As with most other Western countries, Finnish public curricula have adopted a skills-based approach in recent years (Palsa & Mertala, 2019; Niemi, 2015; Uljens & Rajakaltio, 2017; Viinikka & Ubani, 2020). Teacher education has also adapted to the new learning requirements. For instance, the Finnish National Board of Education has recently stated that lifelong learning and anticipation of future needs and competences are core values in the development of teacher education (Niemi, 2015; Rajakaltio, 2014). The importance of support for continuous professional learning has also increased (Niemi, 2012, 2014): the core content of initial teacher education, knowledge and skills, and explicitly research-based development of professionalism are thought to play key roles in coping with the constantly evolving challenges of the profession (Harju & Niemi, 2016).

In this chapter, skills related to religion are conceptualized in terms of "religious literacy." The handling of religion in public education is one of the prevalent issues related to the education of values and interculturality in public education. With regard to religions and worldviews, several policy documents have discussed the skills requirements for teachers and their education for public education today, such as *The Toledo Guiding Principles on Teaching about Religions and Beliefs in Public Schools* by the European Commission (Organization for Security and Co-operation in Europe [OSCE], 2007) and *'Signposts': Policy and Practice for Teaching about Religions and Non-Religious Worldviews in Intercultural Education* by the Council of Europe (Jackson, 2014). These have put forward the case that dialogue skills and media skills are some of the core skills for successful teaching and learning in the context of intercultural and religious education in Europe. However, similarly concerned reports from the UK, for instance (Conroy et al., 2015), and Finland (Räsänen et al., 2018) have surfaced calling for increased up-to-date professional skills for teachers in handling religion in public education, with skills related to religion seen as a part of intercultural professional competence.

This chapter focuses on the question of what aspects religious literacy as a skill for all teachers should entail. The chapter begins by describing the background and content of religious literacy in modern scholarly discussions. Then, a proposition for domains of religious literacy within the professional competence of all teachers is presented. I advocate that religious literacy is not only a content or curricular objective, but that critical teachers should have knowledge of religious literacy as a quality criterion for good practice in public education, and as a legitimacy tool in meeting the demand for recognizing religion in public education and in society. Finally, the chapter presents concluding recommendations for teacher education in the 21st century.

2   What Is Religious Literacy?

"Religious literacy" has lately been increasingly discussed in terms of skills related to religion relevant to several particular public arenas today (Dinham & Francis, 2015). In addition to public education in general (Hannam et al., 2020; Richardson, 2017; Marcus, 2018) or compulsory education in particular (Conroy, 2015, 2016; Dinham & Shaw, 2017; Rissanen et al., 2020), such other specific arenas have included higher education (Jones, 2015) and the academic disciplines of Theology and Religious Studies (Ford & Higton, 2015). In addition, in the media (Pauha & Konttori, 2020; Wakelin & Spencer, 2015) and in church ministry (Clines & Gilliat-Ray, 2015), policies such as welfare (Dinham, 2015), multiculturalism and radicalization (Al-Sharmani & Mustasaari, 2020; Francis & van Eck Duymaer van Twist, 2015; Tiilikainen & Mankkinen, 2020) and human rights (Catto & Perfect, 2015) have been linked with religious literacy. Finally, the concept of religious literacy has also been discussed in terms of professionalism with regard to health and social work (Crisp, 2015; Crisp & Dinham, 2019; Dinham, 2017, 2018), RE teachers (Conroy, 2015, 2016), and as a leadership skill in workplaces in general (Burrell et al., 2018). For instance, recently Conroy (2016) has pushed forward the importance of grounding the objectives of RE in the UK firmly with religious literacy in order to strengthen the profession of RE teachers.

Reportedly, religious literacy has been used as a term in the context of public education at least since the 1950s, albeit scarcely (Hannam et al., 2019, p. 18). However, in the 2000s "religious literacy" resurfaced in the literature. The resurgence of "religious literacy" in public education can be traced to several developments. In a broader societal context, the "re-emergence of religion in public space" acknowledged in the early 2000s by several sociologists and philosophers (Habermas, 2006; Taylor, 2004; Kunzman, 2005) has underlined the need to re-examine the adequacy of citizenship skills regarding religion gained in public education. For instance, in the US Kunzman (2006) has advocated from a pragmatist viewpoint active engagement in public education with diverse religious beliefs with four interconnected arguments (Kunzman, 2006, pp. 517–581):

1. Public schools should help equip students to be citizens who can participate effectively in a liberal democracy.
2. This citizenship should include understanding the diversity of fellow citizens.
3. One vital element of this diversity (and source of civic conflict) for many is religion.
4. Therefore, public school curricula need to foster students' understanding of religious diversity, and a capacity for navigating the resulting conflicts about how we live together.

Consequently, in the policy literature on religion and public education a plea to educate teachers to address religion and non-religious beliefs in a constructive, dialogical and citizen-equipping manner has been put forward (see Jackson, 2014; OSCE, 2007).

Several other quite recent developments integral to the acknowledgement of religious literacy as a concept in the domain of education can also be identified, as Hannam et al. (2019) have described. As regards scientific conceptual developments, one should highlight both Hirsch's (1987) concept of cultural literacy and "New literacy studies" (Brandt & Clinton, 2002; Gee, 1990, 2000; Duranti & Goodwin, 1992), the latter introducing the concept of multiliteracy as an inclusive view of what is considered a "text" and thus laying the basis for introducing several types of literacies (Hannam et al., 2019, pp. 6–7). On the other hand, Hirsch's "Cultural Literacy" (1987) pushed for gaining sufficient knowledge of concepts, contents and terminology related to religion and to the philosophical, theological and sociological aspects related to it in order for the individual to be able to fully take part in and understand sufficiently cultural artefacts such as literature and art (Hannam et al., 2019, p. 7; Hirsch, 1987). Furthermore, with regard to curricular developments, the integrality of "new learning skills" or "21st century skills" (Darling-Hammond, 2006; Newton & Newton, 2014; Niemi et al., 2018; Wang et al., 2018) surfacing in the educational policy and research discourse in the latter decades of the 20th century should not be overlooked as it offers a broader terminological and educational framework suitable for discussing skills related to religion in the secular public education context (see Parker, 2020), although seemingly only a few empirical studies have connected religious literacy and 21st century skills together (e.g., Lipiäinen et al., 2020; Viinikka & Ubani, 2019; Viinikka et al., 2019).

In the current general discussion on religious literacy, scholars such as Prothero (2007), Dinham (2016; Dinham & Francis, 2015) and Moore (2014, 2015) have been essential in defining the concept for modern purposes. While nuances exist, in line with the modern ideals of Western education with regard to knowledge about religions (Kunzman, 2006, 2007), key scholars focus on analytical understanding of culture and society in their conceptions of religious literacy instead of aspects such as developing a personal conviction (i.e. "becoming religious" or "faith formation"). Terminologically, religious literacy comprises two concepts: one referring simply to religion and the other to education. The concept "religious" in religious literacy is usually used in the manner of the American Academy of Religion (2016) in "Religious Studies" to refer to the object of study (as in "Russian studies"). However, the "education" or, specifically, the "literacy" aspect of religious literacy has been less examined. Therefore, in future religious literacy should be examined not only in terms of domains of religious literacy in public education, as in this chapter, but also in terms of what it is to know and become literate in religious literacy, as we seem to lack a science of learning in religious literacy.

In general, knowledge about religion(s) can be perceived to entail critical and analytical understanding of what in other instances has been described as both the sociological category of religion and the anthropological category of religious (see Rothgangel, 2014). For instance, Moore defines religious literacy in the following manner:

> Religious literacy entails the ability to discern and analyze the fundamental intersections of religion and social/political/cultural life through multiple lenses. Specifically, a religiously literate person will possess (1) a basic understanding of the history, central texts (where applicable), beliefs, practices and contemporary manifestations of several of the world's religious traditions as they arose out of and continue to be shaped by particular social, historical and cultural contexts; and (2) the ability to discern and explore the religious dimensions of political, social and cultural expressions across time and place. (Moore, 2014, pp. 379–380)

Similarly concerned with the decline in religious literacy in US society, Prothero describes religious literacy as "the ability to understand and use the basic building blocks of religious traditions – their terms, symbols, doctrines, practices, sayings, characters, metaphors, and narratives" (Prothero, 2007, p. 15) and emphasizes religious literacy as an essential skill in social, political and economic participation in society and the world (Prothero, 2007).

Finally, while agreeing with the societal demand for religious literacy, Dinham (2016; Dinham & Jones, 2012) emphasizes a somewhat functional description of religious literacy. To him, religious literacy can be approached as a type of critical thinking focusing on the sociological category of religion, disposition or attitude towards religion(s), knowledge about religion, and the skill to implement that knowledge in particular situations (Dinham, 2016). The last three domains overlap with what is commonly understood as competence (Baartman et al., 2007), perhaps unsurprisingly as Dinham's main concern has been professional practice (Dinham, 2019; Shaw, 2019).

To sum up, in general, in the recent literature there has been little educational theoretical focus on the dynamics of developing and learning to be "literate" in religious literacy. What we can derive from the above literature, however, is that at the level of the individual religious literacy can be understood as a competence (knowledge, skills and attitudes) for "critical reading" (i.e., identifying, recognizing, understanding, analyzing, distinguishing, evaluating, contesting) of religion in different contexts and being able to apply this competence not only in "the critical reading of religion" but also in applying this set of knowledge, skills and attitudes gained appropriately to different topics and practices. Religious literacy has broad content: it can be seen to relate to religion as a personal, communal, societal, institutional, cultural, local and global phenomenon. This description will be used as the working definition hereafter.

When framing religious literacy, there are two concepts that are important to recognize. First is the question of secularity. It can be said that, by default, religious literacy in Western societies also includes understanding of "secular" and "secularism." In general, secularism (ideology) and secularization (societal process) have been acknowledged as integral in the previous discussions also with regard to demands for religious literacy (and religious illiteracy) (see Dinham, 2017; Moore, 2014; Prothero, 2007). In the literature, secularization is thought to be a contextual process taking place in relation to religion in a given sociocultural context with its local characteristics (Casanova, 2009, 2014) and so, vice versa, is religion – in Western societies discussions related to religion often center on questions of secularism and secularization (Davie, 2000) – yet there are some generalizable aspects of these two.

Furthermore, issues related to religion in public education today in Western societies are also often pinpointed at what in Nordic research is referred to as "secular (Protestant) normativity" (Berglund, 2017; Rissanen, 2018; Rissanen et al., 2020) and "the secularist framework" (Ubani, 2019). The secularist framework can be understood as a

> generic ideological interpretation, where religion is considered as something incompatible with modernity, science and society and is therefore to be restricted to the private sphere, where it will eventually fade out as a part of human progress. At the same time, the relationship between religious institutions, the Churches, state and power becomes scrutinized and heavily criticized. (Ubani, 2019, p. 108)

Admittedly there is little novel in this description with regard to secularism and secularization (Coulby & Zambeta, 2008; Hofstee & van der Kooij, 2013) as such. One aspect identified in the most critical form of the secularist framework is the perceived irrationality of religious truth claims, especially when compared to "scientific," i.e., naturalistic knowledge. Furthermore, the existence of contradicting truth claims between religions or within religions is not compatible with the logic of reason valued in the secularist outlook (see Riitaoja et al., 2010; Ubani, 2018).

The second integral framing concept is worldview and, subsequently, worldview literacy. In recent years there has been an explosion of interest in "worldviews" in education about religion, both in the international research literature (e.g., Chater, 2020; Miedema, 2018; Thalén & Carlson, 2020; Valk, 2017; Åhs et al., 2016) and in policy documents and their related academic commentaries, especially in the UK (CoRE, 2018; Freathy & John, 2019; Hannam & Biesta, 2019). Similarly, in the literature regarding religious literacy, concepts such as "religion and worldview literacy" (Shaw, 2020) or simply "worldview literacy" (Wright, 2009) have been used. However, with regard to religious literacy the use of both terms "religious" and "worldview" together has a totally different meaning to substituting "religious" with "worldview" in "religious literacy."

My use of the term "religion" instead of "worldview" in this chapter is a conscious choice. Regarding the substitution of these terms, Thalén (2020) shares a similar stance to me in his critical assessment of the use of the concept "worldview" in the field of religion and education. According to Thalén, in the educational discourse often little if no "attempts have been made to discern the limitations and pitfalls" associated with the "individualistic and plural use of the concept ... common in educational context" (p. 158). The emergence of "worldviews" in debates on religious education can be perceived as an instance of accommodating developments among individuals and policies in Western societies with regards to pluralization and secularization. In terms of religion, arguably "worldview" would then seem to be suitable for depicting diversity with regard to life stances, whether related to religion or not, or to a mix of views, but even then the term is limited by its potential association with concepts such as "individualistic," "Western rationality" and "Enlightenment." In these senses the use of the term "religion" also has similar challenges, but not to the extent that "worldview" has. Furthermore, "religion" can be used to refer to individual phenomena no matter whether the emphasis is on individual, community, society, institutions or global politics and events. In contrast, in many instances it is debatable whether it is more suitable to use "ideology" than "worldview" when looking at identifiable shared belief and value positions on life, society and reality, especially when discussing political movements or societal actions.

Taking these considerations as a starting point (but acknowledging the different discourses surrounding religion/worldview or religious literacy/worldview literacy debates), in terms of literacy, religion has a strong explicit academic tradition exemplified by international (or at least Western) faculties and scholarly professionals. These approaches and foci, even if diverse in their fields, produce a kind of higher level of knowledge of the phenomenon called religion shared in most, if not all, Western contexts. Arguably, the meaning of "worldview" is still very context dependent. The substitution of "religion" with "worldview" can be seen to imply that the knowledge and skills comprising religious literacy are somehow dated and lack relevance in understanding the different facets of 21st century societies. Finally, this chapter takes a position that if perceived as referring to individuals' perceptions of life, the benefits of approaching the understanding of "worldviews" as literacy, and whether this conception fits with cultural literacy, new literacy or 21st century skills frameworks, needs substantially more elaboration. In this chapter, "worldview" is understood as a potential element of individual and personal aspects of religion, overlapping therefore with religiousness, but when used here, it also denotes an individual's constructed stance to life (beliefs, values), the sources of which may or may not come from religion, but likely draw from several sources, even in the case of those professing to be an adherent of a given religion.

3 The Domains of Religious Literacy in Public Education

3.1 *Religious Literacy as Professional Competence*

Religious literacy is here advocated as an essential skill for good professional pedagogical practice in 21st century public education. Based on this line of thought, religion includes global, cultural, societal, communal and individual aspects that touch everyday life and school life at different levels and should be appropriately handled, regardless of the personal stance towards religion of the people involved (Rissanen et al., 2020; Ubani, 2018). Recent policy (Jackson, 2014; OSCE, 2007) and research literature (Hannam et al., 2019; Rissanen et al., 2020; Ubani & Ojala, 2018) have acknowledged knowledge and skills related to religion (and non-religious beliefs) as important professional tools for teachers of all levels and subjects, not just for teachers of RE or equivalent. In addition, several reports on teachers in public education have highlighted the intersectionality of the topic of religion with respect to issues such as migration, nationalities, minorities, identities and power (e.g., Hammer & Schanke, 2018; Kittelmann-Flensner et al., 2019; Rissanen et al., 2020; Ubani, 2018). With regard to Finnish teacher education, there have been doubts raised whether teacher competence in handling cultural and religious diversity, for instance, has been given enough attention (Lemettinen et al., 2021; Rissanen et al., 2020; Räsänen et al., 2018).

However, here one of the integral questions is what kind and level of ability should all teachers have regarding religion in public education? As stated above, at the level of the individual, religious literacy is the competence for "critical reading" about religion in different contexts and the proper application of this skill. Religion is understood here to be a personal, communal, societal, institutional, cultural, local and global phenomenon with associated aspects. How, then, does this translate to competence in professional pedagogical practice? In the pedagogical sense, religious literacy can be considered a part of the core of teachers' "content knowledge" (Shulman, 1987, p. 8) of religion and to function in the organizing of knowledge about and related to religion, which, incidentally, is an integral part of the subject matter of RE. If expanded, religious literacy can also be perceived as a constituent of pedagogical content knowledge (Shulman, 1986, 1987) with regard to religion: the skill of teaching a certain topic of religion in a manner that promotes learning requires good understanding both of the topic and of its broader context: as Shulman (1987, p. 6) indicates here pedagogical skill should not be seen apart from content knowledge.

However, if religious literacy is seen as a skill that all teachers, regardless of school subject, need in their professional competence, then a broader view of religious literacy is needed. I advocate here that religious literacy as a critical professional skill should entail reflective metacognitive understanding of how to promote religious literacy as a curricular objective, but also understanding of religious literacy as a quality criterion of the modern school and of the political normative aspect inherent in the concept of religious literacy. This perception takes as a predisposition the assumption that teachers' critical reflection on and awareness of their own stance towards religion (see Cox, 1983) are needed: it is the critical analysis of one's own relationship to religion that one could also discuss in terms of religious literacy in itself. In terms of professional practice, this could also be viewed in connection to professional ethics when making decisions on contents, methods and time allocation. However, the domains of religious literacy focused on this chapter, in addition to religious literacy as professional competence, are more explicit instances of religious literacy in public education. As we will later see, through these domains, religious literacy connects in addition to content knowledge also with both pedagogical content knowledge and curricular knowledge, the two other types of pedagogical knowledge advocated by Shulman (1986, 1987). While the first domain presented below, *religious literacy as a curricular objective*, emphasizes content knowledge and pedagogical content aspects, the domain of religious literacy as a quality criterion also requires curricular knowledge, not only pedagogical understanding. Finally, the domain of religious literacy as legitimacy politics can be likened to Shulman's "some other important domains of knowledge" (p. 8) relevant to the successful practice of the teacher with regard to religion in education. This domain can also be seen as heightening the critical quality of curricular knowledge, as it arguably may provide understanding of curricula and power in relation to religion in education and society.

3.2   *Religious Literacy as a Curricular Objective*

The first domain of religious literacy focuses on religious literacy as a pedagogical aim; a knowledge or skill to be acquired in education. This aspect is the prevalent aspect in discussions of religious literacy in public education: the literature mentioned in the previous subsection assumed religious literacy to belong mainly to this domain. Here, the focus is on learning outcomes and curricular aims. The important questions here are: What knowledge of religion is considered relevant, and how should it be taught? This overlaps with content knowledge and pedagogical content knowledge (see Shulman, 1986, 1987). However, concerning the latter form of knowledge, as touched on above, there is little, if any, comprehensive research on teaching and learning religious literacy.

With regard to religious literacy and curricula, in Western curricula the general trend has been away from internalizing religious beliefs towards an objective analytical stance with regard to religion: from learning religion to learning about or from religion (Grimmit, 1967; Hull, 2002; Ubani, 2017). The inclusion or even prevalence of the latter aims regarding learning religion can be seen as prerequisite for a comprehensive sociocultural view of religion and, thus, for what is considered religious literacy. In religious literacy also the concepts of secular, secularism and secularization are needed as conceptual counterparts. Arguably, understanding religion in modern society and culture and the tensions pertaining to it is connected to secularization and vice versa: understanding "secular" and "secularization" requires a sufficient understanding of religion.

Religious literacy as an educational objective has often centered around the subject of religious education (Dinham & Shaw, 2018; Conroy, 2016; Parker, 2020; Wright, 1993, 2000). In most societies in Europe religious education is taught as a separate school subject (Rothgangel et al., 2014). Hence, the wide ongoing debate about developing RE in many Western countries has focused on what kind of knowledge RE should provide and what skills and competencies are most relevant today (Clarke & Woodhead, 2017; Conroy, 2016; CoRe, 2018; Freathy et al., 2017; Lipiäinen et al., 2020; Skeie, 2019).

As stated, the concept of religious literacy has been used in educational discourse for some time. Also in Finnish discussions, religious literacy has been – if undefined – a practical term referring to the outcomes of RE at least since the early 2000s (Hilska, 2003, 2004; Kallioniemi, 2004, 2005) and explicitly in the national core curriculum a decade after that (FNBE, 2014, p. 134). However, the references to religious literacy in Finnish studies have also included the viewpoint of holistic education in early childhood education (Hilska, 2003) and in schools (Rissanen et al., 2020). Broadly speaking, in modern religious education the outcomes of education can be interpreted as pertaining to religious literacy even without mentioning the concept, although not exclusively (see Biesta et al., 2019), although the debate is still ongoing (Parker, 2020; Shaw, 2019) and is not easily resolved. For instance, in the Finnish core curriculum since 1994 (FNBE, 1994, 2014) a concept best translated as "religious general knowledge" has been used broadly connoting objectives related to *Bildung* (see Biesta, 2002). However, depending on the country, several other aims are included in RE, such as aims related to ethics and values that do not easily fall under the umbrella of "religious literacy" so that equating the aims of religious education as "merely" religious literacy is not merited (e.g., Biesta et al., 2019). In addition, lately there has been an increasing initiative to distinguish between religious literacy and worldview literacy by using these concepts in conjugation (Shaw, 2019), which can be taken to indicate that as an overarching objective for RE, religious literacy as such is not comprehensive enough.

Putting RE aside, the literature has increasingly agreed that to educate children and young people successfully about religion, providing knowledge about religion(s) as well as the skills to address religious issues in a constructive manner (Jackson, 2014; OSCE, 2007; Ubani & Ojala, 2018) is the task of whole school education rather than a designated school subject. In countries where public education in RE is provided, one of the key challenges is that RE as a subject is isolated from the rest of the curriculum for a number of reasons depending on the educational system and context. As a result, there is a tendency to restrict education in religions, beliefs and worldviews to the subject of RE, which is used as a catch-all for "all things religious" (Ubani, 2019). This increases the risk of reductionist representations of these aspects of human experience, the world and human history in other subjects. On the other hand, in countries where there is no public RE, the challenge is whether any critical and analytical knowledge and skills related to religion can be obtained: in such situations at one extreme is indoctrination into religion and at the other neglect of religion and reduction of social and cultural phenomena.

3.3 *Religious Literacy as a Quality Criterion*

The second domain concerning religious literacy within the professional competence of the teacher applies to curricular knowledge (see Shulman, 1987) and school practices. Teachers need to develop sufficient critical skills to evaluate how school policies and practices support religious literacy and how to develop them further. The examination of religion in policy documents and public education curricula and practices represents an instance of perceiving religious literacy as a quality criterion. This domain, which is naturally connected with teacher professionalism, has been paid little attention in the literature.

The question of religious literacy as a quality criterion concerns public education as broadly as from early childhood education to higher education and from vocational education to teacher education. However, perhaps the most visible signs of emerging awareness of this domain concerns basic education. For instance, recently several authors have called for critical examination of the actions and practices of the whole school with regard to addressing religions and worldviews (Jackson, 2014; Niemi et al., 2014; Rissanen et al., 2019, 2020; Ubani & Ojala, 2018). In particular, topics such as school celebrations (Niemi, 2019; Niemi et al., 2014), interaction between teachers and parents (Rissanen, 2018) and diets (Hammer & Schanke, 2018) have been brought up along with challenges with regard to Islam in public schools (Berglund, 2017; Buchardt, 2014). Although in those studies the concept of "worldview" is sometimes used to depict diversity in schools, "religion" and "religious literacy" could offer a more thorough understanding of the intersectional processes connecting religion with migration, multiculturalism and citizenship, with the exception, perhaps, of secular outlooks on life. It should be noted that the use or addition of "worldview" alongside or instead of religion in the above literature concerning this domain highlights what has been stated earlier regarding the emphasis on individuality, plurality and diversity.

The focus here with regard to this religious literacy domain is on how religions, their customs and traditions and non-religious beliefs are recognized and negotiated in school practices. This boils down to the question of to what extent school customs are adaptable and inclusive? A challenge here with regard to secularism is the ambiguous position of majority and minority religions and worldviews in schools. For instance, researchers have pointed out that in Finland the position of Lutheranism (the majority religion) is both strong and weak (Ubani et al., 2018). Here cultural heritage is used to legitimize some elements related to Lutheranism in schools, yet Lutheranism also operates within a secularist framework in which its representation is restricted and questioned. On the other hand, religions with a shorter history in Finland, such as Islam, are not considered cultural heritage, but operate within the framework of "multiculturalism" (Ubani, 2019) and arguably have more space to be represented in schools. It seems that different religions operate with different rules in schools according to their position and history in society (Rissanen, 2018; Rissanen et al., 2020; Ubani, 2019; Ubani et al., 2019).

Arguably, in Finland, Protestant and secularist conceptions of religion among educational professionals (Berglund, 2017; Rissanen et al., 2020) are an obstacle to the up-to-date religious literacy of teachers and school practices (Lemettinen et al., 2021; Rissanen et al., 2020). The teacher should be able to examine their own relationship to and understanding of religion to "self-improve" possible biases in how religion is addressed and represented in education.

3.4 *Religious Literacy as Legitimacy Politics*

The third domain emphasizes the role of teachers as critical readers of power when evaluating policies with regard to religion in the public debate and in education. This expands Shulman's (1987) conception of curricular knowledge. As an outcome of this domain, teachers should be required to evaluate their choices of concepts in relation to religion and their role as an authority in relation to students. The question of literacy in educational policy and subsequent discourse can be perceived critically as a question of legitimacy politics. As described earlier, in recent decades Western educational policy and research has been preoccupied with the question of how to best equip citizens for more complex, diverse and global knowledge societies (OECD, 2018). As stated in this discussion, concepts such as "transferable skills," "new learning skills," "life skills" and "21st century skills" have often surfaced. One could argue that in general policymakers, for instance in Finland, have made a conscious choice of concepts (Halinen et al., 2015) that fit well with the Nordic state building ideals of public literacy and quality public education (Buchardt et al., 2013) along with the broader educational trends towards new learning skills (Darling-Hammond, 2006; European Commission, 2013; Newton & Newton, 2014; Niemi & Multisilta, 2016; OECD, 2005; Wang et al., 2018). In Finnish public education, in particular, the terminology of literacy skills has been somewhat emphasized: curricula actively and explicitly promote transversal or multiple literacies (Palsa & Mertala, 2019).

In order to understand the dynamics of the discourse of literacies it is useful to make a distinction between different types of literacies on the basis of their societal status. Barton and Hamilton (1998) have identified dominant and vernacular literacies (Hamilton, 2001; see also Gee, 1990). The dominant literacies are both legally and culturally highly valued institutionalized literacies associated with formal institutions, such as the school. These dominant literacies imply professional experts and teachers who control access to the information with regard to these literacies. The powerfulness of a given literacy is relative to the power of the institution that shapes and maintains it (Hamilton, 2001).

Barton and Hamilton (1998) argue that power structures are present with regard to literacies: while some literacy practices are "supported, controlled and legitimated," others are being "de-valued."

Therefore, it is beneficial if a given area of knowledge or skill is recognized as a "real literacy" (Hamilton, 2001), in other words: among the dominant literacies that are supported and maintained by the establishment and, in our case, educational policy. The use of the concept of religious literacy can therefore be perceived as a political endeavor with the aim of promoting aspects related to religion in society and in education. Here, the aspect of politics and power refers essentially to the use of "literacy" as a legitimizing and justifying tool to promote an area of interest in a socially and politically desirable rhetoric. Similarly to "competence," "literacy" includes not only an aspect of approval in a knowledge society, but also an indication that a lack of this element in one's skillset, for instance, is a deficit and thus to be avoided.

Conceptualizing learning related to religion as "literacy" benefits the case of inclusion of such aims in the national curricula. Alas, "promoting religious literacy" in public education and religious education has been instilled in the political agenda of the multi-faith Finnish Forum of Cooperation of Religions in Finland (Ubani, 2020; Ubani & Tirri, 2014; USKOT, 2020). In the research literature, we can perhaps find parallel cases to religious literacy rather in terms of recognition in the broader academia with respect to the question of intelligences and competences, albeit arguably without a distinct political (in a societal sense) agenda. From there, we can find explicit advocates of spiritual intelligence (Emmons, 2000; Gardner, 2000; Tirri et al., 2006, 2007) and religious competence (Heimbrock & Scheilke, 2001) in the literature around the turn of the millennium, although with limited effect in public education curricula, again due to the sphere of participation. Notably, though, in German *Bundesländer* curricula and literature "competence" has for decades been actively used to describe the aims of religious education (Fricke, 2020).

4   Concluding Remarks: Implications for 21st Century Teacher Education

As societies are and have allegedly moved towards a post-secular age (Habermas, 2006) there is an increasing need to de-construct and re-construct conceptualizations of religion in public education and, therefore, also in teacher education. Although not without challenges (Niemi, 2018), teacher education has been long perceived as forming the basis of the quality of the Finnish education system (Tirri, 2014). According to international evaluation studies (Lee, 2014; Lee & Tan, 2018) teacher education in Finland emphasizes the research ability of teachers: the internalization of a research-based approach is one of the foundational skills of autonomous teachers and functions as the basis of professional "self-improvement" (Lee & Tan, 2018, p. 20). However, as religion in society is a dynamic and evolving phenomenon, skills-based competence with regard to religion is also needed among teachers. Teacher education should adapt to provide sufficient tools for all teachers to handle and understand religion as a dynamic and intersectional phenomenon with global, local, societal, cultural, communal and personal dimensions. In short, it should equip teachers to have critically reflective conceptions of religion in relation to their practice, their pedagogical theory, and professional ethics.

From teacher education this requires deconstructing secularist conceptions of religion in the instruction and evaluation of practices and curricula with regard to the representation of religion. The teachers of today and tomorrow require critical and analytical conceptions of religion within their pedagogical and ethical thinking to enable them to develop a self-improving professional pedagogical approach to religion in public education. It has been argued, for instance, that the handling of religion in Finnish public education is shifting from a secularist framework toward the culturalization of religion within a liberal multiculturalist framework (Ubani, 2019). When compared to the secularist handling of religion, "practical aspects, such as diverse diets, customs and practices are emphasized over diverse truth-claims of religions" (Ubani, 2019, p. 109). If a teacher operates with a secularist professional mindset with regard to religion in public education, this produces a conflict not only with the generic objectives of instruction with regard to dialogue, tolerance and multiculturalist and pluralist recognition, but also with how policy documents perceive religion and multiculturalism in public education (Ubani, 2013).

Shulman in his seminal work asked "What are the sources of teacher knowledge?", "... when did he or she come to know it?" and "How is new knowledge acquired, old knowledge retrieved ... and both combined to form a new knowledge base?" (Shulman, 1987, p. 8). Distinguishing between religious literacy as a professional competence, curricular objective, quality criterion and legitimacy politics offers reflective teacher education a tool for expanding the understanding of skill related to religion(s) in public education. However, in each of these areas authentic research is needed. In terms of curricular objectives, research is needed on how religious literacy develops and evolves in learning. This also holds true for religious literacy as a professional competence; however, here even more emphasis is required for the de-construction of conceptions of the space of religion in modern society and secularization. With regard to quality criteria, it should be examined how to best develop practices where religious and non-religious backgrounds are recognized in a post-secular society. And, finally, in terms of legitimacy politics, critical examination of the stakeholders, voices and motives of participants in the public discussion concerning the space of religion in society and in public education is needed. Critical examination of these issues is required for public education to develop sound and critically developed policies and practices with regard to religions and worldviews in the 21st century school.

References

Åhs, V., Poulter, S., & Kallioniemi, A. (2016). Encountering worldviews: Pupil perspectives on integrative worldview education in a Finnish secondary school context. *Religion & Education*, *43*(2), 208–229. http://dx.doi.org/10.1080/15507394.2015.1128311

Al-Sharmani, M., & Mustasaari S. (2020). Governing divorce practices of Somali Finnish Muslims: Does religious literacy matter? In T. Sakaranaho, T. Aarrevaara, & J. Konttori (Eds.), *The challenges of religious literacy* (pp. 55–66). Springer. https://doi.org/10.1007/978-3-030-47576-5_5

American Academy of Religion. (2019). *AAR religious literacy guidelines*. Retrieved August 6, 2020, from https://www.aarweb.org/AARMBR/Publications-and-News-/Guides-and-Best-Practices-/Teaching-and-Learning/AAR-Religious-Literacy-Guidelines.aspx?WebsiteKey=61d76dfc-e7fe-4820-a0ca-1f792d24c06e

Baartman, L., Bastiaens, T. J., Kirscher, P., & van der Vleuten, C. (2007). Evaluating assessment quality in competence-based education: A qualitative comparison of two frameworks. *Educational Research Review*, *2*(2), 114–129. https://doi.org/10.1016/j.edurev.2007.06.001

Barton, D., & Hamilton, M. (1998). *Local literacies: Reading and writing in one community*. Routledge.

Battelle for Kids. (2009). *A framework for twenty-first century learning*. http://www.p21.org/

Berglund, J. (2017). Secular normativity and the religification of Muslims in Swedish public schooling. *Oxford Review of Education*, 43(5), 524–535. https://doi.org/10.1080/03054985.2017.1352349

Biesta, G. (2002). Bildung and modernity: The future of Bildung in a world of difference. *Studies in Philosophy and Education*, 21(4–5), 343–351.

Biesta, G., Aldridge, D., Hannam, P., & Whittle, S. (2019). *Religious literacy: The way forward for religious education?* Culham St Gabriel's Trust. https://www.reonline.org.uk/news/religious-literacy-a-way-forward-for-religious-education

Binkley, M., Erstad, O., Herman, J., Raizen, S., Ripley, M., Miller-Ricci, M., & Rumble, M. (2012). Defining twenty-first century skills. In P. Griffin, B. McGaw, & E. Care (Eds.), *Assessment and teaching of 21st century skills* (pp. 17–66). Springer.

Brandt, D., & Clinton, K. (2002). Limits of the local: Expanding perspectives on literacy as a social practice. *Journal of Literacy Research*, 34(3), 337–356. https://doi.org/10.1207%2Fs15548430jlr3403_4

Buchardt, M. (2014). *Pedagogized Muslimness: Religion and culture as identity politics in the classroom* (Vol. 27). Waxmann Verlag.

Buchardt, M., Markkola, P., & Valtonen, H. (2013). Introduction. Education and the making of the Nordic welfare states. In M. Buchardt, P. Markkola, & H. Valtonen (Eds.), *Education, state and citizenship* (pp. 7–30). NordWel Studies in Historical Welfare State Research 4. Nordic Centre of Excellence NordWel.

Burrell, D., Rahim, E., Bezio, K., & Goethals, G. (2018). Developing inclusive leaders with religious literacy in the workplace. *Leadership (London, England)*, 14(5), 567–584. https://doi.org/10.1177/1742715018793745

Casanova, J. (2009). The secular and secularisms. *Social Research*, 76(4), 1049–1066.

Casanova, J. (2014). Two dimensions, temporal and spatial of the secular. Comparative reflections on the Nordic Protestant and Southern Catholic patterns from a global perspective. In R. van den Breemer, J. Casanova, & T. Wyller (Eds.), *Secular and sacred? The Scandinavian case of religion in human rights, law and public space* (pp. 21–33). Vandenhoeck & Ruprecht.

Catto, R., & Perfect, D. (2015). Religious literacy, equalities and human rights. In A. Dinham & M. Francis (Eds.), *Religious literacy in policy and practice* (pp. 135–164). Bristol University Press. doi:10.2307/j.ctt1t89c7n.13

Chater, M. (2020). *Reforming RE: Power and knowledge in a worldviews curriculum*. John Catt.

Clarke, C., & Woodhead, L. (2018). *A new settlement revised: Religion and belief in schools*. Westminster Faith Debates. http://faithdebates.org.uk/wp-content/uploads/2018/07/Clarke-Woodhead-A-New-Settlement-Revised.pdf

Clines, J., & Gilliat-Ray, S. (2015). Religious literacy and chaplaincy. In A. Dinham & M. Francis (Eds.), *Religious literacy in policy and practice* (pp. 237–256). Bristol University Press. doi:10.2307/j.ctt1t89c7n.18

Conroy, J. (2015). Religious illiteracy in school Religious Education. In A. Dinham & M. Francis (Eds.), *Religious literacy in policy and practice* (pp. 167–186). Bristol University Press. doi:10.2307/j.ctt1t89c7n.14

Conroy, J. C. (2016). Religious education and religious literacy – A professional aspiration? *British Journal of Religious Education, 38*(2), 163–176. doi:10.1080/01416200.2016.1139891

Coulby, D., & Zambeta, E. (2008). Intercultural education, religion and modernity. Editorial. *Intercultural Education, 19*(4), 293–295. https://doi.org/10.1080/14675980802376812

Cox, E. (1983). *Problems and possibilities for religious education.* Hodder and Stoughton.

Crisp, B. (2015). Religious literacy and social work: The view from Australia. In A. Dinham & M. Francis (Eds.), *Religious literacy in policy and practice* (pp. 207–226). Bristol University Press. doi:10.2307/j.ctt1t89c7n.16

Crisp, B., & Dinham, A. (2019). Are the profession's education standards promoting the religious literacy required for twenty-first century social work practice? *The British Journal of Social Work, 49*(6), 1544–1562. https://doi.org/10.1093/bjsw/bcz050

Darling-Hammond, L. (2006). Constructing 21st century teacher education. *Journal of Teacher Education, 57*(3), 300–314. doi:10.1177/0022487105285962

Davie, G. (2000). *Religion in modern Europe. A memory mutates.* Oxford University Press.

Dede, C. (2009). *Comparing frameworks for "21st century skills."* Harvard Graduate School of Education.

Dinham, A. (2015). Religious literacy and welfare. In A. Dinham & M. Francis (Eds.), *Religious literacy in policy and practice* (pp. 101–112). Bristol University Press. doi:10.2307/j.ctt1t89c7n.11

Dinham, A. (2016). *Comment: Religious literacy: What is the future for religion and belief?* University of Sheffield. https://www.sheffield.ac.uk/news/nr/comment-religious-literacy-what-is-the-future-for-religion-and-belief-1.570731

Dinham, A. (2017). Religious literacy in public and professional settings. In B. Crisp (Ed.), *The Routledge handbook of religion, spirituality and social work* (pp. 257–264). Taylor and Francis. https://doi.org/10.4324/9781315679853

Dinham, A. (2018). Religion and belief in health and social care: The case for religious literacy. *International Journal of Human Rights in Healthcare, 11*(2), 83–90. https://doi.org/10.1108/IJHRH-09-2017-0052

Dinham, A., & Francis, M. (Eds.). (2015). *Religious literacy in policy and practice.* Bristol University Press. doi:10.2307/j.ctt1t89c7n

Dinham, A., & Jones, S. (2012). Religion, Public policy and the academy: Brokering public faith in a context of ambivalence? *Journal of Contemporary Religion, 27,* 185–201. doi:10.1080/13537903.2012.675687

Dinham, A., & Shaw, M. (2017). Religious literacy through religious education: The future of teaching and learning about religion and belief. *Religions, 8*(7). https://doi.org/10.3390/rel8070119

Duranti, A., & Goodwin, C. (Eds.). (1992). *Rethinking context: Language as an interactive phenomenon* (Vol. 11). Cambridge University Press.

Emmons, R. (2000). Is spirituality an intelligence? Motivation, cognition, and the psychology of ultimate concern. *International Journal for the Psychology of Religion, 10*(1), 3–26. doi:10.1207/S15327582IJPR1001_2

European Commission. (2013). *Supporting teacher competence development for better learning outcomes.* http://ec.europa.eu/assets/eac/education/experts-groups/2011-2013/teacher/teachercomp_en.pdf

FNBE. (1994). *Framework curriculum for the comprehensive school.* Finnish National Board of Education.

FNBE. (2014). *Perusopetuksen opetussuunnitelman perusteet 2014* [*National core curriculum for basic education 2014*]. Opetushallitus [Finnish National Board of Education].

Ford, D., & Higton, M. (2015). Religious literacy in the context of theology and religious studies. In A. Dinham & M. Francis (Eds.), *Religious literacy in policy and practice* (pp. 39–54). Policy Press.

Francis, M., & Van Eck Duymaer van Twist, A. (2015). Religious literacy, radicalisation and extremism. In M. Francis & A. Dinham (Eds.), *Religious literacy in policy and practice* (pp. 113–134). Bristol University Press. doi:10.2307/j.ctt1t89c7n.12

Freathy, R., Doney, J., Freathy, G., Walshe, K., & Teece, G. (2017). Pedagogical bricoleurs and bricolage researchers: The case of Religious Education. *British Journal of Educational Studies, 65*(4), 425–443. https://doi.org/10.1080/00071005.2017.1343454

Freathy, R., & John, H. C. (2019). Worldviews and big ideas: A way forward for religious education? *Nordidactica, 4*, 1–27.

Fricke, M. (2020). *FALKO-R: Professional knowledge of teachers of Religious Education (RE). Development of a measuring instrument for subject-specific teacher competence* [Unpublished manuscript]. Institute for Evangelic Theology, University of Regensburg.

Gardner, H. (2000). A case against spiritual intelligence. *International Journal for the Psychology of Religion, 10*(3), 27–34.

Gee, J. P. (1990). *Social linguistics and literacies: Ideology in discourse* (2nd ed.). Falmer-Press.

Gee, J. (2000). The new literacy studies: From 'socially situated' to the work of the social. In D. Barton, M. Hamilton, & R. Ivanic (Eds.), *Situated literacies.* Routledge.

Geisinger, K. (2016). 21st century skills: What are they and how do we assess them? *Applied Measurement in Education, 29*(4), 245–249. https://doi.org/10.1080/08957347.2016.1209207

Griffin, P., Care, E., & McGaw, B. (2012). The changing role of education and schools. defining twenty-first century skills. In P. Griffin, B. McGaw, & E. Care (Eds.), *Assessment and teaching of 21st century skills* (pp. 17–66). Springer.

Grimmitt, M. (1973). *What can I do in RE?* McCrimmons.

Guilland, A., Terzieva, L., & Nieminen, S. (2017). *Teaching and learning transversal competences in the higher education: Learnings from ERASMUS + SOCCES-project.* International Academy of Technology, Education and Development. doi:10.21125/inted.2017.0044

Habermas, J. (2006). Religion in the public sphere. *European Journal of Philosophy, 14*(1), 1–25. https://doi.org/10.1111/j.1468-0378.2006.00241.x

Halinen, I., Harmanen, M., & Mattila, P. (2015). Making sense of complexity of the world today: Why Finland is introducing multiliteracy in teaching and learning 2015. In V. Bozsik (Ed.), *Improving literacy skills across learning. CIDREE yearbook 2015* (pp. 136–153). HIERD.

Hamilton, M. (2001). Privileged literacies: Policy, institutional process and the life of the IALS. *Language and Education, 15*(2–3), 178–196.

Hammer, A., & Schanke, Å. J. (2018). 'Why can't you just eat pork?' Teachers' perspectives on criticism of religion in Norwegian religious education. *Journal of Religious Education, 66*(2), 151–164.

Hannam, P., & Biesta, G. (2019). Religious education, a matter of understanding? Reflections on the final report of the Commission on Religious Education. *Journal of Beliefs & Values, 40*(1), 55–63. doi:10.1080/13617672.2018.1554330

Hannam, P., Biesta, G., Whittle, S., & Aldridge, D. (2020). Religious literacy: A way forward for religious education? *Journal of Beliefs & Values, 41*(2), 214–226. https://doi.org/10.1080/13617672.2020.1736969

Harju, V., & Niemi, H. (2016). Newly qualified teachers' needs of support for professional competences in four European countries: Finland, the United Kingdom, Portugal, and Belgium. *CEPS Journal, 6*(3), 77–100.

Heimbrock, H. G., & Scheilke, C. T. (2001). *Towards religious competence: Diversity as a challenge for education in Europe* (Vol. 3). LIT Verlag.

Hilska, P. (2003). Juhlapyhien vietto monikulttuurisessa päiväkodissa [Celebrations in multicultural daycare centres]. In A. Kallioniemi, A. Räsänen, & P. Hilska (Eds.), *Lapsen sielun maisema [Spirituality of the child]* (pp. 107–126). Studia Paedagogica 30. Helsingin yliopisto [University of Helsinki].

Hilska, P. (2004). Monikulttuurisuuden kohtaaminen [Encountering multiculturalism]. In L. Heinonen, J. Luodeslampi, & L. Salmensaari (Eds.), *Lapsityön käsikirja [Handbook of education of children]* (pp. 73–88). Kirjapaja Oy.

Hirsch, E. (1987). *Cultural literacy: What every American needs to know.* Houghton Mifflin.

Hofstee, W., & van der Kooij, A. (2013). Introduction. In W. Hofstee & A. van der Kooij (Eds.), *Religion beyond its private role in modern society* (pp. 1–11). Brill.

Hull, J. M. (2002). The contribution of Religious Education to religious freedom. In P. Schreiner, J. Taylor, & W. Westerman (Eds.), *Committed to Europe's future. Contributions from education and Religious Education* (pp. 107–110). Comenius-Institut, Protestant Centre for Studies in Education.

Jackson, R. (2014). *'Signposts': Policy and practice for teaching about religions and non-religious worldviews in intercultural education*. Council of Europe Publishing.

Jones, S. (2015). Religious literacy in higher education. In A. Dinham & M. Francis (Eds.), *Religious literacy in policy and practice* (pp. 187–206). Bristol University Press. doi:10.2307/j.ctt1t89c7n.15

Kallioniemi, A. (2000). *Helsinkiläisten lastentarhanopettajien käsityksiä päiväkodin uskonnollisesta kasvatuksesta ja sen toteuttamisesta* [Perceptions of early childhood education teachers about religious education]. Helsingin yliopiston opettajankoulutuslaitos [Department of Teacher Education, University of Helsinki].

Kallioniemi, A. (2005). Varhaiskasvatuksen uskontokasvatus monikulttuuristuvassa maailmassa [Religious education in early childhood education in multicultural world]. In P. Hilska, A. Kallioniemi, & J. Luodeslampi (Eds.), *Uskontokasvatus monikulttuurisessa maailmassa* [Religious education in multicultural world] (pp. 11–37). Kirjapaja Oy.

Kittelmann-Flensner, K., Larsson, G., & Säljö, R. (2019). Jihadists and refugees at the theatre: Global conflicts in classroom practices in Sweden. *Education Sciences, 9*(2), 80. https://doi.org/10.3390/educsci9020080

Kunzman, R. (2005). Religion, politics and civic education. *Journal of Philosophy of Education, 39*(1), 159–168.

Kunzman, R. (2006). Imaginative engagement with religious diversity in public school classrooms. *Religious Education, 10*(4), 516–531.

Lankshear, C., & Knobel, M. (2011). *New literacies. Everyday practices and social learning* (3rd ed.). McGraw-Hill.

Lavonen, J., & Laaksonen, S. (2009). Context of teaching and learning school science in Finland: Reflections on PISA 2006 results. *Journal of Research in Science Teaching, 46*(8), 922–944. https://doi.org/10.1002/tea.20339

Lee, W. O. (2014). Comparative analysis of high performing education systems: Teachers, teaching and teacher education as factors of success. In S. O. Lee, W. O. Lee, & E. L. Low (Eds.), *Educational policy innovations* (pp. 217–229). Springer.

Lee, W. O., & Tan, J. P. L. (2018). The new roles for twenty-first-century teachers: Facilitator, knowledge broker, and pedagogical weaver. In H. Niemi, A. Toom, A. Kallioniemi, & J. Lavonen (Eds.), *The teacher's role in the changing globalizing world. Resources and challenges related to the professional work of teaching* (pp. 11–31). Brill Sense.

Lemettinen, J., Hirvonen, E., & Ubani, M. (2021). Is worldview education achieved in schools? A study of Finnish teachers' perceptions of worldview education as a component of basic education. *Journal of Beliefs and Values*. https//doi.org/ 10.1080/ 13617672.2021.1889218

Marcus, B. (2018). Religious literacy in American education. In M. Waggoner & N. Walker (Eds.), *The Oxford handbook of religion and American education*. Oxford University Press. https://doi.org/10.1093/oxfordhb/9780199386819.013.38

Miedema, S. (2018). Personal world view, existential questions and inclusive pedagogy. Theological and pedagogical underpinnings. In J. Ristiniemi, G. Skeie, & K. Sporre (Eds.), *Challenging life. Existential questions as a resource for education* (pp. 137–155). Waxmann.

Moore, D. (2014). Overcoming religious illiteracy: Expanding the boundaries of Religious Education. *Religious Education, 109*(4), 379–389. doi:10.1080/00344087.2014.924765

Moore, D. (2015). Diminishing religious literacy: Methodological assumptions and analytical frameworks for promoting the public understanding of religion. In A. Dinham & M. Francis (Eds.), *Religious literacy in policy and practice* (pp. 27–38). Policy Press.

Newton, L. D., & Newton, D. P. (2014). Creativity in 21st-century education. *Prospects, 44*, 575–589. doi:10.1007/s11125-014-9322-1

Niemi, H. (2012). Relationships of teachers' professional competences, active learning and research studies in teacher education in Finland. *Reflecting Education, 8*(2), 23–44.

Niemi, H. (2014). Teachers as active contributors in quality of education: A special reference to the Finnish context. In D. Hung, K. Y. T. Lim, & S.-S. Lee (Eds.), *Adaptivity as a transformative disposition for learning in the 21st century* (pp. 179–199). Springer.

Niemi, H. (2015). Teacher professional development in Finland: Towards a more holistic approach. *Psychology, Society and Education, 7*(3), 278–294. doi:10.25115/psye.v7i3.519

Niemi, H. (2018). *Maailman parhaiksi opettajiksi: Vuosina 2016–2018 toimineen Opettajankoulutusfoorumin arviointi* [*To become the best teachers of the world. Evaluation of Teacher Education Forum (2016–2018)*]. Kansallinen koulutuksen arviointikeskus KARVI [Finnish Educational Evaluation Centre FINEEC].

Niemi, H., & Multisilta, J. (2016). Digital storytelling promoting twenty-first century skills and student engagement. *Technology, Pedagogy and Education, 25*(4), 451–468. doi:10.1080/1475939X.2015.1074610

Niemi, H., Niu, S., Vivitsou, M., & Li, B. (2018). Digital storytelling for twenty-first-century competencies with math literacy and student engagement in China and Finland. *Contemporary Educational Technology, 9*(4), 331–353. doi:10.30935/cet.470999

Niemi, P.-M. (2019). Religion and secularity in school festivals–experiences and challenges from Finland. In M. Ubani, I. Rissanen, & S. Poulter (Eds.), *Contextualising dialogue, secularisation and pluralism – Religion in Finnish public education* (pp. 145–164). Waxmann.

Niemi, P.-M., Kuusisto, A., & Kallioniemi, A. (2014). Discussing school celebrations from an intercultural perspective–a study in the Finnish context. *Intercultural Education*, *25*(4), 255–268.

OECD. (2005). *Attracting, developing and retaining effective teachers. Final report: Teachers matter.* OECD Publishing.

OECD. (2018). *The future of education and skills. Education 2030.* OECD Publishing.

Oliver, B., & St Jorre, T. (2018). Graduate attributes for 2020 and beyond: Recommendations for Australian higher education providers. *Higher Education Research & Development*, *37*(4), 821–836.

OSCE. (2007). *The Toledo guiding principles on teaching about religions and beliefs in public schools.* Organisation for Security and Co-operation in Europe, Office or Democratic Institutions and Human Rights. http://www.osce.org/odihr/29154

Palsa, L., & Mertala, P. (2019). Multiliteracies in local curricula: Conceptual contextualizations of transversal competence in the Finnish curricular framework. *Nordic Journal of Studies in Educational Policy*, *5*(2), 114–126. doi:10.1080/20020317.2019.1635845

Parker, S. (2020). Religious literacy: Spaces of teaching and learning about religion and belief. *Journal of Beliefs & Values*, *41*(2), 129–131. doi:10.1080/13617672.2020.1750243

Pauha, T., & Konttori, J. (2020). "There is freedom of religion in Finland, but …" The Helsinki mosque debate. In T. Sakaranaho, T. Aarrevaara, & J. Konttori (Eds.), *The challenges of religious literacy.* Springer. https://doi.org/10.1007/978-3-030-47576-5_2

Prothero, S. (2007). *Religious literacy: What every American needs to know – and doesn't.* Harper Collins.

Rajakaltio, H. (2014). *Yhteisvoimin kohti uudistuvaa koulua. Koulun kehittämisen toimintamalli – täydennyskoulutuksen ja kehittämisprosessin yhteen nivominen.* [*Towards renewing school. The action model of the school development – Integrating in-service-training and the development process*]. Reports and reviews 2014:9. Finnish National Board of Education.

Richardson, M. J. (2017). Religious literacy, moral recognition, and strong relationality. *Journal of Moral Education*, *46*(4), 363–377. https://doi.org.ezproxy.uef.fi:2443/10.1080/03057240.2017.1324771

Riitaoja, A.-L., Poulter, S., & Kuusisto, A. (2010). Worldviews and multicultural education in the Finnish context – A critical philosophical approach to theory and practices. *Finnish Journal of Ethnicity and Migration*, *5*(3), 87–95.

Rissanen, I. (2018). Negotiations on inclusive citizenship in a post-secular school: Perspectives of "cultural broker" Muslim parents and teachers in Finland and Sweden. *Scandinavian Journal of Educational Research.* doi:10.1080/00313831.2018.1514323

Rissanen, I., Ubani, M., & Poulter, S. (2019). Key issues of religion in Finnish public education. In M. Ubani, I. Rissanen, & S. Poulter (Eds.), *Contextualising dialogue, secularisation and pluralism. Religion in Finnish public education* (pp. 203–216). Waxmann.

Rissanen, I., Ubani, M., & Sakaranaho, T. (2020). Challenges of religious literacy in education: Islam and the governance of religious diversity in multi-faith schools. In T. Sakaranaho, T. Aarrevaara, & J. Konttori (Eds.), *The challenges of religious literacy*. Springer. https://doi.org/10.1007/978-3-030-47576-5_4

Rothgangel, M. (2014). Conceptions of religious education and didactical structures. In G. Adam, M. Rothgangel, R. Lachmann, T. Schlag, & F. Schweitzer (Eds.), *Basics of religious education* (pp. 63–80). V&R unipress GmbH.

Rothgangel, M., Jäggle, M., & Skeie, G. (Eds.). (2014). *Religious education at schools in Europe. Part 3: Northern Europe* (pp. 99–120). Vienna University Press.

Räsänen, R., Jokikokko, K., & Lampinen, J. (2018). *Kulttuuriseen moninaisuuteen liittyvä osaaminen perusopetuksessa. Kartoitus tutkimuksesta sekä opetushenkilöstön koulutuksesta ja osaamisen tuesta* [Competence in cultural diversity in basic education. A survey on research and education and support of teachers]. Reports and reviews 2018(6). Finnish National Board of Education.

Shaw, M. (2019). *Teaching and learning about religion and worldviews in English schools: Religion and worldview literacy* [Doctoral dissertation, VID Specialized University, Oslo]. VID Open. https://hdl.handle.net/11250/2648273

Shaw, M. (2020). Towards a religiously literate curriculum – Religion and worldview literacy as an educational model. *Journal of Beliefs & Values, 41*(2), 150–161. doi:10.1080/13617672.2019.1664876

Shulman, L. S. (1986). Those who understand: A conception of teacher knowledge. *American Educator, 10*(1), 4–14.

Shulman, L. S. (1987). Knowledge and teaching: Foundations of the new reform. *Harvard Educational Review, 57*(1), 1–23.

Skeie, G. (2019, June 11–14). *What must be taught and what must be learned in religious education?* Keynote address at the 15th Nordic Conference of Religious Education, Norwegian University of Science and Technology, Trondheim, Norway.

Taylor, C. (2004). The politics of recognition. In A. Guttman (Ed.), *C. Taylor: Multiculturalism. Examining the politics of recognition* (pp. 25–73). Princeton University.

Thalén, P. (2020). World view instead of religion? In O. Franck & P. Thalén (Eds.), *Religious education in a post-secular age: Case studies from Europe* (pp. 157–178). Palgrave Macmillan.

Thalén, P., & Carlsson, D. (2020). Teaching secular worldviews in a post-aecular age. *Religion & Education, 47*(3), 243–256. doi:10.1080/15507394.2020.1785811

Tiilikainen, M., & Mankkinen, T. (2020). Prevention of violent radicalization and extremism in Finland: The role of religious literacy. In T. Sakaranaho, T. Aarrevaara, & J. Konttori (Eds.), *The challenges of religious literacy*. Springer. https://doi.org/10.1007/978-3-030-47576-5_6

Tirri, K. (2014). The last 40 years in Finnish teacher education. *Journal of Education for Teaching, 40*(5), 600–609. doi:10.1080/02607476.2014.956545

Tirri, K., Nokelainen, P., & Ubani, M. (2006). Conceptual definition and empirical validation of the spiritual sensitivity scale. *Journal of Empirical Theology*, 19(1), 37–62.

Tirri, K., Nokelainen, P., & Ubani, M. (2007). Do gifted children have spiritual intelligence? In K. Tirri (Ed.), *Values and foundations in gifted education* (pp. 187–202). Peter Lang.

Tynjälä, P., Virtanen, A., Klemola, U., Kostiainen, E. G., & Rasku-Puttonen, H. (2016). Developing social competence and other generic skills in teacher education: Applying the model of integrative pedagogy. *European Journal of Teacher Education*, 39(3), 368–387. doi:10.1080/02619768.2016.1171314

Ubani, M. (2013). Threats and solutions. Religion and multiculturalism in educational policy. *Intercultural Education*, 24(3), 195–210.

Ubani, M. (2017). Contextualising the contribution of RE scholarly communities and to the developments of RE in Finland over recent decades. *NordDidactica*, 1, 87–108.

Ubani, M. (2018). When teachers face religion in public education. Case examples from Finnish public education. *Journal of Religious Education*, 6(22), 139–150. https://doi.org/10.1007/s40839-018-0064-x

Ubani, M. (2019). Religion and multiculturalism in Finnish public schools. The secularist–culturalist transition. In M. Ubani, I. Rissanen, & S. Poulter (Eds.), *Contextualising dialogue, secularisation and pluralism. Religion in Finnish public education* (pp. 105–126). Waxmann.

Ubani, M. (2020). *Religionsunterricht in Finnland*. Wirelex. https://www.bibelwissenschaft.de/fileadmin/buh_bibelmodul/media/wirelex/pdf/Religionsunterricht_in_Finnland__2020-03-03_07_55.pdf

Ubani, M., & Ojala, E. (2018). Introduction. *Journal of Religious Education*, 66(2), 79–83. doi:10.1007/s40839-018-0067-7

Ubani, M., Poulter, S., & Rissanen, I. (2019). Introduction to contextualising dialogue, pluralism and secularisation. In M. Ubani, I. Rissanen, & S. Poulter (Eds.), *Contextualising dialogue, secularisation and pluralism. Religion in Finnish public education* (pp. 7–16). Waxmann.

Uljens, M., & Rajakaltio, H. (2017). National curriculum development as educational leadership: A discursive and non-affirmative approach. In M. Uljens & R. Ylimäki (Eds.), *Bridging educational leadership, curriculum theory and didaktik* (pp. 411–437). Springer.

Ubani, M., & Tirri, K. (2014). Religious education in Finnish schools. In M. Rothgangel, M. Jäggle, & G. Skeie (Eds.), *Religious education in schools in Europe. Part 3: Northern Europe* (pp. 99–120). Vienna University Press.

USKOT. (2020). *USKOT-foorumin hallitusohjelmatavoitteet* [*The objectives of USKOT-forum*]. https://uskot.fi/2019/04/hallitusohjelmatavoitteet/

Valk, J. (2017). Worldview inclusion in public schooling. In M. Etherington (Ed.), *What teachers need to know: Topics of inclusion* (pp. 233–248). Wipf & Stock.

Viinikka, K., & Ubani, M. (2019). The expectations of Finnish RE student teachers of their professional development in their academic studies in the light of 21st century skills. *Journal of Beliefs & Values*, 40(4), 447–463. doi:10.1080/13617672.2019.1618153

Viinikka, K., & Ubani, M. (2020). A qualitative analysis of Finnish RE students' perceptions of their professional development during their initial teacher education. *Journal of Beliefs & Values*. Advance online publication. doi:10.1080/13617672.2020.1805924

Viinikka, K., Ubani, M., Lipiäinen T., & Kallioniemi, A. (2019). 21st century skills and Finnish student teachers' perceptions about the ideal RE teacher today and in the future. *International Journal of Learning, Teaching and Educational Research*, 18(8), 75–97. doi:10.26803/ijlter.18.8.5

Virtanen, A., & Tynjälä, P. (2019). Factors explaining the learning of generic skills: A study of university students' experiences. *Teaching in Higher Education*, 24(7), 880–894. doi:10.1080/13562517.2018.1515195

Wakelin, M., & Spencer, N. (2015). Religious literacy and the media: The case of the BBC. In A. Dinham & M. Francis (Eds.), *Religious literacy in policy and practice* (pp. 227–236). Bristol University Press. doi:10.2307/j.ctt1t89c7n.17

Wang, Y., Lavonen, J., & Tirri, K. (2018). Aims for learning 21st century competencies in national primary science curricula in China and Finland. *EURASIA Journal of Mathematics, Science and Technology Education*, 14(6), 2081–2095. https://doi.org/10.29333/ejmste/86363

Wright, A. (1993). *Religious education in the secondary school: Prospects for religious literacy*. David Fulton Publishers.

Wright, A. (2000). The spiritual education project: Cultivating spiritual and religious literacy through a critical pedagogy of religious education. In M. Grimmitt (Ed.), *Pedagogies of religious education: Case studies in the research and development of good pedagogic practice in RE* (pp. 107–187). McCrimmon.

Wright, E. (2008). Developing students' worldview literacy through variation: pedagogical prospects of critical religious education and the variation theory of learning for further education. *Journal of Chaplaincy in Further Education*, 5(1), 4–12.

PART 2

Supporting Talent Development with a Growth Mindset

CHAPTER 10

Education of the Gifted and Talented in Finland

Elina Kuusisto, Sonja Laine and Inkeri Rissanen

Abstract

The focus in this chapter is on the education of gifted and talented students in Finland. Firstly, we discuss historical and current developments in Finland's educational policy in relation to the gifted. We show how the egalitarian Finnish educational system has not invested in education for these students, which depends on the initiative of individual teachers. Secondly, we focus on the educational experiences of Finland's gifted and talented through empirical studies that identify family and inner drive as critical factors in talent development. Formal education seems to have a minimal role in these experiences. Thirdly, toward the end of the chapter we ponder further on the lack of understanding in the Finnish school context that gifted and talented students may be in need of support. We also introduce growth mindset pedagogy as one possible route to addressing the needs of these students.

Keywords

giftedness – talented – gifted education – growth mindset pedagogy – Finland

1   **Introduction**

One of the core principles of the Finnish educational system has been equality, indicating that all students regardless of their background are given equal opportunities to develop as human beings. Equality in this context has been generally interpreted as supporting students with learning disabilities and difficulties, leaving the needs of the gifted and talented somewhat neglected. However, and for the first time, the most recent Finnish *National core curriculum for basic education 2014* (Finnish National Board of Education [FNBE], 2016) mentions "talented pupils," and acknowledges the importance of differentiated teaching with them in mind. This implies the strengthening recognition in pre- and in-service teacher education of the need among talented students for challenging learning tasks, and of the need among teachers to develop practices of differentiated teaching.

In this chapter, therefore, we give an overview of historical and current developments in Finnish educational policy related to the education of gifted and talented children. We also summarize empirical studies conducted in Finland that concern the educational experiences of gifted students in the domains of academia, the creative arts, sport, and vocational education. As these studies show, the lack of special education has obstructed the learning paths of these students, and even caused frustration and social exclusion. Studies also demonstrate how inner drive and support from parents and some individual teachers during their school career can be a game changer and guide gifted students towards realizing their talents. Finally, we introduce the notion of growth mindset pedagogy (Rissanen et al., 2019), which is a promising approach to addressing critical aspects in the education of the talented and the gifted in everyday classroom interaction. Mindset theory sheds light on why talented and gifted students may also be fragile and in need of support. A growth mindset pedagogy could help them develop the ability to meet challenges and to cope with failure.

2 The History and Current State of Gifted Education in Finland

2.1 *Building a Nation and a Welfare State – Educational Trends before the 1970s*

Table 10.1 presents the main trends in the Finnish educational system and in gifted education. The roots of the educational system lie in the 16th and 17th centuries when Finnish was established as a literary language, early forms of schooling were in place, and the first university was established (Uljens & Nyman, 2013). Under the Lutheran reformation, the aim of education was to socialize people into religion by teaching reading skills to everyone: for example, the Lutheran Church considered literacy a prerequisite for marriage (Niemi & Sinnemäki, 2019). On the other hand, grammar schools and university education were available for children from families with financial resources, and for those who were considered academically gifted.

The educational system in Finland was sociocentric for a long time, meaning that education was the key element in building *a nation* from the 1800s until the Second World War, and *a welfare state* thereafter (Simola, 2014a). Education was aimed at cultivating individuals to fit into society and its structures. Elementary schooling was established in 1866, and the state gradually assumed responsibility for education. The parallel system stayed in place through the

TABLE 10.1   Educational trends and gifted education in Finland

---

BEFORE THE 1970S: BUILDING A NATION AND A WELFARE STATE
Sociocentrism: Individuals are educated to fit into society
Parallel school system
    Elementary school compulsory for every child in 1921– (est. in 1866)
    followed by vocational education
    Grammar school for the *academically gifted* (established in the 1600s)
    followed by vocational education or academic education at upper-secondary
    school and university (first university established in 1640)
Educational reforms in the 1960s
    Comprehensive school and academic teacher education
Enrichment programs
    Finnish students in the International Mathematical Olympiad in 1965
SINCE THE 1970S: EDUCATING INDIVIDUALS
Individualism: Society is to be changed to serve individuals' needs
Educational system:
    Kindergarten and preschool (age 1–5, 6, respectively)
    Basic education (nine-year comprehensive school for all, age 7–15)
    Secondary education (academic or vocational)
    Higher education
Since the 1970s: Equal opportunities for all
    Free education, materials, meals, transportation, special education for
    students with learning challenges
    A negative stand on differentiated education for gifted children
Since the 1980s: The decentralization of decision-making
    Municipalities (1980s–), schools and teachers (1990s–), parents
    (2000s–) involved in curriculum development
Since the 1990s: Acknowledgement of diversity
    Multiculturalism, EU, refugees, indigenous and historical minorities
    Specified schools established in different domains, e.g., Päivölä Institute
    for mathematically gifted upper-secondary students
Since the 2000s: The ideology of inclusion
    No discrimination at any level, all pupils study together
    Support and enrichment brought to the classroom
Since the 2010s: Differentiated teaching, also for the gifted and talented
    Differentiated teaching defined as the pedagogical basis of all teaching
    Talented students mentioned in the National core curriculum of 2014
    Collaboration between universities and upper secondary schools

two world wars and the establishment of Finland as an independent state in 1917 until the 1970s. Elementary school taught the basics and students moved on to vocational education, whereas grammar schools taught academically gifted students who were able to progress to vocational school or academically-oriented upper-secondary school, and even university. Within this system, teacher education for grammar schools, in other words for subject teachers, has been university-based since the late 1800s. On the other hand, teachers for elementary schools graduated from vocational-level seminars, which became a popular path that allowed students from rural areas to climb the socioeconomic ladder, and this applied especially to gifted females (Simola, 2014b; Tirri, 2014).

Societal changes in the 1960s and influences from the Social Democratic Movement inspired bold educational reforms that ended parallel schooling and established nine-year basic education in a comprehensive school, which offered equal learning opportunities to every student (Simola, 2014a). Academic teacher education was now established for teachers in elementary schools (Tirri, 2014). Quite apart from the educational reforms and in the context of gifted education, participation in the International Mathematical Olympiad became a possibility for Finnish students in 1965, indicating a need for new enrichment programs for gifted students at upper-secondary school (Tirri, 2001).

2.2   Educating Individuals – Trends since the 1970s

The educational paradigm shifted from sociocentrism to individualism in 1970s, meaning that, for the first time in Finnish history, the aim of education was not to socialize students into certain societal structures but to teach them to influence society to serve and meet the needs of individuals (Simola et al., 2014). Finnish educational policy strongly emphasized equality among individuals. In the 1970s this meant that the curriculum was centralized on the national level, and educational investments were made to equalize opportunities and to improve the health of the nation. Basic education was free of charge, including a warm meal, materials, transportation, and special education for students with learning challenges. In this atmosphere, all attempts to develop gifted education was considered elitist, and "a negative stand on differentiated education for gifted children was officially taken in a committee report in 1970" (Tirri & Uusikylä, 1994, p. 69).

The decentralization of decision-making in the 1980s enabled municipalities to create their own curricula, and since then the Finnish National Board of Education has provided a National core curriculum as a general framework to guide education. As a consequence, municipalities (since the 1980s), principals and teachers (since the 1990s), and parents and other stakeholders (since the 2000s) have had more say in designing and organizing teaching. This trend is promising from the perspective of gifted and talented education as well, given the increased opportunities for specialized and individualized teaching (Tirri, 1997; Tirri & Kuusisto, 2013).

More emphasis has been put on individuality, freedom of choice and diversity since the 1990s (Tirri, 1997; Tirri & Kuusisto, 2013). Internationalization through membership of the European Union and the waves of refugees and immigrants led to the recognition of multiculturalism in Finnish society, including the indigenous Samí culture and historical minorities such as Swedish-speaking Finns, Jews, and Tatars. The Finnish Constitution (731/1999) and the Basic Education Act (628/1998) mention pupils' individual needs and abilities as the basis of education, and specifies the importance of being responsive to the age and requirements of students when arranging instruction. These ideas were also emphasized in the professional codes of ethics for teachers published in 1998 (Tirri & Kuusisto, 2013, 2019).

Public debate resurfaced in the 1990s concerning the need for special education for gifted children, resulting in an official educational policy acknowledging special programs for the gifted and granting 32 upper-secondary schools permission to offer a differentiated curriculum in certain subjects (Tirri & Uusikylä, 1994). In 1994, for example, Päivölä Institute established a mathematical track for academically gifted and talented upper-secondary students (E. Lappi, personal communication, August 21, 2020). The number of specialized schools and tracks have been increasing over the years (Tirri & Kuusisto, 2013), although the overall number is low given the total number of schools in Finland.

All in all, changes during the 1990s facilitated acceleration and flexibly scheduled studies (especially at upper-secondary school) for gifted and talented students (Tirri, 1997), and gave teachers more options in differentiating their teaching. Teachers in elementary schools favored differentiation in regular classes, but they were more negative toward the idea of separate schools and classes than their colleagues in secondary schools (Tirri & Uusikylä, 1994). It was reported in another study that Finnish teachers preferred to keep gifted students in normal classes (Ojanen & Freeman, 1994). Interestingly, similar results were reported over 20 years later: teachers continued to support differentiated teaching, but their attitudes toward acceleration and separating gifted students into their own groups were negative. Further and more worryingly, they were quite skeptical about being able to address the needs of gifted students in their teaching (Laine et al., 2019).

Finland signed UNESCO's (1994) Salamanca statement on inclusive education in 1994. However, it was not until almost a decade later, in the 2000s, that inclusive principles appeared on the agenda in the Finnish educational system. Inclusion was understood as ensuring equality and organizing education for students with special educational needs i.e., students with learning disabilities and difficulties (Halinen & Järvinen, 2008). Thus, the understanding of inclusion followed a narrow definition: taking the perspective of some specific groups of students (Ainscow et al., 2006; Armstrong et al., 2011; Tirri & Laine, 2017), among which the gifted and talented were not included at this stage.

2.3 Differentiated Teaching, for the Gifted and Talented, too – Gifted Education Since the 2010s

In 2011 the Finnish National Board of Education published a document entitled "Amendments and Additions to the National Core Curriculum for Basic Education." Some of the changes concerned the section on support for learning and schooling, and support related to the teaching arrangements. One of the main ones was the highlighting of differentiated teaching, which was identified as "the central way to acknowledge the needs of the class and students' differences" (FNBE, 2011, p. 9). Even though the document did not address gifted and talented students specifically, it was applicable to them in that differentiation was seen as a way of offering (1) proper challenges and fostering feelings of success and (2) encouraging students to develop and learn according to their individual strengths (FNBE, 2011).

Gifted and talented students were finally addressed explicitly in the *National core curriculum for basic education 2014*, which mentioned "talented pupils" [in Finnish taitavat oppijat] and "those [who are] advancing faster" [in Finnish nopeammin etenevät] (FNBE, 2014, 2016). The curriculum also gave some specific examples of how to differentiate teaching for these students. Thus, inclusion was now understood from a broad perspective, that is non-discriminatory education for all students (Ainscow et al., 2006). All students regardless of their cultural, religious or socioeconomic backgrounds, disabilities, learning difficulties or giftedness profiles were expected to study together in the same classroom, in which teachers could cater for individual needs by means of co-teaching and multi-professional collaboration (Mäkinen, 2013). From the perspective of gifted and talented students this could have been promising. However, it was revealed in the PISA (Program for International Student Assessment) studies during the 2010s that the achievement outcomes of Finnish students had begun to decline (Kupari et al., 2013; Leino et al., 2019). The decline was evident at both ends of the spectrum: there were more and more students on the lowest levels and fewer on the two highest levels (Hautamäki et al., 2015). Among the high-achieving students, the decline was in all the measured subjects. There may have been many reasons for this strong deterioration (Hautamäki et al., 2015), but in any case the results indicate that schools have not been able to give adequate support to high achievers.

In sum, Finland lacks a formal definition of giftedness or talent, and there are no formal identification criteria. Still, teachers are responsible for identifying the differing needs of students, which they address via differentiated teaching. In this respect, the Finnish educational system follows the so-called differentiation paradigm in gifted education (Laine, 2016a; see also Dai & Chen, 2013). This paradigm stems from the values of equality and inclusiveness, meaning that support for gifted and talented students is organized within the regular classes and mainly in general comprehensive schools. However, it is widely understood that gifted students do not receive sufficient attention at school (Laine, 2016b; Laine et al., 2019). Indeed, the whole topic is rather sensitive in Finland, provoking strong emotions and debate (Laine, 2016b).

Meeting the needs of gifted and talented students and fulfilling the promises of differentiated teaching depends on individual teachers, which could lead to inequality in delivering quality education to the gifted (Laine, 2016a). Finnish teacher education is internationally valued and respected, and Finnish teachers are highly educated. However, they are not currently given any formal and mandatory education about the gifted and their needs: how the topic is handled depends totally on the university. This is an evident weakness and could have far-reaching consequences. Teacher education should thus cover the successful inclusion of students who are different, such as the gifted, in the goal of producing teachers who can reflect on their values, beliefs and attitudes. This, in turn, would influence their pedagogical thinking and teaching practice in an inclusive school system (Tirri & Laine, 2017).

3 Talent Development in Finland – Lessons from Empirical Studies

We will now shift the perspective and take a closer look at studies that investigated gifted and talented people educated within the Finnish egalitarian system described above.[1] Various critical factors for talent development have been identified in these empirical studies, which we summarize below.

In fact, there were relatively few empirical studies on this topic until the Academy of Finland funded a research project entitled "Actualizing Finnish giftedness" in 1999–2007, led by Kirsi Tirri. Studies conducted by Tirri and her colleagues investigated the development of *academic giftedness in mathematics and science,* focusing on Finnish Olympians studying math, chemistry and physics who competed during 1965–1999 (e.g., Tirri, 2001; Tirri & Campbell, 2002; see also Nokelainen & Tirri, 2010; Nokelainen, Tirri, & Merenti-Välimäki,

2007; Tirri & Kuusisto, 2018; Tirri & Nokelainen, 2010; for international comparative studies see e.g., Nokelainen et al., 2004; Nokelainen, Tirri, Campbell et al., 2007; Campbell et al., 2017), and Finnish Academy professors in the field of science (Koro-Ljungberg, 2001; Koro-Ljungberg & Tirri, 2002; Tirri & Koro-Ljungberg, 2002).

Other Finnish studies have explored *creative talents*. Inkeri Ruokonen (2005; Ruokonen et al., 2011) and her colleagues examined the development of musical talent among children aged 6–8 and university students in Finland and Estonia, for example, and Joey Chua (2015) studied the development of talent among Finnish and Singaporean professional dancers. Studies on talent development in *sports* have investigated Finnish Olympic gold medalists (Rahkamo, 2016) and young aspiring elite athletes (Aarresola, 2016). Further, Petri Nokelainen (2010, 2018) and his colleagues have examined the development of *vocational excellence* among Finnish participants in WorldSkills Competitions (e.g., Korpelainen et al., 2009; Nokelainen et al., 2009; Pylväs, 2018; Pylväs & Nokelainen, 2017; see also the international comparative report of Nokelainen et al., 2012).

Table 10.2 summarizes findings from Finnish empirical studies, and highlights critical factors in Finnish talent development that relate to *individual, contextual* and *coincidental factors* in *early childhood, school years*, and *college years and adulthood*.

3.1 Individual Factors in Finnish Talent Development

3.1.1 Natural Abilities – Gifts

Individual factors refer to *natural abilities* or gifts that are usually evident in early childhood. Science Olympians had typically learned to read at the age of three or four, for example (Tirri, 2001). In the case of creative arts and sports, such as dance, early potential could be detected in the right bodily proportions, flexibility, the ability to remember movements and to concentrate (Chua, 2015). In the vocational domain, WorldSkills competitors also showed natural abilities in early childhood, even though in many cases student giftedness was identified by their teacher at vocational school (Korpelainen et al., 2009; Nokelainen, 2010).

3.1.2 Inner Drive

Finnish studies indicate that *inner drive* is even more important than natural ability in talent development. It refers to motivation and persistence to practice, and could also be described as intrinsic motivation (Chua, 2015; Korpelainen et al., 2009), intrinsic characteristics or self-regulatory abilities (Pylväs & Nokelainen, 2017). Research participants studied in early childhood already showed an interest in mathematics and conducting scientific experiments, and in music, dance, or sports (e.g., Aarresola, 2016; Chua, 2015; Ruokonen, 2005; Rahkamo, 2016; Tirri, 2001). Moreover, Olympic athletes who did not differ from other children in terms of natural abilities when they started their sports activities in local clubs, demonstrated resilience as children in practicing longer and more than others (Rahkamo, 2016). It has also been reported that gifted children aged 6–8 realize the importance of effort and practicing, and their inner drive also shows in their positive view of the self and trust in their own learning process (Ruokonen, 2005). Inner drive manifests also in dedication and the power to make choices during school years (age 7–18) (Aarresola, 2016). Science Olympians even call themselves "self-made," indicating a focus on one's own interests, efforts and visions. Koro-Ljungberg and Tirri (2002) recognized the ethics of empowerment among highly successful scientists, indicating independence of thought, a belief in their own internal voices, and goals as leading principles in their work. A similar mentality was identified among Olympic athletes (Rahkamo, 2016). Inner drive has been found to indicate competitiveness in Finnish empirical studies, which is not surprising given that most of the research is closely connected to success in competitions: Olympiads in science (e.g., Tirri, 2001; Tirri & Campbell, 2002), the Olympic Games in sports (e.g., Rahkamo, 2016), and WorldSkills competitions in vocational excellence (e.g., Korpelainen et al., 2009; Nokelainen, 2010; Pyväs & Nokelainen, 2017).

3.2 *Contextual Factors in the Development of Finnish Talent*
Contextual factors refer to family, school, peers, enrichment programs and society that support or hinder talent development. For example, Rahkamo (2016) concludes that Finnish Olympic winners in sports would not have been able to rise to the top alone.

3.2.1 Family
A *supportive family atmosphere* in early childhood and the early recognition of giftedness by parents have been consistently identified as the most important contextual factors in talent development (e.g., Aarresola, 2016; Campbell et al., 2017; Nokelainen et al., 2009). Parental investment in financing their children's hobbies and coaching opportunities in early childhood and during their school years, as well as providing transportation, have made it possible for the gifted to develop, especially in the fields of dance, music, and sports (e.g., Aarresola, 2016; Chua, 2015; Ruokonen, 2005). Hobbies and enrichment programs for children appear to be generally limited in the field of science (see Tirri & Kuusisto, 2013), but even so, parental interest and support have been identified

as critical factors. For example, male science Olympians who had experienced parental encouragement and family discussion about math and science since early childhood acknowledged the positive effect on their talent development. On the other hand, female Olympians had not had similar encouragement from their parents. They were introduced to music and art activities in their childhood, and later in college their parents advised them to choose a career that was more typical for females – such as teaching mathematics as opposed to engineering (Tirri & Koro-Ljungberg, 2002). These experiences illustrate cultural and gender-biased parental expectations, especially in the field of

TABLE 10.2 A summary of the critical factors of talent development identified in Finnish empirical studies

Critical factors	Early childhood (age 0–6)	School years (age 7–18)	College years and adulthood
INDIVIDUAL FACTORS			
Natural abilities	Early potential – early reading – physicality		
Inner drive	Early interest	Persistence to practice	Ethics of empowerment
CONTEXTUAL FACTORS			
Family	Supporting home atmosphere *Early recognition*	Parent in financing and transporting	Choice of partner
School		Teacher's encouragement *Recognition*	
Peers		Peers as a positive and negative influence	International collaboration
Enrichment programs	Hobbies	Coaching, competitions, summer programs, internships	Mentoring, coaching training, studying, working abroad
Society	Moral atmosphere in Finland and attitudes towards the gifted and talented		
COINCIDENTAL FACTORS	Encountering good teachers, mentors and contacts One's own health and the health of close ones		

science. Studies show how parents' own interests and background (e.g., Aarresola, 2016), and their vocation (Korpelainen et al., 2009) typically influence their children's development and interests.

In adulthood, family support may depend on partner choice (Rahkamo, 2016; Tirri & Koro-Ljungberg, 2002). The partners of male scientists took care of the home and children, giving Olympians the opportunity to concentrate on their own careers, whereas it was crucial for females to choose a partner who was willing and able to share household chores and childcaring responsibilities. Combining a career and a family life in general is challenging, and requires compromise especially among female scientists (Tirri & Koro-Ljungberg, 2002).

3.2.2 School

Studies on the gifted and the talented mention the role of *teachers* as positive catalysts who teach the basics (Ruokonen, 2005; Tirri, 2001). Even though teachers in Finland are not educated systematically to recognize and support gifted students (Tirri & Kuusisto, 2013), their encouragement as individuals has been particularly helpful to female scientists and gifted students from middle and low SES backgrounds (Tirri, 2001; Tirri & Campbell, 2002), and has sparked interest in certain vocational paths (Nokelainen, 2010). Teachers are strong gatekeepers in terms of recognizing giftedness and then encouraging students and advising them about acceleration possibilities and enrichment programs in and beyond school hours (e.g., Nokelainen, 2010). However, support from teachers has relied heavily on their individual interests, and in general, gifted students have not been given specific support or challenging learning experiences (Hotulainen & Schofield, 2003; see also Laine et al., 2019).

3.2.3 Peers

Finnish studies on the gifted and talented give a rather ambiguous picture of the role of *peers* in talent development. On the one hand, peers are influential friends with whom hobbies are shared, and this may mark the beginning of a career in sports (e.g., Rahkamo, 2016), but on the other hand they may cause distress in the form of envy, harassment and bullying (e.g., Ruokanen, 2005). These problems are challenging in any domain, but they have been specifically pinpointed by the academically gifted. For example, one third of Finnish Olympians reported experiencing hostility from peers (Tirri, 2001). Female scientists have reported suffering from loneliness and a lack of social contacts in their school years, although their situation improved in upper-secondary school where they were able to find similarly minded peers. Male scientists, in turn, seem to enjoy peer support and interesting hobbies earlier in their school career than females do. Enrichment programs and competitions also provide significant opportunities to socialize with national and international peers, and to create extensive networks (e.g., Kuusisto & Tirri, 2015; Nokelainen et al., 2009; Pylväs, 2018; Tirri et al., 2013). Furthermore, it has been reported that international collaboration in adulthood plays a vital role in talent development in terms of perspectives, strategies and resources (e.g., Chua, 2015; Rahkamo, 2016; Tirri, 2001). All in all, learning and cultivating social and affective skills seem to be worthy of special attention in supporting the holistic education of the gifted within the Finnish school system (Tirri & Kuusisto, 2013).

3.2.4 Enrichment Programs

Enrichment programs in the form of hobbies in early childhood and later coaching, competitions, summer programs, and internships build environments for purposeful and deliberate practicing and training. Workplace learning and coaching for competitions have been identified as major contextual and domain-specific conditions for fostering the development of vocational talent (Pylväs & Nokelainen, 2017). Olympic winners have also identified their coaches as the most significant influencers in their careers, and all five multiple gold-medalists who were interviewed had diligently followed the advice of their coaches (Rahkamo, 2016). Neither coaching nor mentoring has featured strongly in academia, even though some scientists acknowledge the influential role of mentors in their academic careers (Tirri, 2001). Some science Olympians become coaches and mentors themselves, encouraging new generations of Olympians (Tirri, 2001).

It has also been shown in Finnish empirical studies that training, studying or working abroad during college years and in adulthood provides the contextual conditions for talent development, especially among professional dancers (Chua, 2015), athletes (Rahkamo, 2016), and academically talented scientists (Tirri, 2001; Tirri & Koro-Ljungberg, 2002). Even in situations in which their partners had assignments abroad, female scientists utilized the opportunity to enhance their own careers by establishing collaboration at local universities (Tirri & Koro-Ljungberg, 2002).

3.2.5 Society

Society constitutes the ultimate context for talent development. The moral atmosphere in Finland, for example, has allowed Finnish female scientists to make bold choices in fields that typically reflect masculine qualities (Tirri & Koro-Ljungberg, 2002). Nevertheless, as the debate on education for the gifted and talented has shown, giftedness as a notion evokes strong emotions. On the one hand, talented athletes and musicians are treated like celebrities, and the Finnish government supports sport clubs and music institutions. On the other hand, however, in the spirit of Finnish egalitarianism, all forms of differentiated educational tracks and streaming by ability were abandoned in basic education after the comprehensive school reform (Aro et al., 2002). Moreover, special education has been aimed specifically at students with learning disabilities and challenges, leaving the academically gifted and talented in particular to cope alone, to work as teaching assistants, or to become underachievers.

3.3   Coincidental Factors

Coincidental factors refer to issues that influence talent development but that cannot be predicted or influenced. With regard to developing musical talents, university students credited chance for having and finding good teachers, mentors and contacts (Ruokonen et al., 2011). Health issues have also been mentioned: injuries, unexpected accidents and death are not in the control of the people involved, but still have a potentially profound effect on talent development (Aarresola, 2016; Chua, 2015; Tirri & Koro-Ljungberg, 2001).

•••

In sum, empirical studies on the educational experiences of gifted and talented Finnish students highlight the role of inner drive as an individual factor in talent development, and family as a contextual factor. These could be called domain-invariant factors in that they play a role in all the domains studied – academic, creative, sport and vocational. Domain-specific factors could also be identified. In sports and the arts, for example, the role of coaches appears to be crucial, and it is also worth noting that Finnish society thus far offers opportunities for hobbies and professional coaching. On the other hand, similar enrichment programs and coaching designed to develop academic talents are not equally available, or even acknowledged. In the case of vocational excellence, coaching opportunities are offered within the formal educational system in vocational schools, indicating later recognition and starting ages compared to sports and the arts. Moreover, some gender differences were identified in the studies in question. For example, although in theory Finnish society as a whole offers opportunities to female scientists, on a personal level they might face challenges within the family (no parental encouragement and pressure to find a partner to share familial responsibilities) and in their careers.

Our summary also highlights the minimally adopted role of teachers and schools in recognizing, encouraging, and offering learning opportunities to gifted and talented students. According to the empirical evidence, talent development in Finland relies mainly on the individual's inner drive and familial support, thereby possibly leaving the potential of gifted students lacking these advantages untapped. For example, low-SES, immigrant, and single-parent families do not necessarily have the financial or time resources to provide organized coaching for their children. Furthermore, the inner drive of gifted students may remain underdeveloped if they do not have motivating and challenging learning opportunities that help them to build up resilience and persistence in learning. The Finnish educational system aims to offer equal opportunities to all students, but at the same time it seems to fall short in terms of providing learning opportunities for the talented. Consequently, given the lack of a formal educational agenda and the high dependency on the teacher for support, gifted and talented students are not treated equally in the Finnish school system.

4 Towards a Growth Mindset Pedagogy in Gifted Education

This third section introduces growth mindset pedagogy as one possible approach to improving the education of Finland's gifted and talented students. The pedagogical focus is on their particular educational needs, such as cultivating an inner drive, normalizing effort and challenges in learning, and learning to cope with failure. According to the theory of implicit beliefs concerning the nature of basic human qualities related to learning (Dweck, 2000, 2006), teachers and students may have a fixed mindset (entity theory), believing that their basic qualities are stable and unchangeable, or a growth mindset (incremental theory), believing that such qualities are changeable and can be developed. An extensive body of research demonstrates the impact of mindset on motivation, learning and achievement, as well as on adjustment and emotional well-being in school (see e.g., King et al., 2012; Zhang et al., 2017). Mindsets are relatively stable, but they have been successfully changed by means of short interventions (Yeager et al., 2019). More recently, however, research has focused on how students' mindsets develop in their every-day interactions with teachers, and the impact of teachers' mindsets on their pedagogical thinking and practices. It seems to be more typical of Finnish teachers to have a growth rather than a fixed mindset, at least when measured quantitatively on Dweck's scale (Dweck, 2000; Laine et al., 2016): the results from qualitative studies are more ambiguous (Laine et al., 2016). Interestingly, although Finnish teachers seem to think of the academic competence of poorly achieving students as malleable, they tend to hold more fixed views concerning competence stability among high achievers (Rissanen et al., 2018a, 2018b, 2019). Given their views on the stability of giftedness among high achievers, teachers may also be more likely to practice growth mindset pedagogy in teaching low-achievers, and to put less effort into supporting the learning processes of high achievers (Rissanen et al., 2019).

Growth mindset pedagogy is process-focused. It is associated with the teacher's own growth mindset and is likely to cultivate growth mindsets in students. Based on teachers' process-focused (instead of trait-focused) interpretations of students' learning, behavior and achievement, its core principles include: (1) supporting students' individual learning processes, (2) promoting mastery orientation, (3) persistence, and (4) supporting process-focused thinking in students. In general, growth-oriented teachers who believe in the ability of students to learn refrain from practices of consolidation and protection from challenges. They rather put effort into understanding the learning barriers of individual students and helping to surmount them, they use honest feedback, and they help students to overcome their helpless-type responses. It seems that the Finnish educational system leans toward growth mindset pedagogy. The *National core curriculum for basic education 2014* (FNBE, 2014, 2016), for instance, emphasizes aims such as learning-to-learn and creating a mastery-oriented atmosphere. Furthermore, learning (as opposed to achievement) goals and formative assessment are enabled by the minor role given to standardized testing (Rissanen et al., 2019).

However, it is typical in the Finnish educational climate to promote equality by investing effort in supporting the learning of low achievers. Socialization into the system implies that Finnish teachers tend to implement growth mindset pedagogy by supporting the development of a growth mindset and process-focused thinking among low achievers, but do not similarly support high achievers to cope with learning-related difficulties, setbacks and disappointments. Their ethical professional focus seems to be on supporting students with difficulties (Rissanen et al., 2019; Tirri & Kuusisto, 2013). However, research on mindsets shows why gifted students should also be seen as potentially fragile: they may succeed with ease during comprehensive education, but if they develop fixed mindsets they could then experience emotional distress, turn away from challenges or even become dropouts in later stages when "things get difficult" (see Blackwell et al., 2007). In a nutshell, if gifted students learn to attribute success to their talent instead of to their effort and learning processes, they are likely to experience failure as indicative of having reached the limits of their talent, which in turn could predict a tendency to give up and to turn away from challenges, or at least increased stress levels. If they are to develop resilience, well-being and inner drive in learning, they also need to experience growth mindset pedagogy. They should be faced with such challenges during their years of basic education so that they could learn to understand the importance of effort and learning strategies. It is also helpful to experience failure, which would normalize experiences of difficulties in learning and facilitate the development of skills (e.g., emotion regulation) that would help them to cope with setbacks. These are learning-to-learn skills that gifted students also need if they are to reach their full potential in the future, even if they succeed with ease during their basic education. Thus, Finnish teachers should be educated to recognize gifted students as learners with special needs who would benefit from growth mindset pedagogy.

To conclude, we have given an overview of the history and the current state of education for gifted and talented students in Finland. We have also summarized empirical studies focusing on these students to identify the critical factors in talent development and how the gifted and talented experience the Finnish schooling system and its apparent lack of targeted education.

We have presented growth mindset pedagogy as a potential developmental path that would support the Finnish educational system, more specifically its teachers and teacher educators, in meeting the needs of all students equally – including the gifted and talented. The focus in growth mindset pedagogy on malleability beliefs implies that everyone is capable of developing and learning – and also that giftedness and talent are not fixed qualities that make the student concerned less dependent on teacher support. The Finnish reluctance to attend to the needs of gifted students, linked to egalitarian educational ideals, may derive from a dislike of ranking, as well as the pre-conception that well-performing students are also well-off. In an attempt to clarify these ideas we have illustrated how growth-mindset-based pedagogical thinking switches the focus from ranking and achievement while emphasizing the need intentionally to support the development of a growth mindset and related learning-to-learn skills among gifted students. In particular, growth mindset pedagogy gives educators the tools to support emotional learning processes and to foster the kind of resilience that gifted students need as much as other students do.

Notes

1   In addition to the critical factors in the development of Finnish talent that are discussed in this chapter, Finnish studies on the gifted and talented have examined the following issues:
    –   *morality and spirituality among the gifted and talented* (e.g., Nokelainen et al., 2009; Nokelainen & Tirri, 2010; Pehkonen & Tirri, 2003; Tirri & Nokelainen, 2007, 2012; Tirri & Pehkonen, 2002; Tirri et al., 2005, 2009, 2012; Tirri & Ubani, 2005),
    –   *gifted education,* especially the perceptions, attitudes and practices of teachers (e.g., Laine, 2017; Laine & Tirri, 2016; Laine et al., 2016, 2019; Tirri & Uusikylä, 1994; see also international comparative studies Tallent-Runnels et al., 2000; Tirri et al., 2002),
    –   *perceptions of giftedness* in general in Finnish newspapers and among Finnish school children and adolescents (e.g., Laine, 2010; Kuusisto et al., 2017), and
    –   *instrument development* for investigating multiple intelligences and moral sensitivities (Tirri & Nokelainen, 2011), and for identifying giftedness and studying well-being among the gifted and talented (e.g., Hotulainen & Schonfield, 2003; Thuneberg & Hotulainen, 2004).

References

Aarresola, O. (2016). *Nuorten urheilupolut: Tutkimus kilpaurheiluun sosiaalistumisen normeista, pääomista ja toimijuudesta* [*Youth sports paths: A study of norms, capital and agency in socialisation into competitive sports*, Doctoral dissertation, University of Jyväskylä]. JYX Digital Repository. http://urn.fi/URN:ISBN:978-951-39-6791-8

Ainscow, M., Booth, T., Dyson, A., Farrell, P., Frankham, J., Gallannaugh, F., Howes, A., & Smith, R. (2006). *Improving schools, developing inclusion*. Routledge.

Armstrong, D., Armstrong, A. C., & Spandagou, I. (2011). Inclusion: By choice or by chance? *International Journal of Inclusive Education, 15*(1), 29–39.

Aro, M., Rinne, R., & Kivirauma, J. (2002). Northern youth under the siege of educational policy change: Comparing youth's educational opinions in Finland, Sweden, Spain, Portugal, and Australia. *Scandinavian Journal of Educational Research, 46*(3), 305–323. doi:10.1080/0031383022000005698

Basic Education Act. (1998). Act 628. http://www.finlex.fi/en/laki/kaannokset/1998/en19980628.pdf

Blackwell, L. S., Trzesniewski, K. H., & Dweck, C. S. (2007). Implicit theories of intelligence predict achievement across an adolescent transition: A longitudinal study and an intervention. *Child Development, 78*, 246–263.

Campbell, J. R., Cho, S., & Tirri, K. (2017). Mathematics and science Olympiad studies: The outcomes of Olympiads and contributing factors to talent development of Olympians. *International Journal for Talent Development and Creativity, 5*(1–2), 48–60.

Chua, J. (2015). *Dance talent development* [Doctoral dissertation, University of Helsinki]. Helda. http://urn.fi/URN:ISBN:978-951-51-0198-3

Dai, D. Y., & Chen, F. (2013). Three paradigms of gifted education: In search of conceptual clarity in research and practice. *Gifted Child Quarterly, 57*(3), 151–168. doi:10.1177/0016986213490020

Dweck, C. S. (2000). *Self-theories: Their role in motivation, personality, and development. Essays in social psychology*. Taylor & Francis Group.

Dweck, C. S. (2006). *Mindset: The new psychology of success*. Random House Publishing Group.

Finnish Constitution. (1999). Law 731. http://www.finlex.fi/fi/laki/kaannokset/1999/en19990731.pdf

FNBE. (2011). *Perusopetuksen opetussuunnitelman perusteiden muutokset ja täydennykset 2010* [*Amendments and additions to the national core curriculum for basic education 2010*]. Finnish National Board of Education. https://www.finlex.fi/data/normit/37238/oph500112010su.pdf

FNBE. (2014). *Perusopetuksen opetussuunnitelman perusteet 2014* [*National core curriculum for basic education 2014*]. Finnish National Board of Education.

https://www.oph.fi/sites/default/files/documents/perusopetuksen_opetussuunnitelman_perusteet_2014.pdf

FNBE. (2016). *National core curriculum for basic education 2014*. Finnish National Board of Education.

Halinen, I., & Järvinen, R. (2008). Towards inclusive education: The case of Finland. *Prospects, 38*(1), 77–97. doi:10.1007/s11125-008-9061-2

Hautamäki, J., Kupiainen, S., Kuusela, J., Rautopuro, J., Scheinin, P., & Välijärvi, J. (2015). Oppimistulosten kehitys [The development of learning outcomes]. In N. Ouakrim-Soivio, A. Rinkinen, & T. Karjalainen (Eds.), *Tulevaisuuden peruskoulu* [*Comprehensive school of the future*] (pp. 34–39). http://www.minedu.fi/export/sites/default/OPM/Julkaisut/2015/liitteet/okm8.pdf?lang=en

Hotulainen, R., & Schofield, N. J. (2003). Identified pre-school potential giftedness and its relation to academic achievement and self-concept at the end of Finnish comprehensive school. *High Ability Studies, 14*(1), 55–70. doi:10.1080/13032000093508

King, R., McInerney, D., & Watkins, D. (2012). How you think about your intelligence determines how you feel in school: The role of theories of intelligence on academic emotions. *Learning and Individual Differences, 22*, 814–819.

Koro-Ljungberg, M. (2001). *Naming the multiple: Segments of scientific giftedness* [Doctoral dissertation, University of Helsinki]. Helda. http://urn.fi/URN:ISBN:951-45-9844-X

Koro-Ljungberg, M., & Tirri, K. (2002). Beliefs and values of successful scientists. *Journal of Beliefs and Values, 23*(2), 141–155. doi:10.1080/1361767022000010806

Korpelainen, K., Nokelainen, P., & Ruohotie, P. (2009). Ammatillisen huippuosaamisen mallintaminen [Modelling vocational excellence]. *Ammattikasvatuksen aikakauskirja* [*Journal of Professional and Vocational Education*], *11*(1), 33–47.

Kupari, P., Välijärvi, J., Andersson, L., Arffman, I., Nissinen, K., Puhakka, E., & Vettenranta, J. (2013). *PISA12 ensituloksia* [*PISA 2012 preliminary results*]. Ministry of Education. http://www.minedu.fi/export/sites/default/OPM/Julkaisut/2013/liitteet/okm20.pdf?lang=en

Kuusisto, E., Laine, S., & Tirri, K. (2017). How do school children and adolescents perceive the nature of talent development? A case study from Finland. *Education Research International, 2017*. https://doi.org/10.1155/2017/4162957

Kuusisto, E., & Tirri, K. (2015). Disagreements in working as a team: A case study of gifted science students. *Revista de educacion, 368*, 250–272. doi:10.4438/1988-592X-RE-2015-368-287

Laine, S. (2016a). *Finnish elementary school teachers' perspectives on gifted education* [Doctoral dissertation, University of Helsinki]. Helda. http://urn.fi/URN:ISBN:978-951-51-2503-3

Laine, S. (2016b, April 8–12). *The public discussion of gifted education* [Paper presentation]. Annual meeting of the American Educational Research Association, Washington DC, United States.

Laine, S., Hotulainen, R., & Tirri, K. (2019). Finnish elementary school teachers' attitudes toward gifted education. *Roeper Review, 41*(2), 76–87. doi:10.1080/02783193.2019.1592794

Laine, S., Kuusisto, E., & Tirri, K. (2016). Finnish teachers' conceptions of giftedness. *Journal for the Education of the Gifted, 39*(2), 151–167. doi:10.1177/0162353216640936

Laine, S., & Tirri, K. (2016). How Finnish elementary school teachers meet the needs of their gifted students. *High Ability Studies, 27*(2), 149–164. doi:10.1080/13598139.2015.1108185

Leino, K., Ahonen, A. K., Hienonen, N., Hiltunen, J., Lintuvuori, M., Lähteinen, S., Lämsä, J., Nissinen, K., Nissinen, V., Puhakka, E., Pulkkinen, J., Rautopuro, J., Sirén, M., Vainikainen, M.-P., & Vettenranta, J. (2019). *PISA 18 ensituloksia: Suomi parhaiden joukossa* [*PISA first results: Finland among the best*]. Opetus- ja kulttuuriministeriö [Ministry of Education and Culture]. http://urn.fi/URN:ISBN:978-952-263-678-2

Mäkinen, M. (2013). Becoming engaged in inclusive practices: Narrative reflections on teaching as descriptors of teachers' work engagement. *Teaching and Teacher Education, 35*, 51–61. http://dx.doi.org/10.1016/j.tate.2013.05.005

Niemi, H., & Sinnemäki, K. (2019). The role of Lutheran values in the success of the Finnish educational system. In K. Sinnemäki, A. Portman, J. Tilli, R. H. Nelson, J. Saarikivi, P. Hagman, & K. Valaskivi (Eds.), *On the legacy of Lutheranism in Finland: Societal perspectives* (pp. 113–137). Finnish Literature Society.

Nokelainen, P. (2010). Mistä on ammatilliset huippuosaajat tehty? [What are vocational experts made of?]. *Ammattikasvatuksen aikakauskirja* [*Journal of Professional and Vocational Education*], *12*(2), 4–12.

Nokelainen, P. (2018). Modeling the characteristics of vocational excellence: A case study with Finnish WorldSkills Competition competitors. *Talent Development & Excellence, 10*(1), 15–30.

Nokelainen, P., Korpelainen, K., & Ruohotie, P. (2009). Ammatillisen huippuosaamisen kehittymiseen vaikuttavat tekijät [Factors influencing development of vocational excellence]. *Ammattikasvatuksen aikakauskirja* [*Journal of Professional and Vocational Education*], *11*(2), 41–53.

Nokelainen, P., Smith, H., Rahimi, M., Stasz, C., & James, S. (2012). *What contributes to vocational excellence? Characteristics and experiences of competitors and experts in WorldSkills London 2011.* WorldSkills Foundation.

Nokelainen, P., & Tirri, K. (2010). Role of motivation in the moral and religious judgment of mathematically gifted adolescents. *High Ability Studies, 21*(2), 101–116. doi:10.1080/13598139.2010.525343

Nokelainen, P., Tirri, K., & Campbell, J. R. (2004). Cross-cultural predictors of mathematical talent and academic productivity. *High Ability Studies, 15*(2), 229–242. doi:10.1080/1359813042000314790

Nokelainen, P., Tirri, K., Campbell, J. R., & Walberg, H. (2007). Factors that contribute to or hinder academic productivity: Comparing two groups of most and least successful Olympians. *Educational Research and Evaluation, 13*(6), 483–500. doi:10.1080/13803610701785931

Nokelainen, P., Tirri, K., & Merenti-Välimäki, H.-L. (2007). Investigating the influence of attribution styles on the development of mathematical talent. *Gifted Child Quarterly, 51*(1), 64–81.

Ojanen, S., & Freeman, J. (1994). *The attitudes and experiences of head teachers, class teachers, and highly-able pupils towards the education of the highly able in Finland and Britain.* Research Report of the Faculty of Education No. 54. University of Joensuu.

Pylväs, L. (2018). *Development of vocational expertise and excellence in formal and informal learning environments* [Doctoral dissertation, University of Tampere]. Trepo. http://urn.fi/URN:ISBN:978-952-03-0664-9

Pylväs, L., & Nokelainen, P. (2017). Finnish WorldSkills achievers' vocational talent development and school-to-work pathways. International Journal for *Research in Vocational Education and Training, 4*(2), 95–116. doi:10.13152/IJRVET.4.2.1

Rahkamo, S. (2016). *The road to exceptional expertise and success: A study of the collective creativity of five multiple Olympic gold medalists* [Doctoral dissertation, Aalto University]. Aaltodoc. http://urn.fi/URN:ISBN:978-952-60-7177-0

Rissanen, I., Kuusisto, E., Hanhimaki, E., & Tirri, K. (2018a). Teachers' implicit meaning systems and their implications for pedagogical thinking and practice: A case study from Finland. *Scandinavian Journal of Educational Research, 62*, 487–500. https://doi.org/10.1080/00313831.2016.1258667

Rissanen, I., Kuusisto, E., Hanhimäki, E., & Tirri, K. (2018b). The implications of teachers' implicit theories for moral education: A case study from Finland. *Journal of Moral Education, 47*, 63–77. https://doi.org/10.1080/03057240.2017.1374244

Rissanen, I., Kuusisto, E., Tuominen, M., & Tirri, K. (2019). In search of a growth mindset pedagogy: A case study of one teacher's classroom practices in a Finnish elementary school. *Teaching and Teacher Education, 77*, 204–213. https://doi.org/10.1016/j.tate.2018.10.002

Ruokonen, I. (2005). *Estonian and Finnish gifted children in their learning enviroments* [Doctoral dissertation, University of Helsinki]. Helda. http://urn.fi/URN:ISBN:952-10-2001-6

Ruokonen, I., Kiilub, K., Muldmac, M., Vikatc, M., & Ruismäki, H. (2011). "They have always supported my choices": Creative catalysts in university students' learning environments. *Procedia – Social and Behavioral Sciences, 29*, 412–421.

Simola, H. (2014a). Educational science, the state and teachers – Setting up the corporate regulation of teacher education in Finland. In H. Simola (Ed.), *The Finnish education mystery – Historical and sociological essays on schooling in Finland* (pp. 69–94). Routledge.

Simola, H. (2014b). The Finnish miracle of PISA – Historical and sociological remarks on teaching and teacher education In H. Simola (Ed.), *The Finnish education mystery – Historical and sociological essays on schooling in Finland* (pp. 207–223). Routledge.

Simola, H., Heikkinen, S., & Silvonen, J. (2014). The birth of the modern Finnish teacher – A Foucauldian exercise. In H. Simola (Ed.), *The Finnish education mystery – Historical and sociological essays on schooling in Finland* (pp. 95–114). Routledge.

Tallent-Runnels, M., Tirri, K., & Adams, A. (2000). A cross-cultural study of teachers' attitudes toward gifted children and programs for gifted children. *Gifted and Talented International, 15*(2), 103–115.

Thuneberg, H., & Hotulainen, R. (2006). Contributions of data mining for psychoeducational research: What self-organizing maps tell us about the well-being of gifted learners. *High Ability Studies, 17*(1), 87–100. doi:10.1080/13598130600947150

Tirri, K. (1997). How Finland meets the needs of gifted and talented. *High Ability Studies, 8*, 213–222.

Tirri, K. (2001). Finland Olympiad studies: What factors contribute to the development of academic talent in Finland? *Educating Able Children, 5*(2), 56–66.

Tirri, K. (2014). The last 40 years in Finnish teacher education. *Journal of Education for Teaching, 40*, 1–10. doi:10.1080/02607476.2014.956545

Tirri, K., & Campbell, J. (2002). Actualizing mathematical giftedness in adulthood. *Educating Able Children, 6*(1), 14–20.

Tirri, K., & Koro-Ljungberg, M. (2002). Critical incidents in the lives of gifted female Finnish scientists. *Journal of Secondary Gifted Education, 13*(4), 151–163.

Tirri, K., & Kuusisto, E. (2013). How Finland serves gifted and talented pupils. *Journal for the Education of the Gifted, 36*(1), 84–96. doi:10.1177/0162353212468066

Tirri, K., & Kuusisto, E. (2018). What factors contribute to the development of gifted female scientists? Insights from two case studies. In K. S. Taber, M. Sumida, & L. McClure (Eds.), *Teaching gifted learners in STEM subjects: Developing talent in science, technology, engineering and mathematics* (pp. 80–88). Routledge.

Tirri, K., & Kuusisto, E. (2019). *Opettajan ammattietiikkaa oppimassa [Learning teacher's professional ethics]*. Gaudeamus.

Tirri, K., Kuusisto, E., & Aksela, M. (2013). What kind of learning is interactive and meaningful to gifted science students? A case study from the Millennium Youth Camp. In K. Tirri & E. Kuusisto (Eds.), *Interaction in educational domains* (pp. 131–145). Sense Publishers.

Tirri, K., & Laine, S. (2017). Teacher education in inclusive education. In D. J. Clandinin & J. Husu (Eds.), *The Sage handbook of research on teacher education* (Vol. 2, pp. 761–776). Sage. https://doi.org/10.4135/9781526402042.n44

Tirri, K., & Nokelainen, P. (2007). Comparison of academically average and gifted students' self-rated ethical sensitivity. *Educational Research and Evaluation, 13*(6), 587–601. doi:10.1080/13803610701786053

Tirri, K., & Nokelainen, P. (2010). The influence of self-perception of abilities and attribution styles on academic choices: Implications for gifted education. *Roeper Review, 33*(1), 26–32. doi:10.1080/02783193.2011.530204

Tirri, K., & Nokelainen, P. (2011). *Measuring multiple intelligences and moral sensitivities*. Sense Publishers.

Tirri, K., & Nokelainen, P. (2012). Ethical thinking skills of mathematically gifted Finnish young adults. *Talent Development and Excellence, 4*(2), 143–155.

Tirri, K., Nokelainen, P., & Mahkonen, M. (2009). How morality and religiosity relate to intelligence? A case study of mathematically talented adolescence. *Journal of Empirical Theology, 22*, 70–87.

Tirri, K., & Pehkonen, L. (2002). The moral reasoning and scientific argumentation of gifted adolescents. *The Journal of Secondary Gifted Education, XIII*(3), 120–129.

Tirri, K., Tallent-Runnels, M., Adams, A., Yuen, M., & Lau, P. (2002). Cross-cultural predictors of teachers' attitudes toward gifted education: Finland, Hong Kong, and the United States. *Journal for the Education of the Gifted, 26*, 112–131.

Tirri, K., Tallent-Runnels, M. K., & Nokelainen, P. (2005). A cross-cultural study of preadolescents' moral, religious and spiritual questions. *British Journal of Religious Education, 27*(3), 207–214. doi:10.1080/01416200500141181

Tirri, K., Tolppanen, S., Aksela, M., & Kuusisto, E. (2012). A cross-cultural study of gifted students' scientific, societal and moral questions in science. *Educational Research International.* https://doi.org/10.1155/2012/673645

Tirri, K., & Ubani, M. (2005). How do gifted girls perceive the meaning of life? *Gifted Education International, 19*, 366–247. https://doi.org/10.1177/026142940501900310

Tirri, K., & Uusikylä, K. (1994). How teachers perceive differentiation of education among the gifted and talented. *Gifted and Talented International, 9*, 69–73.

Uljens, M., & Nyman, C. (2013). Educational leadership in Finland or building a nation with Bildung. In L. Moos (Ed.), *Transnational influence on values and practices in Nordic Educational Leadership: Is there a Nordic model?* (pp. 31–48). Springer. doi:10.1007/978-94-007-6226-8_3

UNESCO. (1994). *The Salamanca statement and framework for action on special needs education.* https://unesdoc.unesco.org/ark:/48223/pf0000098427

Yeager, D. S., Hanselman, P., Walton, G. M., Murray, J. S., Crosnoe, R., Muller, C., Tipton, E., Schneider, B., Hulleman, C. S., Hinojosa, C. P., Paunesku, D., Romero, C., Flint, K., Roberts, A., Trott, J., Iachan, R., Buontempo, J., Yang, S. M., Carvalho, C. M., ... Dweck, C. S. (2019). A national experiment reveals where a growth mindset improves achievement. *Nature, 573*(7774), 364–369. https://doi.org/10.1038/s41586-019-1466-y

Zhang, J. F., Kuusisto, E., & Tirri, K. (2017). How teachers' and students' mindsets in learning have been studied: Research findings on mindset and academic achievement. *Psychology, 8*, 1363–1377. https://doi.org/10.4236/psych.2017.89089

CHAPTER 11

Recognition, Expectation, and Differentiation for Mathematical Talent Development of Young Gifted English Learners

Jenny Yang, Sonmi Jo, James Campbell and Seokhee Cho

Abstract

This study examines the effect of Project BRIDGE's Math program, an advanced mathematics program with language scaffolding strategies, has on the motivation of gifted English learners (ELs). The premise of the study is the belief that if gifted English learners' talents are recognized and that they are enrolled in a differentiated preparatory program that supports their learning needs, then these students will be motivated to achieve academically. Indeed, the results have shown that young gifted ELs are more motivated in the advanced Project BRIDGE's Math class than in a regular math class with general education students. The study also examines the effects of the teachers' instructional strategies on gifted ELs' academic achievement. Hierarchical linear modelling analyses revealed that out of the six categories of scaffolding strategies, the teachers' use of Talk Moves was found to be the only significant predictor of mathematical reasoning and communication skills' scores. In Project BRIDGE's program, the Talk Moves strategies functioned as tools for teaching content and for creating a nurturing classroom environment. Through Talk Moves, the teachers were able to highlight student ideas, challenge students' reasoning, and facilitate collaborative work.

Keywords

Talk Moves – gifted – English learners – mathematics – motivation – instructional strategies

1   Gifted English Learners: Who Are They?

The number of children from immigrant families in the U.S. and across the world has been rising steadily. Yet, few studies are available on how to provide an equitable education to highly potential students who speak a language other than the mainstream language used in schools. In the U.S., more than 40% of school-aged children will be English learners (ELS) by 2030 (Thomas & Collier, 2001). However, ELS are the least represented in gifted education programs in the U.S. More specifically, ELS' talents in science, technology, engineering, and mathematics (STEM) are grossly under-recognized and underserved. This puts ELS at a severe disadvantage when they try to capitalize on the projected 22% job growth in STEM occupations in the next decade (U.S. Bureau of Labor, 2014). There have been various studies on how to identify gifted ELS. However, there are very few studies on how to nurture STEM talents of ELS (Peters et al., 2014). This study was conducted to evaluate the effectiveness of language scaffolding strategies on young gifted ELS' motivation for learning mathematics and on their mathematical reasoning and communication skills.

In the U.S., analyses of data from a state with a mandate to identify gifted students showed white students who are not ELS, are fifteen (15) times more likely to be identified as gifted than ELS (Siegle et al., 2016). ELS are more likely to experience economic hardships than native-born students, with 23% of current immigrant households living in poverty compared to 13.5% of native-born students in 2010 (Camarota, 2012). Due to their disadvantaged socio-economic status, gifted ELS share common characteristics with other under-represented gifted students. As members of an underserved population, they have had limited exposure to intellectual stimuli in childhood. This lack of intellectual stimuli could be responsible for their lower verbal intelligence test score. Lack of exposure to learning experiences or intellectual stimuli could have been caused by economic poverty, ineffective child care by parents, low esteem for a formal education, lack of an awareness of an appropriate and adequate education, disregard for knowledge and skills, or a lack of verbal interaction (Banks, 1993; Lee et al., 2011; Tomlinson et al., 1997).

2 Review of Literature

2.1 *Talent Development of Young Gifted ELS: Opportunities and Motivation*

Many studies have commonly found two important rules for optimal talent development: (1) Giftedness should be perceived as a developmental process. It changes through learning, practices, and experiences and its catalysts are motivation and opportunities (Dai & Chen, 2013; Sosniak, 1985; Subotnik et al., 2011); and (2) The individual should consciously decide to engage fully in a domain (Arnold, 1995; Sosniak, 1985). These common rules imply that both opportunity and motivation are needed for the talents of gifted ELS to be fully developed. Since they cannot be easily identified as gifted, it is necessary to pre-identify ELs with high academic potential and provide them with appropriate preparatory programs (Siegle et al., 2016), where they can build a love for intense learning and appropriate practices for the gifted student.

2.2   Motivation

Motivation is claimed to be at the center of achievement (e.g., Duckworth et al., 2010; Gagné, 2010; Matthews & Foster, 2009; Nokelainen et al., 2007) and motivation determines an individual's capitalization of talent-development opportunities. Motivation regulates the choice of certain goals, starting work toward a goal, and persevering in that work. In this chapter, motivation is used as an umbrella term which encompasses expectancy-value theory (Atkinson, 1964), intrinsic and extrinsic motivation (Schunk et al., 2008), goal theories (e.g., Performance Goal vs. Mastery Goal in Schunk et al., 2008); Self-Concept, Self-Efficacy, and Malleability of Intelligence (Dweck, 2013); and the Attribution Theory (Weiner, 1985).

Research on achievement motivation has discovered and developed methods for fostering learning goals, or task commitment, which is a love for learning and a desire to persevere on tasks of interest (Ames, 1992; Clinkenbeard, 2012; Maker & Nielson, 1995; Patrick et al., 2006; Renzulli, 1986; Siegle & McCoach, 2005). Increased motivation requires "expectancy" and "value" (Eccles, 2006; Eccles et al., 2005; Graham, 2004). Recognition of students' high academic potential, ideas, thoughts, strengths, efforts, and growth will increase students' expectancy (confidence and efficacy). High expectation from teachers for thinking or achievement will increase students' value of the educational process. Differentiated programs to meet the learning needs of under-represented gifted students will contribute to the development of both expectancy and value.

2.3   Model for Motivational Development of Under-Represented Gifted Students: RED (Recognition, Expectation, and Differentiation)

Those methods for developing achievement motivation of under-represented gifted students, including ELs, can be summarized in three tenets: Recognition of Talents; High Expectations; and the Provision of Differentiated Programs (RED) (Cho, 2016; Cho et al., 2015, 2019).

R (Recognition): Talents of gifted ELs are not readily recognized due to their limited English proficiency. Recognition can be made at two different levels. Recognition occurs at a macro level, when ELs are identified as gifted and provided with advanced educational programs. Recognition occurs at a micro level, when their ideas or responses are highlighted and receive focused and immediate feedbacks. Recognition at both levels are critical for gifted ELs' talent development. Immediate feedback on young students' ideas are found to increase their motivation for learning significantly (Borich & Tombari, 1997; Eggen & Kauchak, 2004; Ericsson et al., 1993; Zahorik, 1987). Small group work and discussions are useful for teachers to recognize talents and provide immediate feedback to young children.

E (Expectation): Expectation influences students' achievement and expectations and accompanying behaviors have a real effect on student performance (Brophy, 1983; Brophy & Good, 1970; Cotton, 1989; Good, 1987; Wineburg, 1987). Younger children are more susceptible to these expectance effects than are older children. Long-Mitchell (2011) found some teachers treat students with low-expectation (e.g., expose them to less learning material and material that is less interesting and less challenging, giving them less time to respond to questions and communicate less warmth and affection to them). Accompanying behaviors of high expectation include provision of rich and challenging learning environments at a macro level and challenging questions for deeper thinking, trust and waiting for students' high-quality response at a micro level.

D (Differentiation): Differentiation is a process for teachers to enhance the match between learners' unique learning needs and various curriculum components, such as learning content, process, depth, and pace (Tomlinson, 1999; Tomlinson et al., 2003). The gifted ELs have unique academic needs due to their limited vocabulary, inexperienced skills, and lack of intense practice habits. At the same time, they need the challenges from an advanced mathematics curriculum that requires higher level thinking and reasoning. The support for gifted ELs can be made through "Sheltered Instruction Observation Protocol (SIOP)" for comprehensible input (Echevarria et al., 2017; Krashen, 1985), and culturally responsive pedagogy (Gay, 2010). These scaffolding strategies can be integrated into an advanced curriculum to simultaneously provide support and challenge to the gifted Els.

Project BRIDGE was created to provide enriched learning experiences for the underserved gifted ELs. The RED model is infused in all the program's elements, from developing its unique curriculum, selection of participating students, and professional development for teachers for the delivery of instructions.

2.4 *Design of Project Bridge's Math Program*

Project BRIDGE's curriculum embodies five key characteristics: (1) presents enriched and cognitively demanding tasks; (2) utilizes creative thinking and problem solving strategies; (3) differentiates the curriculum and instruction to ensure equitable access to challenging mathematics; (4) develops students' reasoning and communication skills; and (5) builds a nurturing classroom environment that supports collaborative learning.

The development process began with the selection of the Mentoring Young Mathematicians (M²) as the base curriculum. The M² math curriculum consists of eight advanced units in Geometry, Measurement, and Numbers & Operations, for grades K to 2. It is a challenging enrichment math curriculum for all students (Gavin et al., 2013) which applied gifted education principles. Project BRIDGE's math curriculum was created by modifying the M² curriculum in order to address the unique needs of gifted ELs. The overarching goal of the modifications was to provide comprehensible input and create opportunities for ELs to engage in content-based language learning. The modifications drew upon the best practices in culturally responsive teaching and sheltered content instruction. The product, BRIDGE Math, is a curriculum that recognizes the talents of gifted ELs, expects them to succeed, and provides the necessary differentiation so that they succeed. Below is a brief overview of the features of BRIDGE math and some examples of the built-in language scaffolding strategies.

2.4.1 Vocabulary Support (VS)

To support gifted ELs' limited vocabulary, teachers explicitly instruct the students in the pronunciation, definition and spelling of a new word. For teaching the word "side" in geometry, the teacher may have students practice spelling the word based on phonics to enforce the correlation between the sounds and letters of the English language. Concrete and visual models are also provided to give students hands-on experiences with the concept. For example, teachers may point to a picture of a triangle with an arrow pointing at one of its sides or ask students to trace their fingers along the side of a rectangle while saying the word out loud. Students are also encouraged to explore the different meanings of the word in various contexts. For example, the teacher may ask students to compare the meaning of the word "side" in "I am on your side." and "This side of the rectangle is longer than the other side." One side indicates allegiance, while the other side is a geometric property. This exercise leads students to investigate the multiple meanings of the word and learn how to use it flexibly. Project BRIDGE recognizes that gifted ELs possess the ability to understand the complexity and nuances of the English language. So, instead of a cursory introduction to the vocabulary, BRIDGE Math allows students the time and the opportunities to explore and extend their understanding of a word in English.

2.4.2 Culturally Responsive Teaching (CRT)

The mathematical ability of gifted ELs may not be readily apparent because of their limited English language proficiency. Coupled with the lack of familiarity with the cultural norms of the United States, a student's understanding of mathematical concepts may not be immediately translated into achievement. For example, a student who is fluent in the use of the metric system may stumble when he or she encounters the English system, and has difficulty navigating its non-standard conversion factors. Project BRIDGE recognizes that the student comes to the program with a wealth of information, and simply needs to build the link between that knowledge and the subject content. BRIDGE Math has included multiple scaffolding language strategies to help students capitalizes on their prior knowledge and cultural resources. One of these language scaffolding strategies is an activity in which students are asked to measure items in the classroom, in inches and in centimeters. This gives students, who have a fundamental understanding of measurement, to generalize their knowledge of the metric system to that of the English system. Teachers can also ask these students to lead a group discussion of their experiences in using both systems and compare the advantages and disadvantages of the two systems. The activity has been structured to provide an environment where the gifted ELs' skills are acknowledged and valued. In turn, the students are expected to be the problem solvers and active participants in classroom activities and discussions. Culturally responsive strategies such as these are effective in connecting mathematics with the students' culture, real life experiences, prior knowledge, and family support systems (Echevarria et al., 2017; Lee et al., 2011; Leonard et al., 2009). BRIDGE Math integrates these strategies as ways to differentiate the curriculum, and also as conduits to build nurturing learning environments.

2.4.3 Talk Moves (TM)

This is a curriculum for gifted students that causes students to grapple with ideas and questions, using critical and creative thinking (Sheffield, 1994, 1999; Tomlinson et al., 2009). The best way to involve students in an in-depth study of mathematical content is through talk. According to Vygotsky's (1978) sociocultural theory, language is the mediator of higher cognitive functions, or simply, one learns through talking. Chapin et al. (2009) found that, through the context of discussions, students were able to develop logical reasoning and learned how to make and support arguments. There are five effective Talk Moves (TM): *Revoicing* is when the teacher repeats what the student said. This is used when what the student said was important but unclear. ("So you're saying ..."); *Repeating* is asking the student to repeat what another student said. ("Can you repeat what he or she just said in your own words?"); *Reasoning* is asking students to explain why they agree or disagree with another student's response ("Do you agree or disagree? Why?"). *Adding on* is to get the student to think more and add to another student's response. ("Would someone like to add something more to this?"): *Waiting* is used to ensure that students have enough time to think about their responses and gather their thoughts before sharing ("Take your time ... we'll wait ..."). Teachers use Talk Moves to facilitate a mathematical discussion in which all students participate in the exchange of multiple perspectives. Through talk, students will become consciously aware of their own thinking processes and build connections between information from different sources. Here, the students begin to act like practicing mathematicians, taking ownership of their learning by asking questions, critiquing their own ideas and the ideas of others, and trying new learning strategies.

2.4.4   Writing Support (WS)

Writing is another literary process for students to explore their thought processes and build their own framework of understanding of mathematical concepts. Some may baulk at the idea of having young EL students write about mathematical reasoning. However, Project BRIDGE believes that these students will adopt the "I do" attitude, if the teacher and their surrounding environments reflect the same. That is why BRIDGE Math consistently offers these students high-level and cognitively demanding tasks. At the same time, the curriculum includes multiple levels of support to help students develop their writing skills. The teachers are trained to provide these types of support flexibly to meet the students' needs. For students with emerging writing skills, they are encouraged to draw and write about their ideas. This dual coding of concept, using both text and pictures, allows students to create multiple representation of an idea. For students who have a firmer grasp of vocabulary and syntactical structures, the teacher may use sentence frames, sentence starters, fill-in, or word banks to facilitate the writing process. Competency in writing can only be accomplished through active practice. That is why the BRIDGE Math program includes daily writing activities to help students analyze, interpret, and communicate mathematical ideas.

2.4.5   Talk Frame (TF)

A Talk Frame is a routine that can be used to help organize mathematical discussions, keeps track of student contributions, and build a framework of information and skills relevant to a key idea (Casa, 2013). First, the teacher and students identify the problem that must be solved, and label it as the question to "Think" about. Then, the teacher gathers ideas from the students, and labels each as a "Talk" point. Here, the students are challenged to critique each other's reasoning and revise, if necessary. It is important for the teacher not to judge the soundness of the ideas or proposed solutions at this point. The teacher may even introduce both correct and incorrect ideas, so that students do not assume that anything that is written on the board is accurate. This builds an environment where an exchange of multiple perspectives is encouraged, misconceptions are treated as opportunities for learning, and students are actively evaluating the validity of evidences that may support the proposed solutions. The teacher facilitates the process for the class to come to one or multiple mathematical conclusions, accepting the fact that there is often more than one way to solve the problem. The main concepts of the lesson are summarized under "We Understand," and here, students can articulate their understanding of key ideas.

The BRIDGE Math program was previously found to be significantly effective for improving mathematics achievement of gifted young ELS compared to those who learned with traditional mathematics curriculum (Cho et al., 2015; Jo et al., 2020). The purpose of this study is to examine motivational level of young gifted ELS participating in Project BRIDGE's program. This research study attempts to find out how student motivation may change when they are challenged with advanced subject content in the BRIDGE Math's program. In addition, this study is also interested in identifying effective instructional strategies that improve gifted ELS' mathematical reasoning and communication skills.

3 Study 1: Motivation for Learning in BRIDGE and Regular Math Classes

3.1 Research Design and Participants

The design of the study is observational. Kindergarten students' (age 5–6) motivational behaviors and levels were observed and compared between regular and after school classes and between before and after Project BRIDGE's program implementation. This study was conducted to examine the possibility of low motivation resulting from fatigue of young kindergarten ELS, if they participate in the after-school Project BRIDGE program. Project BRIDGE's program was implemented in two classes of 10 students each in two urban public schools in the northeast United States for 24 sessions in 8 weeks during afterschool hours.

Teacher nomination was chosen as the pathway for identifying the top 25% of the ELS in the participating schools. For programs that are planned for under-represented gifted students, such as the Project BRIDGE's Math program, it is recommended that the selection should not rely on test scores only (Renzulli, 1986). Instead, diverse criteria, which include teacher nomination, should be used as indicators of above-average ability. This approach is especially important in the identification of primary age students, disadvantaged populations, or culturally different groups. For this study, gifted ELs were recommended by classroom teachers based on their months-long observation of students' behaviors in the mathematic classes using the Scales for Rating the Behavioral Characteristics of Superior Students (Renzulli et al., 2013). These students' language proficiency was at or above intermediate level. Teachers participated in a 5-day professional development event on the RED model, the BRIDGE Math program, and the language scaffolding methodologies integrated into the program. For close classroom observation, four students with either high or low English proficiency and math abilities were recommended by the teachers in each class (see Table 11.1). Each student was assigned to one of the four observers randomly.

TABLE 11.1 Gifted kindergarten EL students observed in each class of two schools (N = 8)

English proficiency	Math ability	Students in school A	Students in school B
High	High	1 (F)	1 (M)
Low	High	1 (M)	1 (M)
High	Low	1 (M)	1 (F)
Low	Low	1 (F)	1 (M)

3.2 Instrument for Observation: BOSS (Behavioral Observation of Students in Schools)

The BOSS enables users to observe students in a school environment and records students' behaviors in real time (Pearson, 2017). It is a 4-point Likert scale that observers record one of 1 to 4 based on student's behaviors and record the categories of six motivating behaviors and 4 non-motivating behaviors. One (1) point for not active, no motivation, to 4-point for active and highly motivated was recorded based on the degree of their motivating behaviors. Four observers were trained to determine the motivational level and behavioral categories. Inter-rater reliabilities were high (r = .78).

3.3 Procedure

Students were observed in two settings: During the regular school hours, students were observed while they learn a school-selected math curriculum with all students. During the afterschool hours, students were observed while they were provided the BRIDGE Math curriculum with other gifted ELs. Each observer documented motivating behaviors of the one target student group for 20 minutes during a one-hour class session of regular and afterschool math classes. Students were observed during the first three (3) and the last three (3) sessions out of a total of 24 sessions. Observations of regular math classes and BRIDGE Math's after-school classes were made on the same days. At the end of the observation period, each student was observed by the assigned observer for a total of 120 minutes. The students' motivating level and the behavioral categories were observed and recorded every three (3) minutes. If students' behaviors were not found among the exemplary behaviors, then their behaviors were described.

3.4 Results

First, surprisingly, young gifted ELs were more motivated during the BRIDGE Math's after-school class than in the regular math class (see Table 11.2). Expected fatigue from long school hours was not found while they were in the BRIDGE Math class. Rather, they were less motivated learning math in their regular day school hours. Second, all gifted ELs' motivating behaviors increased regardless of their level of English proficiency or mathematic ability (see Table 11.3). Students with higher math ability showed more of an increase in motivation than those with lower math ability (see Table 11.3). Interestingly, students with low English proficiency and low math ability showed high motivation from

TABLE 11.2 Student motivation levels in regular and after-school Project BRIDGE's Math classes

After-school BRIDGE math		Regular-school math class	
Before	After	Before	After
3.14	3.36	3.01	3.27

TABLE 11.3 Comparison of motivation levels in students with different levels of English proficiency and math ability, pre- and post-implementation of the BRIDGE math program

Students	Pre-BRIDGE math	Post-BRIDGE math	Gains
High English proficiency and high math ability	2.62	3.53	0.91
Low English proficiency and high math ability	2.63	3.72	1.09
High English proficiency and low math ability	2.62	3.01	0.39
Low English proficiency and low math ability	3.52	3.94	0.42

the beginning and continued to demonstrate a high motivation. Even though statistical analyses were not conducted due to small data size, the trend was apparent enough to demonstrate the efficacy of the BRIDGE Math curriculum for motivating students.

4 Study 2: Effects of Instructional Strategies on Mathematical Reasoning and Communication

4.1 Research Design and Participants

Ninety-two (92) kindergarten ELs and eight (8) teachers from four (4) urban public schools participated in this study. Participating gifted ELs were identified and selected by applying the same criteria described in Study 1 above. The class sizes ranged from 6 to 15 students. The teachers were given a choice to implement one of the three math curricula: BRIDGE, Go Math, or Engage NY, in their afterschool program. The teachers who selected BRIDGE math were invited to participate in a 5-day professional development offered by the Project team. Professional development included training in math content, language scaffolding pedagogy, the RED model, and best practices in TESOL and gifted education. Project BRIDGE teachers also received a copy of the teacher's manual with integrated language scaffolding strategies and a resource box containing visual aids and manipulatives. The teachers taught the Measurement and Geometry units from their chosen curriculum over the course of seven (7) months. The average instructional time was three (3) sessions per week, 45 minutes per session. Since Go Math and Engage NY were already used in the schools, teachers who chose these programs did not receive additional professional development.

4.2 Observation of Teachers' Instructional Strategies

An observation scale was developed to observe and examine the effectiveness of teaching strategies for gifted ELs. First, this Observation Scale was developed through conceptualization and categorization of possible instructional strategies for gifted ELs. Then, to secure content validity, a draft of the Observation Scale was reviewed by educational experts from math, TESOL and gifted education. Finally, the Observation Scale was tested in a pilot study. The Project team trained the observers on the concepts and examples of instructional strategies. Observers were asked to use shorthand for recording during each class session. The shorthand writings were used to count the frequency of specific strategies used. The average inter-rater reliability coefficients between pairs of observers was found to be $r = .71$.

The scale consists of six cognitive and language scaffolding strategies: Vocabulary Supports (VS); Culturally Responsive Teaching (CRT); Writing Support (WS); Talk Moves (TM); Talk Frames (TF); and General Learning Assistance (GLA). Below is a description of the strategies and some of the examples of teacher behaviors that the observers were trained to document (see Table 11.4).

The General Learning Assistance (GLA) strategies were not specifically integrated into Project BRIDGE's program. However, they were frequently observed among the teachers in the pilot study. Therefore, they were added as a sixth category to the observation form in order to capture the full dynamics of the classroom activity. On average, each of the eight teachers were observed on eight separate occasions by two observers during a four-month period. The observers counted the number of times the teachers used instructional strategies from each of the six categories. At the end of each session, the observers tallied the total count for each of the six categories. The minimum count for each category is zero, indicating that the teacher did not use any of the strategies in that category. The scale has no ceiling as there is no pre-designated limit to how many times a teacher may use a strategy during class time. The mean frequency for each category is the average of the total count between the observers.

4.3 Mathematical Assessment: The Open-Response Assessment

The Open-response assessment (Casa et al., 2017) was used to measure the students' mathematical reasoning and mathematical communication skills. This performance assessment had nine (9) questions selected from the Geometry and Measurement areas with a total of 46 possible points. The same test was administered as a pre-test and post-test. The students answered the questions through written and/or verbal response. Students were also allowed to use drawing to visually represent their mathematical reasoning. Project staff were trained for four hours on its administration, using uniform instruction and scoring rubrics. Scores were awarded for the accuracy of the responses, and the diversity of possible solution provided in the response. No deductions were taken for spelling or grammatical errors. The inter-rater reliability between the graders showed high agreement ($r = .96$).

4.4 Data Analysis

A series of Hierarchical Linear Modeling (HLM) analyses were performed to examine the effects of the students' math pretest scores and the teachers' use of each category of instructional strategies on the students' math post-test scores. The two-level hierarchical linear models consisted of students (Level 1)

TABLE 11.4 Observation scale of teachers' instructional strategies for teaching math

Categories	Instructional strategies	Samples of teacher behaviors
VS	Defines key vocabulary, practices pronunciation and spelling, and uses vocabulary in different syntactical structures.	Teacher provides synonyms or known phrases to build a definition for the vocabulary word; teacher points out the prefix and suffix in the word; teacher encourages students to construct their own vocabulary card using images and text; teacher models how to use the vocabulary in everyday and academic language; and the teacher directs students to use the new word in game play, cooperative activities and partner talk.
CRT	Connects new content to real life experiences, cultural background, and students' prior knowledge.	The teacher encourages students to bring their own materials as visual aids and manipulatives; the teacher uses students' interest and hobbies as entry points for class discussions; and the teacher encourages students to talk about how they use their math skills at home.
TM	Restate, revoice, think time, partner talk, add-on, and agree/disagree	The teacher asks the student to restate another student's idea; the teacher asks the students to turn to their partner and explain their ideas to each other; the teacher asks the students to provide a new or different solution than the ones that have been given; and the teacher asks students to explain why they agree or disagree with another student's idea.
TF	Identify the problem, solicit students' responses, and summarize the key idea of the lesson.	The teacher uses talk frame to organize the classroom discussion; the teacher posts the students' responses, either correct or incorrect, into the organizer; the teacher has the students evaluate each possible solution; and the teacher guides the students to arrive at a consensus on the main idea of the lesson.

(*cont.*)

TABLE 11.4 Observation scale of teachers' instructional strategies for teaching math (*cont.*)

Categories	Instructional strategies	Samples of teacher behaviors
WS	Demonstrates writing process to students, helps students organize their reasoning process, and practices guided writing.	The teacher models language structures needed to complete writing task; the teacher helps students revise and edit their writing; the teacher encourages students to use pictures to illustrate their reasoning process; the teacher demonstrates a writing strategy, such as think-aloud or a strong opening sentence; the teacher prompts students to report and summarize information, and make inferences and predictions in their writing.
GLA	Classroom management and instructional practices to facilitate the flow of the lesson.	The teacher uses visual aids and manipulatives; the teacher asks higher order thinking questions; the teacher provides opportunities for students to work independently, in pairs and small groups; and the teacher breaks down the instructions into simple, and sequential steps.

Note: TM = Talk Moves, VS = Vocabulary Supports, CRT = Culturally Responsive Teaching, GLA = General Learning Assistance, TF = Talk Frames, WS = Writing Supports

nested within classrooms Level 2. Students' math post-test scores were entered as a dependent variable. The difference in the post-test scores for students in the same class is represented by the Level-1 variance ($\sigma 2$), and the difference between the average scores of the classes is represented by the Level 2 variance ($\tau 00$). The students' pretest scores were included at Level 1 as a covariate to assess variance between post-test scores of students in the same class. Scores of teachers' use of instructional strategies use were entered at Level 2 to determine if it can explain any variance in scores between classes.

The effect of the teachers' instructional strategies use was calculated using the intraclass correlation coefficient (ICC), R2 and f 2. Interpretation criteria of f2 are 0.02 small effect; 0.15 medium effect; and 0.35 large effect (Cohen, 1992).

4.5 *Results*

Teachers used General Learning Assistance strategies the most ($M = 1.52$), followed by Vocabulary strategies ($M = 1.28$). Then Talk Moves ($M = .56$), Writing Supports ($M = .33$), and Culturally Responsive Teaching strategies ($M = .25$).

The Talk Frame strategies were used the least ($M = .05$). Students' performance on the Open-response assessment was improved from $M = 10.06$ to $M = 19.73$ (see Table 11.5).

TABLE 11.5   Mean and standard deviation of frequency of strategies and math open-response scores

Variables	M	SD
TM	0.56	0.35
VS	1.28	0.34
CRT	0.25	0.12
GLA	1.52	0.40
TF	0.05	0.13
WS	0.33	0.18
Open-response		
Pre-test	10.06	4.79
Post-test	19.73	6.70

Note: TM = Talk Moves, VS = Vocabulary Supports, CRT = Culturally Responsive Teaching, GLA = General Learning Assistance, TF = Talk Frame, WS = Writing Supports

4.6   Effect of Talk Moves

The unconditional model with the post-test score of the Open-response assessment (POST_OPEN) was analyzed (see Table 11.6). The intraclass correlation estimate (ICC) was .42, which means that 42% of the variability in the post-test score of the Open-response assessment lie between classrooms. Thus, it can be inferred that about 58% of the variance lies within classrooms. The pretest scores of the Open-response assessment (PRE_OPEN) were included in the Level 1 model as a grand mean centered. The pretest score was found to be a significant predictor of students' post-test scores ($\gamma 10 = .38$, $t(83) = 3.58$, $p < .001$). The pretest scores can explain 10% of the variance in the post-test scores of the Open-response assessment ($R^2 = .10$). The effect size of the pretest score as a predictor was small to medium ($f2 = .11$). While the pretest scores can account for the differences in post-test scores within the classrooms, a significant amount of variance (ICC = 42%) still exists between the average scores and between classes at Level 2.

To determine if the variance in the average scores between classes can be explained by the teacher's use of Talk Moves as an instructional practice, we inserted teachers' frequency of Talk Moves using (TM) as a grand mean-centered,

TABLE 11.6 Two-level hierarchical linear modeling of Open-response assessment scores with Talk Moves and pre-test scores

Parameter	Unconditional model		Random coefficient model		Contextual model	
	Parameter estimate	SE	Parameter estimate	SE	Parameter estimate	SE
Fixed effects						
Intercept (γ_{00})	19.22***	1.65	19.26***	1.56	19.21***	1.14
TM (γ_{01})					9.02*	3.40
Pretest (γ_{10})			0.38***	0.11	0.39***	0.11
Variance estimate						
Level 1 variance (σ^2)	26.51		24.17		24.22	
Intercept variance (τ_{00})	19.57***		17.26***		8.13***	
Deviance (number of REML parameters)	599.50(2)		569.56(2)		558.18(2)	

Note: TM = teachers' use of Talk Moves, REML = restricted likelihood estimation, Pre-test score were grand-mean centered, ***$p < .001$, **$p < .01$, *$p < .05$

Level 2 predictor in a contextual model. The following shows the contextual model with the post Open-response scores as the dependent variable:

$$POST\_OPEN_{ij} = \gamma_{00} + \gamma_{01}*TM_j + \gamma_{10}*PRE\_OPEN_{ij} + u_{0j} + r_{ij}$$

For students who scored at the mean on the pretest and whose teacher uses TM at the mean, they would have a post-test score of 19.21 (γ_{00} = 19.21, $t(6)$ = 3.62, $p < .001$). With every 1-point increase in the pretest score, the students' post-test scores were expected to increase by .39 (γ_{10}= .39, $t(83)$ = 16.87, $p < .001$). The students' post-test scores would increase by 9.02 points with every 1-point increase in the teacher's use of TM (γ_{01} = 9.02, $t(6)$ = 2.65, $p < .05$). With the insertion of the TM variable, the Level 2 variance estimate (τ_{00}) was reduced from 19.57 to 8.13. This indicates that the teacher's use of TM explains 58% of the variance in the average post-test scores between classes.

TM was the only significant Level-2 predictor that could explain the variance in students' Open-response assessment scores between the classes (see Table 11.7). The teacher's use of other instructional practices, such as VS, CRT, WS, TF, GLA did not have a significant effect on the variance in the assessment

TABLE 11.7 Effects of teachers' use of instructional strategies on students' Open-response assessment scores

Instructional practice	Effect on open-response assessment score				
	Parameter estimate	SE	t-ratio	p-value	Reliability estimate
Vocabulary Support (VS)	−.69	5.36	−.13	.90	.90
Culturally Responsive Teaching (CRT)	3.32	15.23	.22	.84	.90
Writing support (WS)	−.07	10.23	−.01	1.00	.90
Talk Moves (TM)	9.02	3.40	2.65	.04	.79
Talk Frames (TF)	−22.09	11.36	−1.95	.10	.84
General Learning Assistance (GLA)	2.75	4.34	.63	.55	.90

scores. Hence, TM was the only Level-2 predictor in the final contextual model. Altogether, the pretest scores and TM could explain 30% of the variance in the students' post-test scores (R^2 = .30), within and between classes. The effect size of these covariates was large ($f2$ = .43). The results also indicated that the contextual model was moderately reliable (reliability estimate = .79).

5 Discussion

5.1 BRIDGE Program: Effective for Increasing Motivation

Project BRIDGE's math program was found to be effective in motivating young gifted ELs for learning mathematics. Before program implementation, principals and teachers were concerned about possible loss of motivation of kindergarten children after long regular school hours. However, the students that were observed tended to be more engaged and focused during the afterschool BRIDGE Math classes than during the regular day math classes. Probably, it could be that they were recognized as high potential students, expected high achievement with advanced mathematics, and learning with a program that is differentiated to meet their needs could have been instrumental for increasing their motivation. They may also have had the sense of belonging with academic peers as gifted ELs (Worrell, 2012). Gifted ELs, being in a homogenous group of all gifted ELs without native speakers who may overwhelm ELs with their fluent English, might have felt safe and supported. In the BRIDGE Math class, students were allowed to take time to talk and make mistakes, since all students were ELs.

5.2 Talk Moves: Effective Strategies for Mathematical Reasoning and Communication

Among several instructional strategies, only TM was found to be effective in demonstrated gains in the Math Open response assessment scores. TM could have functioned as a tool for immediate recognition of gifted ELs' thoughts, ideas, and high potential and for high expectation of gifted ELs. "Revoicing" and "Repeating" could have functioned as tools for recognition. With "So you're saying …" (*Revoicing*) and "Can you repeat what he or she just said in your own words?" (*Repeating*), students could have felt that their responses were recognized to be significant enough for teachers or other students to pay attention and repeat their statements. With "Do you agree or disagree? Why?" (*Reasoning*), "Would someone like to add something more to this?" (*Adding on*), "Take your time" (*Waiting*), students might realize that they are expected to wait, and they can be trusted to think better and harder.

Project BRIDGE's math program might have been effective for increasing the gifted ELs' motivation because it has incorporated the RED components at a macro level (Cho et al., 2019) through pre-identification and a differentiated preparatory program.

In addition, RED also occurred at a micro level during the discussions using Talk Moves which provided immediate recognition and higher expectations for these young children. The above conjecture should be examined in a future study by collecting data on three variables, instructional strategies used, motivating level, and achievement scores from the same participants.

It seems impossible to deny that other instructional strategies such as Vocabulary Supports, Culturally Responsive Teaching, Writing Supports, Talk Frames, and General Learning Assistance could have facilitated the gifted ELs' building knowledge and skills, which, in turn, could have increased their achievement motivation. However, it can be claimed that mathematical reasoning and communication which are critically needed for gifted ELs to build knowledge, skills and persistence could have been improved the most with Talk Moves.

5.2 Implications for Teacher Education and School Teaching

For talent development of young gifted ELs, RED can be incorporated into the education system through educating teachers and school administrators about pre-identification and the provision of a preparatory program with a differentiated approach. At the classroom level, RED can also be incorporated more easily through Talk Moves.

Findings from this study reveal that SIOP or comprehensible input from the TESOL field may not be effective enough for gifted ELs to develop their mathematical talent. Providing gifted ELs with support for vocabulary learning, comprehension, or writing is not enough. For gifted ELs to develop their mathematical reasoning and communication skills, they need to be in an environment that supports the constant exchange of ideas. Talk Moves is an effective instructional strategy that can be used to facilitate a class-wide discussion and give immediate and focused feedback to individual students. Teachers who use Talk Moves are able to build an encouraging classroom environment where gifted ELs feel safe to take risks and make mistakes while being challenged with problems rather than being protected.

For the gifted ELs to take risks with challenging problems, teachers need to learn how to support gifted ELs participation in classroom discussions (Chapin et al., 2009; Levitt, 2002; Moschkovich, 1999; Reeve, 2006). Teachers should attend professional development programs on how to facilitate student discussions in the classroom, participate in mentoring with a master teacher throughout the academic year. Through observations, it was noticed that most teachers in Project BRIDGE were not fluent in using Talk Moves or used them infrequently in the beginning of the year, and gradually used them more towards the end. It was noticed that teachers with deficit thinking responded to their own prompts, rather than waiting for the students. After professional development and repeated practice, these teachers began to wait for the students to respond, and their wait time increased. With demonstrations and feedback on their instructional skills, teachers could develop competency in using Talk Moves effectively.

References

Ames, C. (1992). Classrooms: Goals, structures, and student motivation. *Journal of Educational Psychology, 84*, 261–271.

Arnold, K. D. (1995). *Lives of promise.* Jossey-Bass.

Atkinson, J. W. (1964). *An introduction to motivation.* Van Nostrand.

Banks, J. A (1993). Approaches to multicultural curricular reform. In J. A. Banks & C. A. M. Banks (Eds.), *Multicultural education: Issues and perspectives* (2nd ed., pp. 3–30). Allyn & Bacon.

Borich, G. D., & Tombari, M. L. (1997). *Educational psychology: A contemporary approach* (2nd ed.). Addison-Wesley Educational Publishers.

Brophy, J. E. (1983). Research on the self-fulfilling prophecy and teacher expectations. *Journal of Educational Psychology, 75*, 631–661.

Brophy, J. E., & Good, T. L. (1970). Teachers' communication of differential expectations for children's classroom performance: Some behavioral data. *Journal of Educational Psychology, 61*, 365–374.

Camarota, S. (2012). *Immigrants in the United States a profile of America's foreign-born population.* Center for Immigration Studies.

Casa, T. M. (2013). Capturing thinking on the talk frame. *Teaching Children Mathematics, 19,* 516–523.

Casa, T. M., Firmender, J. M., Gavin, M. K., & Carroll, S. R. (2017). Kindergartners' achievement on geometry and measurement units that incorporate a gifted education approach. *The Gifted Child Quarterly, 61,* 52–72.

Chapin, S. H., O'Connor, C., & Anderson, N. C. (2009). *Classroom discussions: Using math talk to help students to learn, grades 1–6* (2nd ed.). Math Solutions.

Cho, S. (2016). Motivation and opportunities: The two critical factors for developing talent of under-represented gifted. In S. Lee (Ed.), *Equity and excellence in special education: Empowering students with giftedness or disabilities from economically disadvantaged or multicultural families.* Soonchunhyang University, Asansi, Korea.

Cho, S., Mandracchia, M., & Yang, J. (2019). Nurturing mathematical talents of young mathematically gifted English Language Learners. In S. R. Smith (Ed.), *International handbook of giftedness & talent development in the Asia-Pacific* (pp. 833–856). Springer. https://doi.org/10.1007/978-981-13-3021-6_38-1

Cho, S., Yang, J., & Mandracchia, M. (2015). Effects of M^3 curriculum on Mathematics and English Ppoficiency achievement of mathematically promising English language learners. *Journal of Advanced Academics, 26*(2), 112–142.

Clinkenbeard, P. R. (2012). Neuroscience and young children: Implications for the diversity of gifted programming. In R. Subotnik, A. Robinson, C. Callahan, P. Johnson, & E. J. Gubbins (Eds.), *Malleable minds: Translating insights from psychology and neurosciences to gifted education* (pp. 197–207). National Research Center on the Gifted and Talented, University of Connecticut.

Cohen, J. (1992). A power primer. *Psychological Bulletin, 112*(1), 155–159. https://doi.org/10.1037/0033-2909.112.1.155

Cotton, K. (1989). *Expectations and student outcomes.* Northwest Regional Educational Laboratory.

Dai, D. Y., & Chen, F. (2013). *Paradigms of gifted education: A guide to theory-based, practice-focused research.* Prufrock Press.

Duckworth, A. L., Kirby, T. A., Tsukayama, E., Berstein, H., & Ericsson, K. A. (2010). Deliberate practice spells success: Why grittier competitors triumph at the National Spelling Bee. *Social Psychology and Personality Science, 2*(2), 174–181.

Dweck, C. S. (2013). Mindsets and malleable minds: Implications for giftedness and talent. In R. F. Subotnik, A. Robinson, C. M. Callahan, & P. Johnson (Eds.), *Malleable minds: Translating insights from psychology and neuroscience to gifted education* (pp. 7–18). National Center for Research on Giftedness and Talent.

Eccles, J. S. (2006). A motivational perspective on school achievement: Taking responsibility for learning, teaching, and supporting. In R. J. Sternberg & R. F. Subotnik

(Eds.), *Optimizing student success with the other three R's: Reasoning, resilience, and responsibility* (pp. 199–224). Information Age.

Eccles, J. S., O'Neill, S. A., & Wigfield, A. (2005). Ability self-perceptions and subjective task values in adolescents and children. In K. A. Moore & L. H. Lippman (Eds.), *What do children need to flourish?* (pp. 237–249). Springer.

Echevarria, J., Vogt, M., & Short, D. J. (2017). *Making content comprehensible for English learners: The SIOP model.* Pearson.

Eggen, P., & Kauchak, D. (2004). *Educational psychology: Windows on classroom* (6th ed.). Prentice Hall.

Ericsson, K. A., Krampe, R. T., & Tesch-Römer, C. (1993). The role of deliberate practice in the acquisition of expert performance. *Psychological Review, 100,* 363–406. doi:10.1037/0033-295X.100.3.363

Gagné, F. (2010). Motivation within the DMGT 2.0 framework. *High Ability Studies, 21,* 81–99. doi:10.1080/13598139.2010.525341

Gavin, M. K., Casa, T. M., Firmender, J. M., & Carroll, S. R. (2013). The impact of advanced geometry and measurement curriculum units on the mathematics achievement of first-grade students. *Gifted Child Quarterly, 57,* 71–84.

Gay, G. (2010). *Culturally responsive teaching: Theory, research, and practice* (2nd ed.). Teachers College Press.

Good, T. L. (1987). Two decades of research on teacher expectations: Findings and future directions. *Journal of Teacher Education, 38,* 32–47.

Graham, S. (2004). "I can, but do I want to?" Achievement values in ethnic minority children and adolescents. In G. Philogène (Ed.), *Racial identity in context: The legacy of Kenneth B. Clark. Decade of behavior* (pp. 125–147). American Psychological Association.

Jo, S., Yang, J., & Cho, S. (2020, November). *Teachers' instructional practices and young gifted English learners' Math achievement, concurrent* [Paper presentation]. National Association for Gifted Children, Orlando, FL.

Krashen, S. D. (1985). *The input hypothesis, issues and implications.* Longman Group UK.

Lee, J., Lee, Y. A., & Amaro-Jiménez, C. (2011). Teaching English Language Learners (ELLs) mathematics in early childhood. *Childhood Education; Olney, 87*(4), 253–260.

Leonard, J., Napp, C., & Adeleke, S. (2009). The complexities of culturally relevant pedagogy: A case study of two secondary mathematics teachers and their ESOL students. *The High School Journal; Chapel Hill, 93*(1), 3–22.

Levitt, K. E. (2002). An analysis of elementary teachers' beliefs regarding the teaching and learning of science. *Science Education, 86*(1), 1–22.

Long-Mitchell, L. A. (2011). High-achieving Black adolescents' perceptions of how teachers impact their academic achievement. In J. A. Castellano & A. D. Frazier (Eds.), *Special populations in gifted education: Understanding our most able students from diverse backgrounds* (pp. 99–123). Prufrock Press.

Maker, J., & Nielson, A. (1995). *Curriculum development and teaching strategies for gifted learners* (2nd ed.). Pro-Ed.

Matthews, D. J., & Foster, J. F. (2009). *Being smart about gifted education: A guidebook for educators and parents* (2nd ed.). Great Potential Press.

Moschkovich, J. (1999). Supporting the participation of English language learners in mathematical discussions. *For the Learning of Mathematics, 19*(1), 11–19.

Nokelainen, P., Tirri, K., Campbell, J. R., & Walberg, H. (2007). Factors that contribute to or hinder academic productivity: Comparing two groups of most and least successful Olympians. *Educational Research and Evaluation, 13*, 483–500. doi:10.1080/13803610701785931

Patrick, H., Gentry, M., & Owen, S. V. (2006). Motivation and gifted adolescents. In F. A. Dixon & S. M. Moon (Eds.), *The handbook of secondary gifted education* (pp. 165–195). Prufrock Press.

Peters, S., Matthews, M. S., McBee, M. T., & McCoach, B. (2014). *Beyond gifted education: Designing and implementing advanced academic programs*. Prufrock Press, Inc.

Reeve, J. (2006). Teachers as facilitators: What autonomy-supportive teachers do and why their students benefit. *The Elementary School Journal, 106*(3), 225–236.

Renzulli, J. S. (1986). The three-ring conception of giftedness: A developmental model for creative productivity. In R. J. Sternberg & J. E. Davidson (Eds.), *Conceptions of giftedness* (pp. 53–92). Cambridge University Press.

Renzulli, J. S., Smith, L., Callahan, C., Hartman, R., Westberg, K., Gavin, K., Reis, S., Siegle, D., & Sytsma, R. (2013). *Scales for rating the behavioral characteristics of superior students*. Prufrock Press, Inc.

Schunk, D. H., Pintrich, P. R., & Meece, M. L. (2008). *Motivation in education: Theory, research, and applications* (3rd ed.). Pearson.

Sheffield, L. J. (1994). *The development of gifted and talented mathematics students and the National Council of Teachers of Mathematics Standards* (Research Monograph No. 9404). National Research Center on the Gifted and Talented.

Sheffield, L. J. (1999). Serving the needs of the mathematically promising. In L. J. Sheffield (Ed.), *Developing mathematically promising students* (pp. 43–55). The National Council of Teachers of Mathematics.

Siegle, D., Gubbins, E. J., O'Rourke, P., Dulong Langley, S., Mun, R. U., Luria, S. R., Little, C. A., McCoach, D. B., Knupp, T., Callahan, C. M., & Plucker, J. A. (2016). Barriers to underserved students' participation in gifted programs and possible solutions. *Journal for the Education of the Gifted, 39*, 103–131. doi:10.1177/0162353216640930

Siegle, D., & McCoach, D. B. (2005). *Motivating gifted students*. Prufrock Press.

Sosniak, L. A. (1985). Phases of learning. In B. J. Bloom (Ed.), *Developing talent in young people* (pp. 409–538). Ballantine.

Subotnik, R. F., Olszewski-Kabilius, P., & Worrell, F. C. (2011). Rethinking giftedness and gifted education: A proposed direction forward based on psychological science. *Psychological Science in the Public Interest, 12*(1) 3–54.

Thomas, W., & Collier, V. (2001). *A national study of school effectiveness for language minority students. Long-term academic achievement.* National Center for Bilingual Education. https://escholarship.org/uc/item/65j213pt

Tomlinson, C. (1999). *The differentiated classroom: Responding to the needs of all learners.* Association for Supervision and Curriculum Development.

Tomlinson, C., Brighton, C., Hertberg, H., Callahan, C., Moon, T., Brimijoin, K., Conover, L., & Reynolds, T. (2003). Differentiating instruction in response to student readiness, interest, and learning profile in academically diverse classrooms: A review of literature. *Journal for the Education of the Gifted, 27,* 119–145.

Tomlinson, C. A., Callahan, C. M., & Lelli, K. M. (1997). Challenging expectations: Case studies of high-potential, culturally diverse young children. *Gifted Child Quarterly, 41,* 5–17.

Tomlinson, C. A., Kaplan, S. N., Renzulli, J. S., Purcell, J. H., Leppien, J. H., Burns, D. B., & Imbeau, M. B. (2009). *The parallel curriculum: A design to develop learner potential and challenge advanced learners* (2nd ed.). Corwin Press.

U.S. Bureau of Labor. (2014). *STEM 101: Intro to tomorrow's jobs.* Retrieved January 16, 2018, from https://www.bls.gov/careeroutlook/2014/spring/art01.pdf

Vygotsky, L. (1978). *Interaction between learning and development.* Harvard University Press.

Weiner, B. (1985). An attributional theory of achievement motivation and emotion. *Psychological Review, 92,* 548–573.

Wineburg, S. S. (1987). The self-fulfillment of the self-fulfilling prophecy. *Educational Researcher, 16,* 28–37.

Worrell, F. C. (2012). Mindsets and giftedness: Assumptions and implications. In R. F. Subotnik, A. Robinson, C. M. Callahan, & E. J. Gubbins (Eds.), *Malleable minds: Translating insights from psychology and neuroscience to gifted education* (pp. 153–163). The National Research Center on the Gifted and Talented, University of Connecticut.

Zahorik, J. A. (1987). Reacting. In M. J. Dunkin (Ed.), *International encyclopedia of teaching and teacher education* (pp. 416–423). Pergamon Press.

CHAPTER 12

Reaching for Medals and Vocational Excellence?

WorldSkills Competition Success in Relation to Goal Orientations and Metacognitive and Resource Management Strategies

Petri Nokelainen and Heta Rintala

Abstract

This study investigated Finnish vocational students and WorldSkills competitors' (*N* = 137) self-assessed goal orientations and metacognitive and resource management strategies and their relation to objectively-measured success in international WorldSkills competitions (WSC). Goal orientations and metacognitive and resource management strategies were evaluated with a survey distributed to competitors of four WSCs between 2009 and 2017. Success in a WSC is defined by scores (0–600 points) assessed by an international expert panel after the four-day competition. To examine possible differences, highly successful and other competitors were divided into two groups: one including medal winners and Medallion for Excellence recipients scoring over 500 points (group A) and the other included competitors scoring less than 500 points (group B). The results showed that group A had higher mastery and performance-approach goal orientations than group B; however, the two groups did not differ based on performance-avoidance goal orientations. Regarding metacognitive and resource management strategies, group A self-reported higher metacognitive strategies in their studies (e.g., efficient use of practice time and setting clear goals), but no other statistically significant differences were found between the groups.

Keywords

skills competitions – vocational education – goal orientations – metacognitive and resource management strategies

1   Introduction

Vocational skills competitions, such as international WorldSkills and EuroSkill Competitions and national skills competitions, have established their place as part of vocational education and training (VET). In Finland, national skills competitions are given manifold purposes, including raising awareness of VET, promoting collaboration between education and employers, encouraging continuous development of skills and entrepreneurship, and promoting vocational excellence (SkillsFinland, 2018, p. 4). At the international level, vocational skills competitions provide a platform for feedback, benchmarks, and dissemination of VET systems and practices (WorldSkills International [WSI], 2019, p. 11). Overall, vocational skills competitions present a complementary, even an opposing image of VET, which has at times and in some contexts suffered from its reputation and image as an unattractive choice (Chankseliani et al., 2016; Rintala & Nokelainen, 2020; Ryan & Lőrinc, 2018). Thus, it has been suggested that skills competitions may positively contribute to the image and attractiveness of VET, for instance, through inspiring people by showcasing outstanding performance, demonstrating that VET can offer economic benefits (including awards), and creating a positive image of young people choosing a VET pathway (Chankseliani et al., 2016; see also Virolainen & Stenström, 2014).

This study investigates vocational students competing in global WordSkills Competitions (WSC). WSC is organised once every two years by a host member of WorldSkills International (WSI). WSCs include a variety of skill areas (e.g., painting and decorating, software solutions for business, construction metal work, and hairdressing) that are classified based on occupational sectors that are considered internationally recognised and rather permanent; these include, for instance, construction and building technology, information and communication technology, manufacturing and engineering technology, and social and personal services (WSI, 2019, pp. 9–10). Despite such classification, transversal skills are more and more acknowledged, and since 2013, each competition has taken into account work organisation and self-management, information, communication, and interpersonal skills, and problem solving, innovation, and creativity (WSI, 2019, p. 11). Participants in WSCs are usually selected through national or regional competitions; age is the only eligibility criterion and, depending on the occupational level, the age limit is either 22 or 25 years. After four days of competition, the best competitors in each skill area are awarded gold, silver, and bronze medals. Competitors who perform above the average point score in their skill are awarded a Medallion for Excellence (more than 500 points in competitions prior to 2019). Vocational excellence can be characterised as a combination of practical wisdom and expertise relevant to the vocation (Tyson, 2018), but WSC has offered an interesting context for a line of research (e.g., Nokelainen, 2018; Nokelainen et al., 2012, 2018; Nokelainen & Pylväs, 2017) investigating factors contributing to vocational talent development and excellence. For research purposes, competitors' scores offer a rather objective measurement for vocational skills, thereby providing an opportunity to investigate the differences between the highly successful and other competitors. Although it may be argued that any competition context with the presence of time pressure, observers and audience is different from an authentic working life situation, we assume that the set of vocational skills needed in these two environments are quite similar as the vocational skills competition tasks are modelled after job situations from the real working life.

The present study aims to investigate whether highly successful medal winners and medallion recipients (group A) differ from other WSC competitors scoring fewer than 500 points (group B). Instead of drawing on the wider Developmental Model of Vocational Excellence (DMVE) (Nokelainen, 2018; Pylväs & Nokelainen, 2017), the present study focuses on investigating the role of Finnish competitors' goal orientations and metacognitive and resource management strategies in WSC success.

The present study employs the achievement goal framework (e.g., Ames, 1992; Dweck, 1986; Maehr & Midgley, 1991; Nicholls, 1984; Nicholls et al., 1989) to understand how vocational students interpret and experience achievement context skills. Two major types of achievement goal orientations are *mastery* and *performance*. In mastery goal orientation, the focus is on the task (desire to develop competence and mastery of a new skill area), while in performance-goal orientation the focus is on the self (desire to demonstrate to others an ability in a new skill area) (Ross et al., 2002). However, later studies on achievement goal orientations have often used a trichotomous framework (e.g., Niemivirta et al., 2019), in which *performance-avoidance* has been added as a third goal orientation emphasising avoiding failure in front of others (Elliot & Harackiewicz, 1996). Although it is assumed that goal orientations are relatively stable dispositions and tendencies, the current multiple-goal perspective highlights that mastery and performance-approach goal orientations should not be considered as a dichotomy but rather as a dynamic profile or repertoire of goal orientations (Niemivirta et al., 2019; Poortvliet, 2016; Wimmer et al., 2018). In the context of skills competitions, results have been somewhat inconsistent, since in some cases, medal winners have self-reported higher performance-avoidance goal orientations, while in others, they have self-reported high levels of mastery goal orientation and higher levels of performance-approach goal orientation than their non-winning peers (Nokelainen et al., 2012; Nokelainen & Stasz, 2016). These findings may relate to cultural differences. For example, in the UK context the expectations of success from the vocational skills competitions are present in a more visible manner (e.g., the final number of the competitors is decided after the demonstration of skills during the training period) than in Finland where the composition of the team remains quite stable throughout the training period.

Next to motives and desire to learn, the importance of metacognitive strategies, such as self-regulation and effort, have also been emphasised in the VET context (e.g., Jossberger et al., 2020; Kallio et al., 2018). Individuals may have strong vocation-specific knowledge but still have extensive shortcomings in their metacognitive and resource management strategies. For instance, Jossberger et al. (2020) recently found that well-performing vocational students planned their time and resources, but they monitored work processes and evaluated outcomes rather than their learning behaviours. Previous studies have also suggested that students with mastery goals and high task orientation may also self-report higher levels of self-regulatory strategies (Bouffard et al., 1995; Riveiro et al., 2001).

Based on the issues above, the present study analyses success in WSC and answers the following research questions:

- RQ 1: *How are vocational students' self-reported mastery and performance-goal orientations associated with objective performance measurement in international skills competitions?*
- RQ 2: *How are vocational students' self-reported metacognitive and resource management strategies associated with objective performance measurement in international skills competitions?*

2   Theoretical Framework

2.1   *Goal Orientations*

Goal orientation theories offer a variety of labels, but early studies emphasised two motives for engagement and achievement: mastery goals – also called learning goals (Dweck, 1986), or task-involvement goals (Nicholls, 1984; Nicholls et al., 1989) that highlight personal improvement, and performance goals – also known as ego-involvement goals (Nicholls, 1984) or ability goals (Ames, 1992) that focus on demonstrating abilities and on competition. Mastery goal orientation[1] is related to adaptive patterns of learning (setting personally challenging and valued achievement goals) and performance-approach goal orientation relates to both adaptive (positive expectation of success or judgment: persistently seeking challenge) and maladaptive patterns of learning (negative expectation of success or judgment: avoidance of challenges and withdrawal) (e.g., Dweck, 1986). The third goal orientation, performance-avoidance, is related to maladaptive patterns of learning (Midgley et al., 2000).

A recent review of students' achievement goal orientation profiles (Niemivirta et al., 2019) suggested that mastery goal orientation shows high academic achievement; however, students with either mastery or performance-approach goals perform equally well in the school context. In relation to the context of current study (vocational skills competitions), several studies (e.g., Harackiewicz et al., 1998; Tuominen-Soini et al., 2011; see also Niemivirta et al., 2019) have suggested that a multiple-goal approach (a mixture of mastery and performance-approach goal orientations) might be most successful in selective contexts in which performance and competition are emphasised. When comparing training and competition contexts, competition seems to encourage performance climate and goals rather than mastery goals (van de Pol et al., 2012). Nevertheless, a meta-analysis across work, education, and sport contexts (Van Yperen et al., 2014) found that both mastery and performance-approach goals are positively related to performance, whereas avoidance goals are negatively associated with performance. *In line with this, we hypothesise that higher levels of mastery (H1) and performance-approach goal orientations (H2) and a lower level of performance-avoidance goal orientation (H3) are associated with success in international skills competitions.*

2.2 Metacognitive and Resource Management Strategies

Goal orientations have been shown to relate to metacognitive and resource management strategies (Vrugt & Oort, 2008). Metacognition refers to "awareness of and knowledge about one's own thinking" (Zimmerman, 2002, p. 65). Driscoll (2005, p. 107) expands this definition, adding "… and the self-regulatory behaviour that accompanies this awareness." According to Zimmerman (2002, p. 65), self-regulation refers to a "self-directive process by which learners transform their mental abilities into academic skills." *Metacognitive strategies* are related to cognitive processes, such as critical thinking, problem solving, and creative thinking. These processes advance professional knowledge, deepen one's understanding of knowledge, and increase the transferability of knowledge and skills (Pillay, 1998). In addition to metacognitive self-regulation, vocational students preparing themselves for a skills competition must be able to manage and regulate their studying and practical training. For that, they need *resource management strategies* encompassing time management (e.g., scheduling, planning) and effort regulation (e.g., commitment to completing difficult or uninteresting tasks, even in distracting situations) (Pintrich et al., 1991). In academic contexts, high effort regulation and effective use of time and study environment have been connected to higher achievements (Altun & Erden, 2013; Kim et al., 2015). Similarly, comparisons between the good and the best athletes have suggested that high levels of reflection and effort seem to be associated with high performance levels (Jonker et al., 2010; Toering et al., 2009). *In line with this, we hypothesise that higher levels of metacognitive strategies (H4) and resource management strategies (H5) are associated with success in international skills competitions.*

3 Method

3.1 Participants

Numerical empirical data (N = 137) were collected from the Finnish WSC competitors in 2008–2017. Competitors, mostly secondary level vocational school students, represented Finland in WSCs in 2009 (n = 41, Calgary, Canada), 2011 (n = 35, London, UK), 2013 (n = 42, Leipzig, Germany), and 2017 (n = 19, Abu Dhabi, United Arab Emirates). The sample comprised 64 male (46.7%) and 71 female (51.8%) respondents (two missing values, 1.5%). The average age for the males was 20.0 years (SD = 1.431) and for females was 20.1 years (SD = 1.198). The average age of the respondents was 20.1 years (SD = 1.310). Participants' self-reported grade-point average (GPA) after completion of the ninth grade in middle school was 8.2 (SD = 0.689; max. GPA = 10.0).

According to the t-test, there were no gender-related differences in participants' compulsory school GPA (M_{males} = 8.1, SD_{males} = 0.715; $M_{females}$ = 8.2, $SD_{females}$ = 0.674). Competitors who scored 500 points or higher in the WSC were coded into group A (n = 75, 54.7%), and those with a score lower than 500 points were coded into group B (n = 62, 45.3%). Gender distribution of these groups was quite equal, as the group A had 35 males (46.7%) and the B group had 29 (46.8%) males.

3.2 Instruments

Data were collected with a pen-and-paper questionnaire during the Finnish WSC team training camps 2008–2017. The questionnaire contained 17 five-point Likert scale items (1 = totally disagree through 5 = totally agree) related to goal orientations (nine items) and metacognitive and resource management strategies (eight items). Participants were instructed to focus on their WSC training when answering the questions. In addition to these questions, participants reported their age, gender, and middle school grade-point average.

Goal orientations were measured with nine items adapted from the personal achievement goal orientation section of PALS (Patterns of Adaptive Learning Scales, Midgley et al., 2000; Ross et al., 2002) (Table 12.1). PALS measures goal orientations in three dimensions (sample items in parentheses): (1) *Mastery* (MGO); (2) *Performance-Approach* (PAP); (3) *Performance-Avoidance* (PAV).

Metacognitive strategies (metacognitive self-regulation, elaboration, and critical thinking) were measured in two dimensions (six items) that were adapted from the learning strategies scales of the MSLQ (Motivated Strategies for Learning Questionnaire, see Pintrich et al., 1991): (1) *Metacognitive Strategies in Studies* (MSS) and (2) *Metacognitive Strategies in Training* (MST). *Resource management strategies* (time management and effort regulation) were measured in one dimension (two items adapted from MSLQ): (3) *Time and Resource*

TABLE 12.1   Goal orientation items

	Group A[a]		Group B[b]	
	M	SD	M	SD
Mastery				
– I want to learn as many new things as I can.	4.75	.438	4.55	.563
– I want to be as good as possible in my own skill area.	4.87	.380	4.74	.441
– I try to understand issues presented in the WSC training as thoroughly as possible.	4.51	.705	4.42	.615
Performance-approach				
– I would like others (e.g., trainers and trainees) to respect my craftsmanship.	4.57	.720	4.47	.671
– My aim is to show others that I am in the top level in my skill area.	4.37	.866	4.18	.915
– My aim is to be in the top "A group" in my WSC training team.	4.01	.979	3.71	1.193
Performance-avoidance				
– I don't want to embarrass myself in front of the others.	3.48	.978	3.42	1.049
– I avoid showing others if I am facing difficulties in WSC training exercises.	3.07	1.119	3.03	.940
– It is important to me that my teacher/trainer thinks I am a smart person.	3.53	1.070	3.74	.957

a WorldSkills competition participants with a score of 500 points or above ($n = 75$).
b WorldSkills competition participants with a score of less than 500 points ($n = 62$).

Management (TRM). Metacognitive and resource management strategy items are presented in Table 12.2.

3.3   Statistical Analyses

T and Chi-square tests were applied to identify gender, age, or middle school GPA-related differences between the A and B groups. Results revealed no differences. Pearson product moment bivariate correlations were calculated to examine associations within and between three goal orientation dimensions and three metacognitive and resource management strategies dimensions.

TABLE 12.2 Metacognitive and resource management strategy items

	Group A[a]		Group B[b]	
	M	SD	M	SD
Metacognitive strategies in studies (MSS)				
– I use my practise time efficiently.	3.95	.853	3.66	.788
– I set clear goals for my learning.	3.92	.801	3.82	.713
– Before reading new study material I first glance it through to see what it is about.	3.69	.972	3.52	.954
– I try to elaborate on my own thoughts based on what I have been taught.	3.87	.741	3.77	1.015
Metacognitive strategies in training (MST)				
– During practice I ask myself questions and reflect on the relationship between theory and work tasks.	3.35	1.020	3.42	.967
– I want to receive performance-related feedback from my teachers/trainers.	4.39	.787	4.16	.891
Time and resource management (TRM)				
– I work hard even if I do not like all the exercises relating to my training.	4.00	.771	3.85	.865
– I usually have enough time to practice before the competition or other display of my skills.	3.27	1.070	3.21	1.118

a WorldSkills competition participants with a score of 500 points or above ($n = 75$).
b WorldSkills competition participants with a score of less than 500 points ($n = 62$).

A four-way between-group multivariate analysis of variance (MANOVA) was conducted to investigate whether vocational students' WorldSkills competition success is related to their goal orientations (RQ 1) and metacognitive and resource management strategies (RQ 2). Six dependent variables were included in the analysis. The first three measured goal orientations (MGO, PAP, PAV), the following two measured metacognitive strategies (MSS, MST), and the last measured resource management strategies (TRM). The independent variables in the analysis were: WorldSkills competition success (group A score ≥ 500 points, group B score < 500 points), gender (female, male), age (17–19 years, 20–21 years, 22–25 years), and team (2009 Calgary, 2011 London, 2013 Leipzig, 2017 Abu Dhabi). Assumptions for the data were checked prior to MANOVA; no serious violations of normality, linearity, and univariate and multivariate outliers were detected. However, Levene's test of equality of error variances showed values less than .05, suggesting the use of a more conservative alpha level (e.g., .025, see Tabachnick & Fidell, 1996, p. 80).

4 Results

Table 12.3 presents the correlations between the six dimensions measuring goal orientations and metacognitive and resource management strategies. The upper part of the table presents the correlations of group A (competitors who scored 500 points or more in WSC, $n = 75$), and the lower part presents the correlations for competitors who scored less than 500 points (group B, $n = 62$). In the following, effect sizes of the correlations are interpreted with Cohen's (1988) guidelines: small = .10–.29, moderate = .30–.49, large = .50 and above. As expected, mastery and performance-approach goal orientations correlated positively in both groups (small to moderate effect). Also, the three dimensions measuring metacognitive and resource management strategies correlated

TABLE 12.3 Bivariate correlations between goal orientations and metacognitive and resource management strategies ($N = 137$)

	MGO	PAP	PAV	MSS	MST	TRM
WSC competitor group A[a]						
Mastery Goal Orientation (MGO)	1					
Performance-Approach Goal Orientation (PAP)	.46	1				
Performance-Avoidance Goal Orientation (PAV)	-.01	.38	1			
Metacognitive Strategies in Studies (MSS)	.28	.33	-.10	1		
Metacognitive Strategies in Training (MST)	.24	.34	.05	.50	1	
Time and Resource Management (TRM)	.15	.04	-.05	.58	.33	1
WSC competitor group B[b]						
Mastery Goal Orientation (MGO)	1					
Performance-Approach Goal Orientation (PAP)	.26	1				
Performance-Avoidance Goal Orientation (PAV)	.23	.57	1			
Metacognitive Strategies in Studies (MSS)	.30	.13	.02	1		
Metacognitive Strategies in Training (MST)	.28	.10	-.06	.51	1	
Time and Resource Management (TRM)	.22	.24	.08	.59	.41	1

a WorldSkills competition participants with a score of 500 points or above ($n = 75$).
b WorldSkills competition participants with a score of less than 500 points ($n = 62$).

positively in both groups (moderate to large effect). Interestingly, mastery goal orientation correlated positively with performance-avoidance goal orientation only in group B ($r = .23$, small effect). In addition, this lower performing group clearly had a higher positive correlation between performance-approach and performance-avoidance dimensions ($r = .57$, large effect) than the higher performing group A ($r = .38$, moderate effect). Mastery and performance-approach goal orientations (MGO, PAP) correlated positively (small to moderate levels) and performance-avoidance goal orientation (PAV) had no correlation with metacognitive strategies in studies (MSS) and training (MST), and resource management strategies (TRM) in both groups, except for the group A where no correlation was found between PAP and TRM, and a small negative correlation was present between PAV and MSS.

4.1 RQ 1: How Are Vocational Students' Self-Reported Mastery and Performance-Goal Orientations Associated with Objective Performance Measurement in International Skills Competitions?

In Tables 12.4 and 12.5, the effect sizes (partial eta squared) are interpreted according to Cohen's (1988) guidelines: small = .01–.05, moderate = .06–.13, large = .14 and above. We found a statistically significant difference between exceptionally high achieving competitors (group A, score ≥ 500) and others (group B, score < 500): $F(7, 85) = 2.299$, $p = .034$; Wilks' Lambda = 0.84; partial eta squared = .16. Univariate F-test results showed that mastery goal orientation was related statistically significantly to competition success: $F(1, 91) = 6.114$, $p = .015$; partial eta squared = .06 (moderate effect). High-scoring group A reported higher levels of mastery goal orientation ($M = 4.8$, $SD = 0.395$) than lower-scoring group B ($M = 4.6$, $SD = 0.433$). Performance-approach goal orientation was related statistically significantly to competition success: $F(1, 91) = 7.993$, $p = .006$; partial eta squared = .08 (moderate effect). High-scoring group A reported higher levels of performance-approach goal orientation ($M = 4.5$, $SD = 0.631$) than lower-scoring group B ($M = 4.1$, $SD = 0.712$). No interaction effect between gender, age and WSC group was found. *Hypotheses H1 and H2 were supported: both mastery and performance-approach goal orientations of group A competitors were higher than those in group B. Hypothesis H3 was not supported, as no difference was found between the two groups' performance-avoidance goal orientations.*

4.2 RQ 2: How Are Vocational Students' Self-Reported Metacognitive and Resource Management Strategies Associated with Objective Performance Measurement in International Skills Competitions?

Table 12.5 shows the results related to metacognitive and resource management strategies of the two WSC groups. MSS was related statistically significantly to

TABLE 12.4　Association of achievement goal orientations with WorldSkills competition success

	Group A[a] (n = 75)		Group B[b] (n = 62)		MANOVA
	M[c]	SD	M[c]	SD	
Mastery	4.8	0.395	4.6	0.433	$F(1, 91) = 6.114, p = .015$
Performance-approach	4.5	0.631	4.1	0.712	$F(1, 91) = 7.993, p = .006$
Performance-avoidance	3.4	0.706	3.4	0.711	

a WorldSkills competition participants with a score of 500 points or above.
b WorldSkills competition participants with a score of less than 500 points.
c Estimated marginal means.

TABLE 12.5　Association of metacognition and self-regulation with WorldSkills competition success

	Group A[a] (n = 75)		Group B[b] (n = 62)		MANOVA
	M[c]	SD	M[c]	SD	
Metacognitive Strategies in Studies (MSS)	3.9	0.599	3.6	0.555	$F(1, 91) = 4.062, p = .047$
Metacognitive Strategies in Training (MST)	4.0	0.689	3.7	0.687	
Time and Resource Management (TRM)	3.6	0.709	3.5	0.773	

a WorldSkills competition participants with a score of 500 points or above.
b WorldSkills competition participants with a score of less than 500 points.
c Estimated marginal means.

competition success: $F(1, 91) = 4.062, p = .047$; partial eta squared = .04 (small effect). High-scoring group A reported higher levels of metacognitive strategies in studies ($M = 3.9$, SD = 0.599) than lower-scoring group B ($M = 3.6$, SD = 0.555). No interaction effect between gender, age and WSC group was found. *Hypothesis H4 was partially supported, as metacognitive strategies in studies* were higher in highly-successful group A than in group B. Although metacognitive strategies in training were higher in group A than in group B, there was no statistically significant difference. We consider that the hypothesis H5 was also partially supported, as resource management strategies were higher in group A than in group B.

5   Discussion

Results of correlation analysis showed that mastery goal orientation correlated positively with metacognitive strategies in studies, metacognitive strategies in training, and time and resource management strategies in both high (A, medal winners and medallion recipients) and low (B) achieving competitor groups. However, group B competitors' correlation between mastery goal orientation (focusing on the task) and time and resource management strategies (allocating time for studying/practising) was higher than group A competitors' correlation. Further, correlations between performance-approach goal orientation and use of metacognitive strategies in studies and training were higher in the group A than in the group B, but the correlation with time and resource management was higher in the group B. These findings indicate that high achieving group A competitors utilised *more* metacognitive strategies in studying and training (efficient and reflective studying/training) and *less* time and resource management strategies when striving to master the tasks (mastery goal orientation) and show their ability (performance-approach goal orientation). The group B competitors applied the same strategy for task oriented goals (mastery approach), but a different strategy for ability oriented goals (performance-approach): They put less effort on metacognitive strategies in studying and training and more effort in managing time and resources in order to show their ability.

The first research question sought to study mastery and performance-approach goal orientations in relation to WSC success. Our results correspond with findings of an earlier study (Nokelainen et al., 2012) that medal winners and medallion recipients had higher mastery and performance-approach goal orientations than other WSC participants. This may indicate that adaptive patterns of learning (related to both mastery and performance-goal orientations) during training are related to the effective and versatile development of competencies needed for success in skills competitions. However, the application of maladaptive patterns has also been demonstrated to correlate with high achievement in the context of international skills competitions, as shown in the findings from the UK squad (Nokelainen & Stasz, 2016). The finding related to the third research hypothesis (no difference between groups A and

B in performance-avoidance goal orientation) may be an outcome of cultural (and educational policy) factors. Like was previously indicated in the theoretical framework, Finnish team for the international skills competitions is primarily selected to represent the level of the vocational education training system (instead of 'bringing home' as many medals as possible). Due to this, the Finnish team has always been exceptionally large compared to the size of our country (more than 40 competitors), and included participants also from those vocational fields where competition success is not to be expected. This may lead to a relatively low pressure compared to some other countries and show in competitors' responses to questions that ask their opinion about 'losing their face in front of others.'

The second question investigated metacognitive and resource management strategies in relation to WSC success. Relating to the fourth research hypothesis, the study suggested that highly successful competitors (group A) self-reported higher metacognitive strategies in studies (e.g., efficient use of practice time and setting clear goals). Group A also had higher average values in relation to metacognitive strategies in training (e.g., reflection between theory and practice and the need for performance-related feedback), but no statistically significant difference was present. Regarding our last hypothesis, group A showed higher average values of utilizing resource management strategies, although the mean difference was small and not statistically significant. These findings are in parallel with studies in academic and sport contexts (e.g., Kim et al., 2015; Jonker et al., 2010) highlighting associations between high levels of reflection, effort, and high performance. We measured metacognitive and resource management strategies with three dimensions in this study: (1) *Metacognitive Strategies in Studies* (MSS), (2) *Metacognitive Strategies in Training* (MST), (3) *Time and Resource Management* (TRM). Although they are designed to measure adaptive patterns of learning, we think that the last of them (TRM) may also measure maladaptive patterns of learning, depending on respondents' orientation towards setting his or her learning goals. That is, one may work hard and have a great amount of time for preparation (high score on TRM), but all this makes little difference, if the learning is not focused on the desired goals (low scores on MSS and MST dimensions).

This study shows that high achieving vocational students may endorse both mastery and performance goals. Moreover, the context of WSC has shown that even medal winners may adopt performance-avoidance goals (Nokelainen & Stasz, 2016). However, it is suggested that VET should aim at nurturing adaptive learning patterns including metacognitive learning strategies. In practice, motivational and self-regulated strategies could be enhanced by increasing perceived task value by providing meaningful learning environments and relevant and authentic job-related tasks integrating theory and practice (see e.g., Radovan & Radovan, 2015).

The present study has limitations to be considered. Small sample size ($N = 137$) leads to limitations of statistical power, that is, accepting whether an alternative hypothesis is true. This may have had an influence on the non-significant results related to research hypotheses 4 and 5. Although the sample is small, 85% of the target population (Finnish trainees for the 2009, 2011, 2013, and 2017 WorldSkills competitions) was recruited to participate in a study built on self-reported data. Considering the results, inconsistencies between goal orientations in various samples suggest that there may be a need to acknowledge cultural differences, even in Western cultures, as they may influence motivational processes and social desirability (e.g., King & McInerney, 2014). Furthermore, the association between metacognitive strategies in studies and WSC success should be interpreted with caution because, despite being statistically significant, it was weak ($p = .047$), especially in light of the suggestion to use a more conservative alpha level (e.g., .025) due to inequality-of-error variances. Finally, the context of vocational skills competitions has been scarcely studied: the lack of research on the topic is a challenge but also underscores the need for further research.

Note

1 Mastery goal orientation could also be labelled "mastery-approach goal orientation," but there is no need to do so as our approach will not utilize "mastery-avoidance goal orientations."

References

Altun, S., & Erden, M. (2013). Self-regulation based learning strategies and self-efficacy perception as predictors of male and female students' mathematics achievement. *Procedia-Social and Behavioral Sciences, 106*, 2354–2364.

Ames, C. (1992). Classrooms: Goals, structures, and student motivation. *Journal of Educational Psychology, 84*(3), 261–271.

Bouffard, T., Boisvert, J., Vezeau, C., & Larouche, C. (1995). The impact of goal orientation on self-regulation and performance among college students. *British Journal of Educational Psychology, 65*, 317–329.

Chankseliani, M., James Relly, S., & Laczik, A. (2016). Overcoming vocational prejudice: How can skills competitions improve the attractiveness of vocational education and training in the UK? *British Educational Research Journal, 42*(4), 582–599.

Cohen, J. (1988). *Statistical power analysis for the behavioral sciences.* Erlbaum.

Driscoll, M. (2005). *Psychology of learning for instruction* (3rd ed.). Allyn & Bacon.

Dweck, C. (1986). Motivational processes affecting learning. *American Psychologist, 41*(10), 1040–1048.

Elliot, A. J., & Harackiewicz, J. M. (1996). Approach and avoidance achievement goals and intrinsic motivation: A mediational analysis. *Journal of Personality and Social Psychology, 70*(3), 461–475.

Harackiewicz, J. M., Barron, K. E., & Elliot, A. J. (1998). Rethinking achievement goals: When are they adaptive for college students and why? *Educational Psychologist, 33*(1), 1–21.

Jonker, L., Elferink-Gemser, M. T., & Visscher, C. (2010). Differences in self-regulatory skills among talented athletes: The significance of competitive level and type of sport. *Journal of Sports Sciences, 28*(8), 901–908.

Jossberger, H., Brand-Gruwel, S., van de Wiel, M. W. J., & Boshuizen, H. P. A. (2020). Exploring students' self-regulated learning in vocational education and training. *Vocations and Learning, 13*(1), 131–158.

Kallio, H., Virta, K., & Kallio, M. (2018). Modelling the components of metacognitive awareness. *International Journal of Educational Psychology, 7*(2), 94–122.

Kim, C., Park, S. W., Cozart, J., & Lee, H. (2015). From motivation to engagement: The role of effort regulation of virtual high school students in mathematics courses. *Educational Technology & Society, 18*(4), 261–272.

King, R. B., & McInerney, D. M. (2014). Culture's consequences on student motivation: Capturing cross-cultural universality and variability through personal investment theory. *Educational Psychologist, 49*(3), 175–198.

Maehr, M. L., & Midgley, C. (1991). Enhancing student motivation: A school-wide approach. *Educational Psychologist, 26*, 399–427.

Midgley, C., Maehr, M. L., Hruda, L. Z., Anderman, E., Anderman, L. H., Freeman, K. E., Gheen, M., Kaplan, A., Kumar, R., Middleton, M. J., Nelson, J., Roeser, R., & Urdan, T. (2000). *Manual for the Patterns of Adaptive Learning Scales (PALS).* University of Michigan.

Nicholls, J. G. (1984). Achievement motivation: Conceptions of ability, subjective experience, task choice, and performance. *Psychological Review, 91*, 328–346.

Nicholls, J. G., Cheung, P. C., Lauer, J., & Patashnick, M. (1989). Individual differences in academic motivation: Perceived ability, goals, beliefs, and values. *Learning and Individual Differences, 1*(1), 63–84.

Niemivirta, M., Pulkka, A.-T., Tapola, A., & Tuominen, H. (2019). Achievement goal orientations: A person-oriented approach. In K. A. Renninger & S. E. Hidi (Eds.), *The Cambridge handbook of motivation and learning* (pp. 566–616). Cambridge University Press.

Nokelainen, P. (2018). Modelling the characteristics of vocational excellence: A case study with Finnish WorldSkills competitors. *Talent Development and Excellence, 10*(19), 15–30.

Nokelainen, P., Pylväs, L., & Rintala, H. (2018). Skills competition for promoting vocational excellence. In S. McGrath, M. Mulder, J. Papier, & R. Suart (Eds.), *Handbook of vocational education and training: Developments in the changing world of work.* Springer International. https://doi.org/10.1007/978-3-319-49789-1_69-1

Nokelainen, P., Smith, H., Rahimi, M. A., Stasz, C., & James, S. (2012). *What contributes to vocational excellence? Characteristics and experiences of competitors and experts in WorldSkills London 2011.* https://api.worldskills.org/resources/download/6666/6753/7647?l=en

Nokelainen, P., & Stasz, C. (2016). What contributes to vocational excellence? A study of the characteristics of WorldSkills UK participants for WorldSkills Sao Paulo 2015. *Skope.* http://vocationalexcellence.education.ox.ac.uk/wordpress/wp-content/uploads/2016/05/Project-1-Final-What-contributes-to-Vocational-Excellence.pdf

Pillay, H. (1998). Adult learning in a workplace context. In P. Sutherland (Ed.), *Adult learning: A reader* (pp. 122–136). Kogan Page.

Pintrich, P. R., Smith, D., Garcia, T., & McKeachie, W. J. (1991). *A manual for the use of the motivated strategies for learning questionnaire.* Technical Report 91-B-004. University of Michigan, National Center for Research to Improve Postsecondary Teaching and Learning.

Poortvliet, P. M. (2016). Mastery goals. In V. Zeigler-Hill & T. K. Shackelford (Eds.), *Encyclopedia of personality and individual differences* (pp. 1–4). Springer.

Pylväs, L., & Nokelainen, P. (2017). Finnish WorldSkills achievers' vocational talent development and school-to-work pathways. *International Journal for Research in Vocational Education and Training, 4*(2), 95–116.

Radovan, D. M., & Radovan, M. (2015). Facilitating students' motivation and learning through competence-based didactic units. *Journal of the Institute for Educational Research, 47,* 249–268.

Riveiro, J. M. S., Cabanach, R. G., & Arias, A. V. (2001). Multiple-goal pursuit and its relation to cognitive, self-regulatory, and motivational strategies. *British Journal of Educational Psychology, 71,* 561–572.

Ross, M. E., Shannon, D. M., Salisbury-Glennon, J. D., & Guarino, A. (2002). The patterns of adaptive learning survey: A comparison across grade levels. *Educational and Psychological Measurement, 62*(3), 483–497.

Ryan, L., & Lőrinc, M. (2018). Perceptions, prejudices, and possibilities: Young people narrating apprenticeship experiences. *British Journal of Sociology Education, 39*(6), 762–777.

SkillsFinland. (2018). *Taitaja-kilpailun säännöt* [*The rules of the Taitaja competition*]. http://skillsfinland.fi/download_file/view/231

Tabachnick, B. G., & Fidell, L. S. (1996). *Using multivariate statistics* (3rd ed.). HarperCollins.

Toering, T. T., Elferink-Gemser, M. T., Jordet, G., & Visscher, C. (2009). Self-regulation and performance level of elite and non-elite youth soccer players. *Journal of Sports Sciences, 27*, 1509–1517.

Tuominen-Soini, H., Salmela-Aro, K., & Niemivirta, M. (2011). Stability and change in achievement goal orientations: A person-centered approach. *Contemporary Educational Psychology, 36*(2), 82–100.

Tyson, R. (2018). Educating for vocational excellence. In S. McGrath, M. Mulder, J. Papier, & R. Suart (Eds.), *Handbook of vocational education and training: Developments in the changing world of work*. Springer International. https://doi.org/10.1007/978-3-319-49789-1_70-1

van de Pol, P. K. C., Kavussanu, M., & Ring, C. (2012). Goal orientations, perceived motivational climate, and motivational outcomes in football: A comparison between training and competition contexts. *Psychology of Sport and Exercise, 13*(4), 491–499.

Van Yperen, N. W., Blaga, M., & Postmes, T. (2014). A meta-analysis of self-reported achievement goals and nonself-report performance across three achievement domains (work, sports, and education). *PLOS ONE, 9*(4), e93594.

Virolainen, M., & Stenström, M.-L. (2014). Finnish vocational education and training in comparison: Strengths and weaknesses. *International Journal for Research in Vocational Education and Training, 1*(2), 81–106.

Vrugt, A., & Oort, F. J. (2008). Metacognition, achievement goals, study strategies and academic achievement: Pathways to achievement. *Metacognition and Learning, 3*(2), 123–146.

Wimmer, S., Lackner, H. K., Papousek, I., & Paechter, M. (2018). Goal orientations and activation of approach versus avoidance motivation while awaiting an achievement situation in the laboratory. *Frontiers in Psychology, 9*. https://doi.org/10.3389/fpsyg.2018.01552

WorldSkills International [WSI]. (2019). *Competition rules*. Version 8.2. WSI_OD03_competition_rules_v8.2_EN.pdf

Zimmerman, B. J. (2002). Becoming a self-regulated learner: An overview. *Theory into Practice, 41*(2), 64–70.

CHAPTER 13

Measuring Apprentices' Intrapreneurship Competence in Vocational Education and Training (VET)

An Interdisciplinary Model-Based Assessment

Susanne Weber, Clemens Draxler, Frank Achtenhagen, Sandra Bley, Michaela Wiethe-Körprich, Christine Kreuzer and Can Gürer

Abstract

Teachers should be able to balance content knowledge, pedagogical knowledge and technological knowledge (TPACK) in their various activities on curriculum, instruction, and assessment. Our Germany-wide study focused on measuring intrapreneurship competence. To ensure a valid and reliable assessment, we followed the three-step assessment triangle: cognition, observation and interpretation. We modeled the intended IP competence as an interdisciplinary and interprofessional team, designed a technology-based performance assessment tool that uses authentic work tasks, and analyzed apprentices' behavior via a model-based IRT (Rasch model) approach. Our results identify the distribution of the IP competence of apprentices on four proficiency levels. Since these results are generalizable, single IP tasks can be used by teachers to support and guide apprentices individually with regard to these proficiency levels. Our approach is a blueprint for evidence-based teaching that tackles all areas of TPACK.

Keywords

Technological Pedagogical and Content Knowledge (TPACK) – intrapreneurship competence – technology-based – performance assessment – assessment triangle – Item Response Theory/Rasch Model

1   Measuring Apprentices' Intrapreneurship Competence in
    Vocational Education and Training (VET): An Interdisciplinary
    Model-Based Assessment

Being a good teacher is a big challenge, akin to squaring the circle. Teachers must: know the subject to be taught; consider learners' interests and special needs; design interesting, challenging, and supportive learning activities; create respectful learning environments; monitor learners' behavior and react to misbehavior; arrange physical learning settings; engage learners; offer all learners learning opportunities and participation; communicate with families, colleagues, supervisors, local network partners, etc.; design formative and summative assessments to monitor learning and development processes; give feedback and support; and offer relevant certificates. All of these responsibilities and more can be found in the mountains of literature on teacher education (cf. Hamilton & McWilliam, 2001).

Some believe that good teachers are born (cf. Spranger, 1958; cf. critically: Berliner, 2001) or that teachers and learners share a quasi-therapeutic interrelationship (cf. Oevermann, 1996). According to Shulman (1998) and Oser and Bauder (2013), we perceive teaching as a profession, which means teaching can be learned and applied in many different situations in adaptive ways. Additionally, professionals are (a) entitled to define activities; (b) accountable; (c) available; and (d) integrated into a community (Oser & Bauder, 2013). As cores of these professional components, several competence profiles and standards are defined. These include on a structural level: (a) content knowledge (CK), which means teachers have to know the subject area and domain they are going to teach; (b) pedagogical knowledge (PK), which corresponds to teachers' knowledge of teaching and learning theories; and their intersection of (c) pedagogical content knowledge (PCK), which refers to teachers' knowledge of how to teach the specific content, i.e., the subject matter (Shulman, 1986, 2004). The field of technology expanded this professional competence model into new areas. Mishra and Koehler (2006) developed the TPACK-Model, according to which teachers should have additional knowledge about current technologies (TK) and how this affects the content (TCK) and the pedagogical knowledge (TPK). The arising intersection of all three knowledge areas (Technology, Pedagogical, and Content Knowledge) requires new affordances for teachers to balance them.

Hence, good VET teachers can explore specific VET domains and recognize the role of technology in this content area. For instance, they can formulate subject-specific and occupation-specific competencies as learning goals, (TCK), design technology-supported teaching and learning settings (e.g., video clips, tutorials), and include corresponding assessments (e.g., technology-based assessments) (TPK) in an integrated manner (e.g., authentic workplace simulations; virtual firms; authentic technology-based performance assessments) (TPACK). Such an alignment of curricular, instructional, and assessment-oriented components may lead to efficient and effective learning and development (Pellegrino et al., 2016).

For the field of business, several studies stress the need for innovative behavior in the sense of intrapreneurship (IP) and entrepreneurship to cope and master current workplace affordances (Humburg & van der Velden, 2015). Several VET curricula in Germany and in other European VET contexts postulate this learning goal. Similarly, the European Commission's Europe 2020 strategy claims to foster intrapreneurship to boost entrepreneurial thinking and innovations in existing organizations (Bacigalupo et al., 2016). Intrapreneurship is directed towards innovative behavior for individuals to create innovative project ideas and plan and implement projects within organizational practice. Therefore, individual employees are encouraged to "think-outside-the-box" and be "innovation drivers" (Wiethe-Körprich et al., 2017).

In our contribution, we focused on an authentic technology-based performance assessment (TPACK) of apprentices' intrapreneurship to assess competence gained in the VET instructional fields. In particular, we investigated apprentices participating in the industrial clerk apprenticeship program. In order to run a valid and reliable assessment, we considered the three steps of the assessment triangle to allow inferences from the measurement of data to the theoretical model of latent competence developed a priori (Pellegrino et al., 2001). The assessment triangle encompasses: (a) cognition, which entails addressing which knowledge, skills, and attitudes (competencies the learners should acquire and how they should know them); (b) observation, which involves addressing the challenges tasks learners must master to show their acquired knowledge, skills and attitudes/competence; and (c) interpretation, which concerns observed behavior that can be taken as evidence for the underlying (not directly observable) latent competence of learners and the way these evidences are analyzed, comprised, and structured. This alignment of the assessment triangle is related to Toulmin's (1958) concept of evidence-based reasoning rooted back in his argumentation theory.

Following the application of the assessment triangle, we: (a) modeled the competence of intrapreneurship based on extended domain analyses; and (b) provoked apprentices' intrapreneurship behavior through an integrated, authentic technology-based performance assessment using the virtual enterprise simulation ALUSIM Ltd. (Achtenhagen & Winther, 2014). The challenges and tasks to be mastered in that virtual enterprise represent authentic work tasks and episodes prompting intrapreneurial performance. The apprentices' intrapreneurship behavior is shown when the solution to the tasks is coded according to the evidences formulated in the fixed IP competence model (designed a priori) and analyzed by a corresponding probabilistic item response theory (IRT) model, i.e., the Rasch-Model.

We ran this assessment as a Germany-wide large-scale assessment to generalize the results for a decisive skill in the 21st century. This procedure of modeling and measuring competencies is in line with that of the large international comparative studies like PISA (Blömeke et al., 2015) and TEDS-M (Blömeke et al., 2010). The results showed that a high percentage of apprentices are IP competent. Additionally, through our model-based Rasch-scaling, we can distinguish between easy, medium, and difficult tasks. These insights can help teachers to support and guide apprentices in their learning and development progressions of IP. Furthermore, this approach can serve as a blueprint for evidence-based professional teaching, seeing as it tackles all areas of the TPACK model.

2 Theoretical Considerations

To run this authentic technology-based and model-based performance assessment and verify it as a source for efficient and effective teacher activities, we followed the assessment triangle. This approach emphasizes the stringent alignment of cognition, observation, and interpretation, which leads us to evidence-based reasoning (Pellegrino et al., 2001, 2016). Cognition is related to theoretical assumptions about how individuals acquire knowledge and develop competence in a particular domain. These considerations include an explanation of accepted and expected evidences. All of these considerations are summarized and fixed a priori in a *competence model*. The types of tasks, situations, or episodes that prompt individuals to act so that one can observe their behavior and performance – recognizing the formulated competence model – are described by a *task model*. Finally, methods and analyses described within the *statistical model* should correspond to the theoretical competence model and the quality of tasks for making valid reasonings, interpretations, and inferences on the latent competencies under investigation.

2.1 *Competence Model (Cognition)*
In line with various international comparative Large-Scale Assessments (LSAs) (e.g., OECD, 2014) and approaches in workplace learning and human resource development (e.g., Achtenhagen & Winther, 2014), we define competence as

"the latent cognitive and affective-motivational underpinning of domain-specific performance in varying situations" (Blömeke et al., 2015, p. 3). Such an integrated, holistic definition includes an individual's disposition and performance related to a situational context. This is in accordance with the claims of intrapreneurship/entrepreneurship (Brinckmann et al., 2011; Unger et al., 2011). With regard to the competence model, Hartig et al. (2012) differentiate between a horizontal layer for knowledge, i.e., skill dimensions (width), and a vertical layer for proficiency levels (depth) (Embretson, 2010).

2.2 Task Model (Observation)

After examining IP competence as "a complex ability closely related to performance in real-life settings" (Shavelson, 2012, p. 78), Shavelson (2012) provides seven criteria: complexity, performance, standardization, fidelity, proficiency level, improvement, disposition. The author states:

> A measure of competence should tap complex physical and/or intellectual abilities and skills to produce observable performance on a common standardized set of tasks that simulate with high fidelity the performances that are expected to be enacted in the "real world" ("criterion") situations to which inferences of competence are to be drawn, with scores reflecting the level of performance (mastery or continuous) on tasks where improvement can be made through dispositions for self-regulation, learning, and deliberative practice. (Shavelson, 2012, p. 78)

He applied these criteria with regard to critical thinking, analytical reasoning, problem-solving, and communication competencies within his Collegiate Learning Assessment (CLA) program (Shavelson, 2010), but also later to business planning tasks (Shavelson, 2012, 2013).

2.3 Statistical Model (Interpretation)

The interpretation is usually related to statistical models that characterize or summarize the patterns one would expect to see in the observations given as varying levels of apprentices' competence (Pellegrino et al., 2001). When choosing a suitable statistical model, the formulated competence model's horizontal and vertical structure must be considered. An option within the international discussion on measuring competencies is the Item Response Theory (IRT) (Blömeke et al., 2015; Hartig et al., 2012; Pellegrino & Wilson, 2015). The IRT is a Probabilistic Test Theory (PTT) that estimates apprentices' responses and scales them up on a logit-scale. Thus, a theoretically postulated competence structure (including item fitness, discrimination, and dimensionality) can be empirically proved (Hartig et al., 2012). The Rasch model (Rasch, 1960), one branch of the IRT, allows us to include task difficulties and individuals' abilities regarding the competence under investigation on the same logit-scale. This statistical analysis yields data on the number of competence dimensions on the horizontal layer and insights into the degree of difficulty of the tasks and the number of apprentices solving tasks with a specific difficulty on the vertical layer. For further insights, a particular threshold of proficiency levels can be built into the logit-scale. According to the Hartig procedure, this is done by applying the Gaussian regression analysis (Hartig et al., 2012). Thus, difficulty-generating features (DGFS) of a task (e.g., *cognitive affordance, content-related complexity,* and *unfamiliarity with the required situational actions*) can be used to create predictor variables for the linear regression analysis.

In the following section, we describe how we designed our authentic technology-based performance assessment in accordance with the assessment triangle (Pellegrino et al., 2001).

3   Development of the Authentic Technology-Based Performance Assessment

3.1   *Competence Model (Cognition)*

To define a priori our theoretical IP competence model (cognition), in pre-studies, we ran extensive domain analyses including job advertisements (N = 437) (Trost & Weber, 2012), prior exam reports (N = 205) (Weber et al., 2015), a systematic literature review (Wiethe-Körprich et al., 2017) and several intensive interviews and discussions with VET teachers and trainers. With this sampling procedure, we attempted to capture the width and depth of the latent IP construct to secure curricular and ecological validity (Brinckmann et al., 2011; Pellegrino et al., 2016; Shavelson, 2012).

We found that intrapreneurs are challenged by situational affordances, such as developing innovative new products, markets, or technologies based on newly acquired or (re-)organized resources within a complex bureaucracy (cf. Kuratko et al., 2005). To master these situational affordances, the intrapreneur must apply innovative work behavior, such as: (a) *perceiving problems and opportunities*; (b) *creating a new IP idea*; (c) *planning and monitoring the project*; (d) *implementing the project*; (e) *reflecting on the idea/project*; and (f) *selling the idea/project* (de Jong et al., 2015; Rupprecht et al., 2011). Several authors, such as Pinchot (1985), group these manifold IP skills into two dimensions: *idea generation* (skills 1–2) and *planning and implementing* (skills 3–6).

We also found that the various situational challenges require innovative behavior on different proficiency levels, which can be identified by task difficulty-generating features (DGFs), such as *cognitive affordance, content-related complexity*, and *unfamiliarity with the required situational actions* in theoretical and empirical analyses (Pellegrino et al., 2016). Since competencies, including IP competence, can be learned (Blömeke et al., 2015; Kuratko et al., 2005), we assumed a linear proficiency continuum (Blömeke et al., 2015; Minniti & Bygrave, 2001; Pellegrino et al., 2016; Wilson, 2005) in accordance with international comparative large-scale studies as well as research on intrapreneurship and entrepreneurship.

For the horizontal layer, we modeled the IP competence structure with its six dispositions on innovative work behavior grouped into two dimensions: *idea generation* (dim I); and *planning and implementing* (dim II). Each of the six dispositions was further operationalized through 14 situation-specific skills (cf. Figure 13.1; skills 1.1 ... 6.1) and linked by more detailed observable behavior-related indicators underlying the latent IP competence that is defined as expected and accepted evidences (cf. Figure 13.1, items 1.1.1 ... 6.1.1) (Wiethe-Körprich et al., 2017, p. 57).

On the vertical layer, we modeled the IP proficiency with three identified DGFs: (a) *cognitive affordance* included comprehension (DGF 1a), analyses (DGF 1b), and coping with strategic situations (DGF 1c) (cf. Marzano & Kendall, 2007); (b) *content-related complexity* with regard to the amount and quality of information to be integrated into a decision, action, or judgment included coping with single facts (DGF 2a), relationships (DGF 2b), and overarching concepts (DGF 2c) (Wilson, 2005); and (3) *unfamiliarity with the required situational actions* included coping with abstract school-based task formats (DGF 3a) or coping with authentic contexts (DGF 3b) (Marzano & Kendall, 2007).

3.2 Task Model (Observation)

Based on our IP competence model and our domain analyses, we designed authentic assessment tasks through which we were able to prompt and visualize intrapreneurial performance (Pellegrino et al, 2016; Unger et al., 2011). These tasks were designed to simulate central situational IP challenges found in human resource departments when identifying new means for recruiting new employees (episode 1) and in sales departments when setting up an online shop as a new distribution channel for smartphone covers and bumpers (episode 2) (cf. Kuratko et al., 2005). These challenges required the application of IP knowledge and problem-solving skills (Janesick, 2006; Shavelson, 2012), and a repertoire of different lower and higher-order skills. The tasks were also

Latent IP competence facets	→ Situation-specific skills	→ Observable behavior / evidences
Dimension I (dim I): Idea Generation		
1. Perceiving problems and chances	1.1 Perceive opportunities for IP	1.1.1 The apprentice becomes aware of an IP problem or chance
	1.2 Analyse the situation	1.2.1 The apprentice analyses the perceived IP problem or chance (explicating main and side effects, risks, taking perspectives etc.)
2. Creating new (IP-)ideas	2.1 Create innovative IP ideas	2.1.1 The apprentice generates a new innovative (at least an incremental) IP idea with regard to the perceived IP chance or problem
	2.2 Use creativity techniques	2.2.1 The apprentice applies tools for supporting the idea generating process
Dimension II (dim II): Planning and Implementing		
3. Planning and monitoring (IP-) projects based on the new (IP-) idea	3.1 Arrange work-packages and aspects in sequences and fix them in a GANTT-chart	3.1.1 The apprentice creates a GANTT-chart
	3.2 Procure, assess, and structure information	3.2.2 The apprentice searches for relevant information in documents or data files
	3.3 Use domain-specific terms and techniques	3.3.1 The apprentice applies, for example, a break-even-point by means of complex calculations
	3.4 Use domain-specific tools	3.4.1 The apprentice calculates a break-even-point by means of spreadsheets
	3.5 Reasoned decision	3.5.1 The apprentice decides among alternative solutions in view of disturbances (e.g., changes in market) on the basis of concrete reasons and arguments
	3.6 Identify and analyse risks	3.6.1 The apprentice assesses different risk scenarios
4. Implementing (IP-)projects	4.1 Team work	4.1.1 The apprentice shows that he/she knows and understands central categories of team work
	4.2 Solve problems, manage disturbances	4.2.1 The apprentice analyses and chooses appropriate strategies when team work starts to break down or becomes stuck
5. Reflecting (IP-)ideas/projects	5.1 Reflect whether the project was efficient and effective	5.1.1 The apprentice reflects phases, elements, or the whole project and evaluates them with regard to goal achievement, appropriateness, or success (explicating things that went wrong or well etc.)
6. Selling (IP-)ideas/projects	6.1 Introduce, "defend", justify the project	6.1.1 The apprentice presents his/her IP project and persuades others

FIGURE 13.1   Theoretical competence model for intrapreneurship (cognition)

embedded in a holistic workplace problem (Janesick, 2006). Finally, in our assessment pool, we had apprentices solve 17 tasks with 49 items. The unit of analysis is a single item. Typical performance-based items concern, for example, creating a GANTT chart (item 5, episode 2).

On the horizontal layer, the items captured situation-specific skills, such as arrange work packages and aspects of sequencing and fixing them, procure, assess, and structure information, use domain-specific terms and techniques, and use domain-specific tools (e.g., spreadsheets) corresponding to the disposition planning and monitoring the project. The items also measured apprentices' ability to take a perspective that requires situation-specific skills to perceive opportunities for IP and analyze the situation from the viewpoints of different stakeholders, as in item 42 (episode 1).

On the vertical layer, for example, item 5 was assigned to a medium proficiency level by building on the DGFs coping with relationships (DGF 2b) when apprentices must sequence work packages within a time frame and cope with authentic contexts (DGF 3b), when they have to extract relevant information from documents such as meeting protocols, or fit work packages within a GANTT chart template. Item 42 aimed to measure a higher proficiency level by implementing all three DGFs at their highest levels. To verify our claims, we ran separate think-aloud studies and expert judgments with VET teachers and trainers (Bley, 2017; Bley et al., 2015).

Finally, we implemented the tasks into the virtual enterprise ALUSIM Ltd., which simulates an existing company's production of aluminum boxes (e.g., Nivea) and cans (e.g., Coca Cola). Video clips help the apprentices to rope into the simulated enterprise and situational cases as well as keeping track of the storyline (Janesick, 2006). The modeled virtual enterprise was checked for content correctness and authenticity by practitioners of the modeled firm (cf. Achtenhagen & Winther, 2014) and technical usability (Sangmeister et al., 2018).

To assess the responses (solving performance), we developed a *scoring guide* on a dichotomous and polytomous basis according to our theoretically created IP competence model and defined the evidences (Pellegrino et al., 2016; Shavelson, 2012; Wilson, 2005). Hence, tasks, responses, scoring-rubrics, testing conditions, etc., were the same for all apprentices.

3.3 *Statistical Model (Interpretation)*

In line with our IP competence model (cognition) and task model (observation), we chose IRT, specifically the multidimensional Rasch model – also known as the multidimensional partial-credit model, or PCM – to recognize partial credits. This model is an adequate statistical psychometric approach

Sample task:
"generating a GANTT chart" (task 3)

By email, the test person receives the task to generate a GANTT chart for a new online shop project.

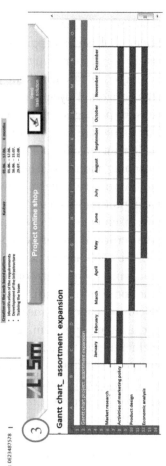

The following documents that are necessary to solve this task are attached to the email:
1. Template of a GANTT chart
2. Protocol of the last team meeting
3. Elaborated GANTT chart of a previous project

FIGURE 13.2   Example task from dimension 1: Creating a GANTT-Chart (observation)

to analyze and condense the observed apprentices' responses and prove our a priori-defined IP competence. We choose this statistical model because we follow on the horizontal layer, the assumption of two IP dimensions (*idea generation* and *planning and implementing*) (cf. Pinchot, 1985), and on the vertical layer, the proficiency along the IP competence continuum (also recognizing partial credits) (Wilson, 2005). Furthermore, this probabilistic Rasch model can simultaneously depict the relationship between the difficulty of tasks (representing IP-situational affordances) and apprentices' abilities (representing apprentices' IP competencies) on a common logit scale (de Ayala, 2009; Wilson, 2005). Furthermore, we intended to generalize the results and to offer VET teachers and trainers a sophisticated base for an evidence-based professional IP teaching model. Hence, we used the Rasch model because it implies that a once-verified model based on a representative sample of the intended population is valid and reliable for every subsample of this particular population, as well as for a small bundle of items (Embretson, 2010; Leutner et al., 2008). Therefore, the Rasch model assumes equal discrimination for all items (de Ayala, 2009; Wilson, 2005). In accordance with Verhelst and Glas (1995), we checked this against a one-parameter logistic model (OPLM) to account for the possibility of discriminating items.

To identify sense-making proficiency levels, we applied the Hartig method (Hartig et al., 2012) to insert thresholds for the proficiency levels on the logit-scale of the IP competence continuum according to the three DGFs identified (*cognitive affordance, complexity,* and *unfamiliarity*). This approach assumes that each DGF that significantly correlates with the item difficulty cumulatively contributes to explaining the item difficulty (Hartig et al., 2012).

Thus, our research questions were whether we succeeded in measuring apprentices' intrapreneurship competence, as per our theoretical model, using an authentic technology-based performance assessment tool (ALUSIM Ltd.) to close the circle for evidence-based reasoning (Toulmin, 1958). Our research questions were:

- Research Question 1 (RQ 1): Can we depict a two-dimensional IP competence model?
- Research Question 2 (RQ 2): Can we depict sense-making proficiency levels?

4   Method, Design, Sample, Data Collection, Analysis

We conducted a Germany-wide study using the authentic technology-based performance assessment tool ALUSIM Ltd. (Winther et al., 2017) and applying testlet designs (Wainer et al., 2007). As suggested by Draxler (2010) and Draxler and Alexandrowicz (2015), the sample size was determined by power analysis. In total, 28 VET schools from seven German states with N = 932 apprentices participated. The sample distribution reflects the typical characteristics of the whole cohort in the program of industrial clerks concerning age (x = 21.24; s = 2.39), gender (64% female), prior education (33% medium general education/*Realschule*; 67% higher general education/*Abitur*), and size of the training company (12% small, 56% medium, 32% large) (BiBB, 2013). Within the analyses, we removed N = 26 cases missing by design. Further systematic omissions could not be identified. The omissions within single cases were considered within the IRT procedure (Wu et al., 2007). A total of 84% of the items (dichotomous and polytomous) were coded automatically based on the coding guide (Pellegrino et al., 2016; Shavelson, 2012); the remaining items were coded manually by two coders (Cohen's Kappa = 0.93).

To answer RQ 1, we applied the Rasch Model – in particular the one- and two-dimensional between-multidimensionality Partial Credit Models (PCMs)[1] (Masters, 1982) using ConQuest v. 3.0 (Wu et al., 2007) – to the horizontal layer of the IP competence model and checked it against the OPLM (One Parameter Logistic Model) (Verhelst & Glas, 1995), considering the adjustments for the discrimination parameters (Weber, Draxler, et al., 2016). Then, we analyzed the item quality using ConQuest statistics by matching the *INFIT* values against the critical benchmarks of de Ayala (2009) and those used in the PISA studies by the OECD (2014).

To answer RQ 2, we applied the Hartig method (Hartig et al., 2012) to the vertical layer to build proficiency levels on a logit-scale. Therefore, experts judged each item concerning the three DGFs a priori. The results were fixed by the means per item. These DGF variables were then dummy-coded (DGF 1a, 2a, 3a are reference categories), and we ran a linear regression analysis using SPSS. The IP competence continuum is defined by adding step-by-step the unstandardized b coefficients to the intercept to explain the variables. The sequence of the explaining variables follows content-related considerations (Hartig et al., 2012).

5 Results

5.1 *Horizontal Layer of IP Competence*

Summing up these findings for RQ 1, we can assume a two-dimensional IP competence structure with *idea generation* (dim I) and *planning and implementing* (dim II) as a continuum. This result confirms our a priori theoretically modeled IP competence model and is in line with the literature, particularly

Pinchot (1985), and consistent with regard to the results of a previous study with N = 357 apprentices of regional firms (Weber, Draxler, et al., 2016).

A comparison of the statistical models (the one- and two-dimensional between-multidimensionality PCMs and the OPLM) shows that the two-dimensional between-OPLM fits the data the best (lowest BIC and AIC scores). The moderate correlations between the two latent dimensions of IP competence (r = .563; *covariance* = .163) support additionally a two-dimensional solution. The results of the scaling process are depicted on the Wright map (Figure 13.3). The EAP/PV reliabilities equal .80 for dimension I (*idea generation*) and .88 for dimension II (*planning and implementing*). These reliability values are comparable to Cronbach's alpha values (OECD, 2014). The ability estimates are well distributed across the logit scale (depicted by the "X"), as is the case for the item difficulties (depicted by item numbers). The item quality analysis shows a mean of –.09 (SD = .68) for dim I and a mean of –.37 (SD = .43) for dim II. The INFIT values (weighted MNSQs), which represent the weighted discrepancy between the empirically observed and theoretically expected responses, are all located within the critical benchmarks of de Ayala (2009), .50 to 1.50, as well as those of the OECD (2014), .80 to 1.20.

5.2 Vertical Layer of IP Competence

With respect to RQ 2, we can identify sense-making proficiency levels based on our three modeled DGFs. The results of the hierarchical linear regression analysis according to the Hartig method (Hartig et al., 2012) show that approximately 50% of the item difficulty can be explained by the three identified DGFs: (a) *cognitive affordance*; (b) *content-related complexity*; and (c) *unfamiliarity*. Based on the statistically significant variables, the main difficulty emerged when strategic situations had to be mastered (b = .458) or when overarching concepts (b = .431) or authentic contexts (b = .328) were involved.

The resulting R^2 lies over the benchmark defined by a minimum of .26 for building thresholds with this method (Hartig et al., 2012). Therefore, we built the first threshold by adding the intercept (–.710) with the unstandardized b coefficient for the significant explanatory variable *unfamiliarity*, coping with authentic contexts (DGF 3b) (–.710 + .328 = –.382), therefore obtaining the lower border of level 2. The second threshold was defined by adding to these results the significant b coefficient for the explanatory variable *content-related complexity*, coping with an overarching concept (DGF 2c) (–.382 + .431 = .049), obtaining the lower border of level 3. For the third threshold, the *cognitive affordance* variable, coping with strategic situations (DGF 1c), was added (.049 + .458 = .507), resulting in the lower border of level 4. This order of adding the DGFs follows the combination of the item characteristics. Thus, as expected

Sample task:
"perspective taking and reasoning" (task 15)

The task is introduced by a video clip describing the situation:

The test person receives the task displayed by the platform screenshot on the right.

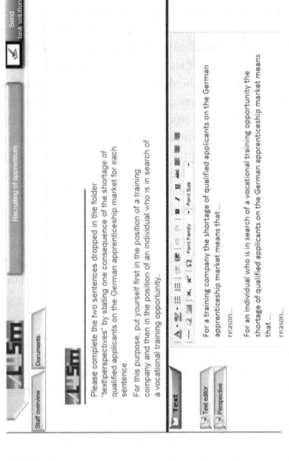

FIGURE 13.3 Example task from dimension II: Perspective Taking and Reasoning (observation)

for the proficiency levels, most of the difficult items combine all three relevant features. Most of the medium difficulty items are characterized by *content-related complexity* and *unfamiliarity*. Finally, most of the first-level items distinguish themselves by *unfamiliarity*.

The proficiency levels on the continuum of IP competence is depicted in Figure 13.4. Level 1 is not defined by any focused DGF and covers apprentices who can master basic IP challenges characterized by familiarity (Marzano &

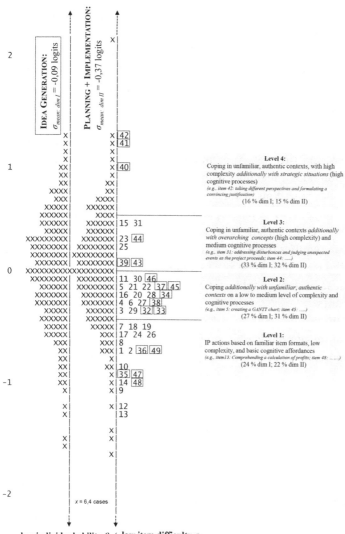

FIGURE 13.4   Empirical IP competence model (Wright-map) (interpretation)

Kendall, 2007), such as school-based task formats, low-complexity tasks that require single content-related facts (Wilson, 2005), and tasks that afford basic cognitive processes such as comprehension (Marzano & Kendall, 2007). For example, in item no. 13, apprentices must comprehend the concept of profit calculation.

The additional difficulty on level 2 is characterized by the degree of *unfamiliarity* with the item format. Apprentices associated with this level can address unfamiliar tasks, such as coping with authentic contexts (DGF 3b) similar to real workplaces. For instance, in item no. 5, apprentices must identify relevant information from a team meeting protocol to sequence work packages and fix them within the GANTT chart.

On level 3, the combination of *unfamiliarity* and *complexity* (DGF 3b and 2c) constitutes the item difficulty. Thus, apprentices on this level can simultaneously act in unfamiliar authentic workplace situations and cope with overarching concepts. For example, in item no. 31, apprentices must address disturbances and judge unexpected events as the project proceeds.

Level 4 combines *unfamiliarity*, *complexity*, and higher cognitive *affordance* (DGF 3b, DGF 2c, and DGF 1c). Apprentices on this level show strategic IP thinking and action skills under uncertainty because they can act in unfamiliar authentic workplace situations, manage authentic tools and context information, address overarching IP concepts, and apply strategic IP knowledge and skills in relevant IP areas such as *idea generation* or *planning and implementation*. Item no. 42 requires these abilities since the apprentices must take the perspective of the training company when new recruiting measures need to be created because of demographic changes and corresponding shortages of qualified applicants.

From a quantitative perspective, 84% of the apprentices achieved level 3, corresponding to the apprenticeship program's curricular goals for industrial clerks. Furthermore, 16% outperformed their colleagues on the highest proficiency level.

6 Discussion, Impact for Teachers

Departing from considerations about good teachers, we postulate teaching here as a profession in which teachers have to balance their activities according to the TPACK model, e.g., subject-related content, pedagogy, and technology (Mishra & Koehler, 2006). We intended to gather data on the IP competence of apprentices (resp. industrial clerks). Therefore, we run an authentic technology-based performance assessment. Our approach aligned cognition (by modelling IP competence on extended domain analyses), observation (by designing an authentic technology-based performance assessment), and interpretation (by using a model-based statistical approach). This alignment allowed us to infer IP competence from the empirical data obtained from a Germany-wide sample in comparison to the latent structure that was theoretically modeled a priori – through evidence-based reasoning (Toulmin, 1958), i.e., curricular and ecological validity. This model-based assessment is in line with current international large-scale studies of the OECD in general, adult education, and teacher education, such as PISA, PIAAC (cf. OECD, 2014), or TEDS-M (Blömeke et al., 2010).

The results support our theoretically assumed competence model with a two-dimensional construct of *idea generation* (dim I) and *planning and implementing* (dim II) on the horizontal layer (RQ1) and four sense-making proficiency levels on the vertical layer that combine *cognitive affordance, complexity*, and *unfamiliarity* (RQ2). Furthermore, these results are in line with a regional pre-study. Even the item difficulties from the regional and Germany-wide studies are within a similar rank order ($r = .871$ for dim I and $r = .802$ for dim II; $p = .000$) (cf. Weber, Wiethe-Körprich, et al., 2016). The results also show patterns comparable to our domain analysis of exam reports from different data sources (Weber et al., 2015).

Hence, we were able to broaden our IP competence understanding through reliable validation and map it on horizontal and vertical layers. By employing simulated authentic performance tasks, we additionally could go beyond classical multiple-choice tasks and self-reports that might be hampered by social desirability biases (task model: observation) (Embretson, 2010; Unger et al., 2011). Through our model-based statistical procedure of probabilistic IRT scaling, we were able to go beyond the total score and mean analyses used in classical test theory, which are often linked to problems of regression to the mean effects (Fayolle & Gailly, 2009; Fretschner & Weber, 2013).

Through Rasch modeling of a representative sample of the intended population, i.e., a huge cohort of apprentices in the area of industrial clerks – one of the most popular German apprenticeship programs – , the results are also valid for every subsample of this particular population, even for a small bundle of items (de Ayala, 2009; Embretson, 2010). This means that VET teachers can use our authentic technology-based performance assessment (all or selected items) to more precisely steer and guide the learning and development of IP competence with regard to the two dimensions (*idea generation* and *planning and implementing*), as well as with regard to the different proficiency levels. This assessment tool focuses on knowledge and skills that individuals have acquired and can apply (Martin et al., 2013; Unger et al., 2011).[2]

Concerning teacher education and the areas and intersections of the TPACK model, our extended domain analyses included visits to real workplaces, discussions with teachers and trainers, analysis of IP projects, job advertisements, etc. to familiarize ourselves with the workplaces of industrial clerks. We found that industrial clerks develop innovative new products, markets, and organizational processes; run information search on new ideas and evaluate them; plan and implement new ideas (CK). We also identified the domain specific tools Enterprise Resource Planning Systems (ERP-Systems) project planning tools (TK) and the use of tools for solving IP challenges and tasks, such as e-mails for delivering work orders and GANTT-charts to plan projects (TCK). Discussing with teachers but also checking existing learning theory (PK), and recognizing learning technology via video clips and video-tutorials (TPK). Furthermore, all professional community participants applied their knowledge on authentic performance task design, including statistical aspects, to fit the theoretical statistical model assumptions (PCK). When implementing the tasks into the virtual enterprise with the support of technicians, we integrated the knowledge into a complex, holistic, authentic, technology-based environment – the virtual enterprise ALUSIM Ltd. (TPACK). We used ALUSIM Ltd. as a performance assessment tool, but it could also be used as a learning tool.

We are aware that possibilities for such interdisciplinary and interprofessional projects – where teachers have the opportunity to participate and integrate research results – are not abundant. Nevertheless, there are plenty of small-scale research questions where teachers can apply the three-step assessment triangle. Teachers may also take the consumer perspective of research (Slavin, 2007, p. 2). Thereby, they may use the research results for an evidence-based teaching. In regard to our results, teachers may take our designed tasks and/or design their own domain-specific tasks (for learning and/or for assessment), hints from our procedure of aligning cognition, observation, interpretation (assessment triangle), discuss good examples for evidences, etc. Evidence-based practice may prompt the awareness of educational professionals on recent advances in their field (Darling-Hammond & Bransford, 2005; Weber & Achtenhagen, 2009). Furthermore, we are aware that such an endeavor of modeling and measuring competencies is neither meaningful nor efficient and effective for all VET competencies. But it seems to be helpful for fostering decisive 21st century skills.

7   Limitations and Outlook

To capture this idea of competence measurement, which implies that individuals should use their ability in several new and changing situations (Blömeke et al., 2015; Shavelson, 2012), we have to develop more tasks, situations, and episodes to extend the item pool. Furthermore, we currently cannot make assumptions about the structural development of IP competencies. For instance, we cannot answer whether the two dimensions merge into one overarching IP competence or split into more than two dimensions on an expert level. These issues can only be investigated using longitudinal approaches. Since the IRT scaling results are related to apprentices, future research should determine whether this IP competence model can also be generalized to other cohorts (e.g., adolescents in general education, bachelor students of business, or employees in organizations).

Acknowledgments

Our project was supported by the ASCOT Initiative (www.ascot-vet.net) of the German Federal Ministry of Education and Research (AZ: 01DB1118) with the aim to visualize work-related skills in the fields of engineering, business, and health.

Notes

1 If one assumes that each test item depicts only one latent dimension, this is denoted as 'between-item-multidimensionality' (Hartig & Höhler, 2009, p. 58).
2 Other projects in the ASCOT-initiative, comparable to ours, also developed blueprints available for pre-commercial development under the new Governmental initiative ASCOT Plus: https://www.bmbf.de/de/bmbf-forschungs-und-transferinitiative-ascot-1228.html

References

Achtenhagen, F., & Winther, E. (2014). Workplace-based competence measurement: Developing innovative assessment systems for tomorrow's VET programmes. *Journal of Vocational Education & Training*, 66(3), 281–295.

Bacigalupo, M., Kampylis, P., Punie, Y., & Van den Brande, G. (2016). *EntreComp: The entrepreneurship competence framework*. Publication Office of the European Union.

Berliner, D. C. (2001). Learning about and learning from expert teachers. *International Journal of Educational Research*, 35(5), 463–482.

BiBB (Federal Institute for Vocational Education and Training). (2013). *VET data report Germany 2012*. BiBB. Retrieved September 16, 2020, from https://datenreport.bibb.de/html/dr2013.html

Bley, S. (2017). Developing and validating a technology-based diagnostic assessment using the evidence-centered game design approach: An example of intrapreneurship competence. *Empirical Research in Vocational Education and Training, 9*(6), 1–32. https://doi.org/10.1186/s40461-017-0049-0

Bley, S., Wiethe-Körprich, M., & Weber, S. (2015). Formen kognitiver Belastung bei der Bewältigung technologiebasierter authentischer Testaufgaben – eine Validierungsstudie zur Abbildung von beruflicher-Kompetenz *Zeitschrift für Berufs- und Wirtschaftspädagogik, 111*(2), 268–294.

Blömeke, S., Gustafsson, J.-E., & Shavelson, R. J. (2015). Beyond dichotomies. *Zeitschrift für Psychologie, 223*(1), 3–13. https://doi.org/10.1027/2151-2604/a000194

Blömeke, S., Kaiser, G., & Lehmann, R. (Eds.). (2010). *TEDS-M 2008. Professionelle Kompetenz und Lerngelegenheiten angehender Mathematiklehrkräfte für die Sekundarstufe I im internationalen Vergleich*. Waxmann.

Brinckmann, J., Salomo, S., & Gemuenden, H. G. (2011). Financial management competence of founding teams and growth of new technology-based firms. *Entrepreneurship Theory and Practice, 35*(2), 217–243. https://doi.org/10.1111/j.1540-6520.2009.00362.x

Darling-Hammond, L., & Bransford, J. (2005). *Preparing teachers for a changing world. What teachers should learn and be able to do*. Jossey-Bass.

de Ayala, R. J. (2009). *The theory and practice of item response theory. Methodology in the social sciences*. Guilford Press.

de Jong, J. P. J., Parker, S. K., Wennekers, S., & Wu, C.-H. (2015). Entrepreneurial behavior in organizations: Does job design matter? *Entrepreneurship Theory and Practice, 39*(4), 981–995. https://doi.org/10.1111/etap.12084

Draxler, C. (2010). Sample size determination for Rasch model tests. *Psychometrika, 75*(4), 708–724.

Draxler, C., & Alexandrowicz, R. W. (2015). Sample size determination within the scope of conditional maximum likelihood estimation with special focus on testing the Rasch model. *Psychometrika, 80*(4), 897–919. https://doi.org/10.1007/s11336-015-9472-y

Embretson, S. E. (2010). Measuring psychological constructs with model-based approaches: An instruction. In S. E. Embretson (Ed.), *Measuring psychological constructs: Advances in model-based approaches* (pp. 1–7). American Psychological Association.

Fayolle, A., & Gailly, B. (2009). Assessing the impact of entrepreneurship education: A methodology and three experiments from French engineering schools. In G. P. West, E. J. Gatewood, & K. G. Shaver (Eds.), *Handbook of university-wide entrepreneurship education* (pp. 203–214). Edward Elgar Publishing.

Fretschner, M., & Weber, S. (2013). Measuring and understanding the effects of entrepreneurial awareness education. *Journal of Small Business Management, 51*(3), 410–428. https://doi.org/10.1111/jsbm.12019

Hamilton, D., & McWilliam, E. (2001). Ex-centric voices that frame research on teaching. In V. Richardson (Ed.), *Handbook of research on teaching* (4th ed., pp. 17–43). AERA.

Hartig, J., Frey, A., Nold, G., & Klieme, E. (2012). An application of explanatory item response modeling for model-based proficiency scaling. *Educational and Psychological Measurement, 72*(4), 665–686. https://doi.org/10.1177/0013164411430707

Hartig, J., & Höhler, J. (2009). Multidimensional IRT models for the assessment of competencies. *Studies in Educational Evaluation, 35*(2–3), 57–63.

Humburg, M., & van der Velden, R. K. W. (2015). Skills and the graduate recruitment process: Evidence from two discrete choice experiments. *Economics of Education Review, 49*, 24–41.

Janesick, V. J. (2006). *Authentic assessment primer*. Peter Lang.

Kuratko, D. F., Ireland, R. D., Covin, J. G., & Hornsby, J. S. (2005). A model of middle-level managers' entrepreneurial behavior. *Entrepreneurship Theory and Practice, 29*(6), 699–716. https://doi.org/10.1111/j.1540-6520.2005.00104.x

Leutner, D., Hartig, J., & Jude, N. (2008). Measuring competencies: Introduction to concepts and questions of assessment in education. In J. Hartig, E. Klieme, & D. Leutner (Eds.), *Assessment of competencies in educational contexts* (pp. 177–192). Hogrefe.

Martin, B. C., McNally, J. J., & Kay, M. J. (2013). Examining the formation of human capital in entrepreneurship: A meta-analysis of entrepreneurship education outcomes. *Journal of Business Venturing, 28*(2), 211–224. https://doi.org/10.1016/j.jbusvent.2012.03.002

Marzano, R. J., & Kendall, J. S. (2007). *The new taxonomy of educational objectives* (2nd ed.). Corwin Press.

Minniti, M., & Bygrave, W. (2001). A dynamic model of entrepreneurial learning. *Entrepreneurship: Theory and Practice, 25*(3), 5–16.

Mishra, P., & Koehler, M. J. (2006). Technological pedagogical content knowledge: A framework for teacher knowledge. *Teachers College Record, 108*(6), 1017–1054.

OECD. (2014). *PISA 2012 technical report*. OECD Publishing.

Oevermann, U. (1996). Theoretische Skizze einer revidierten Theorie professionalisierten Handelns. In A. Combe & W. Helsper (Eds.), *Pädagogische Professionalität* (pp. 70–82). Suhrkamp.

Oser, F., & Bauder, T. (2013). Einleitung: "Professional Minds" – Ein Fribourger Forschungsprogramm. In F. Oser, T. Bauder, P. Salzmann, & S. Heinzer (Eds.), *Ohne Kompetenz keine Qualität* (pp. 9–26). Klinkhardt.

Pellegrino, J. W., Chudowsky, M., & Glaser, R. (2001). *Knowing what students know*. National Academy.

Pellegrino, J. W., DiBello, L. V., & Goldman, S. R. (2016). A framework for conceptualizing and evaluating the validity of instructionally relevant assessments. *Educational Psychologist, 51*(1), 59–81.

Pellegrino, J. W., & Wilson, M. (2015). Assessment of complex cognition: Commentary on the design and validation of assessments. *Theory into Practice, 54*(3), 263–273.

Pinchot, G. (1985). *Intrapreneuring*. Harper & Row.

Rasch, G. (1960). *Probabilistic models for some intelligence and attainment tests.* The University of Chicago Press.

Rupprecht, M., Birner, K., Gruber, H., & Mulder, R. H. (2011). Dealing with diversity in consulting teams: Results of two Delphi studies. *Human Resource Development International, 14*(5), 561–581. https://doi.org/10.1080/13678868.2011.618348

Sangmeister, J., Winther, E., Deutscher, V., Bley, S., Kreuzer, C., & Weber, S. (2018). Designing competence assessment in VET for a digital future. In D. Ifenthaler (Ed.), *Digital workplace learning* (pp. 65–92). Springer.

Shavelson, R. J. (2010). *Measuring college learning responsibly. Accountability in a new era.* Stanford University Press.

Shavelson, R. J. (2012). Assessing business planning competence using the collegiate learning assessment. *Empirical Research in Vocational Education and Training, 4*(1), 77–90.

Shavelson, R. J. (2013). An approach to testing and modeling competence. In S. Blömeke, O. Zlatkin-Troitschanskaia, C. Kuhn, & J. Fege (Eds.), *Modeling and measuring competencies in higher education: Tasks and challenges* (pp. 29–43). Sense Publishers.

Shulman, L. S. (1986). Those who understand: Knowledge growth in teaching. *Educational Researcher, 5*(2), 4–14.

Shulman, L. S. (1998). Theory, practice, and the education of professionals. *The Elementary School Journal, 98*(5), 511–526.

Shulman, L. S., & Wilson, S. M. (2004). *The wisdom of practice: Essays on teaching, learning, and learning to teach.* Jossey-Bass.

Slavin, R. E. (2007). *Educational research in an age of accountability.* Pearson.

Spranger, E. (1958). *Der geborene Erzieher.* Quelle & Meyer.

Toulmin, S. (1958). *The uses of argument.* Cambridge University Press.

Trost, S., & Weber, S. (2012). Fähigkeitsanforderungen an kaufmännische Fachkräfte. Eine kompetenzbasierte Analyse von Stellenanzeigen mittels O*NET. *Zeitschrift für Berufs- und Wirtschaftspädagogik, 108*(2), 217–242.

Unger, J. M., Rauch, A., Frese, M., & Rosenbusch, N. (2011). Human capital and entrepreneurial success: A meta-analytical review. *Journal of Business Venturing, 26*(3), 341–358. https://doi.org/10.1016/j.jbusvent.2009.09.004

Verhelst, N. D., & Glas, C. (1995). The one parameter logistic model. In G. H. Fischer & I. W. Molenaar (Eds.), *Rasch models: Foundations, recent developments, and applications* (pp. 215–238). Springer.

Wainer, H., Bradlow, E., & Wang, X. (2007). *Testlet response theory and its applications.* Cambridge University Press.

Weber, S., & Achtenhagen, F. (2009). Forschungs- und evidenzbasierte Lehrerbildung. In O. Zlatkin-Troitschanskaia, K. Beck, D. Sembill, R. Nickolaus & R. Mulder (Eds.), *Lehrprofessionalität. Bedingungen, Genese, Wirkungen und ihre Messung* (pp. 477–487). Beltz.

Weber, S., Draxler, C., Bley, S., Wiethe-Körprich, M., Weiß, C., & Gürer, C. (2016). Der Projektverbund CoBALIT: Large scale-assessments in der kaufmännischen Berufsbildung – Intrapreneurship (CoBALIT). In K. Beck, M. Landenberger, & F. Oser (Eds.), *Technologiebasierte Kompetenzmessung in der beruflichen Bildung – Resultate aus dem Forschungsprogramm ASCOT* (pp. 75–92). Bertelsmann.

Weber, S., Wiethe-Körprich, M., Bley, S., Weiß, C., & Achtenhagen, F. (2015). Intrapreneurship-Verhalten an kaufmännischen Arbeitsplätzen – Analysen von Projektberichten. *Empirische Pädagogik, 28*(1), 84–105.

Weber, S., Wiethe-Körprich, M., Bley, S., Weiß, C., Draxler, C., & Gürer, C. (2016). Modellierung und Validierung eines Intrapreneurship-Kompetenz-Modells bei Industriekaufleuten. *Unterrichtswissenschaft, 44*(2), 149–168.

Wiethe-Körprich, M., Weber, S., Bley, S., & Kreuzer, C. (2017). Intrapreneurship competence as a manifestation of work agency: A systematic literature review. In M. Goller & S. Paloniemi (Eds.), *Agency at work: An agentic perspective on professional learning and development* (pp. 37–65). Springer.

Wilson, M. (2005). *Constructing measures: An item response modeling approach*. Lawrence Erlbaum Associates.

Winther, E., Seeber, S., Weber, S., Bley, S., Festner, D., Kreuzer, C., Rudeloff, M., Sangmeister, J., & Wiethe-Körprich, M. (2017). *Modellierung und Messung beruflicher Kompetenzen in der kaufmännischen Domäne (CoBALIT). Version: 1*. Berlin: Institut zur Qualitätsentwicklung im Bildungswesen. Dataset. https://doi.org/10.5159/IQB_CoBALIT_v1

Wu, M. L., Adams, R. J., & Wilson, M. (2007). *ACER ConQuest. Version 2.0. Generalized items response modelling software*. ACER Press.

CHAPTER 14

Creative Talent as Emergent Event

A Neurodiversity Perspective

Ananí M. Vasquez, Mirka Koro and Ronald A. Beghetto

Abstract

How might teachers support creative talent in learning environments? Typically, creative talent is conceptualized as a trait possessed by a few, select people. According to the traditional mindset, schools serve as sites whereby educators attempt to identify and nurture the creative talent of the gifted few who possess it. In this chapter, we use a speculative approach to explore, wonder and consider possibilities for an alternative perspective to the creative-talent-as-possession mindset. Specifically, we introduce the concept of *creative talent as emergent event* (CTEE). We define CTEE as dynamic manifestations of diverse strengths, interests, and happenings recognized by oneself and others in the on-going interactions, processes and artifacts of social situations and contexts. We discuss how we derived this definition based on recent perspectives on neurodiversity, which recognizes the multiplicity and dynamic capabilities of all people through limitless modes of interrelating in lived experience. Although our perspective represents a somewhat radical shift from how creative talent is typically conceptualized and approached by scholars and educators, it offers new directions for thinking about how teachers can help realize the creative potential that inheres in teaching and learning practices. We close the chapter by speculating further on possibilities for how educators might move away from a creative-talent-as-possession mindset toward a more inclusive CTEE mindset in and beyond the classroom.

Keywords

creative – talent – event – neurodiversity

1   Introduction

The United States, similar to other westernized societies, has a long history of segregating students according to perceived differences in mental functioning. In the early 20th century, compulsory education laws increased diversity in school populations and the use of intelligence and creativity testing to sort students led to gifted, special and general education siloes within education, each developed along differing historical paths, with differing priorities, discourses and practices (Blanton et al., 2014; Marland, 1972; Rapp & Arndt, 2012). Across these discourses, though, creative talent has typically been conceptualized as a trait possessed by a few, select people. According to the traditional mindset, schools serve as sites whereby educators attempt to identify and nurture the creative talent of the gifted few in preparation for successful and productive adulthoods and in anticipation of great individual contributions to society. This is problematic because it produces inherently exclusionary processes and practices. In this conceptual chapter, we offer an alternative, more inclusive, perspective to this creative-talent-as-possession mindset.

More specifically, we use a speculative approach to introduce the concept of creative talent as emergent event (CTEE). We define CTEE as *dynamic manifestations of diverse strengths, interests, and happenings recognized by oneself and others in the on-going interactions, processes and artifacts of social situations and contexts*. We offer this theoretical construct, or philosophical speculation, in conversation with other scholars and theorists who have promoted a pluralist and developmental view of human potential that is contextually and dynamically shaped (Dai, 2020) and who have envisioned "gift-ed" becoming as transactional, between context and personal qualities (Lo et al., 2019). These related ecological and transactional theories, much like Bronfenbrenner's (1976) systems of influence, have expanded our understanding of the learner. Our definition of CTEE aligns with dynamic and contextual perspectives of talent, but also moves beyond to build on the ideas of talented interactions and smart contexts, contexts that engage talent development and support inclusive participation (Barab & Plucker, 2002). Creative talent describes the quality of the neurodiverse learning event, or set of interactions, as it emerges in a smart context.

CTEE is also informed by recent perspectives on neurodiversity (Manning, 2016). A neurodiversity perspective, rather than a psychological, neurological, biological or behavioral perspective, represents a somewhat radical shift from how creative talent is typically conceptualized and approached by scholars and educators. Neurodiversity here refers not only to the dynamic capabilities of all people, but also to limitless modes of interrelating in lived experience. Using a neurodiversity perspective in speculating how educational experiences might be perceived differently offers new directions for thinking about how teachers can help realize the creative potential that inheres in teaching and learning practices. Although we will not offer specific techniques, we recognize that there are various frameworks and practices that might harmonize with CTEE, including the Enrichment Triad Model (Reis & Renzulli, 2009), Positive Niche Construction (Armstrong, 2012), inquiry-based instruction, active learning, project-based learning, Universal Design for Learning, and possibly Montessori-inspired instruction. These examples are open to the development of dynamic learning environments in which experiences, or learning events, rather than individuals, might be understood as the locus for talent emergence. Educational methods that prioritize independence, such as didactic instruction, over interdependence, or collaborative, experiential learning, will require more substantial shifts in thinking when considering CTEE.

Exploring creative talent through neurodiversity and with a speculative approach expands creativity and talent educational research and practice to more inclusive possibilities. We close the chapter by speculating on how educators might experiment with moving away from a creative-talent-as-possession mindset toward a CTEE mindset in and beyond the classroom.

2 From Creative Talent as Possession to Creative Talent as Event

Although creative talent has typically been conceptualized as a possession of individuals, there are a long line of scholars who have recognized that conceiving of talents and limitations as de-contextualized possessions of individuals is highly problematic (e.g., Barab & Plucker, 2002; Dai, 2016; Dewey, 1938; Lo et al., 2019; McDermott, 1993; Moran, 2020). Lo et al. (2019), for instance, posits that context, personal qualities and development determine giftedness. Using the transactional perspective, individuals become "gift-ed" through dynamic relational flows within their environments. With these shifts, creative talent development is perceived as interactive, relational, contextual and developmental. Creative talent does not reside in an individual's mind, or body, but through an ongoing, processual interaction with their environment.

Additionally, creative talent is not considered singular or one-dimensional, but multiple (Gardner, 2020; Moran, 2020; Tirri & Nokelainen, 2011). Recent work on the concept of neurodiversity has also helped to provoke new conceptions about talent and ability away from singular and static human possessions toward more fluid, emergent and unpredictable events (Manning, 2016). Our conceptualization draws on core tenets of neurodiversity and pushes beyond restrictive pedagogies of sameness toward practices that foreground the creative potential of difference (Beghetto & Yoon, 2020). Neurodiversity celebrates difference, offers an opportunity to rethink "accommodations" and emphasizes neurology as a means to challenge existing norms (Manning, 2016). Erin Manning, in an interview with Evans (2018) states:

> the "neuro" in neurodiversity has opened up the conversation about the category of neurotypicality and the largely unspoken criteria that support

and reinforce the definition of what it means to be human, to be intelligent, to be of value to society. This has been especially necessary for those folks who continue to be excluded from education, social and economic life, who are regarded as less than human, whose modes of relation continue to be deeply misunderstood and who are cast as burdens to society.

CTEE offers a curative to the valorization of neurotypicality, dominant in most westernized societies, which privileges self-sufficiency and independence, reading, writing, speaking and assertive forms of nonverbal communication. High general cognitive intelligence, extroversion and business savvy are often also seen as signs of leadership, creative talent and/or giftedness within this neurotypical mindset. A neurodiversity mindset, in turn, engenders an openness for "multiple modes of relation," including extralinguistic perceptions of rhythm, tone, color, affect, proprioception and movement, in the experience of an event, such as a lesson (Manning, 2013, 2016). It offers a strength-based and ecological approach (see also Armstrong, 2012) that builds on the creative potential of all students, teachers, and situations, while addressing the problem of exclusivity.

What if we think of creative talent less in terms of human capacity for knowledge-gathering or creating and more as processes of relational forces? What if creative talent is not about something we are, but something in the making and doing? And what if some of what we are committed to doing is "refusing to situate movement [of thought, of creative talent] in a reconstituted subject; questioning the place of volition in experience; resisting normopathy as a point of departure; embracing autistic perception," described as direct, felt experience of relational forces as they are forming (Manning, 2016, pp. 129–130). What if creative talent is a fluid and ongoing process? In these initial speculations, neurodiversity is viewed as the "how" of experience. Experience can be perceived through multiple modes of relation. Neurodiversity represents multiplicity and dynamic inter-relationality, while neurotypicality is singular and static. When we discuss event, it is as the "what," or content, of experience. In education, a lesson could be an example of an event. Creative talent, then, is the "what kind," or creative quality, of the event as it unfolds (see Table 14.1).

Taken together, our previous provocations fortify creative talent as neurodiverse event, which emerges in ruptures of the socio-material and historical context. Moreover, these ruptures in otherwise planned learning activities become animated and *sometimes* recognized in the social interactions of teaching (Beghetto, 2016). With CTEE, we also propose that context may promote and potentially generate creative talent. For example, environments and spaces could be smart (Barab & Plucker, 2002), creative talent collective, and

TABLE 14.1 Concepts as used in this chapter and their descriptions

Concepts	Description
Speculation	Practice and process which imagines possibilities and postulates possible futures, potential actions, and draws unthinkable connections
Neurodiversity	Dynamic "how" of experience, multiple modes of relation
Neurotypicality	Singular, static "how" of experience
	Expected/conventional modes of relation
Event	The "what," content, of experience
	Emergent, inter-relational (e.g., a classroom lesson)
Creative talent	Creative quality of an event, experienced through multiple modes of relation

creative talent environments more than the sum of their individual parts. Creative talent events often operate in organic, unexpected and unpredictable ways. Traces of creative talent events, though, might be recognizable and even teachable in some ways.

3   Speculation for Practical Possibilities

Aligned with our contextual and process-oriented perspective we do not offer tools, strategies, and devices for educators and teachers to use. Similarly, we do not want to define what "good teaching" looks like and might entail. Instead, we frame our work in the context of speculation. What might be, what could be, what could be imagined? We ask many questions and "what ifs." Maybe these questions are not even questions but provocations to imagine the possible and also the impossible. By doing this we hope that readers will think, sense, and experiment thus forming their own perspectives, creating their own unique practices and contextualized processes which may stimulate neurodiverse approaches. We do not wish to generate another grand narrative of creative talent (or neurodiversity) which potentially deactivates teachers, educators, parents, and students to follow pre-determined paths and solutions. Instead, we would like to offer options, provoke new thinking and practices toward documenting potentially undiscovered educational events that can serve as reflective artifacts to help prepare or cultivate "readiness" to recognize, engage in, and learn from the manifestation of creative talent.

Our speculative stance is also not new. Indeed, Greek thinkers advanced speculation by being curious, probing, questioning and trying to understand complexities. They were also rigidly systematic and omnivorous in their interests and they did not keep different subjects and disciplines apart. "In one way it [speculative reason] accepts the limitations of a special topic, such as a science or a practical methodology. It then seeks speculatively to enlarge and recast the categorial ideas within the limits of that topic" (Whitehead, 1959, p. 85).

Our world is rapidly changing, and we can no longer stridently predict the most suitable educational futures, even for those of students who have been deemed creative or talented by established identification practices. Instead, we should speculate, postulate, and wonder. While uncertain about the future, creation and invention might be some of the most adaptable processes and tools for moving beyond educational impasses. In this chapter conceptualizations of creative talent are speculative. They are not to be verified or offer fixed solutions. Speculations are not generalizations and they do not build on predictable variables. Instead, they support different kind of science and scholarship. Facts and generalizable variables belong to other kind of scholarship which is based on post-positivism and prediction models. Speculative education practices experiment and ask questions about possibilities. They offer propositions and alternatives which can lead to practical experimentation and transformations in different educational contexts. Speculative practices do not demand or tell teachers what to do but offer alternatives to think about future differently and choose different paths, techniques, and strategies for the future. Speculation offers us a way to propose ideas without imposing ideologies, envision without directing, and imagine without disciplinary borders. Kaljonen et al. (2019) described speculative approaches to experimentation building from the philosophy of science, as being open, hesitant, collective, and participatory. Speculation as a philosophy does not exclude anything and functions as open adventure. In this kind of experimentation educators and students are capable of imagining and creating new practices and framings. Scholarship will move beyond the currently thinkable and doable and may imagine and invent practices of doing otherwise. In speculative work qualities and knowledge are not mental or building-blocks of reality but emergent, becoming within nature, always in relation to others. Relations are real but what they can and will do cannot be known in advance, only continuously be invented (see e.g., Manning, 2016).

With this speculative approach, we continue in uncertainty to explore, invent and question. What speculative possibilities are there for teaching and learning when creative talent is an emergent event?

4   Possibilities of the Lesson-Event

What if we were to consider a lesson-event as a basic educational event? An emerging learning experience is not constrained to a specific time and place, but for a lesson-event, we make determining "cuts" in the learning process to focus on a small portion of the complex interactions within educational experience. What if creative talent is the process(es) of attunement to the dynamic relationships within the lesson-event? These processes of attunement "honor complex forms of interdependence and ... create modes of encounter for ... difference" (Manning, 2016, p. 5). How would conceptualizing creative talent in this way change our teaching and learning practices? Maybe instead of detecting and teaching to individual labels and learning styles, we might design learning environments that engender interactions for learning that are *constantly becoming* through relational interactions in the social, human and material, environment. In attuning to the forming and re-forming relationships, learning, and therefore "ability" or creative talent, instead of being found in the attributes of the students, might be perceived as unfolding through these lesson-events. Doing so would zoom our focus out a bit, providing a broader vantage point for considering the kinds of creative openings that emerge in classrooms. At this point, an example may help clarify our CTEE perspective.

Let's consider a hypothetical, first grade lesson-event. The rationale for including this portion of the lesson-event is to exemplify attunement to creative openings. It is not intended to describe a full math lesson or a process of skills attainment, neither is it a description of a recognized pedagogical approach, such as Montessori.

Four first grade students are gathered around a table, Sean, Marta, Luisa and Ahmed. On the table is a box of base-ten blocks, a box of Unifix cubes, math journals, graph paper, pencils, colored pencils, a stuffed animal, a Hot Wheels sports car and a crumpled tissue. Hanging on these student's chairs are backpacks, sweaters and jackets and near their feet are bottles of water. Nearby are other tables with other students and materials. One of the students pulls a task card from the box by the math shelf. The task cards are student generated and this particular card is signed by Tory and Marco. At the table, one of the students reads the task aloud, then passes the card around so that everyone can read it for themselves. They determine that they do not need to clarify the task with Tory or Marco and begin working on the task. Sean quickly opens the box of base-ten blocks and counts out the first number in the task description. Marta takes the stuffed animal and sportscar and acts out a scene. Ahmed seems interested in Marta's play, but soon turns away to open his math journal. He holds his pencil to his forehead and looks up at the ceiling. Luisa is staring into space and drumming her fingers on the tabletop. A while later, Ahmed has been drawn back into Marta's skit. He finally asks her about it. Soon Sean leaves his blocks to listen to Marta-stuffed animal-sportscar. He brings some of the blocks into the enactment. "Wait!" shouts Ahmed, "You mean ..." Then Ahmed starts to write in his journal. The other three stop what they are doing and huddle over him as he writes out a number sentence. "Yes!" Marta claps. "I don't think so," Sean doubts as he sets up some blocks next to the written numbers in Ahmed's journal. They continue to problem solve together.

This scenario is written through the lens of CTEE, as attunement to the lesson-event, the learning-in-progress through various relational ties between aspects in the classroom environment. These events produced many interconnected units: task card-Tory-Marco-four first grade students, Ahmed-pencil-forehead-ceiling, Marta-stuffed animal-sports car-Sean-blocks-Ahmed-journal, etc. Although the math task, concepts and skills are not mentioned in the scenario, we can imagine the many mathematical concepts that might have emerged during meaning-making in this lesson-event as well as the many possible directions for further conceptual and skill development (e.g., writing number sentences, conservation of number, math reasoning and problem solving, place value, operations). What changes when we shift focus to the learning process, as emergent, rather than as a predetermined product, or result? Might the teacher's responsibility then be to develop the techniques that will open the lesson-event to its more-than features, to perceive the emergent relationships and to guide others in perceiving them as well? What techniques might develop for designing "open" lesson-events? How might classroom routines and structures change using this perspective? What techniques might be useful for developing a CTEE perspective, attunement to creative openings in the lesson-event, as a practice? How might neurodiversity, diverse modes of relation, change other teaching and learning practices? How might we assess creative talent through neurodiversity?

The above example and questions highlight several considerations for how researchers and educators could move away from limiting views of creative talent, including: (1) perspectives that privilege sameness and certainty to those that productively engage with difference and uncertainty, (2) viewing creative talent in overly narrow ways toward a more expansive and inter-relational perspective, and (3) fixed views of human development toward more dynamic and multiple processual pathways. The teacher in the example will not be certain as to which concepts and skills might emerge from the creative openings in this lesson-event, but through attunement and assessment would be able to design multiple pathways for future development.

Educators who embrace difference and uncertainty required for a CTEE perspective might find new possibilities for teaching and learning (Beghetto,

2020), some of which might include ways of noticing creative talent in learning environments. If we imagine a lesson as an event and classroom learning as a field of experience, the modes of relation that emerge and are always uncertain and generating difference. Even when a lesson-event is repeated for a different class or a subsequent year, it is never the same lesson-event. A specific event, although similar to past events, might have "startled the original task, opening it up toward its more-than" (Manning, 2013, p. 79). In a classroom, for example, a math problem might be solved in a way that the teacher has never seen before or a new word is created. These solution strategies and word creations emerge through difference, the interconnected units of relationships within the classroom environment, rather than the structured sameness in predetermined lessons with prescribed outcomes. What if creative talent, as neither singular nor stable, is also becoming through/with these events? Engaging with uncertainty and difference, then might involve a practice of attunement to creative talent as multiplicity.

5 Multiplicity in Emerging Creative Talent Events

The quality of an experience, not yet consciously understood, is sensed, felt as an affective attunement, a form of emergent relation between/with more than one person and/or thing (Manning, 2013). In this way, the teacher and the student are not viewed as discrete individuals, or "selves," but are co-constituted with other individuals. An individual, then "is a durational multiplicity, a becoming of continuity, not a continuity of becoming" (Manning, 2013, p. 23). New interconnected units intersect, generating tendencies, or attunements, which may take form and become consciously recognized as a certain concept, idea, gift or creative talent. In the classroom, educators may sense interests, motivations, aptitudes and dispositions, which change throughout the school year, or even a school day, across subject areas, with different grouping situations and with changes in materials. Jose and Lily in solving multiplication math story problems with Unifix cubes creates shifting connections with multiple potentialities. Maya, Robin, Luis, Danny, a raw egg and a ten-foot drop create others. A personal narrative, a speech-to-text app, Mrs. Brown and Jose, yet another. How might these potentialities become recognized as multiplicity of creative talent?

Manning (2016) explains that there is a "different kind of knowing, a knowing in the event, in nonlinear event-time, a knowing that, while impossible to parse, delights in the force of conceptual invention" (p. 24). Attuning to the emergence of creative talent in the learning environment involves noticing that which is unfolding, including speed, sounds, smells, absences, silences, vibrations, other forms of relatedness, and movement. How might we experience movement in a lesson-event through a CTEE lens? How might movement move us across spaces (classroom, school, community, world, physical and virtual)? How might movement move us to conscious thought, to concept, or idea, creation, to creative thinking? What patterns or rhythms might we notice? What might this movement mean for creative talent, or the attunement to creative talent events in formation?

Oftentimes educators map out classrooms and design routines for movement within and between classroom spaces. Teachers consider heavily used routes (seat to drinking fountain, door to seat, carpet areas to seats, seats to supply shelves) and ensure that those routes are clear from distractions and easy to navigate. Movement from the classroom to other areas on the school grounds, such as the lunchroom, special area classes or fire drill locations is also planned. One dominant, or neurotypical, expectation is that students be limited in movement by a connection to their seats (Vasquez et al., in press). The connection to seats includes the expectation for sitting upright, feet on the floor, for many hours a day. Students then are to communicate from the waist up as tables and desks visually hide the rest of their bodies. Hands and feet are to be kept still to limit noise. This image depicts how neurotypical learning is based on teacher/student, knower/learner, mind/body dichotomies. If the teacher-knower can keep the student-learner still enough, they are able to fill the student-learner's mind more easily.

The math lesson scenario above was written with attunement to the creative openings of the lesson-event and one of the processes attuned to was movement. The students had chairs and a common workspace, the table. There was also a specific location in the classroom from which to retrieve the task card. Cues in the environment move learners toward thought even before they are consciously aware. Movement of thought is an intuitive co-composing, or a co-creating as interconnected units, in the event (Manning, 2016). So, if teachers-learners practice attunement to the movement of the lesson-event, might they become more intuitive co-composers and more apt to notice creative talent in its becoming? What if we attune to movement in the math scenario? What shifts in our readiness for the emergence of creative talent events might we sense? When students are fixed in desks, what kinds of creative movements and expressions might be missed? What are the potential creative openings emerging from the movements of the task card or the stuffed animal? Where is the teacher in this movement and what kinds of creative possibilities might emerge from different movements of the teacher? Might we imagine a lesson-event in which there are no chairs? Or one in which there are no walls?

Could we visualize lesson-events, even math class, in movement: role-playing, singing, dancing, building, engineering, huddling, drumming. Imagine the multiplicity of creative talent in becoming. What kinds of creative openings might our attunement to these movements reveal?

5.1   How Might We Document and Learn from Emergent Creative Talent Events?

CTEE, as opposed to a pedagogy of sameness, does not hold to a narrow conception of experiencing the world, therefore dynamic learning pathways must replace educational tracks and intervention plans. Attuning to the multiplicity of creative talent acknowledges difference and uncertainty in developing educational programming. With infinite modes of creative talent and ways to develop creative talent(s), how might educators design pathways? CTEE means that planning for learning, (creative talent development) is uncertain. There is a multiplicity of modes (not domains) for creative talent and for development. Education systems need to offer dynamic pathways (not special, gifted or general education and not dependent on labels), but individually designed and flexible opportunities for developing creative talent by attuning to learning environments and lesson-events.

In recognizing that creative talent development is an emergent event that is in constant co-construction with the educational environment, we recommend that educators approach it with a flexible approach. Educational programming could, for instance, provide students with opportunities to engage creative expression in everyday, general education settings. Educators can establish a range of creative openings in their curriculum by taking smaller steps, such as allowing students to meet learning goals in different ways to larger efforts aimed at allowing students to identify their own problems to solve and their own ways of solving them (Beghetto, 2020). Doing so may help promote our attunement to the emergent creative talent events because it leverages a fuller range of possibilities. Designing these kinds of educational experiences within the general education setting, with flexible opportunities to delve deeper into specific problems or concentrations, can go a long way in developing openings for the emergence of creative talent events.

This is an important departure from traditional curriculum design, which tends to be focused on the "average student" who learns along a linear trajectory at an average pace. Designing educational experiences based on a wide exposure general education setting with flexible opportunities to delve deeper into specific problems or concentrations follows a CTEE perspective and reflects the multiplicity and neurodiversity of creative talent. Individualized pathways will organically emerge from these educational experiences and teachers will need to be attuned to shifts in learning.

In what follows we further speculate on practical possibilities for educators and researchers to consider when moving toward an approach that recognizes creative talent as an emergent and neurodiverse event.

5.2 What If Teams of Educators, Parents, and Students Worked Together to Document Events of Creative Talent?

What if schools used a team approach to document "living biographies" of creative talent events throughout the school year? These would be event stories that draw on emergent, snap-shot descriptions of events wherein the emergence and facilitation of creative talent would be centered. This would be a collective responsibility, described from multiple perspectives. These snapshots can be based on observations, discussions, created products and any supporting documentation that illustrates the neurodiverse and emerging creative talent events in and across school, home, and educational settings. These snap shots can also be used as the basis for developing collective event narratives that could be curated and assembled from multiple perspectives in shared, open-ended documents (e.g., a Google Doc). Educators could then adopt the motto in their classrooms of "everybody documents, and we document all the time" (Beghetto, 2018, p. 117) as a way to identifying the forces and flow of activities involved in the emergence of creative talent events. By documenting these events teachers, students, parents may be in a better position to ready themselves for when such events become activated in and beyond the classroom. These biographies can also serve as artifacts that can support future ecological thought and action of teachers, students, and parents.

5.3 What If We Provided Multiple Openings for Students?

Given the broad horizon of possibilities for how creative talent events emerge in unpredictable and multiple ways, what if educators were careful not to limit students by placing them into predetermined pathways? What if, instead, students had multiple opportunities to explore and engage in cross-domain, cross-field, and interdisciplinary collaborations, projects, and experiences? Curricular and extracurricular planning, viewed from a neurodiversity perspective, recognizes that creative talent can organically emerge from multiple provocations, perspectives, and improvisational experiences. This moves educators away from trying to neatly fit students into a pre-determined talent trajectory and toward becoming more attuned to how creative talent events emerge. Creative talent events not only emerge through current interconnected interests and strengths, but also from encounters with uncertainty, which may (or may not) provoke the development of yet-to-be-determined interests and strengths. Viewed from this vantage point, activities like mentorships, apprenticeships, self-directed projects, and courses and clubs are viewed not only as interest or strength-based activities, but as encounters with the possible (Glăveanu, 2021).

5.4   *What If We Viewed Creative Talent as an Inconclusive Series of Events across Life?*

A CTEE perspective asserts that when creative talent is viewed as possession of the few, then the always and already existing creative potential of talent events, which extends beyond particular individuals to everchanging interconnected units, fails to be realized. As we have discussed at length, viewing creative talent as an emerging event helps us move away from such narrow conceptions. What if instead of limiting creative development pathways for a few, we facilitated flexible, untimed, non-linear creative events across life and life events? What if the focus was not on trying to develop specific creative talent (e.g., trying place young people into pre-determined trajectories), but rather encourage students to engage in and reflect on a multiplicity of creative experiences they are having now and across the lifespan?

6   Concluding Thoughts

In this chapter we introduced an alternative way of conceptualizing creative talent. Specifically, we offered the concept of creative talent as emergent event (CTEE) as an effort to provoke movement away from a de-contextualized and atemporal view of creative-talent-as-possession and toward a much more dynamic and neurodiverse conception that recognizes the multiplicity of capabilities of all people which get animated and sometimes recognized in the on-going interactions, processes, and artifacts of social situations and contexts. The concept of CTEE adds theoretical, empirical and practical value to the field. Theoretically, the concept of CTEE invites researcher and practitioners to rethink the creative-talent-as-possession mindset and move toward new, more generable and inclusive possibilities for understanding creative talent as an emergent event. Empirically, our concept of CTEE offers researchers a new lens for developing collaborative designs with educators to document and learn from emergent creative talents events in and across educational contexts. We highlighted the example of "living biographies" or "event stories" as one possible direction for moving empirical work forward. Practically, CTEE offers educators with a new way of thinking about how they conceptualize, design, and respond to learning experiences aimed at supporting the emergence of creative talent events. In this way CTEE serves as a starting point for considering new theoretical, empirical and practical possibilities for conceptualizing, documenting, and supporting creative talent as an ongoing series of emergent events.

Through our speculation on CTEE, we only propose that educators consider how teaching and learning might change if talent was understood as emergent in learning contexts. Teachers and researchers might experiment with the idea of attuning, or noticing, during their lesson-events. Through this attunement, we advocate the development of learning environments that support the growth of all students through collaborative experiences. This might mean allowing for more flexibility in learning approaches, including more time for exploration and apprenticeship, or mentoring, experiences. It would be the goal that the primary setting for developing CTEE would be general education. CTEE, though, can occur in any setting and could be further developed in mentorships and experiences outside of school. Indeed, schools might consider flexible approaches to scheduling for mentorship, or collaborative specialization learning, as well as opportunities for dual enrollment and the attainment of specialization certificates (e.g., technical and career certifications) prior to high school graduation for all students. We are not advocating a large-scale restructuring of schooling, but a shift in perspective on talent development and a close noticing of the creative talent that might emerge in each lesson taught. From that point on, we can all continue to speculate on the possibilities.

Our approach is, of course, not free from limitations. As with any speculative and nascent perspective, additional work is needed to determine how the CTEE concept compliments and potentially transforms the way in which researchers and practitioners think about, document, and support creative talent in and across educational settings. CTEE is not a ready-made or finalized concept, rather it is representing a set of provocations and speculations which is informed by (but ultimately goes beyond) existing neurodiversity perspectives and pedagogical approaches. Consequently, the potential benefits and limitations of this approach are contingent on how researchers and practitioners work with this concept and help to give it shape in their particular contexts. To that end we invite you (as the reader) to take up this concept and consider it in light of your own professional endeavors aimed at understanding, documenting, and supporting emerging creative talent events. We close by briefly offering a few additional provocations that we hope can move you forward in this direction:

– *What kinds of possibilities for creative talent as emerging event might you imagine in your classrooms and educational contexts?*
– *How might you imagine talent events beyond the "unimaginable"? and*
– *How might our educational and creative experiences change as a result of this re-imagination?*

References

Armstrong, T. (2012). *Neurodiversity in the classroom: Strength-based strategies to help students with special needs succeed in school and life*. ASCD.

Barab, S. A., & Plucker, J. A. (2002). Smart people or smart contexts? Cognition, ability, and talent development in an age of situated approaches to knowing and learning. *Educational Psychologist, 37*, 165–182.

Beghetto, R. A. (2016). Creative openings in the social interactions of teaching. *Creativity: Theories – Research – Applications, 3*, 261–271.

Beghetto, R. A. (2018). *What if? Building students' problem-solving skills through complex challenges*. ASCD.

Beghetto, R. A. (2020). Uncertainty: A gateway to the possible. In V. P. Glăveanu (Ed.), *The Palgrave encyclopedia of the possible*. Palgrave.

Beghetto, R. A., & Yoon, S. A. (2020). Change through creative learning: Toward realizing the creative potential of translanguaging. In C. A. Mullen (Ed.), *Handbook of social justice interventions in education*. Springer.

Blanton, L. P., Pugach, M. C., & Boveda, M. (2014, September). *Teacher education reform initiatives and special education: Convergence, divergence, and missed opportunities*. CEEDAR Center. https://ceedar.education.ufl.edu/wp-content/uploads/2014/09/LS-3_FINAL_09-20-14.pdf

Bronfenbrenner, U. (1976). The experimental ecology of education. *Educational Researcher, 5*(5), 5–15.

Dai, D. Y. (2016). Envisioning a new century of gifted education: The case for a paradigm shift. In D. Ambrose & R. J. Sternberg (Eds.), *Giftedness and creative talent in the 21st century: Adapting to the turbulence of globalization* (pp. 45–64). Sense Publishers.

Dai, D. Y. (2020). Rethinking human potential from a talent development perspective. *Journal for the Education of the Gifted, 43*(1), 19–37.

Dewey, J. (1938). *Experience and education*. Collier MacMillan.

Evans, B. (2018, January 2). *Histories of violence: Neurodiversity and the policing of the norm*. Los Angeles Review of Books. https://lareviewofbooks.org/article/histories-of-violence-neurodiversity-and-the-policing-of-the-norm/

Gardner, H. (2020). Of human potential: A 40-year saga. *Journal for the Education of the Gifted, 43*(1), 12–18.

Glăveanu, V. P. (2021). *The possible: A sociocultural theory*. Oxford University Press.

Kaljonen, M., Peltola, T., Salo, M., & Furman, E. (2019). Attentive, speculative experimental research for sustainability transitions: An exploration in sustainable eating. *Journal of Cleaner Production, 206*, 365–373.

Kaufman, J. C., & Beghetto, R. A. (2009). Beyond big and little: The four C model of creativity. *Review of General Psychology, 13*, 1–12.

Lo, C. O., Porath, M., Yu, H., Chen, C., Tsai, K., & Wu, I. (2019). Giftedness in the making: A transactional perspective. *Gifted Child Quarterly, 63*(3), 172–184.

McDermott, R. (1993). The acquisition of a child by a learning disability. In J. Lave & S. Chaiklin (Ed.), *Understanding practice: Perspectives on activity and context* (pp. 269–305). Cambridge University Press.

Manning, E. (2013). *Always more than one: Individuation's Dance.* Duke University Press.

Manning, E. (2016). *The minor gesture.* Duke University Press.

Marland, S. P. (1972). *Education of the gifted and talented: Report to the Congress of the United States by the U.S. Commissioner of Education and background papers submitted to the U.S. Office of Education* (2 Vols.). (Government Documents, Y4.L 11/2: G36). U.S. Government Printing Office.

Moran, S. (2020). Life purpose in youth: Turning potential into a lifelong pursuit of prosocial contribution. *Journal for the Education of the Gifted, 43*(1), 38–60.

Rapp, W. H., & Arndt, L. (2012). *Teaching everyone: An introduction to inclusive education.* Paul H. Brookes Publishing Co.

Reis, S. M., & Renzulli, J. S. (2009). The schoolwide enrichment model: A focus on student strengths and interests. In J. S. Renzulli & E. J. Gubbins (Eds.), *Systems & models for developing programs for the gifted & talented* (2nd ed., pp. 323–352). Prufrock Press, Inc.

Tirri, K., & Nokelainen, P. (2011). *Measuring multiple intelligences and moral sensitivities in education.* Sense Publishers.

Vasquez, A. M., Wells, T. C., & Johnson, G. L. (in press). From technique to technicity: Explorations of chairs, neurodiversity, and schooling. *Reconceptualizing Educational Research Methodology.*

Whitehead, A. (1959). *The function of reason.* Beacon Press.

CHAPTER 15

A Socio-Cultural Approach to Growth-Mindset Pedagogy

Maker-Pedagogy as a Tool for Developing the Next-Generation Growth Mindset

*Jenni Laurell, Aino Seitamaa, Kati Sormunen,
Pirita Seitamaa-Hakkarainen, Tiina Korhonen and Kai Hakkarainen*

Abstract

The purpose of this chapter was to examine mindset research from a sociocultural perspective, analyze the interrelation between mindset and social representations, and expand mindset discourse from intelligence and giftedness to the creativity domain with maker-pedagogy. Although mindset research has traditionally been anchored in personality psychology, the present chapter argues that mindsets reflect social and cultural practices of schooling and associated cultural beliefs and social identities. Experienced societal and educational realities shape implicit ability beliefs and reflect social representations shared by families, teachers, and peers. Because the rapidly transforming knowledge society requires all citizens to solve non-routine problems and pursue novelty and innovation, it is critical that young people believe in their potential to stretch their intellectual and creative capabilities and build new talents through sustained efforts. Hence, deliberate cultivation of a growth mindset is not only beneficial for young people's educational and professional trajectories but also a societal necessity.

Keywords

growth-mindset pedagogy – mindsets – maker-pedagogy – knowledge-creating learning – social representations

1   Introduction

Humans are facing increasingly severe problems and risks related to climate change, sustainability, and radical inequality. Investigators are concerned with the growing ingenuity gap (Facer, 2011; Homer-Dixon, 2001) between such challenges and current educational practices, which do not empower students' growth mindset. Productive participation in the emerging innovation-driven knowledge-creation society and building a sustainable future will require the cultivation of sophisticated knowledge-creation competencies by all citizens. Instead of merely promoting intellectual elites, all citizens need better capabilities to see things from fresh perspectives, enhanced self-efficacy, and deliberate stretching of competencies and associated identities as potential knowledge creators (Paavola et al., 2004; Paavola & Hakkarainen, 2014). The revolution of socio-digital technologies is profoundly transforming the tools and environments of human activity and collectivizing all spheres of human learning, working, and everyday activities (Hakkarainen et al., 2015). Human capabilities are extended through social learning, collaboration, and knowledge and competence sharing. Today's increasingly challenging problems require people to capitalize on their heterogeneously distributed knowledge and competences to jointly achieve results far beyond what they could achieve on their own. However, schools have only started to capitalize on the power of social-collaborative learning and teaching enabled by the development of socio-digital technologies.

The dominant tradition of viewing intelligence, giftedness, and creativity as pre-given and fixed individual abilities is increasingly problematic. Research on people's implicit ability beliefs, that is, their mindsets, has traditionally relied on personality psychology and narrow social cognition aspects, whereas the more profound social and cultural aspects of mindsets, highlighted by recent societal changes, have received little attention. The purpose of the present chapter is to reflect on mindset research from a sociocultural perspective conceptually and theoretically. We propose that implicit theories, i.e., assumptions and lay beliefs regarding intelligence, giftedness, and creativity, are embedded in and internalized from socio-historically developed social representations (Moscovici, 1961). These social and cultural connections are critical when studying young people's mindsets, fostering a growth mindset, and developing the growth-mindset pedagogies required by the ongoing societal and digital transformations. We will first review the dominant individualist tradition of mindset research and associated interventions and provide sociocultural interpretations of these findings. Second, we will examine social representation theories and their application for studying mindsets in educational contexts. Third, we will address the creativity mindset and associated efforts to bring maker culture elements to schools and foster maker mindsets.

2 Mindset Research and Its Educational Significance

Mindset research is based on the study of implicit theories of human qualities, such as intelligence, giftedness, and creativity. Such "theories" are defined as laypeople's mental representations and, in the present context, as subjective beliefs and assumptions regarding capabilities held and used at school and in everyday life. More specifically, in Carol Dweck's mindset research, participants believe human capabilities are either non-malleable or malleable; however, such beliefs appear unrelated to independently measured intellectual abilities (Macnamara & Rupani, 2017). A fixed mindset (also called entity theory) is a belief that personal abilities are unchangeable and stable. In contrast, subscribers of the growth mindset (also called an incremental theory) view these abilities to be dynamic and subject to development and enhancement (Dweck, 2017). There is considerable evidence that intelligence mindsets form the core of meaning systems that play an essential motivational role in personal educational and professional pursuits (Claro et al., 2016).

Implicit ability beliefs are embodiments of mindsets people most commonly hold. Fixed, and growth mindsets exist in all people and usually vary between situations and contexts. Generally, young people tend to prefer one mindset over others, but it is common to hold different mindsets in various domains (e.g., intelligence, giftedness) (Dweck, 1999; Kuusisto et al., 2017). Mindsets of intelligence could explain why some people care more about *"proving"* their cognitive ability while others care more about *"improving"* theirs (Dweck & Leggett, 1988). People with an intelligence-related growth mindset orient toward developing their capabilities through sustained efforts and appear less judgmental toward others (Dweck et al., 1995). While a fixed mindset leads young people to give up and avoid challenges that could provide learning opportunities, a growth mindset encourages the agent to seek challenges, be persistent, and put in long-standing efforts to overcome obstacles and develop intellectually (Molden & Dweck, 2006).

What is exciting about mindset research is its expansion to interventions, which have yielded promising results (Bettinger et al., 2018; Paunesku et al., 2015; Yeager et al., 2016). A growth mindset can be taught to students through social, emotional learning interventions that strive to motivate and empower students to take responsibility for their learning (Yeager & Dweck, 2012; Yeager & Walton, 2011). For instance, Blackwell et al. (2007) conducted an eight-session intervention for seventh students whose math grades had deteriorated. The mindset intervention group read an article aloud called "You Can Grow Your Intelligence," which argued that the brain is like a muscle, and you need to work and try hard to learn. The group discussed how learning makes people smarter and to avoid labels of dumb or stupid. The study reported significant changes in the intervention group's math grades and mindsets after the intervention. The authors stated that changing the way students think about math and learning made them more motivated because they now understood that they are in charge of their learning. Learning about growth-mindset dynamics decreased the effects of stress on students' academic performance and exclusion after the transition to high school (Yeager et al., 2014). Yeager et al. (2019) argue for self-administered, brief, and scalable interventions conducted through a website for students. These scalable interventions are cost-effective and can be administered to all students. However, Dweck and her school's approach to the mindset appear to undertheorize the cultural mediation involved in associated interventions. Such mediation occurs when providing students with scientific knowledge about the super-plasticity of the human mind (Donald, 1991); such reflections remediate subsequent learning efforts. Correspondingly, asking students to write letters for subsequent cohorts of students about their struggles of overcoming belonging uncertainties can be understood as Vygotskian (1978) double stimulation (i.e., creating artifacts for remediating learning processes). Further theoretical analyses of various intervention tasks could improve our understanding of the socio-cultural reasons for their effectiveness.

3 Mindsets as Social Representations

The research on implicit ability beliefs superficially differentiates between implicit (i.e., laypeople's beliefs and opinions) and explicit theories (i.e., scientific theories) (Furnham, 1988). Investigators have tended to consider these two types of cultural knowledge as inherently separate from one another; many studies have focused on examining how implicit beliefs influence how we assess ourselves and others around us from an individualized perspective (Glăveanu, 2011). Thus, it is critical to ask where implicit beliefs and assumptions about intelligence, giftedness, and creativity, actually originate. Sociocultural research views all human attributes as profoundly socially and culturally mediated. Mental representations in general, and implicit ability beliefs in particular, do not come from the depths of the human mind but are appropriated from the social environment and enacted cultural practices, representing internalized cultural models (Holland et al., 1998; Vygotsky, 1962, 1978). Cultural practices mediate our views of prototypically intelligent, gifted, or creative persons and how we value their characteristics. In contrast to Runco (1999), who sees such implicit ability beliefs as mindsets residing in the individual's mind and personality, we believe that such beliefs are appropriated from the social and cultural environment and shared with others through everyday cultural-communicative practices and acquired values and attitudes.

The theory of social representations explains how individuals appropriate and apply dominant representations regarding, for instance, intelligence. Moscovici (1961, 2000) proposed the idea that human cognition cannot be seen as simple mental structure; rather, it is mediated socially and historically. Shared social representations are defined as a system of values, attitudes, and practices with two functions: to create order by which the socio-material world is controlled and ease communication within the community (Sakki et al., 2014). Conceptions of intelligence, giftedness, and creativity can be seen as emotion-laden social representations that provide meaning and value to everyday events and communicate our experiences to others (Mugny & Carugati, 1989). We argue that mindsets cannot be treated as mere mental representations but as fundamentally social constructions manifested in our language and social interaction. Thus, implicit beliefs are connected to prevailing social and cultural realities and associated socially mediated knowledge structures. They are shaped through interaction with family, friends, teachers, and media, mediating developmental and educational cognitive socialization.

Moscovici's theory of social knowledge addresses the transformation of knowledge as it "travels" through different communities and social milieus (Moscovici, 2000; see also Vygotsky, 1962). Hence, the popularization of the dominant differential psychological theories on intelligence, giftedness, and creativity shaped implicit theories through anchoring and objectification. Anchoring involves merging the phenomenon as a natural part of the social group's existing beliefs, assumptions, and meanings systems, while objectifying saturates communicative processes through the target phenomenon (Moscovici, 2000, p. 49). Notions of intelligence are simplified and selectively constructed according to participants' cultural practices and norms. Mindset interventions are impactful because they prove new, more expansive ways of objectifying and anchoring the targeted ability concepts and, thereby, provide novel possibilities for action and development.

Kärkkäinen et al. (2008) found that students' conceptions of the malleability of their academic competence became more pessimistic throughout the school years. Students tend to internalize the fixed mindset embedded in institutionalized categorization practices and develop their sense of ability through normative assessment practices and everyday feedback. The authors argued that "classroom practices convert the school's view on [students'] abilities into children's representations of their competencies" (p. 446). A fixed mindset may appear adaptive for making sense of strongly stratified societies with intensive cognitive categorization. Hacking (1999) argued that scientific categorizations affect people's ways of making sense of themselves and their subsequent activities and development trajectories. With the so-called looping effect, people tend to take up and act upon human categorizations they are subjected to, gradually changing their identities (see also Holland et al., 1998). Consequently, educational categorization practices may transform the kind of people students consider themselves to be, shaping their activity, learning, and development significantly ways, thereby leading to the concrete social construction of reality. Simultaneously, teachers', parents', and other stakeholders' implicit or explicit categorizations constrain and limit young people's intellectual and creative development.

Räty et al. (2004) defined two spheres of education – restrictive and promotional spheres – arguing that both are current prevailing school practices. The promotional sphere is related to the school's goal to develop every student's skills and competence and incorporate a belief that competencies can be developed and stretched; hence, school institutions tend to have a growth mindset. The restrictive sphere of education, in contrast, is related to school assessment practices that compare students' abilities and rank and assess students. These competing ideas produce a paradox in school practices, where teachers operate and make rapid pedagogical decisions and assumptions about students. Räty et al. (2018) suggested that students' "ability self" – a conception of one's ability "profile," which includes the mindsets and feelings of self-efficacy – develops through one's history and is influenced by normative comparisons imposed by school institutions.

When educational institutions view intelligence as fixed and stable, children tend to be categorized into groups of, for example, more or less able, intelligent, or unintelligent. A longitudinal study by Boaler et al. (2000) revealed that placing students into math "ability" groups creates a set of expectations for teachers that overrides their awareness of individual capabilities. Teachers constructed students as successes or failures based on their location in a "set," not due to their personal academic qualities, and had preconceptions about students' appropriate level and pace of studying in their selected math ability group. Adopting ability-grouping appeared to signal teachers that it was appropriate to use different pedagogical strategies from those they used with mixed-ability classes. Nevertheless, in their famous Pygmalion study, Rosenthal and Jacobson (1968) told the teacher that a group of ordinary students were exceptionally talented. After one year, the students' academic achievements and the teacher's assessment of their capabilities were far above the mean. It follows that a teacher's attributions and judgments of students are highly significant for their development. What if teachers treated all students as highly intelligent, gifted, and creative?

People live in vast social realities that shape how they see the world around them. For instance, Hart and Risley (1995) revealed drastic differences in early socialization for children with educated parents versus those living on social support. Children of educated parents heard three times more words directed to themselves, and educated parents systematically encouraged their children, whereas the latter discouraged their children. It is unsurprising that the former tend to develop a growth mindset and the latter a fixed mindset (Claro et al., 2016). Moreover, these realities are shaped by the social identities forced upon vulnerable social groups. Stereotypical characteristics may be positive or negative and may have little to do with fact. A stereotype can place an added burden on the student (e.g., stereotype threat), which can interfere with learning and achievement (Master et al., 2016). Notably, a student does not need to believe it to feel this burden. Teaching students under a stereotype threat about the growth mindset provides them with a new way of seeing their abilities and potential (Good et al., 2003). Mindset interventions have been especially significant for students under a stereotype threat and those with a low socioeconomic status (Sisk et al., 2018).

To conclude, it is critical to understand that mindsets are largely developed and maintained by the institutional practices of schooling, the school's pedagogical culture, and the overall sociocultural environment. The theory of social representation provides valuable knowledge regarding the sociocultural mediation of mindsets. School is a demanding and hectic environment, where it is easy to make quick stereotypical judgments about students' abilities. Teachers should be aware of the ways school as an institution, generates different cognitive and other categorization practices. Discrimination create maladaptive social representations shaping students' views of their capabilities. Consequently, teachers need tools to fight the fixed mindset. It is crucial to shed light on how mindsets are enacted in teachers' everyday practices of interacting with students and interpreting their daily learning.

4   Cultivating the Growth Mindset at Schools

Following Vygotsky (1978), we assert that all skilled activities considered to represent intelligence, giftedness, or creativity stem from culture and tradition and are then elaborated through interaction with cultural ideas, tools, practices, communities, and networks. Intelligence, talent, and creativity are culturally mediated capabilities that grow through participating in expanding cognitive-cultural communities and networks. Humans are biologically cultural, ultra-social, and hyper collaborative in nature (Rogoff, 2003; Tomasello,

2019). Despite the prevailing digital divides, the socio-digital revolution has made such networks accessible for students in industrialized countries. A radical transformation in teaching and schooling practices is needed to realize the power of social-collaborative learning for all students.

As indicated above, teachers' implicit beliefs about intelligence and giftedness can influence their interpretation of students' behavior, learning, and achievements, which may affect their pedagogical thinking and practices of motivating students (Rissanen et al., 2018). To identify students' fixed mindsets and foster a growth mindset, teachers should cultivate a growth mindset themselves by being adaptive rather than routine experts (Hatano & Inagaki, 1992) and actively participating in developing the school's operational culture (e.g., Hildrew, 2018). Teachers with a growth mindset regard emotional processes, learning strategies, and contextual factors as the leading indicators of students' behavior, learning, and achievements and try to influence them instead of seeking explanations in fixed abilities (Boaler, 2019; Rissanen et al., 2018).

Rissanen et al. (2019) framed a growth-mindset pedagogy according to process-focused pedagogical thinking, the promotion of a mastery orientation in classrooms, and allowing challenges and creative ideas to flourish in classrooms (Kuusisto et al., 2017). This means emphasizing progress and learning goals over achievement and performance (i.e., formative rather than summative assessment) (Rissanen et al., 2019; Ronkainen et al., 2018). Supporting students' individual learning processes is vital. Teachers must understand the influence of psychological processes, contextual factors, and learning strategies as these may create barriers to students' motivation and learning. (e.g., Sormunen et al., 2020). Teacher with a growth mindset support students in overcoming these barriers (Rissanen et al., 2019). Such teachers are naturally optimistic about student learning and development and offer them "the gift of confidence" (Mahn & John-Steiner, 2003). Nevertheless, students' motivation is challenged by the increasing gap between their super-social and peer-supported out-of-school activity and teacher-led reproductive and individualist learning at school. Our study reveals that active socio-digital participants are increasingly disengaged and alienated by traditional school learning (Hietajärvi et al., 2020). The learning sciences focus on radically transforming prevailing educational practices by promoting knowledge-creating pedagogies that highlight collaboration in solving open-ended problems and building knowledge and artifacts to answer future challenges (Hakkarainen et al., 2004).

Technology-enhanced learning environments provide ample opportunities for organizing challenging projects and engaging students in knowledge creation; such projects are suitable for the phenomenon-based pedagogy of

Finnish new curriculum (Finnish National Board of Education, 2016; Riikonen, Kangas, et al., 2020). Engaging students in collaborative learning practices capitalizes on heterogeneously distributed knowledge and competence in a way typical of workplace communities. Socio-digital technologies enable transforming school places into spaces of learning; emerging digital fabrication technologies allow students to pursue challenging maker projects, sparking intellectual, technical, and aesthetic challenges (Riikonen, Seitamaa-Hakkarainen, et al., 2020). Within this development, it is crucial to expand growth-mindset interventions beyond the intelligence and giftedness domains toward creativity; the ethos of future education should be that every student is a potential creator and inventor.

Dougherty (2013) highlighted the importance of cultivating students' maker mindset, which involves tolerating risks and failures and engaging in iterative experimental play to develop ideas into reality, giving learners "the full capacity, creativity, and confidence to become agents of change in their personal lives and their community" (p. 11). Teachers should facilitate a creative growth mindset and foster students' capabilities. Creating novelty is a social-collaborative process, and engaging students in inventing and making artifacts releases their hidden social-collaborative learning powers. Tang et al. (2016) argued that a growth mindset is especially beneficial for creative activities and future creative achievements. A creativity-related growth mindset has been positively linked to greater academic risk-taking behavior and lower academic stress (Yamazaki & Kumar, 2013). Maker-pedagogy engages students in iterative creative efforts and learning safely from productive failures (Sinervo et al., 2020). People who do not believe that creativity can be developed naturally see little reason to engage in creative activity or develop their skills (O'Connor et al., 2013). Consequently, we argue that the creativity-related mindset should be addressed when implementing mindset interventions in school.

5   Maker-Centered Co-Invention Projects at School

To cultivate students' creativity-related mindset, we have organized a series of co-invention projects at ten schools in the capital area of Helsinki and rural schools (Härkki et al., 2021; Riikonen, Seitamaa-Hakkarainen et al., 2020). These projects have had an inclusive ethos, including all students, regardless of their cultural or socio-economical background or stereotypical judgments about their abilities. The projects aim to cultivate all students' creative and innovative skills together with critical thinking, collaboration, and communication (Sinervo et al., 2020). Moreover, the projects intend to provide diverse students with a sense of contribution. Students experience doing something worthwhile together, each student's efforts and accomplishments matter, and the whole team jointly achieves something that no one could have achieved alone. Each project was orchestrated by teachers representing different school subjects, including craft education, science, and visual arts.

Students were given an open-ended innovation challenge, such as designing functional and aesthetically pleasing artifacts that make daily activities easier and integrate digital (e.g., circuits or robotics) elements. Students worked on a compact but heterogeneous team across each longitudinal maker project. While traditional school learning relies on linear pedagogy, focusing on pre-established goals, content, stages, and outcomes, maker-centered learning relies on nonlinear pedagogy, involving emergent objects, stages, and unforeseen results (Härkki et al., 2021; Riikonen, Kangas, et al., 2020). It changes classroom dynamics and empowers students who may not do well in traditional school studies.

The co-invention process involved creative and critical thinking through evaluating ideas, defining constraints, making models, and testing the prototypes. Periodically, the teams presented their ideas and plan to the whole class and received peer feedback. The prime ideation and prototype of the co-invention were made, and subsequently the students developed the prototype further. Through the several cycles of ideation and making phases, students learned the iterative nature of the creative process and learning: they could improve their design ideas, learn from their mistakes, and develop their ideas further. These aspects align with the growth-mindset pedagogy, where learning is seen as progress, and mistakes and failures are critical for learning. Moreover, it was significant for students to share their designs with parents and a broader audience. It was an empowering experience for students to finalize their long-term process, and they were proud of their achievements (Sinervo et al., 2020).

In one invention project, the 13 student mixed-ability teams (mainstream students and special educational needs [SEN] students) came up with a wide variety of co-inventions (Sinervo et al., 2020). The teams' co-inventions focused on three primary purposes: (1) improving cleanliness, (2) providing reminders, or (3) addressing well-being (hygiene, health, and nutrition issues). Some highly original solutions for known problems were found, including vacuuming the carpet and a gel comb for styling hair, although the teams could not construct fully functional solutions. On the gel comb team (three SEN and two mainstream students), the innovation was a driving force for all students, and they were engaged in and committed to their co-invention: they made five different prototypes from wood, recycled materials, and Three Dimensional (3D) printing. The team put considerable effort into making the gel come out of the comb but encountered unsolvable problems with fluid dynamics. Committing factors for the SEN students on the gel comb team included adequate task differentiation, necessary support, and a sense of contribution. All of the SEN students felt that the malfunctioning invention was a success: "We made a prototype at least, and we did our best."

According to the SEN students' interviews, it provided a sense of contribution to something worthwhile. One of the students with severe SEN, who was in charge of drawing, stated, "I am good at drawing," His role was agreed upon with other team members. It also provided experiences of the maker mindset in terms of a persistent attitude, tireless working, and valuing all contributions. The need for teacher support was evident in providing SEN students with an exact role on the team. From the SEN students' perspective, the co-invention project improved their attitudes towards collaborative tasks. As Sormunen et al. (2020) discovered, working as full members of a group can promote SEN students' social acceptance by peers and promote inclusion. It can also develop students' growth mindset, as it provides opportunities to learn about their strengths, agency, and empowering learning experiences. In this open-ended co-invention project, students could practice and learn a variety of things, from design to collaboration and, primarily, how to engage in long-term working without a structured and detailed lesson plan. Our experiences indicate that participation in creative technology use fosters students' construction of personal and collaborative agency and identity as a knowledge creator (Paavola, Lipponen, & Hakkarainen, 2004). The co-invention projects show that treating all young people as "super talented" without stereotypical labeling is critical for advancement. People treated in this way may, miraculously, start pursuing ideas and making positive contributions to their team.

6   Concluding Remarks

The present chapter examined mindsets from a sociocultural perspective. We argued that, rather than mere personal dispositions, mindsets could be understood as internalized social representations mediated by prevailing social and cultural practices. Mindsets are shared between teachers, parents, and peers, although specific aspects of such social mediation warrant further study. As long as mindsets are considered to represent only individual dispositions, teachers and school leaders may not understand the critical role of pedagogic practices and a supportive school culture in facilitating a growth mindset. Thus, it is urgent to examine the social foundations of mindsets and provide schools and teachers actionable means for fostering a growth mindset (Dweck, 2017).

However, more research is needed on how mindsets are enacted in teachers' everyday interactions with students and how educational institutes' operating culture affects students' mindsets.

Teachers may not be capable of eliciting a growth mindset if they do not have one. The dialogical processes of building a school's growth-mindset culture are dependent on transforming pedagogic and operational culture and developing teachers' ability to recognize students' mindsets and foster all students' development, learning, and well-being (Esses et al., 1993). Consequently, it is crucial to engage teachers in orchestrating and conducting mindset interventions (see also Rissanen et al., 2019). When the school's operational and pedagogical culture deliberately empowers students' and teachers' growth mindsets, we may start talking about "growth-mindset school" (see also Hildrew, 2018).

The rapid societal transformations related to the socio-digital revolution demand more positive perspectives on the malleability of human capabilities. Cultivating a growth mindset in the domain of creativity, beyond intelligence and giftedness, is critical. To make mindset interventions more impactful, the social nature of mindsets should be considered by transforming the prevailing individualist and acquisition-oriented educational practices and promoting social-collaborative learning and knowledge creation (Paavola & Hakkarainen, 2014). To prepare young generations for societal changes and capitalize on the novel pedagogical possibilities of digitalization, educational institutions and teachers must cultivate a growth mindset across intelligence, giftedness, and creativity in collaboration with rigorous academic research. Accordingly, educational institutions should engage students in structured creative maker practices using socio-digital technologies. Such practices allow students to experience agency and learning experiences in which they are super-talented innovators.

Acknowledgment

This study was supported by grant (312527) of the Strategic Research Council of the Academy of Finland for the Growing Mind project (https://growingmind.fi/).

References

Bettinger, E., Ludvigsen, S., Rege, M., Solli, I. F., & Yeager, D. (2018). Increasing perseverance in math: Evidence from a field of experiment in Norway. *Journal of Economic Behavior & Organization, 146*, 1–15. https://doi.org/10.1016/j.jebo.2017.11.032

Blackwell, L. S., Trzeniewski, K. H., & Dweck, C. (2007). Implicit theories of intelligence predict achievement across an adolescent transition: A longitudinal study and an intervention. *Child Development*, 78(1), 246–263.

Boaler, J. (2019). *Limitless mind. Learn, lead and live without barriers.* Harper One.

Boaler, J., Wiliam, D., & Brown, M. (2000). Students' experiences of ability grouping – Disaffection, polarisation and the construction of failure. *British Educational Research Journal*, 26(5), 631–648. https://doi.org/10.1080/713651583

Claro, S., Paunesku, D., & Dweck, C. (2016). Growth mindset tempers the effects of poverty on academic achievement. *Proceedings of the National Academy of Sciences of the United States of America*, 113(31), 8664–8668. https://doi.org/10.1073/pnas.1608207113

Donald, M. (1991). *Origins of the modern mind: Three stages in the evolution of culture and cognition.* Harvard University Press.

Dougherty, D. (2013). The Maker mindset. In M. Honey & D. E. Kanter (Eds.), *Design, make and play: Growing the next generation of STEM innovators* (1st ed., pp. 7–11). Routledge.

Dweck, C. (1999). *Self-theories: Their role in motivation, personality and development.* Psychology Press.

Dweck, C. (2017). *Mindset: The new psychology of success* (2nd ed.). Random House.

Dweck, C., Chiu, C.-Y., & Hong, Y.-Y. (1995). Implicit theories and their role in judgments and reactions: A word from two perspectives. *Psychological Inquiry*, 6(4), 267–285. https://doi.org/10.1207/s15327965pli0604_1

Dweck, C., & Leggett, E. L. (1988). A social-cognitive approach to motivation and personality. *Psychological Review*, 95(2), 256–273.

Esses, V. M., Haddock, G., & Zanna, M. P. (1993). Values, stereotypes, and emotions as determinants of intergroup attitudes. In D. M. Mackie & D. L. Hamilton (Eds.), *Affect, cognition and stereotyping. Interactive process in group perception* (pp. 137–166). Academic Press.

Facer, K. (2011). *Learning futures: Education, technology, and social change.* Routledge.

Finnish National Board of Education. (2016). *National core curriculum for basic education 2014.*

Furnham, A. (1988). *Lay theories: Everyday understanding of problems in the social sciences.* Pergamon Press.

Glăveanu, V. P. (2011). Is the lightbulb still on? Social representations of creativity in a western context. *The International Journal of Creativity & Problem Solving*, 21(1), 53–72.

Good, C., Aronson, J., & Inzlicht, M. (2003). Improving adolescents' standardized test performance: An intervention to reduce the effects of stereotype threat. *Applied Developmental Psychology*, 24(6), 645–662.

Hacking, I. (1999). *The social construction of what?* Harvard University Press.

Hakkarainen, K., Hietajärvi, L., Alho, K., Lonka, K., & Salmela-Aro, K. (2015). Socio-digital revolution: Digital natives vs digital immigrants. In J. D. Wright (Ed.), *International encyclopedia of the social and behavioral sciences* (2nd ed., Vol. 22, pp. 918–923). Elsevier.

Hakkarainen, K., Palonen, T., Paavola, S., & Lehtinen, E. (2004). *Communities of networked expertise: Professional and educational perspectives*. Elsevier.

Hart, B., & Risley, T. R. (1995). *Meaningful differences in everyday experiences of young American children*. Brookers.

Hatano, G., & Inagaki, K. (1992). Desituating cognition through the construction of conceptual knowledge. In P. Light & G. Butterworth (Eds.), *Context and cognition: Ways of knowing and learning* (pp. 115–133). Harvester.

Hietajärvi, L., Lonka, K., Hakkarainen, K., Alho, K., & Salmela-Aro, K. (2020). Are schools alienating digitally engaged students? Longitudinal relations between digital engagement and school engagement. *Frontline Learning Research, 8*(1), 33–55. https://doi.org/10.14786/flr.v8i1.437

Hildrew, C. (2018). *Becoming a growth mindset school. The power of mindset to transform teaching, leadership and learning*. Routledge.

Holland, D., Lachicotte, W., Skinner, D., & Cain, C. (1998). *Identity and agency in cultural worlds*. Harvard University Press.

Homer-Dixon, T. (2001). *The ingenuity gap: How can we solve the problems of the future?* Vintage Canada.

Härkki, T., Vartiainen, H., Seitamaa-Hakkarainen, P., & Hakkarainen, K. (2021). Co-teaching in non-linear projects: A contextualized model of co-teaching to support educational change. *Teaching and Teacher Education, 97*. https://doi.org/10.1016/j.tate.2020.103188

Kärkkäinen, R., Räty, H., & Kasanen, K. (2008). Children's notions of the malleability of their academic competencies. *Social Psychological Education, 11*, 445–458. https://doi.org/10.1007/s11218-008-9062-2

Kuusisto, E., Laine, S., & Tirri, K. (2017). How do school children and adolescents perceive the nature of talent development? A case study from Finland. *Education Research International, 2017*, 4162957. https://doi.org/10.1155/2017/4162957

Macnamara, B. N., & Rupani, N. S. (2017). The relationship between intelligence and mindset. *Intelligence, 64*, 52–59. https://doi.org/10.1016/j.intell.2017.07.003

Mahn, H., & John-Steiner, V. (2002). The gift of confidence: A Vygotskian view of emotions. In G. Wells & G. Claxton (Eds.), *Learning for life in the 21st century. Sociocultural perspectives on the future of education* (pp. 47–58). Blackwell.

Master, A., Cheryan, S., & Meltzoff, A. N. (2016). Motivation and identity. In K. R. Wentzel & D. B. Miele (Eds.), *Handbook of motivation at school* (2nd ed., pp. 300–319). New York.

Molden, D., & Dweck, C. (2006). Finding "meaning" in psychology: A lay theories approach to self-regulation, social perception, and social development. *American Psychologist, 61*(3), 192–203.

Moscovici, S. (1961). *La psychanalyse, son image et son public*. PUF.

Moscovici, S. (2000). The phenomenon of social representations. In R. Farr & S. Moscovici (Eds.), *Social representations* (pp. 3–70). Cambridge University Press.

Mugny, G., & Carugati, F. (1989). *Social representations of intelligence*. Cambridge University Press.

O'Connor, A., Nemeth, C., & Akutsu, S. (2013). Consequences of beliefs about the malleability of creativity. *Creativity Research Journal, 25*(2), 155–162. https://doi.org/10.1080/10400419.2013.783739

Paavola, S., & Hakkarainen, K. (2014). Trialogical approach for knowledge creation. In S. C. Tan, H. J. So, & J. Yeo (Eds.), *Knowledge creation in education* (pp. 53–72). Springer Education Innovation Book Series.

Paavola, S., Lipponen, L., & Hakkarainen, K. (2004). Modeling innovative knowledge communities: A knowledge-creation approach to learning. *Review of Educational Research, 74*, 557–576. https://doi.org/10.3102/00346543074004557

Paunesku, D., Walton, D., Romero, C., Smith, E., Yeager, D., & Dweck, C. (2015). Mind-set interventions are scalable treatment for academic underachievement. *Psychological Science, 26*(6), 748–793.

Räty, H., Kasanen, K., Kiiskinen, J., Nykky, M., & Atjonen, P. (2004). Children's notions of the malleability of their academic ability in their mother tongue and mathematics. *Scandinavian Journal of Educational Research, 48*(4), 413–426. http://goi.org/10.1080/0031383042000245807

Räty, H., Komulainen, K., Harvorsén, C., Nieminen, A., & Korhonen, M. (2018). University students' perceptions of their 'ability selves' and employability: A pilot study. *Nordic Journal of Studies in Educational Policy, 4*(2), 107–115. https://doi.org/10.1080/20020317.2018.1453221

Riikonen, S., Kangas, K., Kokko, S., Korhonen, T., Hakkarainen, K., & Seitamaa-Hakkarainen, P. (2020). The development of pedagogical infrastructures in three cycles of maker-centered learning projects. *Design and Technology Education: An International Journal, 25*(2), 29–49.

Riikonen, S., Seitamaa-Hakkarainen, P., & Hakkarainen, K. (2020). Bringing maker practices to school: Tracing discursive and materially mediated aspects of student teams' collaborative making processes. *International Journal of Computer Supported Collaborative Learning, 15*, 319–349.

Rissanen, I., Kuusisto, E., Hanhimäki, E., & Tirri, K. (2018). Teachers' implicit meaning systems and their implications for pedagogical thinking and practice: A case study from Finland. *Scandinavian Journal of Educational Research, 62*(4), 487–500. https://doi.org/10.1080/00313831.2016.1258667

Rissanen, I., Kuusisto, E., Tuominen, M., & Tirri, K. (2019). In search of a growth mindset pedagogy: A case study of one teacher's classroom practices in a Finnish elementary school. *Teaching and Teacher Education, 77*, 204–213.

Rogoff, B. (2003). *The cultural nature of human development*. Oxford University Press.

Ronkainen, R., Kuusisto, E., & Tirri, K. (2019). Growth mindset in teaching: A case study of a Finnish elementary school teacher. *International Journal of Learning, Teaching and Educational Research, 18*(8), 141–154. https://doi.org/10.26803/ijlter.18.8.9

Rosenthal, R., & Jacobson, L. (1968). Pygmalion in the classroom. *Urban Review, 3*, 16–20. https://doi.org/10.1007/BF02322211

Runco, M. A. (1999). Motivation, competence and creativity. In S. Elliot & C. Dweck (Eds.), *Handbook of motivation and competence* (pp. 609–623). Guilford Publications.

Sakki, I., Mäkiniemi, J.-P., Hakoköngäs, E., & Pirttilä-Backman, A.-M. (2014). Miten tutkia sosiaalisia representaatioita? [How to study social representations?]. *Sosiaalilääketieteellinen aikakauslehti, 51*, 317–329.

Sinervo, S., Sormunen, K., Kangas, K., Hakkarainen, K., Lavonen, J., Juuti, K., Korhonen, T., & Seitamaa-Hakkarainen, P. (2020). Elementary school pupils' co-inventions: Products and pupils' reflections on processes. *International Journal of Technology Design and Education*. Advance online publication.

Sisk, V., Burgoyne, A., Sun, J., Bultler, J., & Macnamara, B. (2018). To what extent and under which circumstances are growth mind-set important to academic achievement? Two meta-analyses. *Psychological Science, 29*(4), 549–571. https://doi.org/10.1177/0956797617739704

Sormunen, K., Juuti, K., & Lavonen, J. (2020). Maker-centered project-based learning in inclusive classes: Supporting students' active participation with teacher-directed reflective discussions. *International Journal of Science and Mathematics Education, 18*(4), 691–712. https://doi.org/10.1007/s10763-019-09998-9

Tang, M., Werner, C., & Karwowski, M. (2016). Differences in creative mindset between Germany and Poland: The mediating effect of individualism and collectivism. *Thinking Skills and Creativity, 21*, 31–40.

Tomasello, M. (2019). *Becoming human: A theory of ontogeny*. The Belknap Press.

Yamazaki, S., & Kumar, V. K. (2013). Implicit theories of intelligence and creative ability: Relationship with academic risk-taking and academic stress. *International Journal of Creativity and Problem Solving, 23*, 25–40.

Yeager, D. S., & Dweck, C. (2012). Mindsets that promote resilience: When students believe that personal characteristics can be developed. *Educational Psychologist, 47*(4), 302–314.

Yeager, D. S., Hanselman, P., Walton, G. M., Murray, J. S., Crosnoe, R., Muller, C., Tipton, E., Schneider, B., Hulleman, C. S., Hinojosa, C. P., Paunesku, D., Romero, C., Flint, K., Roberts, A., Trott, J., Iachan, R., Buontempo, J., Yang, S. M., Carvalho, C. M., ... Dweck,

C. S. (2019). A national experiment reveals where a growth mindset improves achievement. *Nature, 573*(7774), 364–369. https://doi.org/10.1038/s41586-019-1466-y

Yeager, D., Johnson, R., Spitzer, B., Trzesniewski, K., Powers, J., & Dweck, C. (2014). The far-reaching effects of believing people can change: Implicit theories of personality shape stress, health, and achievement during adolescence. *Journal of Personality and Social Psychology, 106*(6), 867–884. https:///doi.org/10.1037/a0036335

Yeager, D. S., Romero, C., Paunesku, D., Hulleman, C. S., Schneider, B., Hinojosa, C., & Dweck, C. S. (2016). Using design thinking to improve psychological interventions. *Journal of Educational Psychology, 108*(3), 374–391.

Yeager, D. S., & Walton, G. M. (2011). Social-psychological interventions in education: They're not magic. *Review of Educational Research, 81*(2), 267–01.

Vygotsky, L. S. (1962). *Thought and language*. MIT Press.

Vygotsky, L. S. (1978). *Mind in society: The development of higher psychological processes*. Harvard University Press.

CHAPTER 16

Experimental Evidence on Connections between Speech and Music

Possible Applications on Learning

Minna Huotilainen and Teija Kujala

Abstract

Some researchers consider music and speech as alternative means of communication, containing somewhat similar but still distinct acoustic features to carry information from the player, singer, or speaker to the listener. These low-level similarities in speech and music as acoustic signals form the starting point for experimental research comparing automatic neural processes in perceiving music and speech. Importantly, there is also evidence that learning occurs in these low-level neural processes due to exposure and training. We review the influence of music on language systems. We also discuss some recent evidence showing that musical training can have a positive effect on speech perception and neural processing of speech signals. Finally, we propose some possible applications of music interventions on learning of speech perception in early childhood education and in schools.

Keywords

speech – music – brain – learning – dyslexia – hearing impairment

1 Key Similarities between Processing of Speech and Music

There are notable similarities between speech and music on several levels of processing. The power of using music as a means of education depends partially on these similarities. Educators have named musical skills as one of the subjects where fixed mindsets are more frequent: pupils with a fixed mindset are more likely to talk about "musical talent" and to interpret their own mistakes as a lack of musical ability rather than lack of effort or time spent practicing (Dweck, 2006). This chapter discusses the experimental and especially neural foundations of the applicability of music in education, namely, the similarities of speech and music, brain plasticity and transfer effects, as well as experimental evidence of the use of music in special education. Finally, we also present some thoughts on how teachers can apply this knowledge in their work in using music as a means of education.

The shared properties of language and music have been investigated on several domains, starting from low-level acoustic similarities to structural similarities and even shared evolutionary origins (Patel, 2007). Both speech and music are learned through interactions with other individuals, utilizing audition as the main channel but also strongly influenced by non-vocal communication, such as facial and bodily expressions and movements. They consist of successive acoustic events that unfold over time, both operating in rhythmic, tonal and timbre domains. Further, both speech and music use high-level hierarchical structures of combinations of these acoustic events, thus forming new representations derived from the combinations. In speech, an example would be combining phonemes or syllables in a row to form words and sentences with meaning, while in music, melodies are formed from successive tones and chords are formed from simultaneous tones (see Table 16.1).

For decades, the low-level similarities in the mode of expression of speech and music have inspired teachers and educators to investigate the possibilities of music in helping children's language development and learning. Even more evidence on the shared mechanisms was found after it became possible to study the neural correlates of speech and music perception. For example, although some studies indicate lateralization of brain areas, i.e., stronger responses in the left temporal lobe for speech and in the right for music (Zatorre et al., 2002), the very basic acoustic analysis of both speech and music is carried out in overlapping temporal-lobe cortical areas. Further, violations of structure, i.e., ungrammatical words in speech or out-of-key notes in music, were found to give rise to similar changes in the event-related potential (ERP) called P600 (Patel et al., 1998). Functional magnetic resonance imaging (fMRI) studies have identified overlapping cortical areas in the inferior frontal gyrus to be responsible for the processing of both musical and linguistic structure (Friederici et al., 2003; Tillmann et al., 2003, see also Peretz et al., 2015; Rogalsky & Hickok, 2011, for critical discussions on studies assessing musical and linguistic structural processing). Naturally, these high-level similarities between speech and music have also inspired educators to use music as a teaching method outside the musical domain and especially for language learning.

Currently, in the light of acoustic, behavioral and neural investigations, there is a strong consensus of the close connections between speech and music perception. The most overwhelming evidence comes from the low-level acoustic features such as similarities in the perception of musical timbres and phonemes, similarities in perceiving melodies and speech intonation patterns, and overlapping requirements for memory and attentive processes due to the unfolding-in-time nature of both speech and music. These similarities can help us understand how, practically, musical activities could support pupils with speech- and language-related problems. The process of achieving a positive transfer effect from practicing musical activities to learning speech- and language-related skills is dependent on the capacity of the auditory system to change after exposure, training and teaching, efficiently occurring in active interaction between human beings. This neural learning-related process is called brain plasticity. Plasticity, the brain's ability to change, is a core mechanism which is always involved when an individual learns something, whether it is new melodies, phonemes, or some complex knowledge at school. Below we review some of the main findings specifically related to plasticity in the auditory system, which has a central role in music and language processing.

2 Plasticity and Learning in the Auditory System

There is a broad consensus that the auditory system of the human brain can change its function and structure according to exposure (spending time in environments where one is exposed to certain sounds), training (engaging in tasks for a long enough time) and teaching on a larger scale (being given information and activities by a teacher or a coach, being supported and scaffolded towards expertise via tasks and training). Plasticity of the auditory system can be investigated on several levels ranging from the cellular, synaptic, and network levels up to systems level. For the purpose of this text, it is most beneficial to use the framework of cognitive neuroscience where brain plasticity is often described as measurable structural and/or functional changes in the brain that are associated with changes in behavior and are caused by exposure or training.

In the area of auditory-system plasticity, two time scales are usually separated (Galván, 2010). Long-term plasticity involves effects occurring on the time scale of years. For example, being exposed to a certain native language for decades results in plastic changes in the auditory system, making it easy to recognize the phonemes of the native language. Short-term plasticity, however, would occur in time scales from minutes to weeks. For example, in order to learn to sing a new simple song one might need to practice it for a few minutes per day for a few weeks. Thereafter, the brain would automatically react to hearing any modified notes in this simple melody. Typically, long-term plasticity is studied in cross-sectional studies (comparing two groups of people

TABLE 16.1   Key similarities and differences between the acoustic signals and expressive features of speech and music

Features specific to music		Features specific to speech	
Features specific to music, distant from speech	Features specific to music, close to speech	Features specific to speech, close to music	Features specific to speech, distant from music
High-level features			
	– Building emotional and sometimes cognitive content and meaning via music	– Building cognitive and often emotional content and meaning via speech	
Mid-level features			
– Harmony and scales – Chord structure and progression			– Semantics, i.e., specific meaning of words – Grammar
Low-level features			
– Fundamental frequency/pitch – Timbre: recognition of a musical instrument on the basis of spectral content and fast spectral changes – Timing: using rhythm and sound duration as expressive elements – Memory requirement: keeping previous tones in memory in order to combine them into a coherent melody		– Fundamental frequency/pitch – Timbre: recognition of a phoneme on the basis of formants, i.e., spectral content, as well as fast spectral changes – Timing: using sound duration and sometimes rhythm as expressive elements (e.g., short and long vowels) – Memory requirement: keeping previous syllables and words in memory in order to combine them into coherent words and sentences	

Note: At the lowest level of expression, both speech and music use frequency content and timing of sounds as features. This similarity opens the possibility to direct transfer effects: skills learned in musical activities are directly benefitting the perception of frequency content and sound timing in speech perception. For the mid-level features, differences are obvious, reflected in the different processing systems of speech and musical sounds in the brain. Finally, similarities occur at the highest level, where both speech and music use structured, meaning-loaded expressions and use similar acoustic characteristics to express emotions.

who have had different types of long-term exposure or training), although longitudinal follow-up studies also exist. Short-term plasticity is typically studied in experiments where pre- and post-tests are administered and training occurs between them. It is often not possible to use double-blind randomized controlled trials, but forming matched intervention groups is considered to be important in order to control for family background and genetic factors.

The auditory system shows plasticity to music even without any musical training, merely due to exposure to a certain musical culture. For example, tonality (Toiviainen & Krumhansl, 2003) and meter (Hannon et al., 2004) are musically relevant phenomena that the auditory system is also shown to be sensitive to in individuals without any musical training. Our innate musicality allows our brains to form models of tone and meter simply when exposed to a certain musical culture. Plasticity resulting from music exposure is even observed in animal studies (Rickard et al., 2005), showing that no prior knowledge or music training is required for the beneficial structural and functional music effects to emerge.

Musical training can influence the auditory system greatly and at several levels. At the brainstem, which is a very early part of the auditory pathway, changes in response patterns have been observed due to musical training (Wong et al., 2007). The changes at this level allow the auditory system to extract information from sounds more accurately. This was proposed to be one of the mechanisms via which musical training affects the perception of all sounds, including speech sounds. Further, in the primary and surrounding auditory cortices, musical training was found to enhance neural structure and function (Bermudez et al., 2009; Schneider et al., 2002). Some studies have shown that the plasticity extends to higher-order cortical areas (Lappe et al., 2008).

Like music, language learning can also occur through passive exposure and by actively training language functions. For instance, it was shown that representations of new word-forms, that is, new words that do not have pre-existing meanings, are formed when the individual is exposed to them even when not paying attention to the stimuli (Kimppa et al., 2018; Shtyrov et al., 2010). Furthermore, these studies found that the representations are formed very rapidly, in less than 15 minutes in adults (Shtyrov et al., 2010) and within 6 minutes in children (Kimppa et al., 2018).

These findings on automatic and rapid learning of words have changed our view on language learning mechanisms. Learning of new languages usually requires extensive training. In grammar learning, which is a central task in school in language-learning classes, one has to engage attention and memory mechanisms to achieve the proficiency of the new language. The acquisition of the phonology of a new language often calls for effort, and there can be a large variation between individuals in how they master the pronunciation even after extensive training.

3 Transfer Effects from Musical Training to Speech Perception and Neural Processing of Speech Signals

When a skill acquired in a specific domain has an influence on processes in another, unrelated domain, a transfer has occurred. Based on several observations, it was hypothesized that there can be a transfer from musical practice to language, more specifically, to speech processing (Besson et al., 2011; Kraus & Chandrasekaran, 2010; Patel, 2011, 2014). First, a large body of literature has shown superior auditory functions in musicians. Second, speech and music share similarities. Both of them include the processing of acoustic cues such as timbre, pitch, duration, and intensity, and involve sound sequences that are in a structured fashion unfolding in time. Third, there is an overlap of subcortical and cortical brain structures for music and speech processing (Koelsch et al., 2005; Schön et al., 2010), suggesting that they have shared neural resources (Patel, 2011, 2014).

Phoneme awareness is one of the most frequently used measures of speech perception in studies of transfer effects of musical training (Anvari et al., 2002). Linnavalli et al. (2018) used a block-randomized intervention design where language skills were followed up for two years in four separate measurement sessions, including both testing of language skills and ERP measurements of children's brain responses to changes in speech sounds. They found that even though the children's speech perception skills advanced on average, attending musical play school during the follow-up period advanced the skills even faster.

There are several other studies in which participating in a music programme was found to advance language skills. Degé and Schwarzer (2011) found strong transfer from musical training to phonological awareness in German 6-year-olds. Gromko (2005) found clear effects of 4-month music instruction on phoneme segmentation fluency in American 5–6-year-old children. Thomson et al. (2013) found strong effects on phonological awareness in British 9-year-olds, who participated in musical rhythmic training. Myant et al. (2008) showed positive effects on reading ability in British 4-year-olds, who participated in musical activity in nursery. Register (2004) found better early literacy skills in American 5–6-year-olds after different types of video and audio music programmes. Bolduc and Lefebvre (2012) found increased phonological awareness in French 5-year-olds who took part in a music programme. Chobert et al. (2011,

2014) found effects at the level of syllables. Clearly weaker effects of musical training have also been reported. For example, Cogo-Moreira et al. (2013), Herrera et al. (2011) and Yazejian and Peisner-Feinberg (2009) found small or even contrary effects of musical training on phoneme awareness in their studies in Brazilian, Spanish, and American children. It should be noted that the number of participants in these three last studies was not small, altogether 472 children. Overall, musical training in children is accompanied by positive effects on phoneme awareness in most studies, but not all.

Rhyming is a frequently used task in testing the effects of musical training on language skills. Moritz et al. (2013) used a rhyming discrimination task and found effects of musical training. Similarly, Herrera et al. (2011) found effects of musical training on rhyming tasks in two languages, and the results of Moreno et al. (2011) and Thomson et al. (2013) were very similar. In contrast, Yazejian and Peisner-Feinberg (2009) and Myant et al. (2008) found very small or even contrary effects on rhyme recognition.

There are also studies showing transfer effects from musical training to reading skills. Moreno et al. (2009) found clear effects of musical training on non-word reading skills. Similar findings but with smaller effects were found by Cogo-Moreira et al. (2013) and Herrera et al. (2011) on word-reading, and Register (2004) and Gromko (2005) on letter naming. In conclusion, many intervention and follow-up studies show positive effects of musical training on several language-related skills at varying levels from the very low-level skills like perception all the way to higher-level skills like reading, but the findings are not consistent and may depend on the age of the children, the type of musical training, and the language characteristics. Some correlational studies with Finnish learners show similar findings (Milovanov et al., 2008, 2009), thus further supporting the connection.

4 Music in Special Education

Using music in early childhood education has a long tradition in many countries. In Finland, musical play schools are well structured and the activities are organized mainly by professional early childhood music educators with a Master's degree, and musical activities during early childhood education are considered important. Teachers know that music is also a great method for other subjects like reading and mathematics for 1st and 2nd grade students (Rantala, 2017; Ruokonen, 2016). Musical methods of teaching native and foreign language skills are important and effective for all learners, but they are especially important for learners with language-learning problems, since musical activities were shown to develop several key skills in speech perception, including speech segmentation (François et al., 2013).

There are several groups of special learners whose responses to different types of musical interventions have been studied, and there are even some promises for very early interventions (Virtala & Partanen, 2018). In high-quality research, the protocol would include randomizing children into groups of interventions or waiting-list control groups, documenting the intervention, and testing prior to and after the intervention for changes in cognitive and/or academic skills. Unfortunately, not all intervention studies in music adhere to these requirements, and there are some critical voices about the field in terms of publication bias (Rothstein et al., 2005) and applicability in healthy children (Tervaniemi et al., 2018). There are, however, several groups of special learners for whom the results of intervention studies are especially important for educators.

In a large training program in at-risk communities, several benefits of musical training to language skills were found (Kraus et al., 2014a, 2014b). Music intervention holds promise in alleviating a range of problems in, for example, the autism spectrum (Maw & Haga, 2018), attention deficit and hyperactivity disorder (Rickson, 2006), and developmental language-related dysfunctions, such as dyslexia (Habib et al., 2016). Next, we will review studies on the influence of music intervention in children with dyslexia and hearing-impairment as examples.

4.1 Children with Dyslexia

Dyslexia is one of the most common neurodevelopmental disorders (prevalence 5–10%; Snowling & Melby-Lervåg, 2016), which can be devastating for the individual, first in the challenge of learning to read and then learning by reading. The early negative learning experiences and feelings of inferiority compared to peers can also lead to low learning motivation. Therefore, it is of high importance to find efficient means to alleviate dyslexia and particularly to prevent it with interventions applied before school entrance. All teachers encounter learners with dyslexia during their career due to its high prevalence.

For the development of language and literacy skills, phonological awareness was proposed to be crucial (Ramus et al., 2013; Serniclaes et al., 2004). Phonological perception is based on speech-sound categorization ability on the basis of very short timing differences, which are challenging for dyslexic children (Serniclaes et al., 2004). Although many perceptual dysfunctions are associated with dyslexia, phonological deficits were suggested to be its major cause (Ramus, 2014; Snowling & Melby-Lervåg, 2016).

Overy (2003) was among the first in determining the efficacy of music intervention in children with dyslexia. The results, albeit obtained with a small group size (N = 9) and lacking a proper matched-control group, were promising. They showed that rhythmic training improves phonological awareness and spelling skills in children with dyslexia. A study with an intervention group (N = 114) and a control group without intervention (N = 121), both having reading difficulties, corroborated these results (Cogo-Moreira et al., 2013). Interventions included musical improvisation, composition, and interpretation. It was found that this training improved both literacy skills and educational achievement in children with dyslexia (Cogo-Moreira et al., 2013).

A training method called Cognitive Musical Training (CMT) was also found to have a positive influence on dyslexic children (Habib et al., 2016). It has auditory exercises in duration, pitch, tempo, rhythm, and pulsation, motor exercises (e.g., tapping on rhythm), and cross-modal tasks. This intervention program was found to significantly improve the perception of phoneme categories and temporal speech components in dyslexic children. Furthermore, it enhanced auditory attention, phonological awareness (syllable fusion), reading abilities, and repetition of pseudo-words.

Phonological deficits in dyslexic children were proposed to be linked to misalignments between maximum speech-signal amplitudes and fluctuations in neuronal excitability in the auditory areas (Power et al., 2013). Consistent with this view, adult dyslexic musicians were found to outperform non-musician dyslexic individuals in temporal auditory processing tests, particularly in those assessing processing of "rise time" and temporal envelope (Bishop-Liebler et al., 2014). Moreover, dyslexic musicians were found to be better than dyslexic non-musicians in tests of reading skills and phonological awareness.

Corroborating this, rhythm perception and production tasks and performance on a metric perception task predicted phonological processing and both reading accuracy and speed in dyslexic individuals (Flaugnacco et al., 2014). Some further evidence for the beneficial effects of music, particularly rhythmic training, was found by Slater et al. (2013). They determined the influence of 1 year of musical training focusing on the perception of rhythm (tapping in synchrony with a given tempo), pitch, and improvisation in 8-year-old children who were at risk for learning disability. This training was found to yield beneficial effects on performance in a synchrony tapping task, in which the children who underwent the training had better skills than matched controls.

Moreover, rhythmic stimuli were found to have a rapid influence on performance in a language task (Przybylski et al., 2013). Reading- and language-impaired children were presented with a rhythmic prime (a sequence of notes played either regularly or irregularly), which was immediately followed by a syntactically correct or incorrect spoken sentence (e.g., "John has/have forgotten his violin"). The regular compared with irregular rhythmic primes clearly resulted in better performance in the syntactic task.

The influence of music intervention on dyslexia has also been determined at the neural level. ERPs to syllables and changes in their voice onset time, vowel duration, and vowel frequency were recorded from dyslexic children before and after training that included either learning to play various instruments or painting exercises (Frey et al., 2019). It was found that neural discrimination of the voice onset time and vowel duration changes improved in the musical training group but not in children who did painting exercises.

The results presented above are consistent with the observations of scientists, teachers, and clinicians that music has a positive influence on basic scholarly skills. This might result from the partly overlapping neural network processing speech and music (Friederici et al., 2003; Tillmann et al., 2003). Additionally, the improving influence of music on mood and brain's reward system (Sihvonen et al., 2017) can be expected to facilitate these effects.

4.2   *Hearing-Impaired Children*

One group of children who need specific support for their auditory functions is children with a hearing impairment. Even children who were born deaf can be helped by inserting cochlear implants (CI) in their inner ear. CI has proven to be very successful in allowing these individuals to communicate with speech. Yet, these children have difficulties in acquiring spoken language skills due to many of them having, for example, a limited receptive and expressive vocabulary (Lund, 2016; Percy-Smith et al., 2013). Children with CI often experience difficulties when listening to speech in noisy conditions. Furthermore, around half of children with CIs have poor expressive syntactic, morphological, and narrative production skills (Boons et al., 2013), as well as phonological awareness and verbal IQ (for a review, see van Wieringen & Wouters, 2015).

According to recent evidence, music can positively influence a wide range of language-related skills in children with CI. This was evident in a study collecting questionnaire data on musical activities, particularly singing, and assessing language skills in 5–13 year-old children with CI or normal hearing (Torppa et al., 2020). The language skills tested were verbal intelligence, phonological awareness, word finding performance, and perception of stress in words and sentences. It was found that musically active children with CIs performed comparably to normal-hearing controls in all language tasks in these tests, whereas the performance of those who were not musically active was poorer and they made more errors in phonological and semantic word finding tasks than normal-hearing controls.

Rhythmic priming, which has been shown to enhance speech perception (Cason & Schön, 2012), was found to improve language production in children with CIs. In a study determining the effect of rhythmic priming on phonological production, children with hearing aids were asked to repeat sentences which did or did not follow a rhythmic prime (Cason et al., 2015). The rhythmic prime either matched or did not match the stress contrasts (i.e., meter) of the sentence. It was found that the children had a better phonological accuracy in producing sentences in the matching than mismatching conditions. These results imply that musical rhythmic priming enhances phonological production in children with CI.

Speech hearing for individuals with CI is particularly challenging in noise, which is ubiquitous in modern city environments. Noise may be present in classrooms and particularly in kindergartens, making learning and interaction with teachers and peers difficult. Music can alleviate this problem as well. It was found that children who regularly sang at home had a better perception of speech in noise as compared with children who had less musical activity (Torppa et al., 2018). This study also illuminated neural correlates of these functions by finding that in the regularly singing group, a higher accuracy in speech in noise perception was associated with faster P3a ERP responses to sound changes (Torppa et al., 2018). Besides showing the beneficial effects of music activities on perceiving speech in noisy conditions, these results suggest that the improved speech in noise perception of the children who sang is associated with better attention-shifting mechanisms. Generally, the use of music is recommended in the lives of children with CIs both as a hobby and as a teaching method (Torppa & Huotilainen, 2019).

5 How Good Teachers Use Music Interventions in Education to Support Learning

For decades, teachers have used the close connection between speech and music both at the acoustic level and in emotional expressions (see Table 16.1). The recent evidence highlighting these connections and showing transfer effects between musical training, use of music as a teaching method, and learning of native and foreign language skills further strengthens this connection and can make the use of music more specific and goal-driven in different learning situations and for different types of learners.

One important field of music intervention applications is learning and language disorders, such as dyslexia and in children with hearing problems. These children have challenges in developing sufficient language skills, which are the fundamental basis for any learning of knowledge at school. Both children with dyslexia and those with hearing deficits need support for the building blocks of speech: accurate perception of its acoustic features. Therefore, music, which facilitates the brain's overall plasticity through a wide neural network involving reward and learning systems (Sihvonen et al., 2017), and specifically stimulates the auditory system, is a feasible means to support language development in these groups.

Beneficial influences of music on dyslexic and hearing-impaired pupils have been shown both by correlational and intervention studies. Many teachers enjoy music, and this may motivate them to use music in their teaching. In the professional use of music in education, however, teachers should not only rely on such personal likes and dislikes but should base their choice of teaching methods on scientific evidence. Critical thinking towards any oversimplified and overoptimistic views on using music in education is needed (Tervaniemi et al., 2018). For example, short-term improvements in some test results after music listening have been misinterpreted to reflect long-term and broad beneficial changes in any cognitive or mental abilities, including intelligence. At the same time, more well-controlled comparative studies on the use of musical vs. other teaching methods are needed for different subject matters. When requiring teachers to base their teaching methods on scientific evidence it should be noted, however, that researchers should put effort on translating their findings to actionable knowledge appropriate for guiding teachers' professional practices.

Teacher training is one of the key factors affecting the use of music in education. For teachers, growth mindset is of crucial importance, highlighted by using phrases like "don't know *yet*" instead of a deterministic belief of being incompetent (Tirri & Kuusisto, 2019). Growth mindset, and taking neural plasticity seriously, is also needed in the teachers' own musical training and learning to use music as a method of teaching. Previously, training of early childhood education teachers contained a lot of artistic work and musical training. When the training was moved to universities, the amount of musical training unfortunately decreased. In their training, the scientific understanding on why music is important in early childhood education was brought up, which is important, but practical skills are also needed in order for teachers to feel competent using music in their work in early childhood education, as well as to continue their own learning in the field of music. The same holds partially true for school teacher education. Teacher training should both educate future teachers on the reasons music is so important for learning and also how it can practically be used in everyday educational contexts. In addition, class teacher training should give the motivation and the means for all teachers to develop their own musical skills throughout their career.

There is enough evidence to say that music is a powerful resource that can advance learning (Tervaniemi et al., 2018). Good teachers are aware of the possibilities of music for helping their pupils learn different subject matter and exercise growth mindset. They are inspired by new research in educational sciences and they experiment with music interventions in their daily teaching in order to find the best ways of using music for each learner that they work with. They use music not only as *content* of education, but also *a means* of education.

References

Anvari, S. H., Trainor, L. J., Woodside, J., & Levy, B. A. (2002). Relations among musical skills, phonological processing, and early reading ability in preschool children. *Journal of Experimental Child Psychology, 83*, 111–130. doi:10.1016/S0022-0965(02)00124-8

Bermudez, P., Lerch, J. P., Evans, A. C., & Zatorre, R. J. (2009). Neuroanatomical correlates of musicianship as revealed by cortical thickness and voxel-based morphometry. *Cerebral Cortex, 19*, 1583–1596.

Besson, M., Chobert, J., & Marie, C. (2011). Transfer of training between music and speech: Common processing, attention, and memory. *Frontiers in Psychology, 2*, 94.

Bishop-Liebler, P., Welch, G., Huss, M., Thomson, J. M., & Goswami, U. (2014). Auditory temporal processing skills in musicians with dyslexia. *Dyslexia, 20*, 261–279. doi:10.1002/dys.1479

Bolduc, J., & Lefebvre, P. (2012). Using nursery rhymes to foster phonological and musical processing skills in kindergarteners. *Creative Education, 3*, 495–502. doi:10.4236/ce.2012.34075

Boons, T., De Raeve, L., Langereis, M., Peeraer, L., Wouters, J., & van Wieringen, A. (2013). Expressive vocabulary, morphology, syntax and narrative skills in profoundly deaf children after early cochlear implantation. *Research in Developmental Disabilities, 34*, 2008–2022.

Cason, N., Hidalgo, C., Isoard, F., Roman, S., & Schön, D. (2015). Rhythmic priming enhances speech production abilities: Evidence from prelingually deaf children. *Neuropsychology, 29*, 102–107. doi:10.1037/neu00 00115

Cason, N., & Schön, D. (2012). Rhythmic priming enhances the phonological processing of speech. *Neuropsychologia, 50*, 2652–2658. doi:10.1016/j.neuropsychologia.2012.07.018

Chobert, J., François, C., Velay, J. L., & Besson, M. (2014). Twelve months of active musical training in 8- to 10-year-old children enhances the preattentive processing of syllabic duration and voice onset time. *Cerebral Cortex, 24*, 956–967. doi:10.1093/cercor/bhs377

Chobert, J., Marie, C., François, C., Schön, D., & Besson, M. (2011). Enhanced passive and active processing of syllables in musician children. *Journal of Cognitive Neuroscience, 23,* 3874–3887. doi:10.1162/jocn_a_00088

Cogo-Moreira, H., Brandão de Ávila, C. R., Ploubidis, G. B., & Mari, J. D. J. (2013). Effectiveness of music education for the improvement of reading skills and academic achievement in young poor readers: A pragmatic cluster-randomized, controlled clinical trial. *PLoS ONE, 8,* 59984. doi:10.1371/journal.pone.0059984

Degé, F., & Schwarzer, G. (2011). The effect of a music program on phonological awareness in preschoolers. *Frontiers in Psychology, 2,* 124. doi:10.3389/fpsyg.2011.00124

Dweck, C. S. (2006). *Mindset: The new psychology of success.* Random House.

Flaugnacco, E., Lopez, L., Terribili, C., Zoia, S., Buda, S., Tilli, S., Monasta, L., Montico, M., Sila, A., Ronfani, L., & Schön, D. (2014). Rhythm perception and production predict reading abilities in developmental dyslexia. *Frontiers in Human Neuroscience, 8,* 392. doi:10.3389/fnhum.2014.00392

François, C., Chobert, J., Besson, M., & Schön, D. (2013). Music training for the development of speech segmentation. *Cerebral Cortex, 23,* 2038–2043.

Frey, A., Francois, C., Chobert, J., Velay, J. L., Habib, M., & Besson, M. (2019). Music training positively influences the preattentive perception of voice onset time in children with dyslexia: A longitudinal study. *Brain Science, 9,* 91. https://doi.org/10.3390/brainsci9040091

Friederici, A. D., Rüschemeyer, S. A., Hahne, A., & Fiebach, C. J. (2003). The role of left inferior frontal and superior temporal cortex in sentence comprehension: Localizing syntactic and semantic processes. *Cerebral Cortex, 13,* 170–177.

Galván, A. (2010). Neural plasticity of development and learning. *Human Brain Mapping, 31*(6), 879–890.

Gromko, J. E. (2005). The effect of music instruction on phonemic awareness in beginning readers. *Journal of Research in Music Education, 53,* 199–209. doi:10.1177/002242940505300302

Habib, M., Lardy, C., Desiles, T., Commeiras, C., Chobert, J., & Besson, M. (2016). Music and dyslexia: A new musical training method to improve reading and related disorders. *Frontiers in Psychology, 7,* 22. https://doi.org/10.3389/fpsyg.2016.00026

Hannon, E. E., Snyder, J. S., Eerola, T., & Krumhansl, C. L. (2004). The role of melodic and temporal cues in perceiving musical meter. *Journal in Experimental Psychology and Human Perception and Performance, 30,* 956–974.

Herrera, L., Lorenzo, O., Defior, S., Fernandez-Smith, G., & Costa-Giomi, E. (2011). Effects of phonological and musical training on the reading readiness of native- and foreign-Spanish-speaking children. *Psychology of Music, 39,* 68–81. doi:10.1177/0305735610361995

Kimppa, L., Shtyrov, Y., Partanen, E., & Kujala, T. (2018). Impaired neural mechanism for online novel word acquisition in dyslexic children. *Scientific Reports, 8,* 12779. doi:10.1038/s41598-018-31211-0

Koelsch, S., Gunter, T. C., Wittfoth, M., & Sammler, D. (2005). Interaction between syntax processing in language and in music: An ERP study. *Journal in Cognitive Neuroscience, 17*, 1565–1577.

Kraus, N., & Chandrasekaran, B. (2010). Music training for the development of auditory skills. *Nature Reviews in Neuroscience, 11*, 599–605. doi:10.1038/nrn2882

Kraus, N., Slater, J., Thompson, E. C., Hornickel, J., Strait, D. L., Nicol, T., & White-Schwoch, T. (2014a). Auditory learning through active engagement with sound: Biological impact of community music lessons in at-risk children. *Frontiers in Neuroscience, 8*, 351. doi:10.3389/fnins.2014.00351

Kraus, N., Slater, J., Thompson, E. C., Hornickel, J., Strait, D. L., Nicol, T., & White-Schwoch, T. (2014b). Music enrichment programs improve the neural encoding of speech in at-risk children. *Journal of Neuroscience, 34*, 11913–11918. doi:10.1523/JNEUROSCI.1881-14.2014

Lappe, C., Herholz, S. C., Trainor, L. J., & Pantev, C. (2008). Cortical plasticity induced by short-term unimodal and multimodal musical training. *Journal of Neuroscience, 28*, 9632–9639.

Linnavalli, T., Putkinen, V., Lipsanen, J., Huotilainen, M., & Tervaniemi, M. (2018). Music playschool enhances children's linguistic skills. *Scientific reports, 8*, 1–10.

Lund, E. (2016). Vocabulary knowledge of children with cochlear implants: A meta-analysis. *Journal of Studies in Deaf Education, 21*, 107–121.

Maw, S. S., & Haga, C. (2018). Effectiveness of cognitive, developmental, and behavioural interventions for Autism Spectrum Disorder in preschool-aged children: A systematic review and meta-analysis. *Heliyon, 4*(9), e00763. https://doi.org/10.1016/j.heliyon.2018.e00763

Milovanov, R., Huotilainen, M., Esquef, P. A., Alku, P., Välimäki, V., & Tervaniemi, M. (2009). The role of musical aptitude and language skills in preattentive duration processing in school-aged children. *Neuroscience Letters, 460*, 161–165. doi:10.1016/j.neulet.2009.05.063

Milovanov, R., Huotilainen, M., Välimäki, V., Esquef, P. A., & Tervaniemi, M. (2008). Musical aptitude and second language pronunciation skills in school-aged children: Neural and behavioral evidence. *Brain research, 1194*, 81–89. https://doi.org/10.1016/j.brainres.2007.11.042

Moreno, S., Friesen, D., & Bialystok, E. (2011). Effect of music training on promoting preliteracy skills: Preliminary causal evidence. *Music Perception, 29*, 165–172. doi:10.1525/mp.2011.29.2.165

Moreno, S., Marques, C., Santos, A., Santos, M., Castro, S. L., & Besson, M. (2009). Musical training influences linguistic abilities in 8-year-old children: More evidence for brain plasticity. *Cerebral Cortex, 19*, 712–723. doi:10.1093/cercor/bhn120

Moritz, C., Yampolsky, S., Papadelis, G., Thomson, J., & Wolf, M. (2013). Links between early rhythm skills, musical training, and phonological awareness. *Reading and Writing, 26*, 739–769. doi:10.1007/s11145-012-9389-0

Myant, M., Armstrong, W., & Healy, N. (2008). Can music make a difference? A small scale longitudinal study into the effects of music instruction in nursery on later reading ability. *Educational Child Psychology, 25*, 83–100.

Overy, K. (2003). Dyslexia and music: From timing deficits to musical intervention. *Annals of New York Academy of Sciences, 999*, 497–505. doi:10.1196/annals.1284.060

Patel, A. D. (2007). *Music, language, and the brain.* Oxford UP.

Patel, A. D. (2011). Why would musical training benefit the neural encoding of speech? The OPERA hypothesis. *Frontiers in Psychology, 2*, 142. doi:10.3389/fpsyg.2011.00142

Patel, A. D. (2014). Can nonlinguistic musical training change the way the brain processes speech? The expanded OPERA hypothesis. *Hearing Research, 308*, 98–108. doi:10.1016/j.heares.2013.08.011

Patel, A. D., Peretz, I., Tramo, M., & Labreque, R. (1998). Processing prosodic and musical patterns: A neuropsychological investigation. *Brain and Language, 61*, 123–144.

Percy-Smith, L., Busch, G., Sandahl, M., Nissen, L., Josvassen, J. L., Lange, T., Rusch, E., & Cayé-Thomasen, P. (2013). Language understanding and vocabulary of early cochlear implanted children. *International Journal of Pediatric Otorhinolaryngology, 77*, 184–188.

Peretz, I., Vuvan, D., Lagrois, M. É., & Armony, J. L. (2015). Neural overlap in processing music and speech. *Philosophical Transactions of the Royal Society of London B: Biological Sciences, 370*, 20140090. doi:10.1098/rstb.2014.0090

Power, A. J., Mead, N., Barnes, L., & Goswami, U. (2013). Neural entrainment to rhythmic speech in children with dyslexia. *Frontiers in Human Neuroscience, 7*, 777. doi:10.3389/fnhum.2013.00777

Przybylski, L., Bedoin, N., Krifi-Papoz, S., Herbillon, V., Roch, D., Léculier, L., Kotz, S., & Tillmann, B. (2013). Rhythmic auditory stimulation influences syntactic processing in children with developmental language disorders. *Neuropsychology, 27*, 121–131. doi:10.1037/a0031277

Ramus, F. (2014). Neuroimaging sheds new light on the phonological deficit in dyslexia. *Trends in Cognitive Sciences, 18*(6), 274–275.

Ramus, F., Marshall, C. R., Rosen, S., & van der Lely, H. K. (2013). Phonological deficits in specific language impairment and developmental dyslexia: Towards a multidimensional model. *Brain, 136*, 630–645.

Rantala, E. (2017). *Musiikki opetuksen eheyttäjänä: luokanopettajien kokemuksia ja käsityksiä oppiainerajat ylittävästä musiikinopetuksesta alkuopetuksessa* [Music in integrating teaching: Experiences of class teachers] [Master's thesis, University of Jyväskylä]. JYX Digital Repository. http://urn.fi/URN:NBN:fi:jyu-201705292553

Rickard, N. S., Toukhsati, S. R., & Field, S. E. (2005). The effect of music on cognitive performance: Insight from neurobiological and animal studies. *Behavioral and Cognitive Neuroscience Reviews, 4*, 235–261. https://doi.org/10.1177/1534582305285869

Rickson, D. J. (2006). Instructional and improvisational models of music therapy with adolescents who have Attention Deficit Hyperactivity Disorder (ADHD): A comparison of the effects on motor impulsivity. *Journal of Music Therapy, 43*, 39–62.

Register, D. (2004). The effects of live music groups versus an educational children's television program on the emergent literacy of young children. *Journal of Music Therapy, 41*, 2–27. doi:10.1093/jmt/41.1.2

Rogalsky, C., & Hickok, G. (2011). The role of Broca's area in sentence comprehension. *Journal in Cognitive Neuroscience, 23*(7), 1664–1680. https://doi.org/10.1162/jocn.2010.21530

Rothstein, H. R., Sutton, A. J., & Borenstein, M. (2005). *Publication bias in meta-analysis.* John Wiley & Sons.

Ruokonen, I. (2016). *Esi- ja alkuopetuksen musiikin didaktiikka* [Didactics in music in preschool and first and second grades]. Finn Lectura.

Schneider, P., Scherg, M., Dosch, H. G., Specht, H. J., Gutschalk, A., & Rupp, A. (2002). Morphology of Heschl's gyrus reflects enhanced activation in the auditory cortex of musicians. *Nature Neuroscience, 5*, 688–694.

Schön, D., Gordon, R., Campagne, A., Magne, C., Astesano, C., Anton, J. L., & Besson, M. (2010). Similar cerebral networks in language, music and song perception. *NeuroImage, 51*, 450–461.

Serniclaes, W., Van Heghe, S., Mousty, P., Carre, R., & Sprenger-Charolles, L. (2004). Allophonic mode of speech perception in dyslexia. *Journal of Experimental Child Psychology, 87*, 336–361.

Shtyrov, Y., Nikulin, V., & Pulvermüller, F. (2010). Rapid cortical plasticity underlying novel word learning. *Journal of Neuroscience, 30*, 16864–16867. https://doi.org/10.1523/JNEUROSCI.1376-10.2010

Sihvonen, A. J., Särkämö, T., Leo, V., Tervaniemi, M., Altenmüller, E., & Soinila, S. (2017). Music-based interventions in neurological rehabilitation. *Lancet Neurology, 16*, 648–660. doi:10.1016/S1474-4422(17)30168-0

Slater, J., Tierney, A., & Kraus, N. (2013). At-risk elementary school children with one year of classroom music instruction are better at keeping a beat. *PLoS ONE, 8*, e7725. doi:10.1371/journal.pone.0077250

Snowling, M. J., & Melby-Lervåg, M. (2016). Oral language deficits in familial dyslexia: A meta-analysis and review. *Psychological Bulletin, 142*, 498.

Tervaniemi, M., Tao, S., & Huotilainen, M. (2018). Promises of music in education? *Frontiers in Education, 3*, 74. https://doi.org/10.3389/feduc.2018.00074

Thomson, J. M., Leong, V., & Goswami, U. (2013). Auditory processing interventions and developmental dyslexia: A comparison of phonemic and rhythmic approaches. *Reading and Writing, 26*, 139–161. doi:10.1007/s11145-012-9359-6

Tillmann, B., Janata, P., & Bharucha, J. J. (2003). Activation of the inferior frontal cortex in musical priming. *Brain Research Cognitive Brain Research, 16*, 145–161.

Tirri, K., & Kuusisto, E. (2019). *Opettajan ammattietiikkaa oppimassa* [*Learning teachers' professional ethics*]. Gaudeamus.

Toiviainen, P., & Krumhansl, C. L. (2003). Measuring and modeling real-time responses to music: The dynamics of tonality induction. *Perception, 32*, 741–766.

Torppa, R., Faulkner, A., Kujala, T., Huotilainen, M., & Lipsanen, J. (2018). Developmental links between speech perception in noise, singing, and cortical processing of music in children with cochlear implants. *Music Perception, 36*, 156–174.

Torppa, R., Faulkner, A., Laasonen, M., Lipsanen, J., & Sammler, D. (2020). Links of prosodic stress perception and musical activities to language skills of children with Cochlear iwmplants and normal hearing. *Ear and Hearing, 41*, 395–410.

Torppa, R., & Huotilainen, M. (2019). Why and how music can be used to rehabilitate and develop speech and language skills in hearing-impaired children. *Hearing Research, 380*, 108–122.

van Wieringen, A., & Wouters, J. (2015). What can we expect of normally-developing children implanted at a young age with respect to their auditory, linguistic and cognitive skills? *Hearing Research, 322*, 171–179.

Virtala, P., & Partanen, E. (2018). Can very early music interventions promote at-risk infants' development? *Annals of the New York Academy of Sciences.* Blackwell Publishing Inc. https://doi.org/10.1111/nyas.13646

Wong, P. C. M., Skoe, E., Russo, N. M., Dees, T., & Kraus, N. (2007). Musical experience shapes human brainstem encoding of linguistic pitch patterns. *Nature Neuroscience, 10*, 420–422.

Yazejian, N., & Peisner-Feinberg, E. S. (2009). Effects of a preschool music and movement curriculum on children's language skills. *NHSA Dialogues, 12*, 327–341. doi:10.1080/15240750903075255

Zatorre, R. J., Belin, P., & Penhune, V. B. (2002). Structure and function of auditory cortex: Music and speech. *Trends in Cognitive Sciences, 6*, 37–46.

EPILOGUE

Growth Mindset and Purpose in Critical-Democratic Citizenship Education

Wiel Veugelers

1   Learning about Finnish Education

Finland has attracted a lot of attention in recent decades. The country achieves high scores in most international rankings that concern welfare. In education it is even world champion. Finland scores highly in international comparative studies on language, science and mathematics, and also on citizenship. The country is well known for technology, design and the arts. Many young females are part of the government. Finnish people are perceived as nice and caring. You meet them all around the world.

I met Kirsi and other Finnish scholars such as Hannele Niemi, Eero Ropo and Tero Autio in the 1990s at conferences in the USA and Europe. Kirsi and I started working together and we became good friends. In the background there was always the question of why Finland was doing so well and why many Finnish people were so nice. And they have to overcome some critical issues with me: I like warm sunny weather, and I like hanging around with friends on terraces drinking local beer or wine. This is not that easy in Finland, but I have found out that Finnish people also like these things, they are very sociable, and they try to live a Mediterranean life, even close to the Arctic Circle.

I have visited Finland as a professional many times during the past 25 years, twice with a group of 15 school leaders and teachers at Dutch secondary schools (Veugelers & O'Hair, 2005; Veugelers & Zijlstra, 2004). We were on an educational pilgrimage and we wondered what made Finnish education so excellent. At that time Dutch educational change focussed on enhancing self-regulated learning and flexibility in learning and teaching arrangements, as well as using more technology in classrooms. We were surprised that Finnish schools were quite traditional from our perspective: a central role for teachers, not much individual working among students or group work, and not a lot of technology. We had many discussions with Finnish teachers and school leaders, and with Kirsi and her colleagues at the universities of Helsinki and Tampere.

It became clear to us that the Finnish teachers had a caring orientation in their pedagogical approach, and they knew a lot about the progress of each student. The students sat around the teacher. We were also surprised by the friendly and relaxed climate in schools and classrooms. Teachers and most students worked consciously and hard. There was a sphere of cooperation among the schools, in contrast to the competition we experience in the Netherlands. Trust on all levels was the central value. We learned about the values of care and cooperation in education.

1.1 International Conferences

Kirsi and I worked together a lot with Fritz Oser of the University of Fribourg, and our academic circle extended over Europe and the US. Moral education was the central theme – not in a preaching sense, but more about what a good life is, what justice is and how to develop moral autonomy among students. We worked together in symposia at AERA, AME and EARLI. We inspired each other to make our research internationally relevant. We had different theoretical perspectives: Kirsi focussed more on moral development and the central role of teachers, and I was more concerned with linking the moral and the political in education, and with tensions in policy and practice. Kirsi always emphasised the need to do good empirical research, whereas I was very focussed on the theoretical concepts. We challenged each other in those symposia, and we established links with other researchers from all over the world.

1.2 The Book Series 'Moral Development and Citizenship Education'

Fritz Oser and I launched the book series 'Moral Development and Citizenship Education' in 2008, first with Sense Publishers and now with Brill Sense (Oser & Veugelers, 2008). Kirsi became a member of the editorial board and published two books in the series. The first one was an edited volume, *Educating Moral Sensibilities in Urban Schools* (Tirri, 2008), to which scholars from all over Europe, and some from North America contributed. The book succeeded in showing the relevance of moral sensibilities in human development, and how these sensibilities are embedded in different cultural and social contexts. My contribution to this book, entitled 'Youngsters in transformative and reproductive processes of moral and citizenship education,' is one of my all-time favorite articles (Veugelers, 2008). My aim was to integrate different perspectives on the moral development of youngsters: sociology (reproduction/transformation), developmental psychology (autonomy development), and pedagogy (the moral role of teachers).

Kirsi's second book in the series was a monograph written together with Petri Nokelainen (Tirri & Nokelainen, 2011), in which they created empirical instruments for measuring multiple intelligences and moral sensitivities including the spiritual, the environmental, the ethical, the emotional, the intercultural, and the interreligious. They clearly showed that it is possible to acquire all these sensitivities and to teach them in classrooms. Fifteen books have now been published in this series. Fritz Oser passed away in September 2020: Kirsi will now become the second editor of the series.

1.3 Education for Democratic Intercultural Citizenship

We had very concrete cooperation in the Erasmus Programme 'Education for Democratic Intercultural Citizenship' (EDIC): collaboration involving the Universities of Barcelona, Bath-Spa, Helsinki, Prague, Thessaloniki, Tallinn, and my own university, the University of Humanistic Studies in Utrecht. Initially, before we were restricted to members of the European Union, Fribourg, Brighton and Kibbutzim College in Tel Aviv also belonged to the EDIC network. We started off with intensive two-week programs involving 14 teachers and 20 students from all the universities, in 2013 in Utrecht, and in 2014 in Barcelona. We succeeded in forming an Erasmus Strategic Partnership in 2016, which enabled us to work on joint curriculum development. We continued our Intensive programs, now as a driver of curriculum development. In Prague, in 2017, we experienced together and discussed local educational, social, cultural, culinary, and political sensibilities.

The 2018 intensive program was held in both Tallinn and Helsinki: again, a very cultural experience. We learned in Helsinki about the history and the current state of Finnish education, and about the central role of moral education. We also found out how students were selected for teacher education based on their moral sensibilities, and how they developed a holistic, engaged and caring view of education.

As an Erasmus Strategic Partnership, we jointly wrote a book entitled 'Education for Democratic Intercultural Citizenship' (Veugelers, 2019), which received the 2020 book award of the SIG Moral Development and Education of the American Educational Research Association.

During the same period, we were also involved in the research project Teaching Common Values, at the request of the European Parliament (Veugelers et al., 2017). Our research investigated the policy and practice of teaching the common values of democracy and tolerance in all 28 EU Member States. Kirsi conducted the case study on Finland (Tirri, 2017). As she wrote: 'Citizenship education is a vital means of getting students involved and teaching them to be ethical, active members of society, thus promoting tolerance and respect towards diversity' (p. 85). In our overall analyses we showed that Finland, compared with the other 27 EU Member States, attach more importance to teaching the common values of democracy and tolerance: this is incorporated into the general laws and the curriculum documents, and schools have a lot of autonomy to develop these values (Veugelers et al., 2017, p. 40).

1.4 *Moral Sensitivity and Global Citizenship*

Another cooperative venture was our joint supervising of the PhD research of Ingrid Schutte of the Hanze University of Professional Studies in Groningen. Ingrid met Kirsi at conferences on talent development. They started a research project on ethical sensitivity among talented students. Ingrid wanted to link ethical sensitivity to global citizenship education. After hearing me speaking at a Dutch conference Ingrid told Kirsi about my research and suggested to include me in their project as well. Ingrid was surprised that we already had strong cooperation. Together, Kirsi and I supervised Ingrid's thesis at the University of Humanistic Studies. Her research clearly showed that, for the purpose of global citizenship teachers and students should have or develop ethical sensitivity: they should be aware when moral values are at stake. It was good for me to learn more about the research Kirsi was doing, and for Kirsi to link ethical sensitivity to specific content, in this case global citizenship. One of the studies conducted in connection with the thesis, entitled 'Preparing Students for Global Citizenship: The Effects of a Dutch Undergraduate Honors Course' (Schutte et al., 2017), was published in a special issue of the journal *Education Research International* edited by Kirsi, entitled 'Education for Creativity and Talent Development in the 21st Century'.

1.5 *The Californian Sun: Growth Mindset and Purpose*

Kirsi moved partly to California at the beginning of this millennium, and she joined Stanford University in Palo Alto. What a pity that I have never visited her in Stanford: we met a few times in San Francisco at AERA, but never at Stanford. Before focussing on the scientific relevance of California, let me offer an anecdote. Kirsi and I were both at the conference of the Association of Moral Education held at Notre Dame University in South Bend Illinois in 2008. As the reception was coming to an end I told her that Brian Wilson was playing here in town that night. Brian Wilson was the leader of the Beach Boys, one of my 'guilty pleasures' in the 'sixties'. He was playing with his new band. We went to the local concert hall and when we arrived the show had already started; we could hear the song 'Californian Girls'. We asked for two tickets, the lady at the office box gave them and added: you don't need to pay, the people haven't arrived. We had great seats in the 5th row, right in front of the band. They played all the old Beach Boys songs and the new album, 'That Lucky Old Sun'. California at its best!

At Stanford Kirsi started to work will Bill Damon and included the concept of 'purpose' in her work. She also worked with Carol Dweck and started using the concept of 'growth mindset'. Both concepts have become pivotal in her work over the past decade. Together with her colleagues – in particular Elina

Kuusisto – she introduced them in our EDIC program. They challenged our conceptual and didactic work and the students like their activities a lot.

In the second part of this Epilogue I would like to discuss Kirsi's work on both concepts, and I will analyse it from my theoretical perspectives. We have already done that to a certain extent at many conferences and in EDIC meetings. Having the opportunity to contribute to this book about Kirsi's work gives me the possibility to write these reflections down as a critical friend. First, I will present the theoretical framework that I use to analyse moral and citizenship education, and then I will discuss the ideas that Kirsi and her colleagues have about growth mindset and purpose. I will link these ideas through the concept of critical-democratic citizenship.

2 Critical-Democratic Citizenship

Educational systems, schools within a system, and teachers within a school: they may all have different educational goals, even with regard to citizenship and citizenship education. Our surveys among teachers have revealed three clusters of educational goals: discipline, autonomy, and social involvement (Leenders et al., 2008). (See Veugelers, 2007, 2017 for more conceptual explorations of these clusters.) Discipline is a central concept in character education (Lickona, 1991); autonomy in the moral development theory of Kohlberg (Power et al., 1989); and social involvement ranges from care (Noddings, 2002) to social justice and solidarity (Freire, 1985). Upon further analysis of our data we constructed three types of citizenship, expressing different orientations:

> The first type is *adaptive* citizenship. This type scores high on discipline and social involvement. Socially involved not in a political sense, but in a moral commitment to each other, especially your own community. For autonomy, the scores are not so high for the adaptive type.
>
> The second type, *individualised* citizenship, scores high on autonomy and fairly high on discipline but relatively low on social involvement. This type has a strong focus on personal development and freedom, not on the social.
>
> The third type, *critical-democratic* citizenship, scores high on social involvement and on autonomy. On discipline this type scores low. We call this type critical-democratic because of its focus on the social and on society, a critical engagement with the common good, and a democracy that leaves room for individual autonomy and personal articulation.

> The types of citizenship are ideal-typical constructions. In people's views and in educational practice we find many hybrid forms of citizenship and citizenship education. But these three types of citizenship and citizenship education clearly demonstrate that citizenship is not a matter of bad or good citizenship, and that different orientations in the political nature of citizenship and citizenship education are possible. It shows that nations, schools and teachers can make choices in their educational goals and in their practice of citizenship education. (Veugelers & De Groot, 2019, p. 19)

I believe that a human and democratic society needs critical-democratic citizens who combine autonomy and social involvement: care, social justice and solidarity (Veugelers, 2017, 2020).

2.1   Growth Mindset and Critical-Democratic Citizenship

Carol Dweck's mindset theory refers to the set of beliefs concerning whether intelligence, personality, and morality can (a growth mindset) or cannot (a fixed mindset) be developed.

> Learning mindsets refer to implicit beliefs about whether or not human qualities such as intelligence, giftedness, and personality can be developed; a growth mindset (the incremental theory) holds that they can, while a fixed mindset (the entity theory) holds that these qualities are innate and fixed. A teacher's mindset has an impact on how, and even on whom, she or he instructs (Dweck, 2000; Rissanen et al., 2018, 2019). (Kuusisto & Tirri, 2019, p. 82)

Kuusisto and Tirri (2019) place a growth mindset in the framework of 'Education for Democratic Intercultural Citizenship':

> It can be said that teachers' moral and professional responsibility in a democratic society is to have a growth mindset towards every student regardless of background or current competencies. Students with learning and behavioural problems as well as gifted students need to have tasks that provide sufficient challenges and opportunities to learn from their mistakes. Studies show that in intercultural societies students may face stereotyping, meaning that racial or gender stereotypes may unconsciously hinder the learning process (Aronson, Fried, & Good, 2002). However, knowledge about mindsets and how beliefs systems work is one of the best educational tools for cultivating intercultural and demo-

cratic citizenship so that every student is supported in developing their agency and becoming active citizens who realise their potential to the full. (Kuusisto & Tirri, 2019, p. 82)

A growth mindset could be described as a kind of openness and support of the individual as part of becoming autonomous. It is a psychological theory that shows how autonomy can be developed, and the kind of mechanisms that are involved. In this sense it is an essential part of the autonomy pillar of critical-democratic citizenship. Openness in a growth mindset is, as indicated above by Kirsi and Elina, a crucial precondition for an intercultural and democratic society. Its reflective character is also necessary for autonomy development and living in a democratic society.

Is a growth mindset in itself enough to become a critical-democratic citizen? I think not: what is missing is the social component, the component that links autonomy to living together and to society. A growth mindset has no specific direction, and without a social context it could become individualistic. In her theoretical work Kirsi approaches this moral component through the concept of 'purpose'.

The concept of growth mindset and the way Kirsi and her colleagues have researched it make an important contribution to the work on education for a democratic intercultural society. It constitutes the psychological foundation of this kind of learning.

I am curious to know how this concept of growth mindset can be linked to other psychological concepts and approaches I am using in my research such as critical thinking and efficacy. Research on critical thinking relies on the search for different perspectives, and their analysis and comparison should stimulate the formation of one's own opinions (Walters, 1994). From a critical perspective, critical thinking is not only a logical activity, and moral values are involved in the process (Walters, 1994). Indeed, moral values are criteria in the process of judging perspectives and arguments (Veugelers, 2002, 2010). In a similar way, one could pose the question: How can the use of different perspectives and moral values as criteria be incorporated into the idea and practice of a growth mindset?

Another question concerns the linking of a growth mindset with the concept of efficacy, on which Bandura (1995) in particular has conducted seminal research. Efficacy is the way individuals themselves judge their capacities. Internal efficacy concerns how they judge their own capacities; external efficacy relates to judgements about the opportunities society gives them to use their own capacities. Both forms of efficacy are relevant to moral and citizenship development (Haste, 2004; De Groot, 2013). Adding the external to the internal perspective on efficacy avoids its attribution as only a personal cause. External efficacy connotes the experience of being able to exercise internal efficacy. The growth-mindset approach is about internal efficacy in particular; that is its strength. Constraints on the use of one's own capacities seem less central within such a framework. Finding a balance between internal and external efficacy could facilitate the defining of a realistic perspective on a growth mindset.

2.2 Purpose in Life, the Link with Society

We conclude that growth mindset is an open perspective. In the recent work of Kirsi and colleagues the concept of 'purpose' gives more meaning to the direction in which a person can develop. Not everything can be purposeful, however: it is about relationships with other people. They use the work of Bill Damon, also from Stanford, to structure this thinking. Here is a quotation from the chapter 'Teachers' moral competence in pedagogical encounters' (Kuusisto & Tirri, 2019) in the book *Education for Democratic Intercultural Citizenship*:

> The notion of 'purpose' is the most profound phenomenon of human experience, as it provides reasons not only for acting ethically but also for living. Research has found powerful links between the pursuit of positive purpose and life satisfaction (Damon, 2008). In the view of Damon, purpose promotes pro-social behaviour, moral commitment, achievement, and high self-esteem. Purpose has a social orientation; therefore, individualism or a strong orientation to one's own life is not considered to be a purpose. (p. 83)

Kirsi and Elina make purpose more clear and more teachable.

> Our goal is to educate teachers who can reflect on the educational purposefulness of their calling from different points of view and who can help their students find purpose in their lives (Bundick & Tirri, 2014). Democratic societies need citizens who are engaged in civic and political activities (Veugelers et al., 2017). Teachers can stimulate participation in civic activities as a means of promoting what will eventually be an effective democracy. This can be achieved by building purpose, which includes beyond-the-self aspirations; in other words, supporting societal participatory skills and a responsible attitude towards the community and the future (Damon, 2008; Tirri, 2017, p. 85). (Kuusisto & Tirri, 2019, p. 83)

Kirsi and Elina clearly put purpose in a societal context: it is a moral and social direction, and giving purpose is a process. I have sometimes joked with Kirsi about the concept of purpose. Is loving football or loving a glass of wine a purpose? She explicitly stated that purpose must have a moral and a social direction. Loving football in itself is not a purpose, loving to play football together and in a fair way is a kind of purpose. However, purpose should be part of a larger normative frame of reference. In that way, finding purpose is a way of developing a meaningful life and contributing to a just society.

In itself the concept of purpose is not very political, but it could be put into a political context. The political spectrum is still quite broad, and it depends on the perspectives introduced. Developing a growth mindset and purpose could be placed in a critical-democratic citizenship framework with a combination of autonomy and social commitment.

Kirsi always emphasises how strongly moral values and ethical sensitivity are embedded in Finnish society and education. A caring orientation is the norm, in all aspects of life. It is as if, with such a strong moral foundation, politics is less manifest and there is less societal polarisation. A community feeling that binds the nation and links it with the world is strong all over the country. The research of Kirsi and her group contributes to this moral climate in a critical and engaged way. It is an example of ethical sensitivity, growth mindset, and purpose.

References

Bandura, A. (1995). *Self-efficacy in changing societies*. Cambridge University Press.
De Groot, I. (2013). *Adolescents' democratic engagement*. University of Humanistic Studies.
Freire, P. (1985). *The politics of education: Culture, power and liberation*. Bergin & Garvey.
Haste, H. (2004). Constructing the citizen. *Political Psychology, 25*(3), 413–440.
Kuusisto, E., & Tirri, K. (2019). Teachers' moral competence in pedagogical encounters. In W. Veugelers (Ed.), *Education for democratic intercultural citizenship* (pp. 81–106). Brill | Sense.
Leenders, H., Veugelers, W., & De Kat, E. (2008). Teachers' views on citizenship in secondary education in the Netherlands. *Cambridge Journal of Education, 38*(2), 155–170.
Lickona, T. (1991). *Educating for character*. Random House.
Noddings, N. (2002). *Educating moral people*. Teachers College Press.
Oser, F., & Veugelers, W. (Eds.). (2008). *Getting involved. Global citizenship development and sources of moral values*. Sense Publishers.
Power, F., Higgins, A., & Kohlberg, L. (1989). *Lawrence Kohlberg's approach to moral education*. Columbia University Press.

Schutte, I., Kamans, E., Wolfensberger, M., & Veugelers, W. (2018). Effects of an international undergraduate honors course on awareness of global justice. *Education Sciences, 8,* 82. doi:10.3390/educsci8020082

Tirri, K. (Ed.). (2008). *Moral sensibilities in urban education.* Sense Publishers.

Tirri, K. (2017). Finland – Promoting ethics and equality. In W. Veugelers, I. de Groot, & V. Stolk (Eds.), *Research for CULT Committee – Teaching common values in Europe* (pp. 83–90). Brussels: European Parliament, Policy Department for Structural and Cohesion Policies.

Tirri, K., & Nokelainen, P. (2011). *Measuring multiple intelligences and moral sensitivities in education.* Sense Publishers.

Veugelers, W. (2002). Teachers, values and critical thinking. In S. R. Steinberg (Ed.), *Multi/Intercultural conversations* (pp. 199–215). Peter Lang.

Veugelers, W. (2007). Creating critical-democratic citizenship education: Empowering humanity and democracy in Dutch education. *Compare, 37*(1), 105–119.

Veugelers, W. (2008). Youngsters in transformative and reproductive processes of moral and citizenship education. In K. Tirri (Ed.), *Moral sensibilities in urban education* (pp. 79–91). Sense Publishers.

Veugelers, W. (2010). Moral values in teacher education. In P. Peterson, E. Baker, & B. McGaw (Eds.), *International encyclopedia of education* (Vol. 7, pp. 660–665). Elsevier.

Veugelers, W. (2017). The moral in Paulo Freire's work: What moral education can learn from Paulo Freire. *Journal of Moral Education, 46*(4), 412–421.

Veugelers, W. (Ed.). (2019). *Education for democratic intercultural citizenship.* Brill | Sense.

Veugelers, W. (2020). Different views on global citizenship. In D. Schugurensky & C. Wolhuter (Eds.), *Global citizenship education and teacher education* (pp. 20–39). Routledge.

Veugelers, W., & De Groot, I. (2019). Theory and practice of citizenship education. In W. Veugelers (Ed.), *Education for democratic intercultural citizenship* (pp. 14–41). Brill | Sense.

Veugelers, W., De Groot, I., & Stolk, V. (2017). *Research for cult committee – Teaching common values in Europe.* European Parliament, Policy Department for Structural and Cohesion Policy. http://bit.ly/2pm5Yh9

Veugelers, W., & O'Hair, M. J. (Eds.). (2005). *Network learning for educational change.* Open University Press.

Veugelers, W., & Zijlstra, H. (2004). Networks of schools and constructing citizenship in secondary education. In F. Hernandez & I.F. Goodson (Eds.), *Social geographies of educational change* (pp. 65–78). Kluwer/Springer Publishers.

Walters, K. (1994). *Re-thinking reason. New perspectives in critical thinking.* SUNY.

Index

21st century skills   9, 84, 166, 167, 169, 170, 173, 178, 274

academic achievement   49, 52, 149, 217, 243, 301
active learning   80, 86, 224, 281, 282
adaptive patterns of learning   243, 251, 252
  maladaptive patterns of learning   243, 252
  Patterns of Adaptive Learning Scales (PALS)   245
affordance   258, 259
  cognitive   262, 263, 267, 269, 272, 273
  situational   262, 267
agency   1, 5, 7, 27, 37, 45–48, 50, 51, 99, 100, 119, 122, 158, 306, 307, 337
apprentice   11, 257–262, 265, 267–269, 271–273, 275, 291, 293
assessment   11, 29, 40, 41, 44, 76, 78, 86, 102, 167, 172, 209, 228, 231–234, 257–263, 265, 267, 272–274, 287, 300, 301, 303
  model-based assessment   257, 258, 273
  Program for International Student Assessment (PISA)   24, 79, 200, 260, 268, 273
  Teaching and Learning International Survey (TALIS)   43, 76, 77, 79, 87
  triangle   257, 259, 260, 262, 274
Australia   1, 76, 87, 149
Australian Values Education Program (AVET)   9, 148, 150, 162
authentic/authenticity   7, 57–63, 67, 118, 123, 257, 259, 260, 263, 265, 267, 269, 272–274
  instruction/pedagogy   60, 63, 105, 149
  moral   7, 57, 59, 61–67, 69
autonomous/autonomy   1, 5, 6, 7, 24, 28, 37–40, 43–46, 49, 51, 61, 78, 85, 180, 332, 333, 335–337, 339

basic education   177, 195, 197–200, 207, 209, 210
Bioecological Systems Model   7, 91, 93, 97, 98, 99, 104, 131
  ecological systems theory   129, 131
  educational ecosystems   6, 19, 21, 22, 27–29

brain   12, 150, 298, 313, 314, 315–318, 322
  event-related potential (ERP)   314, 318, 322, 323
  plasticity   12, 299, 314, 315, 317, 324
  storming   7, 56, 79, 81, 85, 86
Bronfenbrenner, Urie   93, 97–99, 281

Canada   245
character/character strengths/personal characteristics   2, 4, 5, 6, 22, 24, 52, 61, 62, 67, 68, 69, 102, 120–121, 141, 151, 157, 158, 337
character education   105, 161, 335
citizenship education   13, 131, 141, 331–336
  International Civic and Citizenship Education study (ICCS)   131
cognition   100, 152, 257, 259, 260, 262, 264, 265, 273, 274, 297, 300
competence   2, 3, 7, 9, 11, 20, 22, 24, 26, 28, 38, 50, 52, 75–77, 80–84, 86, 87, 134, 140, 158, 167, 168, 171, 173–175, 177, 179–181, 208, 242, 257–265, 267–269, 271–275, 297, 300, 301, 304, 338
  model   258, 260–264, 267, 268, 271, 273, 275
  moral   38, 48, 76, 338
  occupation-specific   258
  professional   2, 7, 28, 134, 168, 173–175, 177, 181, 258
  profiles   258
  subject-specific   258
Complex Dynamic Systems (CDS)   93, 97, 101–103, 106
content knowledge   3, 174, 175, 258
creative talent   9, 12, 281, 286–288
  as emergent event (CTEE)   11, 12, 202, 280–282, 284, 285, 288–293
creative thinking   220, 222, 244, 289
creativity   282–284
critical thinking   159, 171, 244, 261, 304, 305, 324, 337
cultural literacy   9, 169, 173
culture   1, 24, 26, 37, 39, 41, 42, 47, 49, 51, 65, 78, 81, 82, 92, 96, 136, 141, 142, 151, 158, 170, 176, 199, 222, 253, 297, 302, 303, 306, 307, 317

culturally responsive pedagogy/Culturally Responsive Teaching (CRT)   220–222, 228–234
curriculum/curricula   4, 7, 10, 22–25, 27, 28, 38, 40–44, 46, 50, 59, 66, 69, 76, 78, 80, 82, 84, 86, 92, 136, 137, 148, 149, 152, 153, 167, 169, 175–177, 179, 180, 195, 197–200, 209, 220–225, 227, 259, 290, 304, 333

Damon, William   8, 93, 94, 103, 334, 338
Developmental Model of Vocational Excellence   242
developmental systems   7, 93, 97, 99
Dewey, John   5, 49, 161
differentiated programs   219
differentiation   10, 199–201, 217, 220, 221, 306
Dinham, Adam   170, 171
diversity   1, 5, 8, 21, 25, 26, 28, 129–142, 169, 172, 174, 177, 197, 199, 228, 280, 333
  diverse   12, 29, 47, 84–86, 136, 140, 167, 169, 173, 178, 180, 224, 281, 287
  superdiversity   9, 141
Durkheim, Emile   114
Durkheimian   113
Dweck, Carol   12, 208, 298, 299, 334, 336
dyslexia   12, 320–324

early childhood education and care (ECEC)   131, 133, 134, 136
Education for Democratic Intercultural Citizenship (EDIC)   333, 335, 336, 338
Enrichment Triad Model   281
entrepreneurship   167, 241, 259, 261, 263
equality   5, 10, 25, 29, 77, 83, 131, 195, 198, 200, 201, 209, 248, 253,
equity   2, 6, 19–30, 40, 49, 131
ethic/ethical/ethics   26, 58, 61, 136, 140–142, 156, 175, 176, 180, 199, 203, 204
ethical code   24, 27, 82
ethical education   6, 9, 76, 136, 141, 333, 334, 339 (*see also* moral education)
ethical sensitivity   6, 334, 339 (*see also* moral sensitivity)
European Commission   23, 167, 259
Evangelic Lutheranism   112, 135
  Lutheran, Lutheranism   137, 138, 178, 196

Finland/Finnish   1, 7–11, 23, 24, 26, 62, 75, 76, 78–81, 84–86, 111–118, 120, 121, 123, 129–131, 133–140, 167, 174, 176, 178–180, 195–210, 240–242, 245, 252, 304, 319, 331, 333, 339
fixed mindset   209, 289, 300, 302, 303, 313, 336
  entity theory   208, 298, 336

Germany/German   3, 11, 13, 180, 259, 260, 267, 268, 273, 318
gifted   10, 11, 195–210, 217–222, 224–227, 233–235, 281, 290, 299, 301, 336
gifted education   10, 196–198, 201, 210, 218, 221, 227
giftedness   9–12, 200–203, 205, 206, 208, 210, 218, 282, 283, 297–300, 302–304, 307, 336
goal   7, 8, 11, 22, 24, 47, 63, 64, 66, 67, 75, 77, 92–96, 99, 100, 103–105, 111, 115, 130, 149, 158, 201, 203, 209, 219, 221, 240, 242–253, 258, 259, 272, 290, 293, 301, 303, 305, 323, 336, 337
  ability   243
  achievement goal orientation profiles   242, 243, 245, 250
  ego-involvement   243
  learning   77, 219, 243, 252, 258, 259, 290, 303
  mastery   242–244, 249, 251
  orientation   11, 242–253
  performance   242, 243, 251, 252
  performance-avoidance   242–244, 249, 252
  task-involvement   243
grade-point average (GPA)   245, 246
growth mindset   9, 10, 12, 13, 209, 297, 299, 301, 302, 304, 306, 307, 324, 335–339
  incremental theory   208, 298, 336
  malleability of intelligence   210, 300, 307
  pedagogy   10, 12, 196, 208–210, 297, 303, 305

hearing impairment   320, 322
Hirsch, E. D.   9, 169

identity   2, 4, 5, 8, 23, 27, 43, 45–47, 50, 58, 95, 98, 100–102, 105, 111–113, 118–123, 134, 306
ideology   112, 173, 197
innovation   7, 23, 77, 80, 82, 86, 241, 259, 297, 305
innovative behavior   259, 263

inquiry-based instruction 281
instructional strategies 10, 224, 227–230, 233–235
intelligence 4, 12, 179, 218, 281, 283, 297–304, 307, 324, 336
   multiple 9, 210, 332
intercultural 167, 168, 333, 336, 337, 338
   sensitivity 133, 134, 142
interdisciplinary 11, 257, 258, 274, 291
interreligious 333
   sensitivity 133, 134, 139, 142
intervention 8, 39, 45, 94, 96, 104, 150, 155, 208, 290, 297–300, 302, 304, 307, 317–325
intrapreneurship (IP) 11, 257–261, 263, 264, 267

knowledge creating learning 297, 303, 307

learning activities 65, 68, 151, 152, 258, 283
learning environments 1, 4, 9, 11, 26, 29, 65, 76, 82–84, 87, 149, 151, 153–155, 158, 160, 161, 220, 222, 252, 258, 282, 286
literacy/literacies 9, 84, 136, 166–179, 181, 320, 321

maker-pedagogy 12, 296, 304
mathematics 11, 201, 203, 204, 218, 220, 222, 224, 233, 319, 331
meaning in life 93
Medallion for Excellence 241
mentoring 105, 204, 206, 235
mentoring young mathematicians 221, 293
metacognition 244, 250
metacognitive strategies 11, 243, 244, 250–253
Metacognitive Strategies in Studies (MSS) 245, 247–250, 252
Metacognitive Strategies in Training (MST) 245, 247–250, 252
mindset 9, 10, 12, 13, 209, 297, 299, 301, 302, 304, 306, 307, 324, 335–339
   implicit beliefs 10, 141, 208, 299, 300, 336
Moore, Diane 11, 257, 258, 273
moral 7, 38, 48, 57, 59, 61–67, 69, 76, 338
   authenticity 7, 57, 59, 62, 65
   competence 38, 48, 76, 338
   dilemma 26, 136
   education 7, 141, 161, 332–334
   purpose 5, 7, 37, 47–49, 51

   qualities 59, 61
   sensitivity 141, 334 (see also ethical sensitivity)
Moscovici, Serge 300
motivation 5, 47, 52, 65, 84, 100, 113, 141, 155, 158, 202, 208, 218–220, 224, 225–227, 233, 234, 288, 303, 320, 324
multiculturalism 168, 177, 178, 181, 197, 199
music 12, 117, 202–204, 206, 207, 313–325

Narvaez, Darcia 149, 152, 156, 160
neurodiversity 11, 12, 280–284, 287, 290, 291, 293
Niemi, Hannele 6, 19, 22, 331

OECD 38, 76, 79, 269, 273
Olympiads 203
   International Mathematical Olympiad 197, 198
   science Olympian 202–204, 206
Olympic Games 203
   winner 203, 206
Orthodox Church 135
Oser, Fritz 26, 112, 258, 332, 333

Pargament, Kenneth 114
pedagogical content knowledge 3, 174, 175, 258
pedagogical knowledge 49, 175, 258
pedagogical thinking 201, 208, 210, 303
problem solving 167, 220, 244, 261, 287
   skills 241, 263
profession/professional/professionalism 2, 6, 7, 27, 28, 37, 38, 41, 47, 50, 51, 68, 80, 131, 134, 168, 173–175, 177, 181, 258
   identity 2, 5, 43, 46, 49, 51
   knowledge 2, 3, 5, 59, 76, 77, 86, 244
project-based learning 282
Prothero, Stephen R. 170
purpose 5–8, 38, 46–52, 60, 63, 67, 69, 92–106, 112, 122, 170, 224, 241, 297, 315, 331, 334
   commitment 51, 95, 96, 103
   development 7, 8, 91–106
   exploration 95, 96, 103, 105
   in life 92, 93, 104, 338
   interventions 94, 96
   youth 8, 92–97, 100, 106
purposeful teacher 5, 7, 92

purposeful teaching   5–7, 92, 93
  teaching purpose   8, 46–49, 52, 60, 63, 67, 338
Pygmalion   301

quality   2, 3, 6, 9, 19–30, 44, 45, 47, 49, 51, 57–59, 63, 64, 66, 67, 78, 80, 87, 105, 141, 149, 156, 157, 160, 168, 174, 175, 177, 178, 180, 181, 201, 220, 260, 263, 268, 269, 281, 283, 284, 288, 320

religion/religious/religiosity/religiousness   1, 9, 94, 112–121, 123, 130, 131, 135–142, 158, 167–181, 196
  education   7, 119, 121, 136, 140, 167, 172, 176, 179, 180
  literacy   9, 166–179, 181

sacred   8, 111–123
Schwartz, Shalom   8
Science, Technology, Engineering, and Mathematics (STEM)   92, 218
Scotland   86w
secular/secularization   113, 114, 130, 140, 170–172, 176, 177, 180, 181
self-regulation   99, 100, 243–245, 250, 261
Shulman, Lee   3, 174, 175, 178, 181, 258
skills   2–5, 9–12, 20, 42, 49, 61, 66, 76, 81–84, 86, 95, 136, 139, 162, 166–171, 173, 174, 176–180, 196, 202, 206, 209, 210, 218, 220–224, 228, 229, 234, 235, 240, 241, 263, 265, 272–274, 286, 287, 301, 304, 313, 315, 316, 318–324, 338
  competitions   11, 203, 240–244, 246–248, 250–253
  higher-order   263
  lower-order   263
social representations   12, 297, 300, 302, 306
sociocultural perspective   297, 306
socio-digital revolution   303, 307
socio-digital technologies   297, 304, 307
special educational needs (SEN)   12, 200, 305
speech   12, 288, 314–318, 320–324
spiritual/spirituality   1, 5, 7, 8, 100, 112–114, 116, 119, 121, 123, 130, 179, 210, 332
stereotype threat   302
subject didactics   3
subject-specific pedagogy   3

talent   1, 6, 9–12, 25, 195–197, 199–210, 217–221, 234, 235, 241, 280–293, 301, 302, 306, 313, 334
  development   9, 10, 12, 201–207, 210, 218–220, 234, 241, 281, 282, 290, 293, 334
Talk Moves (TM)   10, 11, 222, 223, 228, 230–235
teacher beliefs   4, 46, 141, 303, 324
teacher competences   3, 76, 83, 140, 158, 174
teacher education   1–4, 7–9, 13, 19, 20, 23–25, 27, 28, 58, 59, 62, 69, 75–88, 129, 131, 132, 135, 141, 142, 162, 167, 168, 174, 177, 180, 181, 195, 197, 198, 201, 234, 258, 273, 274, 324, 333
Teacher Education Forum   7, 79, 81, 84, 87
teacher education traditions   1, 2
teacher educator   3, 51, 58, 76, 77, 81, 83–85, 87, 210
teacher professionalism   6, 7, 27, 37, 38, 41, 47, 50, 51, 68, 80, 131, 177
teacher role   6, 19, 21–24, 27, 39, 60, 61, 68, 78, 87, 92, 93, 178, 205, 306, 331, 332
Technological, Pedagogical and Content Knowledge (TPACK)   258–260, 272, 274
technology   11, 77, 80, 218, 241, 258–260, 262, 267, 272–274, 303, 306, 331
Tirri, Kirsi   6, 13, 92, 112, 120, 123, 156, 201, 203, 336
trajectory/trajectories   10, 93, 100, 130–134, 142, 290, 291, 301

UNESCO   199
  Salamanca statement   199
United Arab Emirates   245
United Kingdom   77, 87, 152, 156, 157, 167, 168, 172, 242, 251
United States   1, 5, 169, 170, 217, 218, 222, 224, 280, 332

values   1, 4, 9, 20, 22, 23, 25, 27, 40, 46, 49, 50, 58, 59, 62, 63, 68, 75, 92, 111–116, 119–123, 130, 132–134, 140, 148–151, 156, 158, 173, 176, 252, 268, 269, 283, 300, 332–334
  education   6–9, 28, 29, 129, 131, 135, 136, 141, 142, 148, 150–161, 167, 219
vocational education   11, 177, 196–198, 240, 252, 253, 258
Vocational Education and Training (VET)   11, 240, 241, 243, 252, 253, 257–259, 274
  teacher   11, 258, 262, 265, 267, 273

vocational excellence   11, 202, 203, 207, 240–242
vocational skills   241, 242
vocational skills competition   240–242, 253
Vygotsky, Lev   222, 302
Vygotskian   299

WorldSkills Competitions (WSC)   11, 202, 203, 240–244, 246–248, 250–253
WorldSkills International (WSI)   11, 240, 241
worldview   27, 130–136, 138–142, 167, 172, 173, 176–178, 181

Printed in the United States
by Baker & Taylor Publisher Services